The Man Behind the Myth

Seeing Jesus As He Really Is

by

Rodney M. Howard-Browne

ALBURY PUBLISHING
Tulsa, Oklahoma

The Man Behind the Myth
Seeing Jesus As He Really Is
ISBN 1-57778-102-3
Copyright © 1999 by Rodney M. Howard-Browne
P. O. Box 292888
Tampa, Florida 33687

Published by ALBURY PUBLISHING
P. O. Box 470406
Tulsa, Oklahoma 74147-0406

Contents

What Was Jesus Really Like?

Have you ever wondered, *What was Jesus really like?* As a child growing up in the Church, I listened to preachers preach about Jesus, Sunday after Sunday. The desire in my young heart was to find out more about Him. I remember praying often that He would walk off the pages of the Bible and walk in my heart. I felt, *I've got to see Him. I want to know Him.*

I discovered that the only way I could see and know Jesus was to read the Gospels. Then later, as I read the Gospels over and over, I started seeing a different picture of Him than I'd heard coming from the pulpit. I heard people say that Jesus wouldn't do this and Jesus wouldn't do that, but when I read the Gospels and found out what He did do, I saw that He was radical. He didn't fit in with the religious. As a matter of fact, Jesus would be kicked out of most churches today! They wouldn't invite Him to speak at most conferences, and He would not be welcome in certain ministerial fellowships and denominations. Why? Because apart from being totally unorthodox, they wouldn't be able to predict what He might do next!

There have been many theories over the years concerning Jesus, from those that were sound scripturally to those that were just plain blasphemous. But the Gospels tell it like it is. That's why I've included the books of Matthew, Mark, Luke, and John in the back of this book — so you can read about Jesus yourself and see Him as He really is.

As I studied the Gospels, I began to realize that through centuries of religion and tradition, the Church has relegated Jesus to a stained glass window. They've put Him in a religious picture found in children's Bible storybooks. This religious, traditional treatment of Jesus has caused the world to have a warped, one-dimensional view of Him. Blinded by religious tradition, they don't see Jesus as He really is.

Look at the very beginning of the gospel of John:

In the beginning was the Word, and the Word was with God, and the Word was God.

The same was in the beginning with God.

All things were made by him; and without him was not any thing made that was made.

In him was life; and the life was the light of men.

And the light shineth in darkness; and the darkness comprehended it not.

There was a man sent from God, whose name was John.

The same came for a witness, to bear witness of the Light, that all men through him might believe.

He was not that Light, but was sent to bear witness of that Light.

That was the true Light, which lighteth every man that cometh into the world.

He was in the world, and the world was made by him, and the world knew him not.

JOHN 1:1-10

You could express this last verse in the context of the Church today: Jesus was in the Church, and the Church was made by Him, but the Church knew Him not. The Bible says,

He came unto his own, and his own received him not.

But as many as received him, to them gave he power to become the sons of God, even to them that believe on his name:

Which were born, not of blood, nor of the will of the flesh, nor of the will of man, but of God.

And the Word was made flesh, and dwelt among us, (and we beheld his glory, the glory as of the only begotten of the Father,) full of grace and truth.

JOHN 1:11-14

Now here's the problem. The world today can't see Jesus, because He's not here in the visible realm. The only Jesus the world can see is through those whose lives He has changed, the ones who have received Him, believers — **to them gave he power to become the sons of God, even to them that believe on his name** (John 1:12). The only Jesus the world can see is in the lives of Christians. If people are ever going to read the Bible, it will probably be because they have first seen something special and supernatural in the life of a believer. It will be because Jesus touched that believer in such a way that His life shines through them.

People will say, "There's something about this person. They're not like the other people I know. There's something different about their life — the way they walk, the way they talk. There's a sparkle in their eyes. It's something better than religion — it's reality. They know Jesus, and I have to meet Him."

I know that if people could see Jesus as He really is, they would love Him as I do. The cry of my heart is that Jesus would become real to you as you read this book. I pray that He will walk off the pages of the Gospels, into your life, and walk up and down in your heart!

If you want to know Jesus right now, or if you have never been absolutely certain that you are born again, just turn to the Salvation Prayer on page 229 of this book. You are one prayer away from knowing Jesus personally and intimately. This is not a religion; this is a new life in God!

Chapter 1

Who Is Jesus?

I had to go to the Gospels to see Jesus and then to know Him. I used to spend a lot of time, as I was growing up, thinking about His conception and His birth, His life as a baby, as a child, as a boy, a teenager, and then a man.

Although Jesus' life and ministry fulfilled all the Old Testament prophecies for the first coming of the Messiah, the details are always astounding and unpredictable. The prophecy said the Messiah would be born in Bethlehem (see Micah 5:2), but no one could have guessed exactly *how* the King of kings would arrive on the scene.

> *Now the birth of Jesus Christ was on this wise: When as his mother Mary was espoused to Joseph, before they came together, she was found with child of the Holy Ghost.*
>
> *Then Joseph her husband, being a just man, and not willing to make her a publick example, was minded to put her away privily.*
>
> *But while he thought on these things, behold, the angel of the Lord appeared unto him in a dream, saying, Joseph, thou son of David, fear not to take unto thee Mary thy wife: for that which is conceived in her is of the Holy Ghost.*
>
> MATTHEW 1:18-20

Something really hit me when I first read this. How would you like to be Joseph or Mary?

"Joseph, I'm pregnant, okay? Now listen, I know this is going to sound crazy, and I love you with all my heart, but I have not allowed another man to touch me. I'm a virgin, but I'm pregnant. Oh, and the angel of the Lord told me that God was the father."

Joseph's not married and his lady, Mary, is pregnant. Talk about embarrassing! How in the world do you explain to your family and friends how your girlfriend got pregnant if you say you haven't done anything? "Mary's pregnant, and I know we're not married yet, but this is different. This is not what you think it is."

"You're not even married, you haven't had marital relations, and she's pregnant? Yeah, right. Don't lie to us, Joseph."

Do you understand what we're dealing with here? These are not saints; they are normal, everyday people. So Joseph came to the only conclusion he could. He was going to have to break off his engagement to Mary. I mean, who's going to believe he didn't touch her — and just forget that crazy story about the angel of the Lord!

But then the angel of the Lord spoke to Joseph in a dream and said, "Don't break off your engagement with Mary! This whole thing is of God." Now Joseph can say for sure, "No, I am not lying! I'm telling you the truth! I never touched Mary and neither has anyone else. An angel came to me and said that the baby was conceived by the power of the Holy Spirit." But can you imagine the frustration? This has never happened before. This is a unique, one-of-a-kind event. Who will believe him? What will family and friends say about this?

Thank God for the Word of the Lord that came to Joseph through the angel. Knowing that this was done by the hand of God was the only reason he and Mary could endure the shame and reproach. I guarantee you, there were family members, close friends, and neighbors who said, "Yeah, we know what Joseph and Mary have been doing!"

"But we didn't do it! The Holy Ghost did it! The angel of the Lord spoke the Word and that's it. We promise you, before God, we did not do anything!"

For me, this is where it all begins: Jesus' supernatural conception. He was born of a *virgin*. Jesus entered humanity in controversy, as the rock of offense, the stumbling block — because the whole thing was *supernatural*.

And she shall bring forth a son, and thou shalt call his name JESUS: for he shall save his people from their sins.

Now all this was done, that it might be fulfilled which was spoken of the Lord by the prophet, saying,

Behold, a virgin shall be with child, and shall bring forth a son, and they shall call his name Emmanuel, which being interpreted is, God with us.

MATTHEW 1:21-23

Thank God, Joseph and Mary could go back to the Word of God and say, "It says that a virgin shall be with child, and shall bring forth a son." And this description of Jesus by the angel showed us who Jesus is — Emmanuel, God with us, God manifested in the flesh.

Then Joseph being raised from sleep did as the angel of the Lord had bidden him, and took unto him his wife:

And knew her not till she had brought forth her firstborn son: and he called his name Jesus.

MATTHEW 1:24-25

Now in John 1:1 we read, **In the beginning was the Word and the Word was with God, and the Word was God.** This "Word" was Jesus prior to His coming on the scene in human flesh. Jesus didn't come into existence the day He was born. He preexisted with the Father and the Holy Spirit, the "three in one."

The Father said to the Son, "You need to become a man and pay the price for man's sin."

The Son said, "I will go. I will become a man."

The Word was spoken as a seed into the womb of Mary — not a seed from a natural man — but the Word of God was spoken into the womb of Mary. And she conceived and brought forth Jesus the God-man, who was without sin, without spot, and without blemish.

Why did God have to do it that way? Ever since Adam sinned in the Garden of Eden, man had been separated from God by his sin. So God needed a *sinless* man to pay the price for sinful mankind. Only a man who was without sin could pay the penalty for sinful man. God and man came together in one person — Jesus Christ — in order to cut an unbreakable covenant between God and man.

Jesus said that He would give Himself. "I'm the one. I will become a man and pay the price for man's sin so man can have the choice to come back to the Father." So the Word came into the womb of a virgin, and nine months later Jesus came forth just like a regular baby. Now, the baby Jesus didn't fly around the crib, you know! He had diapers. He had to cut His baby teeth. He did all this and everything any other child would do.

Just think about Jesus' boyhood. What was it like for Him growing up in an ordinary family with brothers and sisters and a mother and father? What was it like for them and for Him, knowing that He had a supernatural mission, that He came from heaven to the earth to die for the sin of mankind?

When Jesus was a young man, twelve years of age, He and His family went to the temple in Jerusalem to pay their taxes. Joseph and Mary were already heading home when they realized He was missing. So, they went back to Jerusalem. They found Him in the temple, discussing the things of God with the priests. When they discovered Him they were angry, asking Him where He had been. He said, "Did you not know that I must be about My Father's business?" (See Luke 2:49.)

Jesus knew what His mission was. Even as a young boy, he knew He had to be about His heavenly Father's business. Somebody would say, "But Your father's business is working in the carpentry shop. What do You mean, You're about Your Father's business?" The young Jesus had to live like a regular human among regular people — all the while knowing He was different — VERY different!

What was it like for Him as a teenager? Imagine all the pressures of growing up and coming to adulthood that teenagers have. There must have been pressure that He faced when the young girls showed interest in Him. The Bible tells us that Jesus was tempted in all the ways that we are, yet He was without sin. (See Hebrews 4:15.) If you look at history you will find that the Jews during this time period would get married young. Many of the young boys were trained in the family business by the age of thirteen, and some of them had their wives chosen for them by their parents years in advance.

You wonder what other people were thinking about Jesus. "Maybe there is something wrong with Him. He shows no interest in women." When He was twenty-nine years old and not married, you can understand why people might have thought there was something wrong with Him!

On top of that, Jesus kept talking about the fact that His kingdom was not on this earth. Where did He come from? Was He from another planet? He was not interested in political things and didn't really care who was in power. He had no hatred for anyone, including the government of the day.

> Jesus kept talking about the fact that His kingdom was not on this earth. Where did He come from? Was He from another planet?

He could have grown up with a chip on his shoulder because, when he was just a toddler, all the little Hebrew boys in Bethlehem, two-years-old and younger, had been slaughtered by Herod — who was trying to kill the "King of the Jews." Yet Jesus never said, "I'll overthrow these Jewish traitors and Roman dogs. We'll raise up an army and take them out." Not once did He ever mention it. He must have seemed odd, different in many ways from His brothers and sisters, and He was not interested in following His earthly father's footsteps either.

But all these pressures were forming Him and shaping Him, preparing Him for the greatest mission ever known to man. Jesus' eternal purpose was greater than just what was happening at that time. God does not see things the way we see them. Those things which we think are so important often are not an issue to Him, as He sits in eternity.

Finally the day came when Jesus came to the Jordan to be baptized. John the Baptist baptized Jesus and God Himself spoke from heaven and proclaimed Him to be His own beloved Son. Jesus was led by the Spirit into the wilderness, where He fasted for forty days and forty nights and was tempted by the devil. But He soundly defeated Satan with the Word of God. (See Luke 4:1-15.) When Jesus came out of the wilderness, the power of the Holy Spirit was all over Him to preach, teach, heal, and deliver.

Everywhere Jesus went during His earthly ministry, He left a trail of people who were set free and healed, who went away walking and leaping and praising God. We count three people raised from the dead: the widow's boy outside the city of Nain (see Luke 7:11-16), Jairus' daughter (see Luke 8:49-56), and Lazarus (see John 11:43-45). What's more, at the end of his gospel, John said,

And there are also many other things which Jesus did, the which, if they should be written every one, I suppose that even the world itself could not contain the books that should be written.

JOHN 21:25

Miracles were not the only unusual occurrences in Jesus' ministry, however. He habitually hung out with the despised tax collectors and sinners. He didn't act like them, but He didn't condemn them or make them feel inferior either. That's why they loved to be around Him, because they felt He accepted them as they were. Then, when He looked at them with eyes of love, and taught them the truth about God, they *wanted* to get rid of their sin to get closer to Him.

Jesus has never been repulsive like religion can be. When you see Hollywood's idea of what they think God and God's people are like — condemning, mean, angry, and uncompassionate — you know that they get it straight from religion. Religion focuses on your sin and condemns you for it; but Jesus focuses on setting you free. His love and goodness lead you to repent and give you the power to overcome the sin in your life. Religion locks you into sin; Jesus is the lover of your soul who sets you free from sin.

> *God so loved the world, that he gave his only begotten Son, that whosoever believeth in him should not perish, but have everlasting life.*
>
> *For God sent not his Son into the world to condemn the world; but that the world through him might be saved.*

JOHN 3:16-17

That was His whole mission. There was never a time that Jesus did not keep in mind the divine purpose and plan for His life. He came with one goal, and that was to pay the price at Calvary for your sin and my sin. He was born to die — in a remarkable, unparalleled act of love.

Yet if you listen to some preachers today, you'd think that God only sent His Son into the world to tell the world, "You are sinners and I am angry with you. I want you to burn in the flames of hell." Somehow they think that this is the gospel of Jesus Christ. Jesus never came with a message of condemnation. Jesus came with a message of love and forgiveness. We can see this demonstrated through the story of the woman who was caught in adultery:

> *And the scribes and Pharisees brought unto him a woman taken in adultery; and when they had set her in the midst,*
>
> *They said unto him, Master, this woman was taken in adultery, in the very act.*

Now Moses in the law commanded us, that such should be stoned: but what sayest thou?

This they said, tempting him, that they might have to accuse him. But Jesus stooped down, and with his finger wrote on the ground, as though he heard them not.

So when they continued asking him, he lifted up himself, and said unto them, He that is without sin among you, let him first cast a stone at her.

And again he stooped down, and wrote on the ground.

And they which heard it, being convicted by their own conscience, went out one by one, beginning at the eldest, even unto the last: and Jesus was left alone, and the woman standing in the midst.

When Jesus had lifted up himself, and saw none but the woman, he said unto her, Woman, where are those thine accusers? Hath no man condemned thee?

She said, No man, Lord. And Jesus said unto her, Neither do I condemn thee: go, and sin no more.

JOHN 8:3-11

Jesus said, **Go, and sin no more.** He released her from her sin, and He is still releasing people from their sin today. He does not condone sin, but He has compassion on and forgives sinners. He releases people from their guilt and condemnation.

But religion does not release you from guilt and condemnation. Religion has to make you feel guilty in order to survive, because religion is a parasite that thrives on your guilt. As long as you're guilty, you're caught in religion's trap. You'll go through all the rituals and try to keep all the laws, and when you can't do it, you'll be even more guilty and condemned. It's a vicious cycle that only Jesus can break.

When you're released from your guilt and sin by receiving Jesus as your Lord and Savior, you're free from religion's control. The power of God is not only working on the inside of you, but it works through you. You can cast out devils, heal the sick, and raise the dead just like Jesus did! Religion does not want you to do that.

That's why Jesus was a total oddity to the religious world. He came in total opposition to the religious system of the day and wreaked havoc. The religious people were the ones who put Him on the cross. They were the ones who said, "We've got to get rid of Him." Jesus had a power they did not understand — the power of unconditional love which sets men and women free and allows them to know God personally, for themselves. But religion says, "Do what we say and *we'll* tell you what God says."

The history of Jesus is greater than any James Bond 007 movie. Jesus the God/Man came to the earth and took on human flesh for the purpose of paying the price and becoming the eternal sacrifice for man's sin. God-and-man-in-one did it, so that all we have to do is say, "I believe!" and salvation becomes ours.

Jesus speaks to me. His body speaks to me of the fact that He is a human being and understands everything I'm going through. (See Hebrews 2:17,18.) The beatings He endured speak to me that by His stripes He bore my sicknesses and carried my diseases. His blood shed on the cross speaks to me that He washed away my sin. (See Isaiah 53:5.) And His resurrection speaks to me that because He lives, I can also live — really live! I'm talking about eternal life! I'm talking about everlasting life! (See Galatians 2:20.)

We know that Jesus could have walked away at any time. Even on the cross, He could have called thousands of angels to help Him. (See Matthew 26:53.) But He gladly laid His life down for us. Heaven's court of justice was waiting to be satisfied, the price for sin had to be paid, and Jesus did it — for you and me.

Who is Jesus?

He is the God/Man who paid the price for our sin so that we could know God and be set free from sin and all religious bondage. Hallelujah!

Chapter 2

Seeing Jesus Clearly

*W*hen Jesus came into the coasts of Caesarea Philippi, he asked his disciples, saying, Whom do men say that I the Son of man am?

And they said, Some say that thou art John the Baptist: some, Elias; and others, Jeremias, or one of the prophets. He saith unto them, But whom say ye that I am?

MATTHEW 16:13-15

Jesus asked the disciples two questions. "Whom do *men* say that I am?" And then, "Whom do *you* say that I am?" I believe that these two questions will be asked of you as you read this book. Jesus wanted to know who His disciples thought He was, and now He wants to know who *you* think He is.

Simon Peter answered and said, Thou art the Christ, the Son of the living God.

And Jesus answered and said unto him, Blessed art thou, Simon Bar-jona: for flesh and blood hath not revealed it unto thee, but my Father which is in heaven.

And I say also unto thee, that thou art Peter, and upon this rock [of revelation] I will build my church; and the gates of hell will not prevail against it.

MATTHEW 16:16-18 (INSERT MINE)

I want you to notice something. Peter saw something that day. His eyes were opened and he saw who Jesus really was. As we step into this new millennium, what the world needs more than anything is to see Jesus clearly. Unfortunately, most people see Jesus through the eyes of religion and tradition.

When we went to Disney World to see their Christmas production one year, we saw people put out their cigarettes and stand there with tears rolling down their cheeks, singing about the babe who was born in Bethlehem. Everybody can get tearful about a baby. If you keep Him as a baby, you don't have to accept Him as the Lord of your life.

Jesus is born at Christmas and He dies at Easter. At Easter, Jesus is on the cross. The world again stands with tears rolling down their cheeks, this time about the fact that Jesus died. But you know what? They still don't make Him their Lord. To be born again and make heaven their home, they have to invite the *risen* Lord Jesus to come and make His home on the inside of them. They have to see, and believe, that the tomb is empty.

The world says that Jesus was just a good man. Some say He was a prophet in a long line of prophets. Others say He was an eccentric. Some say He was a martyr. And others say He was a fairy tale. Children are raised to believe in the tooth fairy, the Easter bunny, Santa Claus, and Jesus Christ. We've put Jesus in there with the fairy tales, and when children eventually find out the fairy tales are not real, they start to wonder about Jesus too. But Jesus is not a fairy tale; He's a living reality.

What is very interesting is that every year is marked on the calendar as the year of our Lord. 2000 AD. Anno Domini — AD — is Latin for "year of our Lord." You don't see it written down as "Year of Buddha 2000," or "2000 Mohammed," or "2000 Confucius." One man split the time of a whole planet, and His name is Jesus. It's more than just coincidence.

Jesus came to earth as a human being. He was born of a virgin and lived a sinless life. He went to the cross of Calvary and paid the price for our sin. Then He rose from the dead, sat down at the right hand of the Father, and sent the Holy Ghost to live in the hearts of those who believe. So now you and I can come and simply surrender our lives to Him, and the Holy Ghost can come into our hearts and give us a new life. I thank God for the reality of the risen, resurrected Lord Jesus Christ.

If you want to see Jesus clearly, take your Bible or go to the back of this book and read through the gospels of Matthew,

Mark, Luke, and John. Underline everything He did and everything He said. Put yourself in every verse. I've been at the pool of Bethesda. "When did you go there?" you might ask. I went there in the pages of the Word of God!

> *Now there is at Jerusalem by the sheep market a pool, which is called in the Hebrew tongue Bethesda, having five porches.*
>
> *In these lay a great multitude of impotent folk, of blind, halt, withered, waiting for the moving of the water.*
>
> JOHN 5:2-3

I've been there. I've seen it in the Spirit! When you walk through the pages of the Word of God, Jesus will walk right off the pages of the Gospel and into your heart. The living reality of the resurrected Lord will walk up and down in your heart. The Bible says, **Blessed are they that have not seen, and yet have believed** (John 20:29). I haven't seen, but I believe. I haven't seen with my natural eye, but I've seen Him with the eye of my spirit in the pages of the Word of God.

The Word says, **Lo, I come in the volume of the book** (Hebrews 10:7). We must see Him as He really is — not through the eyes of religious tradition, but through the eyes of the Holy Spirit and God's Word.

Jesus was not a barefoot, scrawny, weak-kneed individual with a lamb under His arm who spoke in Elizabethan English, "For yea, as thou hast gathered here this day." That's not Jesus, that is religion and tradition. If you read the Bible, you'll see that the reputation Jesus had among the religious people was that of a gluttonous man and a winebibber, because He hung around with the sinners. Religious people don't want to be around sinners, and they didn't like Jesus because He convicted them of their hard-heartedness.

> Religious people don't want to be around sinners, and they didn't like Jesus because He convicted them of their hard-heartedness.

21

Jesus was also a man's man. If He walked in the door, your head would turn; and when He spoke, He would get your attention. People sometimes say to me, "Rodney, just be nice. Just be like Jesus." I say, "Man, you haven't read about Jesus!" He was straight; He was right down the line with His message. There was no gray area with Him; it was either white or black. He was merciful to sinners, but to religious people His words cut like a knife.

For example, we see His incredible mercy in the Garden of Gethsemene when Peter chopped off the ear of Malchus, the high priest's servant. Malchus was trying to arrest Jesus. But rather than treating him as an enemy, Jesus bent right down, picked up the ear, stuck it back on, and healed him.

On the other hand, when He was dealing with religious people — the Pharisees and the Sadducees, the "wouldn't sees" and the "couldn't sees" — He was extremely blunt. In Matthew 23 He called them **a generation of vipers.** He called them **blind leading the blind** and **white-washed sepulchres, full of dead men's bones.** He said, **If you make any converts,** (which He doubted) **you're gonna make them twice the devils of hell that you are** (Matthew 23:27, author's paraphrase). That's Jesus!

We have this religious idea of what we think Jesus is like. But as you go through the gospels, you begin to see Him as He really is! If He walked the earth today, He would run cross-grain with religious tradition. Religious tradition tries to keep Him on the cross or in the crib. Jesus would be persecuted by many of today's religious leaders.

Take, for example, casting out demons. The religious Pharisees and Sadducees told Jesus that He was of the devil and that He cast out devils by the devil. Religious people are still saying that today. So you're in good company when people accuse you of the same thing!

Many churches make the world think that whenever you come around God, you've got to be morbid and sad. Too many religious, traditional churches put people off from serving Jesus because they have no life, no joy. But Jesus said, **I am come that**

they might have life, and that they might have it more abundantly (John 10:10). That's the Jesus of the gospels; in fact, that's the Jesus of the whole Bible!

Let's go on a journey through the Bible, from Genesis to Revelation, and let's see how Jesus is portrayed through the Word of God. [1]

In Genesis, He is the Seed of the Woman.

In Exodus, He is the Passover Lamb.

In Leviticus, He is our High Priest.

In Numbers, He's our Pillar of Cloud by day and our Pillar of Fire by night.

In Deuteronomy, He is the Prophet like unto Moses.

In Joshua, He is the Captain of our salvation.

In Judges, He is our Lawgiver.

In Ruth, He is our Kinsman Redeemer.

In First and Second Samuel, He's our Trusted Prophet.

In Kings and Chronicles, He is our Reigning King.

In Ezra, He's our Faithful Scribe.

In Nehemiah, He's the Rebuilder of the broken walls.

In Esther, He's our Advocate.

In Job, He's our Ever-Living Redeemer.

In Psalms, He is the Lord, our Shepherd, so we shall not want.

In Proverbs, He is our Wisdom.

In Ecclesiastes, He is our Goal!

In the Song of Solomon, He is our Lover and our Bridegroom.

In Isaiah, He's the Prince of Peace.

In Jeremiah and Lamentations, He is the Weeping Prophet.

In Ezekiel, He's the Wonderful Four-faced Man.

---

[1] This is from a message I heard as a boy, which had a great impact on my life, "The Fourth Man," by Oral Roberts.

In Daniel, He's the Fourth Man in the burning, fiery furnace.

In Hosea, He's the Eternal Husband, forever married to the backslider.

In Joel, He's the Baptizer in the Holy Ghost.

In Amos, He's our Burden-bearer.

In Obadiah, He's our Savior.

In Jonah, He's the Great Foreign Missionary.

In Micah, He's the Messenger with beautiful feet.

In Nahum, He's our Avenger.

In Habakkuk, He's the Evangelist pleading for revival.

In Zephaniah, He's the Lord, mighty to save.

In Haggai, He's the Restorer of the lost heritage.

In Zechariah, He's the Fountain springing up with everlasting life.

In Malachi, He's the Son of Righteousness, rising with healing in His wings.

In Matthew, He's the Messiah.

In Mark, He's the Wonder Worker.

In Luke, He's the Son of Man.

In John, He's the Son of God.

In Acts, He's the Holy Ghost, moving among men.

In Romans, He's the Justifier.

In First and Second Corinthians, He's the Sanctifier.

In Galatians, He's the Redeemer from the curse of the law.

In Ephesians, He is the Christ of unsearchable riches.

In Philippians, He's the God who supplies ALL of our needs.

In Colossians, He's the fullness of the godhead bodily.

In First and Second Thessalonians, He's our Soon-coming King.

In First and Second Timothy, He's the Mediator between God and man.

In Titus, He is the Faithful Pastor.

In Philemon, He's the Friend of the oppressed.

In Hebrews, He's the Blood of the everlasting covenant.

In James, He is the Lord who raises the sick.

In First and Second Peter, He's the Chief Shepherd, who shall soon appear.

In First, Second, and Third John, He is Love.

In Jude, He's the Lord coming with ten thousand of His saints.

In Revelation, He is King of kings and Lord of lords.

Jesus is Abel's sacrifice and Noah's rainbow. He's Abraham's ram and Isaac's well. He's Jacob's ladder and Ezekiel's burden. He's Judah's scepter, Moses' rod, David's slingshot, and Hezekiah's sundial. He's the Church's Head and is risen from the dead. He is a Husband to the widow and a Father to the orphan.

To those traveling by night, He's the Bright and the Morning Star. To those in the lonesome valley, He's the Lily of the Valley, the Rose of Sharon, the Honey in the Rock and the Staff of Life. He's the Pearl of Great Price. He's the Rock in the weary land. He's the Counselor. He's the Everlasting Father. The government is upon His shoulders. He's Peter's shadow, John's pearly white city. He's Jesus of Nazareth, the Son of the Living God.

He's the One who owns the cattle on a thousand hills. He's the One who split the Red Sea. He's the One who took the children of Israel out of Egypt into the promised land. He's the One who humbled Himself, came to earth, healed the sick, raised the dead, cleansed the lepers, opened the eyes of the blind, and turned the water into wine.

He's the One who fed the five thousand, walked on water, and cast out devils. He's the One who humbled Himself, once again, and became obedient unto death — even the death of the cross. He's the One who died on the cross, rose from the dead, ascended to the right hand of the Father, and ever liveth to make intercession for us. And He's coming back very, very soon. He is Jesus Christ of Nazareth, King of kings and Lord of lords.

Jesus said, **I and my Father are one** (John 10:30). He said, "If you've seen Me, you've seen the Father." (See John 14:9.) Jesus was God manifest in the flesh.

> *I am Alpha and Omega, the first and the last...*
>
> *And I turned to see the voice that spake with me. And being turned, I saw seven golden candlesticks.*
>
> *And in the midst of the seven candlesticks one like unto the Son of man, clothed with a garment down to the foot, and girt about the paps with a golden girdle.*
>
> *His head and his hairs were white like wool, as white as snow; and his eyes were as flames of fire;*
>
> *And his feet like unto fine brass, as if they burned in a furnace; and his voice as the sound of many waters.*
>
> *And he had in his right hand seven stars: and out of his mouth went a sharp twoedged sword; and his countenance was as the sun shineth in his strength.*
>
> *And when I saw him, I fell at his feet as dead. And he laid his right hand upon me, saying unto me, Fear not; I am the first and the last. I am he that liveth, and was dead; and behold, I am alive for evermore, Amen; and have the keys of hell and of death.*
>
> REVELATION 1:11-18

See Jesus clearly!

Chapter 3

What Happens When Jesus Shows Up?

T
he Spirit of the Lord is upon me, because he hath anointed me to preach the gospel to the poor; he hath sent me to heal the brokenhearted, to preach deliverance to the captives, and recovering of sight to the blind, to set at liberty them that are bruised,

To preach the acceptable year of the Lord.

LUKE 4:18-19

This is the message Jesus declared all during His earthly ministry. **The Spirit of the Lord is upon me, because he hath anointed me to preach the gospel...** and the Gospel is *Good News!* There are too many *bad news* preachers in the earth today. All they want to do is bring doom and gloom. Some people seem to think they're Old Testament prophets, called to rail out against sin. But thank God we're under a new covenant. The message of this new covenant is the same message that Jesus proclaimed: the Spirit of the Lord is upon *me,* and He has anointed *me* to preach the Gospel, the Good News.

The Gospel is Good News, my dear friend. Good News! I bring you Good News! I bring you glad tidings. *I bring you Good News! Hallelujah!* I get happy just thinking about the Good News!

We all know the world is full of bad news. You can turn on television news and all you hear is bad news. The last thing you need is a preacher bringing you more bad news. We need to hear the Good News of the Gospel: that Jesus still saves, Jesus still heals, Jesus still sets free, and that Jesus is coming again. That's the Gospel!

The problem is that many Christians are confused. They have a little bit of the old covenant, a little bit of the new covenant, and they've made up their own covenant. Their own covenant brings them under condemnation and bondage one minute, and it sets them free the next. In their confusion, they think God is blessing them one moment and the next moment He is saying, "I'm going to kill you." They walk around waiting for God to beat them and hurt them for reasons known only to Him.

> I want you to know that when Jesus walks in the door, the very atmosphere of the room changes. When Jesus walks in the door, sickness and death and poverty and the curse of hell go out the back door, saying, "It's time for us to leave."

That's not the Good News! The Good News is the same as it was when Jesus walked the earth. Do you know why it's still the same? Because Jesus is still the same. Jesus has not changed!

The question I pose to you is, "What happens when Jesus shows up?" What happens when Jesus walks in the door? I want you to know that when Jesus walks in the door, the very atmosphere of the room changes. When Jesus walks in the door, sickness and death and poverty and the curse of hell go out the back door, saying, "It's time for us to leave."

When Jesus walks in the door, you will know that He is there. You can see His nature and His character in Matthew, Mark, Luke, and John. What happens when He shows up? Jesus answered that Himself.

The thief cometh not, but for to steal, and to kill, and to destroy: I am come that they might have life, and that they might have it more abundantly.

JOHN 10:10

He that committeth sin is of the devil; for the devil sinneth from the beginning. For this purpose the Son of God was manifested, that he might destroy the works of the devil.

1 JOHN 3:8

How God anointed Jesus of Nazareth with the Holy Ghost and with power: who went about doing good, and healing all that were oppressed of the devil; for God was with him.

ACTS 10:38

I have good news for you: God is *good;* Jesus is *good.* God wants to bless you! Jesus wants to bless you! People ask me, "What's all this joy in your meetings? Why joy? What is the purpose? Don't you know it's the *Holy* Spirit, not the *joy* spirit?"

Joy is a fruit of the Spirit, although it is not the only fruit of the Spirit. When the Holy Spirit does His work in your life, you will have all nine fruits of the Spirit: love, joy, peace, patience, kindness, goodness, faithfulness, gentleness, and self-control (see Galatians 5:22-23 NIV). Joy is noticeable, however, because it is very much an outward expression others can see.

Jesus brings joy. When Jesus shows up, He says to you, "Be of good cheer." When Jesus shows up, He says, "Rejoice! Rejoice! Rejoice!" When Jesus shows up, He says, "Be strong."

In the book of Acts, chapter 8, we see that when Philip went down to the city of Samaria and preached Jesus Christ to them, there was great joy in the city. What happens when Jesus shows up? There is great joy!

A glad heart makes a cheerful countenance.

PROVERBS 15:13 AMP

Someone wrote, "But Rodney, Jesus didn't jump up and down, do cartwheels, and run around the place." Maybe Jesus didn't, but people He touched *did.* They went around walking and leaping and praising God! Oh, hallelujah!

Another person said, "You don't have to get so emotional." I'm telling you right now, when Jesus touches you, you want to shout it from the rooftops! If you say you had an encounter with the Living God and are not stirred in your heart all the way through your emotions — then I question whether you had a real touch. Only people who have *not* had a personal encounter with the power and presence of God tell us that we should not have an emotional response to the reality of the touch of God in and on our lives. God is real, Jesus is real, the Holy Spirit is real, and if I meet them face-to-face — I am going to know about it and so is everybody else!

If you can have an emotional response to something other than the Lord, such as a spouse, a child, a sporting event, a great triumph, or a great tragedy — then it's only logical that your emotions would respond to the love and power of God in your life. Emotions are not all bad. Emotions which come out of your carnal nature, such as bitterness and lust, should be controlled and eliminated by the power of God. Our emotions, like the other areas of our life, should be controlled by our spirit and the Holy Spirit — not by our flesh and our sin. But to express good emotions is normal and healthy.

*And my language and my message were not set forth in persuasive (enticing and plausible) words of wisdom, but they were in demonstration of the [Holy] Spirit and power [a proof by the Spirit and power of God, operating on me and stirring in the minds of my hearers the most **holy emotions** and thus persuading them].*

1 CORINTHIANS 2:4 AMP (EMPHASIS MINE)

According to the Gospel, when Jesus walks in the door, He meets your every need. As the Holy Spirit moves on people in our meetings, many times they are filled with joy. Critics have said, "Well, it doesn't really seem there's any purpose in what's happening in your meetings, because nobody's life depends upon receiving joy."

The problem is that people are always looking for some great significance and reading other things into everything Jesus did. But the desire of Jesus' heart was simply to meet people's needs, whatever they might be; to show us that God has provided for us in every situation.

Jesus walked into the wedding in Cana of Galilee and what did they need there? They had run out of wine. His turning the water into wine was a miracle, to be sure, but it wasn't essential. Nobody's life depended upon the miracle. He was just showing His glory. He was manifesting His power. John 2:11 says, **This beginning of miracles did Jesus in Cana of Galilee, and manifested forth his glory.**

You ask, "What is Jesus doing in the meetings you conduct?" Quite simply, He's doing what He's always done. He's just showing forth His glory and meeting the needs — big and small — of the people. Jesus walked into that wedding feast and was pushed into that miracle by His mother. He turned the water into wine to manifest His glory and meet the need.

What does that tell you? It tells you that Jesus wants to bless you. He is interested in the smallest details of your life. He wants to take care of you. He wants to meet your every need, just like He did for the disciples in Mark 4:35-41. Jesus is sleeping in the back of the boat as He and His disciples are taking a cruise across the lake. Alas, a storm arises and the waves roll and the winds howl. The disciples are afraid and they run back and awaken Jesus.

What happened when Jesus showed up? He commanded, "Peace, be still!" and the wind obeyed.

I want you to know, He can still calm the storms in your life! It doesn't matter what your storm looks like. It doesn't matter what you're facing. Jesus still calms the storm for you.

You might think, "Well, maybe He's sleeping in the back of the boat." Then why don't you just go lie down at the back of the boat with Him and take a nap too? As long as He's sleeping, you can rest too. He'll calm the storm for you.

Jesus also casts out demons. After calming the storm, Jesus and the disciples came to the country of the Gadarenes where a man with an unclean spirit met Him. (See Mark 5:1-6.) The devils possessing the man took one look at Jesus and said, "Uh-oh, we have to go! We can't stay here anymore! Where can we go? Oh, there's a bunch of swine; let's go into those swine." The devils know they can't stay around when Jesus walks in the door.

What's more, Jesus forgives sin. In Matthew 9:2-8, He walked up to a man with palsy and said, "Your sins are forgiven you," and he was healed. When Jesus shows up, it's the absolute opposite of when the Pharisees show up. When the Pharisees and the Sadducees and the wouldn't-sees and couldn't-sees show up, they bring rocks! They're ready to stone you to death for your sins. When Jesus shows up, He forgives sin! It's easy for Him to forgive sin and heal the sick because it's His nature and His purpose to forgive.

Jesus heals sickness. In Mark 5:25-34, a woman had been sick for twelve years with an issue of blood. She had spent all that she had on medical doctors, who were unable to help her. When she heard that Jesus was going to pass by, she said, "If I can just touch the hem of His garment, I'm going to be made whole."

As the woman touched the hem of Jesus' garment, the power of God, the anointing of the Holy Spirit that was on the life and the ministry of Jesus, flowed out of Him into her, and she was made whole. He said to her, **Go in peace, and be whole of thy plague** (Mark 5:34).

When Jesus shows up, He'll heal you. It doesn't matter what you're facing. You might have an incurable disease right now, a disease that has been diagnosed as terminal. I want you to know that Jesus still heals today. Hallelujah! He's the same yesterday, today, and forever. (See Hebrews 13:8.)

Jesus provides for us. In Matthew 14:15-21, Jesus had been followed into a desert place by a multitude of people who didn't have anything to eat. He took a little boy's lunch, blessed it, and multiplied it. Then He fed thousands with five loaves and two fishes. That's what happens when Jesus shows up!

Jesus shows mercy to sinners. Luke 19:2-9 tells the story of Jesus meeting a sinner. As He walked along a road, He saw a man named Zacchaeus sitting up in a tree. He said, "Come down, Zacchaeus. Let's go to your house." You might feel stuck way up in a tree right now, but I want you to know that Jesus will show up and say, "Come on down; let's go to your house." And believe me, when you experience Jesus' unconditional love and compassion, you will do what Zacchaeus did — drop everything and go with Jesus!

Jesus will raise us from the dead. In Mark 5:22-24 and 35-43, Jairus, one of the rulers of the synagogue, fell down in the dusty road at Jesus' feet and said, "My daughter is sick at home." Jesus went with Jairus to his home, but before they got there, they heard that she had died. Jesus told Jairus to continue believing, and because He walked into that house, the young girl was raised from the dead. When Jesus shows up, He brings new life!

Look at Luke 7:11-15. Jesus found a funeral procession outside the city of Nain. He called the boy right up out of the coffin and gave him back to his mother. When Jesus shows up, He'll raise the dead!

He came to the tomb where His dear friend Lazarus had been dead for four days. Lazarus' sisters were grieving. "Master," they said, "if You'd come earlier, this would not have happened. He's dead now and stinketh." But what happened when Jesus showed up? He said, "Roll away the stone." And then He said, "Lazarus, come forth!" And he did!

You might be right in the middle of a situation where you have no hope, where things you've been believing and trusting God for look dead. They look like they're buried in the tomb, stinking. But I want you to know that the same Jesus who walked the shores of Galilee two thousand years ago comes to you and says, "Roll away the stone and come forth!" Hallelujah! He brings life!

It doesn't matter what your circumstances are. When Jesus comes on the scene, impossible situations can be turned around. It doesn't matter what the devil says. It doesn't matter what other people say. When Jesus walks in the door, everything changes.

When Jesus walks in the door, there's no more argument. There's no more question, for He is *the Answer*. How can there be a question remaining when He is the Answer?

When Jesus walks in the door, there's no more loss of direction. How can there be a loss of direction when He is *the way?* When He walks in the door, there are no more lies. How can there be lies when He is *the truth?* When He walks in the door, there's no more death. How can there be death when He is *the life?* (See John 14:6.)

What happens when you've been in your boat all night fishing, but have caught nothing? You've fished and you've fished — and you know how to fish because you're a fisherman by trade — but you've caught absolutely nothing. Then Jesus shows up and gives you clear direction: "Cast your nets on the other side." (See John 21:1-6.)

You might be a minister of the Gospel and you've been fishing for souls all your life. You've been fishing for years in Podunk Hollow but you've caught no fish. Jesus comes to you now and says, "Cast your nets on the other side." Watch in wonder as hundreds of fish jump into your net!

Your first thought might be to say, "Rodney, you can't be serious. Surely Jesus won't meet every need —not *every single* need. Some He'll meet, yes, but surely not every need."

Yes! He'll meet every need, every one! Some people think His power is only for life-and-death situations. But that's not true. In fact, Jesus used His power not only to touch people in every area of their lives, but to meet the needs of His own ministry as well. When the disciples needed tax money, for instance, Jesus said to Peter, "Go down and catch the first fish. The money you need is in his mouth." (See Matthew 17:24-27.)

When you have a need, no matter how simple or how complicated it is, when Jesus shows up, He's going to meet that need. That is the Gospel! *It's Good News!*

Jesus is also our Miracle Worker. Think about this for a moment: Jesus walked on water. Nobody benefited from that miracle except Him. So why, then, did He walk on water? He walked on water because He needed to get to the other side! He sent the disciples on across the lake, because when you're in ministry, you need to get away from people and pray sometimes. Then he walked on the water to catch up with them. When Jesus walked on water, it did not seem like a necessity, but a luxury. He could have waited for another boat!

If the Pharisees had gotten hold of Jesus, they would have said, "You're abusing God's power! How dare you walk on water for your own benefit? Who do You think You are? From now on, please refrain from walking on water and always take a boat like everyone else. Look at You, taking God's power and using it for Yourself."

I believe that Jesus walked on water to show us that He had control over the elements as a sign and a wonder. But I also believe that He did it to show us that if we are obeying and serving God, we can trust Him to make a way for us where there is no way. Most of the time we have no faith for the supernatural, but God wants us to know that His supernatural power is there for us when we need it.

> *And Jesus looking upon them saith, With men it is impossible, but not with God: for with God all things are possible.*
>
> Mark 10:27

We could go on and on telling what happens when Jesus shows up. He showed up at the Pool of Bethesda, around which lay a great multitude of blind, crippled, maimed, and withered people. What happened when Jesus showed up? He found a man who had been there for a long time because he didn't have anybody to help him get into the pool. Jesus tells you the same thing He told that man, **Rise, take up thy bed, and walk** (John 5:8).

Do you realize that all we need in our churches, all we need in America, is for Jesus to show up? When He walks in the door, He is going to make a difference.

The problem is that some people are waiting for Prophet Doodad to show up; they're waiting for Evangelist Dingaling or Apostle Bucketmouth to come along. "Oh, if only he would come to our town, if only he would come and hold a crusade, it would be so wonderful." But you don't need any man; you need Jesus Christ, the Son of the Living God.

You say, "Rodney, I would love for Jesus to show up in my house. I would love for Jesus to show up in my church. I would love for Jesus to show up in my town."

Well, the truth is that if you are born again, Jesus will show up when you show up, because He's in you! He is in you and **greater is he that is in you, than he that is in the world** (1 John 4:4)!

Jesus also gives *you* power. He said to His disciples, **Behold, I give unto you power to tread on serpents and scorpions, and over all the power of the enemy** (Luke 10:19). When Jesus shows up, He gives you power and authority, the same power and authority that He walked in on the earth.

You're waiting for Jesus to show up and He's waiting for you to show up. He already did show up. Jesus has done everything He can do to bring you everything you need. He is waiting for you to believe it, to receive it for your life, and to see it manifested. Jesus is here right now, visiting your house! Just receive your need as being met as it would have been if Jesus had come to your house during His earthly ministry. You have a better covenant. The new covenant is better than the old. The only thing standing in your way is doubt and unbelief.

Jesus replied, Have I been with all of you for so long a time, and do you not recognize and know Me yet, Philip? Anyone who has seen Me has seen the Father. How can you say then, Show us the Father?

Do you not believe that I am in the Father, and that the Father is in Me? What I am telling you I do not say on My own authority and of My own accord; but the Father Who lives continually in Me does the (His) works (His own miracles, deeds of power).

Believe Me that I am in the Father and the Father in Me; or else believe Me for the sake of the [very] works themselves.

[If you cannot trust Me, at least let these works that I do in My Father's name convince you.]

I assure you, most solemnly I tell you, if anyone steadfastly believes in Me, he will himself be able to do the things that I do; and he will do even greater things than these, because I go to the Father.

JOHN 14:9-12 AMP

If Jesus lives in us, we can do the same things that He did. He even said we would do greater works. All we have to do is to take Him at His Word and believe it. When we show up, Jesus shows up! And when Jesus shows up, all of heaven's power is on the scene to save, heal, deliver, and set free!

Chapter 4

Jesus and His Methods

One of the things that really intrigued me about the ministry of Jesus was the methods He used to reach people. Whatever method He used, He was always led by the Holy Spirit. In the gospels, we see that Jesus was anointed by the Holy Spirit to minister to people. Everything He did was by the prompting and the leading of the Holy Spirit.

> *And Jesus, when he was baptized, went up straightway out of the water: and, lo, the heavens were opened unto him, and he saw the Spirit of God descending like a dove, and lighting upon him:*
>
> MATTHEW 3:16

> *How God anointed Jesus of Nazareth with the Holy Ghost and with power: who went about doing good, and healing all that were oppressed of the devil; for God was with him.*
>
> ACTS 10:38

God anointed Jesus with the Holy Ghost to do everything He did. To study Jesus' methods and the anointing He operated under, I want us to look at the ministry of Jesus through the eyes of a religious person or a skeptic — someone who does not believe. This might sound strange, but let's pretend that we don't know Him at all. We don't know who He really is. We're hearing about Him for the first time. Would His methods be acceptable in our day and time?

I am positive that if Jesus were here today in the flesh, He would be kicked out of most churches and would not be invited to speak at most conferences because of His methods. If

> I am positive that if Jesus were here today in the flesh, He would be kicked out of most churches and would not be invited to speak at most conferences because of His methods.

His methods were put under scrutiny, many would not receive Him today, just as they did not receive Him yesterday.

Let's look at some of the methods Jesus used that would cause a problem today.

1. He was constantly with sinners and was accused of being a gluttonous man and a winebibber (a drunk). (See Matthew 11:19.)

2. He healed on the Sabbath day. (See Luke 13:14-17.)

3. His disciples did not wash their hands when they ate, which was against Jewish law. (See Matthew 15:2.)

4. His disciples did not keep the traditions of the elders. (See Mark 7:5.)

5. He and His disciples harvested food to eat on the Sabbath. (See Matthew 12:1.)

6. He walked on water when He could have taken a boat. (See Matthew 14:25-32.)

7. He went over to the country of the Gadarenes and cast demons out of a man, which resulted in a whole herd of swine running down a hill into the sea and drowning. The local people, who made their living by raising pigs, then begged Him to leave their country. (See Mark 5:1-20.)

8. When they needed tax money, He told His closest followers to go fishing and get the money out of the fish's mouth. (See Matthew 17:24-27.)

9. He stopped a funeral procession and raised a boy from the dead. (See Luke 7:12-15.)

10. He spat in the ground, made clay, put it on a blind man's eyes, and told him to go wash in the pool of Siloam. (See John 9:1-7.)

11. He called a Syrophenician woman a dog. (See Mark 7:25-30.)

12. He got angry and cursed a fig tree. (See Mark 11:12-14, 20-21.)

13. He got angry in the temple, overturned the moneychanger's tables, and beat the moneychangers with whips. (See Matthew 21:12-13.)

14. At one of His meetings, His followers got out of order and ripped the roof off a house to lower a crippled man down through the hole — and He didn't mind! (See Mark 2:2-5.)

15. He made strong statements like, "Unless you eat of My flesh and drink of My blood you have no life in you." (See John 6:53.)

16. He told a man who wanted to follow Him — when he wanted to go home and bury his father — "Let the dead bury the dead." (See Matthew 8:21-22.)

17. He stood by the offering, watched it being taken up, and called His disciples to come and observe. (See Mark 12:41-44.)

18. He allowed people to go walking and leaping and praising God in His services. (See Luke 19:37-40.)

19. He allowed a woman to pour expensive perfume on His head when the money could have been given to the poor. (See Matthew 26:7-13.)

20. He didn't show up to attend the funeral of Lazarus, a dear friend, and waited four days before raising him from the dead. (See John 11:1-45.)

21. He called respected religious leaders the "blind leading the blind," (see Matthew 15:12-14) and "white-washed sepulchres full of dead men's bones" (see Matthew 23:27). He called them a "generation of vipers" (see Matthew 23:33) and said they were of "their father the devil" (see John 8:44).

22. He caused unclean spirits to cry out with loud voices in the synagogue. (See Luke 4:33-34.)

23. He let a woman, who was caught in adultery, go when she should have been stoned. (See John 8:1-11.)

24. He offended a rich young ruler by telling him to sell all he had and give it to the poor. (See Luke 18:18-23.)

25. He forgave a man of his sin and healed him — then said that both were easy. (See Matthew 9:2-6.)

26. He accepted people just as they were. (See Luke 19:2-10; John 8:1-11; 4:7-30.)

27. He breathed on His disciples and said, **Receive ye the Holy Ghost.** (See John 20:22.)

28. He spat on His hands, touched a deaf boy's tongue and ears, and healed him. (See Mark 7:32-35.)

29. He was not polite enough to His mother when He said, **Woman, what have I to do with thee?** (See John 2:4.)

These methods would get Him kicked out of most churches today. He would not be accepted in the religious world.

Jesus was radical.

Chapter 5

What *Did* Jesus Do?

Have you seen the wristbands that everybody's wearing? W.W.J.D. What Would Jesus Do? It's a craze that's gone across America. There are probably millions of people wearing those wristbands. W.W.J.D. is a question that many people ask today. We could sit and speculate for hours over what Jesus would do. But I want to come from the angle of what Jesus *did* do. W.D.J.D. — What Did Jesus Do?

At the end of the book of John, the Bible says **Jesus did many other things as well. If every one of them were written down, I suppose that even the whole world would not have room for the books that would be written** (John 21:25 NIV). What did He do? He did a bunch of things, and they all had to do with God's relationship with mankind, because He loves mankind so much.

If you look at religion and you look at Jesus, you get two totally different pictures. Religion is rigid, argumentative, and judgmental. But Jesus is loving and forgiving. He always comes with compassion, with arms wide open, and He never holds anything against anybody.

Because of His compassion for people, Jesus had to destroy the works of the devil. First John 3:8 says, **For this purpose was the Son of God manifested, that he might destroy the works of the devil.** I'll tell you, Jesus hates the devil, the devil hates Him, and two thousand years ago on the cross of Calvary, Jesus totally destroyed the works of the devil. There He paid the price for our sin, for our sickness, for our disease, for our mental turmoil, for our anguish, poverty, and lack.

It is evident from looking at the gospels of Matthew, Mark, Luke, and John that Jesus' whole ministry was directly opposed to the devil and to his works. Most importantly, He stripped the devil of any authority he had over man by paying the price for the sin of man. When Adam fell from grace in the Garden of Eden and exiled himself and all mankind from the presence of God, it was only Jesus who could come and pay the price to bring man back into the presence of God.

Can you imagine what it was like for Adam to be in the presence of God — to not know a day of sin in his life, to know God's provision, to know God's plan, and to know His joy and His peace — and then suddenly, because of his own disobedience, he is cut off? Suddenly he's on the outside looking in, cast away from the presence of God.

Thank God Jesus reversed what Adam did. My Bible tells me, **For God so loved the world, that he gave his only begotten Son, that whosoever believeth in him should not perish** (John 3:16). And that's the Good News. Jesus came to buy us back so that we can come back into the presence of God. Jesus says,

Come unto me, all ye that labour and are heavy laden, and I will give you rest. Take my yoke upon you, and learn of me.... for my yoke is easy, and my burden is light.

MATTHEW 11:28-30

The yoke of religious tradition is hard and its burden is heavy. If you are finding that serving God is hard, you need to jettison religion and discover Jesus afresh. Jesus' message today is, "I love you. I forgive you. Come to Me. You're tired, you're bruised, you're battered, you're weary, you're torn. Come unto Me and I'll give you rest. I'll give you what you need."

People are always looking for the latest fix, the latest joy, the latest thrill. They try to escape from reality through movies, computer games, virtual reality, drugs, sex, or alcohol, but they are wasting their time. The only true joy, the only true satisfaction, comes from Jesus and knowing Him as your personal Lord and Savior.

When Jesus comes into your life, He changes you, He sets you free, and He breaks the yoke of sin and bondage off you. God never made you to be a slave to sin. God made you to be lord and master of the sin. The Bible says that when you're bought with a price, when you're washed in the blood of Jesus, when you become a new creation in Christ Jesus, sin shall no longer have dominion over you. (See Romans 6:14.)

How wonderful it is to be a new creature. Aren't you glad that you're a new creature today? Oh, Hallelujah! The Bible says old things are passed away. Behold, all things are become new. (See 2 Corinthians 5:17.)

If you have given your life to Jesus, if you have been born again and washed in the blood of Jesus, you should not spend any time talking about the past. Don't allow people to say, "Hey, do you remember what we did ten years ago? You know how bad...."

Just look at them with a puzzled look on your face and say, "What are you talking about? That person's dead. Yeah, I used to do those things, but then Jesus came. He touched me. My life will never be the same again. Who you talking about?"

"Well, you remember we robbed the bank. Remember, we used to deal drugs. Remember, we used to do this and that."

"Sorry, I don't know who you're talking about. That person's dead. That person's gone. I'm a new creature in Christ Jesus. I've been washed in the blood of Jesus. I've been cleansed by the blood of Jesus."

The apostle Paul said, "Receive us because we've wronged no man." (See 2 Corinthians 7:2.) If you study the life of Paul before he was converted, when he was still Saul of Tarsus, you'll see how Saul threatened the Church and slaughtered the people of God. Yet Paul boldly wrote, "Receive us for we've wronged nobody."

How could he say that? It's because he was a new man. He knew that he'd had an encounter with God. He knew that the old man had died on the road to Damascus. When he had a head-on collision with Jesus of Nazareth, his name changed from Saul to Paul, and his name was written down in the Lamb's Book of Life. He knew on that day he was crucified with Christ. That's why he could say,

I am crucified with Christ: nevertheless I live; yet not I, but Christ liveth in me: and the life which I now live in the flesh I live by the faith of the Son of God, who loved me, and gave himself for me.

GALATIANS 2:20

"Receive us," Paul said, "because we've wronged nobody."

Someone said, "Oh, I know you."

"No, you don't."

"Oh yeah, I know you. I know what you were like."

"No, you don't. All you know is somebody who died." How can I say that? It's all because of *what Jesus did do.* Adam was cast out of the presence of God, but Jesus came as a second Adam to make us welcome there. He opened the door. He made a way and said, "Come."

Not only did Jesus pay the price for our sin on the cross, but He also paid the price for our sickness and disease. Sickness and disease don't come from heaven. I've never heard of a heavenly flu, have you? I've heard of Asian flu, I've heard of swine flu, I've heard of Hong Kong flu, but none of them are mine because I'm a citizen of heaven!

That's one area where the reality of Jesus conflicts with religious tradition. There are people in the religious world who believe that sickness and disease are God's plan for His people. What kind of a god is sitting in heaven trying to teach mankind a lesson, trying to bring them closer to him by afflicting mankind with sickness and disease? That's a lie from the pit of hell!

I want you to know that Jesus is the Healer as well as the Savior. Why would He save you from hell only to make you live in hell all your life on earth? No, He came to save you, heal you, and set you free!

There are many people bound by sickness and disease who believe that God put that on them. And that's a lie of the devil. God's not a monster and His idea of abundant life is not a life filled with pain and suffering. If our earthly parents did to us what we accuse God of doing, the authorities would lock them away for life. God's not a child molester; God's not a child abuser. There is one who is abusing and his name is Satan. Jesus came to destroy the works of the devil and to pay the price so that you and I could go free.

> *Who his own self bare our sins in his own body on the tree, that we, being dead to sins, should live unto righteousness: by whose stripes ye were healed.*

> 1 PETER 2:24

Two thousand years ago, Jesus bore the stripes upon His back so that today you could have health. Today you can have divine healing. I'll tell you, it doesn't matter what sickness or disease is coming against you right now. The name of Jesus is greater than any cancer, greater than any arthritis, greater than any tumor, greater than any heart condition, greater than any lung problem that you might ever face. The name of Jesus!

At the mention of His name, sickness and disease have to bow. Why? Because Jesus paid the price on the cross of Calvary. That's why the cross was so powerful. That's the finished work of the cross. When Jesus hung on the cross He said, "It is finished." He didn't say "There's still more that has to be done." No! He said, "It is finished. This is it. I've paid the price. You can go free. This is the year of jubilee. Shout it from the mountaintops! Shout it from the rooftops!" Tell the world the Good News! He saves, He heals, He delivers!

Jesus also paid the price for our peace. Watch people who don't believe. They're tormented. They can't sleep at night and have to take special tablets to go to sleep. The Bible says, He gives his beloved sleep. (See Psalm 127:2.) And yet, people are worried — worried about tomorrow, worried about the future, worried about the close of the millennium. But the Prince of

Peace has come and paid the price that you and I can have peace of mind.

Do you remember the day the war stopped in your head? Before you met Jesus there was a battle going on in your mind constantly, but the day He came you had peace. It was not a peace that the world gives, but the peace that He gives you. Now you can lie down at night and sleep, and you don't have to be afraid. You don't have to worry about a thing because you know that He's with you. You know that you dwell in the secret place of the Most High. You know you abide in the shadow of the Almighty. (See Psalm 91:1-2.) You know that He's your shepherd. (See Psalm 23:1.)

Not only did Jesus pay the price for our sin, our sickness, and our fears, but also for our poverty. Poverty's not a blessing. Poverty is a stinking curse! Heaven's not in a state of poverty. God's not sitting in the middle of a rubbish dump with flies hanging around the throne and angels slipping on rotten banana peels. No, we're going to a city where the roses never fade and where the streets are lined with crystal-clear gold.

Poverty is a curse, and since you are no longer under the curse, poverty's not for you. It's not your inheritance. You don't have to have it in your life. You have to resist poverty just like you would sickness and sin. You have to say, "No, poverty! I'm not going to allow you to come. You've come this far, but no further. You're not coming into my house. You're not going to dictate to my family. You're not going to dictate to my life. I come against you in the name of Jesus."

You just have to make the decision. In Deuteronomy 30:19, God said,

I call heaven and earth to record this day against you, that I set before you life and death, blessing and cursing: therefore choose life, that both thou and thy seed may live.

The choice is yours. Somebody said, "Well, we can't choose. It's just whatever will be will be. *Que sera, sera.*" I want you to know, the choice is ours to choose life. We can make a decision. Fathers, you can make a decision for your house. As for me and my house, we are going to serve the Lord. As for me and my house — it's time to draw a line in the sand. It's time to tell the devil, "You've come this far and you're coming no further. I rebuke sickness and disease, poverty, lack, depression and oppression, fear, bondage, and all that hell has to offer." And you tell him to get the *hell* out of your life! You can tell the devil to get the hell out and then you can let the heaven in. Hallelujah!

When heaven comes down, everything begins to change. Sin says, "I can't hang around here any longer; I need to leave."

Sickness and disease say, "Uh-oh, I can't stay. I have to leave."

Poverty says, "I can't hang around. I've got to go."

Fear says, "I can't hang around anymore. I must leave."

Torment says, "I can't stay; I've got to go."

Why? Because Jesus is here, and He paid the price on Calvary two thousand years ago so that you and I could go free.

What did Jesus do? He acted like His Father. Jesus said, **I seek not my own will, but the will of the Father which hath sent me** (John 5:30). He said, **I and my Father are one** (John 10:30). **He that hath seen me hath seen the Father** (John 14:9). So if we read about Jesus in Matthew, Mark, Luke, and John, we're going to get a portrayal of what the Father's like.

Over 70 percent of the life and ministry of Jesus was healing the sick, casting out devils, and setting the captives free. If Jesus dedicated 70 percent of His ministry to it, I would say it's important, wouldn't you? Our job is to get people saved, but once we get them saved, we want to get them healed. Once we get them healed, we want to get them free and walking in the blessings of heaven.

Salvation is an all-inclusive term. It comes from the Greek word *sozo*, which means soundness, wholeness, healing, preservation, deliverance, blessing, and provision — all of the goodness of God wrapped up in the finished work of the cross of Calvary (see

W. E. Vine's Expository Dictionary of Biblical Words, "save," Thomas Nelson Publishers, 1985). And it's all yours for the taking. You just have to say, "Thank You, Lord. I take it now. I take it by faith. Jesus is my Savior, Jesus is my Healer, Jesus is my Prince of Peace, Jesus is my Provider."

> But you know what? I want *all* that Jesus has for me. You know why? Because I've found out *what Jesus did.*

You could be saved, yet still be walking in anguish because you haven't taken Him as your Prince of Peace. You could be saved, yet still be walking in sickness because you haven't taken Him as your Healer. You could be saved, yet still be walking in poverty because you haven't taken Him as your Provider. But you know what? I want *all* that Jesus has for me. You know why? Because I've found out *what Jesus did.*

Somebody said, "Where did you find out what He did?" I found out in the pages of Matthew, Mark, Luke, and John. Jesus was the expressed will of the Father. He was God manifest in the flesh. He didn't do anything that He didn't first see His Father do. In other words, the Father loves — Jesus loves. The Father saves — Jesus saves. The Father forgives — Jesus forgives. The Father heals — Jesus heals. The Father delivers — Jesus delivers. He never did anything other than what His Father wanted Him to do.

And His will has not changed. I know that's true because my Bible says in Hebrews 13:8 (NIV), **Jesus Christ is the same yesterday and today and forever.** You have to settle that in your heart, because religion and tradition will try to distract you away from the truth. You have to make a decision in your heart to receive and accept the Word of God. God doesn't lie. I'm going to stand upon the Word of God, because everything else will fade away, but the Word will not.

What did Jesus do? He was born of a virgin, lived a sinless life, took our place at the cross of Calvary where you and I should have died for our sin. He died that you and I might live. He rose from the dead to be the head of His body, the Church. Then He gave us His resurrection power — the power of the Holy Spirit

— to do His works. Now, when I've found out what Jesus did do, that puts a responsibility on me to go and do what Jesus did.

But I can still avoid taking responsibility if I keep asking, "What would Jesus do?"

"Well, I don't know what He would do. Who knows what He would do?"

"We don't know. Do you know?"

We're just speculating. So whenever we come across a sick person, if we don't know what Jesus did, we'll say, "If it be Thy will, Lord, save this dear brother. Looooord! If it be Thy will, please heal Sister Bucketmouth. Lord, if it be Thy will, please provide for Brother Doodad."

But if you know exactly what Jesus *did* do, you know what His will *is*. You know what He *would* do. He's mighty to save, mighty to heal, mighty to deliver, mighty to forgive. So then, what must we do? We must take responsibility for what we know and do what He did — and what He told us to do. He said,

> *Go ye into all the world, and preach the gospel to every creature....*
>
> *And these signs shall follow them that believe; In my name shall they cast out devils; they shall speak with new tongues;*
>
> *They shall take up serpents; and if they drink any deadly thing, it shall not hurt them; they shall lay hands on the sick, and they shall recover.*
>
> MARK 16:15,17-20

We have the same commission He had. **For this purpose the Son of God was manifested, that he might destroy the works of the devil** (1 John 3:8). For this purpose are you and I made manifest, that we might destroy the works of the devil, set the captives free, destroy the yokes of bondage, and break the chains that have bound people for years. Hallelujah!

So with the knowledge of what Jesus did do, there's a responsibility that comes to me. I can't wander in the Land of Questions anymore because I have the Answer, and His name is Jesus, the solution to every problem. He gave us the power to do His works. He told us to go into all the world. Go. Two-thirds of God's name is "go." The other two-thirds of His name is "do."

What would Jesus do? Well, what did He do? He did it all. A lot of the things people think Jesus would do are nonessentials, but what He did do, eternity depends upon. We're not going to be held responsible for some myth of what we *think* Jesus would do. We'll be held responsible for what He *did* do.

Somebody said, "Why do you want the Holy Ghost in your life?" Because Jesus told the disciples to tarry at Jerusalem until they were endued with power from on high. And we can assume that if He said that, He knew that it was important. So that's what I want to do — I want Him to pour out His power upon me. I want Him to empower me and anoint me to go and reach the lost. He said, **Ye shall receive power, after that the Holy Ghost is come upon you; and ye shall be witnesses** (Acts 1:8).

Being a witness isn't running around with a T-shirt with a fish on it or having a "Honk if you love Jesus" sticker on your car. Being a witness is showing people there's something different about your life even when you say nothing. They can see Jesus in your eyes. They can hear Jesus in your voice. They can feel Jesus in your touch. The world is waiting to see Him made manifest in these last days.

It's time to do it. What would Jesus do? Matthew, Mark, Luke, and John tell us. Then it's not, What Would Jesus Do, it's what will *you* do? What are you going to do? He's waiting. He will do it when you do it.

We say, "Oh God, please do it."

God's saying, "I have already done My part in Jesus. It's your move now. You move and I will meet you at your point of faith."

I remember when I was praying, "Lord, if I were You, I'd do more than what I'm doing."

The Lord said to me, "Son, if I were you, I'd do more than what I'm doing."

I said, "Lord, I'm waiting for You."

He said, "Son, I'm waiting for you."

"You mean that, Lord?"

"Yes. Get up and go. Do it."

"Lord, can I wait for conditions to be right?"

"No."

"Oh God, there's opposition."

"Good, then I'll be with you."

"Oh God, there's persecution."

"Good. Now you know what I faced. Count it all joy. Rejoice!"

What must we do? What Jesus did: heal the sick, raise the dead, cast out devils, and preach the Good News of the Lord Jesus Christ everywhere we go. That commission doesn't leave any gray areas. People come upon a car wreck or somebody just had a heart attack and everybody runs around like a chicken with its head chopped off. What would Jesus do? He'd walk right in there and say, "Arise, in Jesus' name."

Somebody might say, "Well, you're just bold." No, it's got nothing to do with being naturally bold. If you've seen Him do it, you can do it. As you obey, He will make you supernaturally bold. Somebody might say, "But I'm not some great preacher." You don't have to be! Are you born again? Are you washed in the blood of Jesus? Is your name written in the Lamb's Book of Life? Have you accepted Him as your Lord and Savior? Then He lives on the inside of you and His Holy Spirit is right there to lead you and empower you.

What did Jesus do? Go do it!

It's time to rise up and do what Jesus would want us to do in the circumstances of life. The world is dying and needs a solution, and that solution is Jesus. You know He wants to save people more than we want them to be saved. He wants to heal people more than we want them to be healed. He wants to deliver people more than we want them to be delivered. He wants revival in America more than we want revival in America. He wants to shake whole cities in this nation more than we want to see whole cities shaken.

He's waiting for us while we're waiting for Him. He's waiting for us to get with the program, to say, "Oh, all right, Lord, whatever You want to do. I'll be the glove if You'll put Your hand in me, then do whatever You want to do. Whatever You want me to do, I'll do it. Wherever You want me to go, I'll go."

Jesus wants the Holy Spirit to live *big* on the inside of you. When you wake up and realize what you have on the inside, it's going to be explosive. You're going to say, "Blessed be the name of the Lord God forevermore! He's put His power and anointing on the inside of me! I might not have the education. I might not even know how to speak properly. But I know God lives on the inside of me. What would Jesus do? Just watch. I'm going to show you what He would do. Take up your bed and walk. Be healed. Be forgiven. Be free. I'll show you what He would do."

What would Jesus do? A friend of mine, someone in the ministry whom I really respect, was preaching out West many years ago. While he was preaching, a person in the meeting had a heart attack and died. The moment he heard that he prayed, "Don't expect me to do something about that. I mean the person's dead, you know. It's time to die. They needed to die." You know how people start reasoning.

But the Lord said to him, "What would Peter do if he was here right now?"

He said, "Lord, Peter would go back and raise that lady from the dead. But Lord, Peter's not here."

The Lord said to him, "What would I do?"

He said, "Lord, I know You'd go back there and raise that woman from the dead."

And the Lord said, "I'm in you. I'm in you. I'm in you."

So he ran back there and he said, "I command life in Jesus' name."

God breathed new life back in that woman, and she came off that floor totally healed by the power of God. When she went back to the doctor, he couldn't believe what he saw. She had been suffering from one of the worst heart conditions he'd ever seen, but now her heart was that of a baby.

What would Jesus do? Rise up big on the inside of you. That's what He would do. What did He do? He did it all. What does He want to do? He wants to do it *all* through you and me!

Chapter 6

The Blood of Jesus

*B*ut now in Christ Jesus ye who sometimes were far off are made nigh by the blood of Christ.

EPHESIANS 2:13

From the earliest times, blood has been a vital part of man's relationship with God, because life itself is in the blood. (See Leviticus 17:11.) Blood had to be shed to pay for the sins men committed — the life of the blood to cover the death found in sin. Under the old covenant, the blood of bulls and goats was used to temporarily cover the sin of the people. As the people exercised their faith in the blood to cover their sin, God looked down through the blood and counted then righteous in His sight.

But God wanted a more permanent relationship with man than what the blood of bulls and goats could give. The sacrifices of animals only temporarily covered the sin of the people. God wanted to make a way for man's sin nature to be wiped out by His righteousness, by His eternal life. Only the sinless, righteous, eternal blood of Jesus could do that.

God said, "I must send My Son and He will shed His eternal, sinless blood." This was not just the case of a *man* dying. Jesus was God and man combined, 100 percent God, 100 percent man. He was God manifest in the flesh, coming to redeem us and pay the price for the sin of the world.

That's why the blood of Jesus is so precious to you and me today. When we talk about His blood, it's not that we're gross or bloodthirsty. This is totally different. It's the blood of Jesus that has given us life. It's His blood that has ransomed us. It's His blood that has set us free. It's His blood that has removed every sin and every guilt from our life. It's His blood that has made us new creatures in Christ Jesus. It's His blood that gives us access to the throne of God in heaven. It's His blood that protects us. Hallelujah!

The blood of Jesus is so precious, because without it you and I would be lost. Without the blood of Jesus, we would be sacrificing animals with the high priest once a year. But we don't have to do that anymore. We have a high priest in the heavens, Jesus Christ, the Son of the Living God, and He has paid the price for the sin of the world. Like that old song says, "There's a fountain filled with blood drawn from Emmanuel's veins, and sinners plunged beneath that flood lose all their guilty stains." Today, tonight, tomorrow, and next week the blood is still flowing from Calvary. It has not dried up. It is eternally alive and it is precious. It's the blood that gives us identity. When the enemy sees you, he can't touch you because he sees the blood.

Let's look at what Jesus says about His blood. In Matthew 26:28, Jesus said, **For this is my blood of the new testament, which is shed for many for the remission of sins.** The word "remission" is totally different from the word "atone." Atone means to cover. Under the Old Covenant, the sins of people were atoned for, or covered. The blood of the bulls and goats would merely cover the sin.

But remission means to wipe out and do away with so that it's not there. There's no record of it. There's no trace of it. You can't find it. It's gone. It's been done away with. In John 6:53-54, Jesus speaks of this remission in the Last Supper:

Then Jesus said unto them, Verily, verily, I say unto you, Except ye eat the flesh of the Son of man, and drink his blood, ye have no life in you.

Whoso eateth my flesh, and drinketh my blood, hath eternal life; and I will raise him up at the last day.

It's the blood of Jesus that gives us eternal life. If you're born again, you're living in eternity right now. You are never going to die. You might die physically, but you're alive to God. You're going to live forever with Him. When you die physically, you're just going to step outside your body and go straight on to be with the Lord. John 6:55-56 goes on to say:

> *For my flesh is meat indeed, and my blood is drink indeed.*
>
> *He that eateth my flesh, and drinketh my blood, dwelleth in me, and I in him.*

That's why we can say, **For in him we live, and move, and have our being** (Acts 17:28), because the blood has made us one with Him. Paul, describing that first communion in 1 Corinthians 11:25 says:

> *After the same manner also he took the cup, when he had supped, saying, This cup is the new testament in my blood: this do ye, as oft as ye drink it, in remembrance of me.*

In other words, every time we partake of communion, we remember what took place two thousand years ago at the cross of Calvary. We drink the wine and remember Jesus shed His blood for our sin. We eat the bread and remember that His body was broken for our healing.

When we go back to the Old Testament, we can see the whole plan of redemption portrayed in types and shadows, in patterns established with the children of Israel. Look at the Exodus, when the children of Israel left their bondage in Egypt. When we study the story, we see that they could not leave Egypt until they had the lamb in them and the blood over them. In the same way, you and I cannot leave Egypt — the life of sin — until we have the Lamb in us and the blood over us.

Let's read the story, starting in Exodus 12:

> *The Lord spake unto Moses and Aaron in the land of Egypt, saying,*

This month shall be unto you the beginning of months: it shall be the first month of the year to you.

Speak ye unto all the congregation of Israel, saying, In the tenth day of this month they shall take to them every man a lamb, according to the house of their fathers, a lamb for an house:

And if the household be too little for the lamb, let him and his neighbour next unto his house take it according to the number of the souls; every man according to his eating shall make your count for the lamb.

Your lamb shall be without blemish, a male of the first year: ye shall take it out from the sheep, or from the goats:

And ye shall keep it up until the fourteenth day of the same month: and the whole assembly of the congregation of Israel shall kill it in the evening.

And they shall take of the blood, and strike it on the two side posts and on the upper doorpost of the houses, wherein they shall eat it.

And they shall eat the flesh in that night, roast with fire, and unleavened bread; and with bitter herbs they shall eat it.

Eat not of it raw, nor sodden at all with water, but roast with fire; his head with his legs, and with the purtenance thereof.

And ye shall let nothing of it remain until the morning; and that which remaineth of it until the morning ye shall burn with fire.

And thus shall ye eat it; with your loins girded, your shoes on your feet, and your staff in your hand; and yet shall eat it in haste: it is the Lord's passover.

EXODUS 12:1-11

God told them that this was a meal they had to eat, and then they needed to be ready to leave. "We're coming out of bondage," they said. "We're coming out of slavery! God is delivering us, but we can't leave Egypt till we have the lamb in us and the blood over us. So we first inspect the lamb to make sure it has no blemish. Then we kill the lamb, and with a branch of hyssop we put the blood on the doorposts and the lintels of the house. That way, when the angel of death passes over, it will not stop by and touch the firstborn. And then we're going to leave."

> *For I will pass through the land of Egypt this night, and will smite all the firstborn in the land of Egypt, both man and beast; and against all the gods of Egypt I will execute judgment: I am the Lord.*

EXODUS 12:12

Can you imagine sitting in your house knowing the angel of death is coming by, but knowing because you've smeared blood on the doorposts and the lintels, he cannot touch you? *You are under the blood.* Then next door, you hear a scream, because they had no blood.

I believe the blood was so powerful that if an Egyptian family found out what was going on and just did what they saw the Hebrews doing, their firstborn was saved. Wherever the blood of the lamb was, there was safety and deliverance.

It's the same with salvation. God doesn't care if you're white, black, yellow, green, or turquoise. He doesn't care what denomination you are, what nationality you are, male or female, bond or free. He just looks for the blood. It's the blood of Jesus that cleanses us from every guilt and every stain. It's His blood that makes us whole and makes us one.

Now let's look at Hebrews 9:6-24.

> *Now when these things were thus ordained, the priests went always into the first tabernacle, accomplishing the service of God.*
>
> *But into the second went the high priest alone once every year, not without blood, which he offered for himself, and for the errors of his people.*

So every time the High Priest came around, there had to be blood, because it was by blood that he could gain access into the Holy of Holies, into the presence of God. It's the blood that gives us access to the very presence of God. If it weren't for the blood, when you got in the presence of God, you'd drop dead. It says here, **which he offered for himself.** Notice, it didn't exclude the priest, **and for the errors of the people.** Let's continue with verse 8:

The Holy Ghost this signifying, that the way into the holiest of all was not yet made manifest, while as the first tabernacle was yet standing:

Which was a figure for the time then present, in which were offered both gifts and sacrifices, that could not make him that did the service perfect, as pertaining to the conscience;

Which stood only in meats and drinks, and divers washings, and carnal ordinances, imposed on them until the time of reformation.

But Christ being come an high priest of good things to come, by a greater and more perfect tabernacle, not made with hands, that is to say, not of this building;

Neither by the blood of goats and calves, but by his own blood he entered in once into the holy place, having obtained eternal redemption for us.

For if the blood of bulls and goats, and the ashes of an heifer sprinkling the unclean, sanctifeth to the purifying of the flesh:

How much more shall the blood of Christ, who through the eternal Spirit offered himself without spot to God, purge your conscience from dead works to serve the living God?

And for this cause he is the mediator of the new testament, that by means of death, for the redemption of the transgressions that were under the first testament, they which are called might receive the promise of eternal inheritance.

For where a testament is, there must also of necessity be the death of the testator.

For a testament is of force after men are dead: otherwise it is of no strength at all while the testator liveth.

Whereupon neither the first testament was dedicated without blood.

For when Moses had spoken every precept to all the people according to the law, he took the blood of calves and of goats, with water, and scarlet wool, and hyssop, and sprinkled both the book, and all the people,

Saying, This is the blood of the testament which God hath enjoined unto you.

Moreover he sprinkled with blood both the tabernacle, and all the vessels of the ministry.

And almost all things are by the law purged with blood; and without shedding of blood is no remission.

It was therefore necessary that the patterns of things in the heavens should be purified with these; but the heavenly things themselves with better sacrifices than these.

For Christ is not entered into the holy places made with hands, which are the figures of the true; but into heaven itself, now to appear in the presence of God for us.

HEBREWS 9:8-24

On earth was this earthly tabernacle made with hands, and that earthly tabernacle was a duplicate of the heavenly tabernacle. But man could not go into that heavenly tabernacle. So whenever it was taking place on the earth, God looked at it as though it were being done in heaven. But it wasn't sufficient. That's why Jesus had to come — He was the final sacrifice.

After Jesus said, "It is finished," and died on the cross, the veil of the earthly temple was torn in two, from top to bottom. (See John 19:30 and Matthew 27:51.) The Holy Ghost came out of an earthly tabernacle that was made with the hands of men, never again to live therein, but to come and live in your heart and my heart. And that's why we become temples of the Living God. For God has said, "I will dwell in them. I will walk in them. I will be their God. They will be My people." (See 2 Corinthians 6:16.) You are the temple of the living God, and the blood of Jesus washes you clean so He can come and live on the inside of you. Hallelujah!

Now, look at that last verse: **For Christ is not entered into the holy places made with hands, which are the figures of the true; but into heaven itself, now to appear in the presence of God for us.** When Jesus ascended, He went right into heaven to the real temple, not the type and shadow on earth. He took His own blood and made sure that heaven's court was satisfied, that the price for the sin of man was paid.

And it was paid for good.

Nor yet that he should offer himself often, as the high priest entereth into the holy place every year with blood of others;

For then must he often have suffered since the foundation of the world: but now once in the end of the world hath he appeared to put away sin by the sacrifice of himself.

HEBREWS 9:25-26

It's done. There's no more sacrifice. And yet it seems the modern-day church is always trying to sacrifice something. I'm convinced that if some people could, they would sacrifice another bull or goat, because they don't know what was purchased at Calvary. They don't know when Jesus said, "It is finished," He meant it.

As it is appointed unto men once to die, but after this the judgment:

So Christ was once offered to bear the sins of many; and unto them that look for him shall he appear the second time without sin unto salvation.

HEBREWS 9:27-28

The blood of Jesus has the purchasing power to redeem a sinner from the jaws of hell. I don't care who they are or what they've done. The blood can set them free. We were purchased with that blood.

> *Take heed therefore unto yourselves, and to all the flock, over the which the Holy Ghost hath made you overseers, to feed the church of God, which he hath purchased with his own blood.*
>
> ACTS 20:28

I don't care who they are or what they've done. The blood can set them free.

If you're the Church of the Lord Jesus Christ, you do not belong to yourself anymore. You belong to Him. You have been purchased by His blood. I belong to Jesus. I've been purchased by His blood. I'm His personal property. Written on my heart is "Personal Property of the Lord Jesus Christ."

Jesus left His mighty throne in glory to come to earth to pay the price to buy me. He must have thought I was worth something, because He came to pay the price. He came Himself to pay the price. He didn't send anybody else. He came Himself.

And it's a signed deal! This is not something that still has to be negotiated. The deal has been done. The God-Man, Jesus Christ of Nazareth, the Son of the Living God, 100 percent God, 100 percent man, came down and on behalf of man and on behalf of God, He cut the covenant in Himself to make sure that it couldn't go wrong on either side. It was done within Himself. Hallelujah!

Because of the blood of Jesus, we join the family of God and we're entitled to all that relationship implies.

> *In whom we have redemption through his blood, the forgiveness of sins, according to the riches of his grace.*
>
> EPHESIANS 1:7

> *In whom we have redemption through his blood, even the forgiveness of sins.*
>
> COLOSSIANS 1:14

And, having made peace through the blood of his cross, by him to reconcile all things unto himself; by him, I say, whether they be things in earth, or things in heaven.

COLOSSIANS 1:20

Through the blood we're justified. Through the blood we've been reconciled. My sins are forgiven and I'm part of the family of God.

And that's not all.

Much more then, being now justified by his blood, we shall be saved from wrath through him.

ROMANS 5:9

The day is coming when there will be a terrible judgment for all those who have rejected Jesus Christ — God's love and redemption extended to us — but not for you and me. For the believer, there will be the judgment seat of Christ which is going to be totally different. Every one of us will stand before Jesus to give an account of what we've done with our life, our calling, our ministry, and to give an account for every idle word spoken. And the Bible says our works will be tried as with fire. Some works will be wood, hay, and stubble and burn up. Some will be gold, jewels, and precious stones and we'll carry them into eternity with us.

That's why I believe the Bible says He's going to wipe away the tears from our eyes, because many people will get to heaven and be ashamed that they never did more with what was purchased for them on the cross. Everything you're doing right now is going to count for eternity. Every act of kindness, every act of generosity, every time you help somebody and bring them to Jesus, you're laying up treasure in heaven.

Don't take it lightly! Jesus came and gave His all. The least I can do is give my all because of what He did for me at Calvary. The least I can do is to be 100 percent committed to Him. The least I can do is live a holy life. The least I can do is live a sanctified life. The least I can do is renew my mind to the Word of God. The least I can do is put my flesh under. That's the least I can do!

The blood of Jesus not only cleanses me from sin and saves me from judgment, but it protects me from the enemy. When the enemy comes by me, he can't touch me, because he sees the blood. "Oh, he belongs to Jesus," the devil says, "I can't touch him. I have no authority over him. I can't put sickness and disease on him for long. I'll try, but I can't make it stick. He just keeps getting healed all the time."

People sometimes look at me and say, "Well, you're just a real bold individual." But you have to understand. I wasn't always that way. I was very shy. But I'm made bold because of the blood of Jesus. Hebrews 10:19-20 says:

> *Having therefore, brethren, boldness to enter into the holiest by the blood of Jesus,*
>
> *By a new and living way, which he hath consecrated for us, through the veil, that is to say, his flesh.*

I can be bold because of the blood — not arrogant — bold. When you stand in front of somebody who is sick, you can be *bold.* You can lay your hands on them and know that the power of God is going to come into them and that sickness and disease are going to have to go. You can be bold when you speak to devils, and they're going leave.

Where does that boldness come from? People are trying to get bold by reading self-help books, but that's just confidence in human ability. People who are bold by the blood of Jesus don't trust in their own ability. They have no confidence in the flesh, but they have boldness in the blood, boldness in the name of Jesus, boldness in the Word of God. By the blood of Jesus we can be bold.

Now, just because we can come boldly to the throne of grace to obtain mercy doesn't mean we can just sin, knowing that the blood will cover it. No! We've got to treat the blood with total respect. Hebrews 10:29 says,

Of how much sorer punishment, suppose ye, shall he be thought worthy, who hath trodden under foot the Son of God, and hath counted the blood of the covenant, wherewith he was sanctified, an unholy thing, and hath done despite unto the Spirit of grace?

That's why we don't play with sin. If you have a problem with sin in your life, deal with it. Put it out. If you don't put it out, it will take you out. It's not a game. The verse before that, Hebrews 10:26, says if we sin willfully after we hear the truth, then we have no forgiveness. To sin willfully means to go ahead and practice sin, thinking it doesn't matter because we know that God will just forgive us one of these days. We can't live like heathens and then go back to the throne of grace after we're done.

You don't want to touch sin. It will kill you! It will destroy you. Keep it away from your thought life. Treat sin like your worst enemy, like you would a burglar coming into your house at night.

"Does that mean I need to live a holy life?" Yes! And you can, because if Jesus said you can live a holy life, then I believe you can live a holy life. And I'm not talking about being religious, pious, or "holier than thou." If Jesus said you could, you can.

"But can I do it?" Yes, you've got the power to live a holy life. You're not weak when it comes to temptation. That's a lie from hell. You're strong. You can do it. You've got faith in the blood of Jesus, and because you've got faith in the blood, you can do it; you can overcome.

"Well, then, how do I get this blood to work in my life?" You have to walk in the light. First John 1:7 says, **But if we walk in the light, as he is in the light, we have fellowship one with**

another, and the blood of Jesus Christ his Son cleanseth us from all sin. Just walk in the light. Everywhere you go, make sure you're walking in the light. If there's any darkness, don't put your foot in it. It's a pile of something that you don't want to get into! Walk in the light.

If we walk in the light as He is in the light, then we will have fellowship one with another. The first sign that somebody's backsliding is when they break fellowship with other Christians. That's why the Bible says not to forsake fellowship with other believers. (See Hebrews 10:25.)

On the other hand, when you get on fire for God, suddenly your unsaved friends won't want to be around you. What's happening is that you're now walking in the light and they want to walk in darkness. Your light is convicting them.

How do you activate the reality of the blood on a daily basis? You do it by testifying. Look at Revelation 12:11: **They overcame him by the blood of the Lamb, and by the word of their testimony; and they loved not their lives unto the death.** To make the blood a reality in your life, find somebody to tell your conversion to every day. Tell them about what Jesus did for you. If Jesus has really touched you, you cannot tell somebody else without getting excited. It takes you right back and you get all refreshed.

Activate the power of the blood daily in your life by telling the story. "Hallelujah! I was lost, but He found me," you can tell them. "I was blind, but now I can see. I was bound, but now I'm free. He washed me in His blood. He set me free. He cleansed me. He delivered me from all my guilt and all my shame. I've fallen in love with Jesus, and I just want to tell you about Him, how wonderful He is! Because of His blood, I'm His child and He loves me!"

Chapter 7

The Name of Jesus

*N*ow *Peter and John went up together into the temple at the hour of prayer, being the ninth hour.*

And a certain man lame from his mother's womb was carried, whom they laid daily at the gate of the temple which is called Beautiful, to ask alms of them that entered into the temple;

Who seeing Peter and John about to go into the temple asked an alms.

And Peter, fastening his eyes upon him with John, said, Look on us.

And he gave heed unto them, expecting to receive something of them.

Then Peter said, Silver and gold have I none; but such as I have give I thee: In the name of Jesus Christ of Nazareth rise up and walk.

And he took him by the right hand, and lifted him up: and immediately his feet and ankle bones received strength.

And he leaping up stood, and walked, and entered with them into the temple, walking, and leaping, and praising God:

And all the people saw him walking and praising God:

And they knew that it was he which sat for alms at the Beautiful gate of the temple: and they were filled with wonder and amazement at that which had happened unto him.

And as the lame man which was healed held Peter and John, all the people ran together unto them in the porch that is called Solomon's, greatly wondering.

And when Peter saw it, he answered unto the people, Ye men of Israel, why marvel ye at this? or why look ye so earnestly on us, as though by our own power or holiness we had made this man to walk?

ACTS 3:1-12

Then Peter began to preach to the people about Jesus, in whose name he had just healed the lame man. Although about five thousand people got saved, the religious leaders arrested Peter and John. (See Acts 4:1-4.) They had only one question for them:

By what power, or by what name, have ye done this?

Then Peter, filled with the Holy Ghost, said unto them, Ye rulers of the people, and elders of Israel...

*Be it known unto you all, and to all the people of Israel, that **by the name of Jesus Christ of Nazareth,** whom ye crucified, whom God raised from the dead, even by him doth this man stand here before you whole...*

*Neither is there salvation in any other: **for there is none other name under heaven given among men, whereby we must be saved.***

ACTS 4:7-8,10,12 (EMPHASIS MINE)

Then the men of the council got together and conferred among themselves:

Saying, What shall we do to these men? for that indeed a notable miracle hath been done by them is manifest to all them that dwell in Jerusalem; and we cannot deny it.

*But that it spread no further among the people, let us straitly threaten them, **that they speak henceforth to no man in this name.***

*And they called them, and commanded them **not to speak at all nor teach in the name of Jesus.***

But Peter and John answered and said unto them, Whether it be right in the sight of God to hearken unto you more than unto God, judge ye.

For we cannot but speak the things which we have seen and heard.

ACTS 4:16-20 (EMPHASIS MINE)

That name really stirred them up, didn't it? Now, look at verses 23 through 31 (EMPHASIS MINE):

> *And being let go, they went to their own company, and reported all that the chief priests and elders had said unto them.*
>
> *And when they heard that, they lifted up their voice to God with one accord, and said, Lord, thou art God, which hast made heaven, and earth, and the sea, and all that in them is:*
>
> *Who by the mouth of thy servant David hast said, Why did the heathen rage, and the people imagine vain things?*
>
> *The kings of the earth stood up, and the rulers were gathered together against the Lord, and against his Christ.*
>
> *For of a truth against thy holy child Jesus, whom thou hast anointed, both Herod, and Pontius Pilate, with the Gentiles, and the people of Israel, were gathered together,*
>
> *For to do whatsoever thy hand and thy counsel determined before to be done.*
>
> *And now, Lord, behold their threatenings: and grant unto thy servants, that with all boldness they may speak thy word,*
>
> *By stretching forth thine hand to heal; and **that signs and wonders may be done by the name of thy holy child Jesus.***
>
> *And when they had prayed, the place was shaken where they were assembled together; and they were all filled with the Holy Ghost, and they spake the word of God with boldness.*

The name of Jesus has been given to the Church as the Church's possession. Jesus gave us His name. A name is only as good as the person from whence it comes. How good a name is depends on what authority is backing up that name. When somebody knocks on your door and says, "I stand here by the authority of the police department," even though you don't know this particular policeman, you open up because you recognize the authority of the police. If you stand in the name of someone, then you'd better make certain they have what it takes to back you up.

That's why the chief priests and elders asked Peter and John, "By what name have you done this?" They wanted to know whose power was backing the disciples up.

We come in the same name — Jesus — **a name which is above every name.** The name that, even at the mention of it, **every knee should bow, of things in heaven, and things in earth, and things under the earth** (Philippians 2:10). At the mention of that name, **every tongue should confess that Jesus Christ is Lord** (Philippians 2:11).

Have you ever wondered why there is only one name that is taken in vain? Only the name of one God is taken in vain: Jesus. You don't hear people scream in pain and say, "Oh, Buddha, I stubbed my toe," or "Oh, Mohammed, I jammed my finger." You don't see people hit their thumb with a hammer and say, "Oh, Confucius!" They always use the name of Jesus. Even the worst sinner uses the name of Jesus. Why? The devil knows only Jesus' name has authority and power and he tries to get people to disrespect that name by using it as a curse. But he finds himself in big trouble when believers, washed in the blood, find out that he has no defenses against that name!

Jesus has given His name to you and me. It's our possession. It belongs to us. Hallelujah! We have authority over every evil thing in that name. In that name, sickness has to go. In that name, disease has to go. In that name, poverty has to go. In that name, oppression has to go. In that name, death has to go. When the believer speaks that name in faith, something's going to happen!

In John 16:23-24, Jesus says this about our use of His name:

And in that day ye shall ask me nothing. Verily, verily, I say unto you, Whatsoever ye shall ask the Father in my name, he will give it you.

Hitherto have ye asked nothing in my name: ask, and ye shall receive, that your joy may be full.

Jesus wants us to use His name so that our joy may be full. He also wants us to know the power of His name:

And these signs shall follow them that believe; In my name shall they cast out devils; they shall speak with new tongues;

They shall take up serpents; and if they drink any deadly thing, it shall not hurt them; they shall lay hands on the sick, and they shall recover.

MARK 16:17-18

There are many people who believe in Jesus, but they don't believe in the power of His name, so they don't cast out devils or heal the sick. When you believe in His name, you can. I believe in that name, that name that's above every name, that name that's above cancer, that name that's above arthritis, that name that's above depression, that name that's above every sickness and disease. I believe that name is higher than any other name on the face of the earth — Jesus.

What authority stands behind that name? All of heaven is behind that name. When we mention that name, heaven stands at attention. When we mention that wonderful name, all heaven stands up and says, "Did you call?" When we mention that name, the angels of God move to and fro saying, "He mentioned that name! She mentioned that name!"

There's a story that I heard many years ago about a lady whose beloved husband died, but she would not let him go. She stood by the bed and said, "I'll not let you go. In the name of Jesus, come back." And he was raised from the dead.

The man testified later that he went to heaven and an angel came to him and said, "You have to go back. She's using that name. Although you'd love to stay, you'll have to go back. She's using that name."

That name carries authority.

And Jesus came and spake unto them, saying, All power is given unto me in heaven and in earth.

Go ye therefore, and teach all nations, baptizing them in the name of the Father, and of the Son, and of the Holy Ghost:

Teaching them to observe all things whatsoever I have commanded you: and, lo, I am with you always, even unto the end of the world. Amen.

MATTHEW 28:18-20

Jesus said, "I have been given all power and all authority. You go in My name, teach them in My name, and I will come to back up My name. So when you speak My name, I'm going to come. I will come and confirm My Word with signs following." (See Mark 16:20.)

Now a person can acquire a name three ways. In the world, people acquire names first of all by inheritance. Prince Charles inherited his name and title. There's no way that a commoner could be called a prince. You have to be born into the royal family.

Secondly, you could acquire a name by bestowal. It could be bestowed or conferred upon you. A university can confer a doctorate or the queen could knight you Sir Whoever. That name would be conferred upon you because of your achievements in a certain field.

A name can also be acquired by conquest. William the Conqueror or Emperor Napoleon got their names and their kingdoms by conquest in battle.

But Jesus got His name all three ways. He got His name first by inheritance.

In the beginning was the Word, and the Word was with God, and the Word was God....

And the Word was made flesh, and dwelt among us, (and we beheld his glory, the glory as of the only begotten of the Father,) full of grace and truth.

JOHN 1:1,14

God hath fulfilled the same unto us their children, in that he hath raised up Jesus again; as it is also written in the second psalm, Thou art my Son, this day have I begotten thee.

ACTS 13:33

God, who at sundry times and in divers manners spake in time past unto the fathers by the prophets,

Hath in these last days spoken unto us by his Son, whom he hath appointed heir of all things, by whom also he made the worlds;

Who being the brightness of his glory, and the express image of his person, and upholding all things by the word of his power, when he had by himself purged our sins, sat down on the right hand of the Majesty on high;

Being made so much better than the angels, as he hath by inheritance obtained a more excellent name than they.

For unto which of the angels said he at any time, Thou art my son, this day have I begotten thee? And again, I will be to him a Father, and he shall be to me a Son?

And again, when he bringeth in the first begotten into the world, he saith, And let all the angels of God worship him.

HEBREWS 1:1-6

The second way Jesus got His name was by bestowal:

Wherefore God also hath highly exalted him, and given him a name which is above every name.

PHILIPPIANS 2:9

In *The Amplified Bible*, Philippians 2:9-11 says:

Therefore [because He stooped so low] God has highly exalted Him and has freely bestowed on Him the name that is above every name,

That in (at) the name of Jesus every knee should (must) bow,
in heaven and on earth and under the earth,

And every tongue [frankly and openly] confess and acknowl-
edge that Jesus Christ is Lord, to the glory of God the Father.

His name was bestowed because of His achievements, because Jesus paid the price on the cross and defeated sin, death, hell, and the grave, and then rose again. He is giving us that same power with which He overcame sin, and He said, "You go in My name." So when you and I stand in front of darkness and we say, "In the name of Jesus," darkness knows the power behind that name!

But you can't do this without knowing the Person behind the name. It's not going to work. In Acts 19:13-16, the seven sons of Sceva saw Paul casting out devils in the name of Jesus. They said, "Well, we'll just go and do the same thing in the name of Jesus Christ whom Paul preaches."

They used the name, but the demon said, "Well, Jesus I know. Paul I know, but who are you?" And the demon leaped on them, tore their clothes off, and they ran from the place naked.

So not just anybody can use that name! It's only for the believer. It's only for the one who knows what that name represents. People come to me all the time and say, "Well, I used the name and nothing happened." It's got to become a living reality on the inside of you. I know when I speak that name of Jesus, something is going to happen, because I have faith in the authority bestowed upon that name.

First, Jesus got His name by inheritance; second, He got it by bestowal; and third, He got it by conquest.

Who hath delivered us from the power of darkness, and hath
translated us into the kingdom of his dear Son.

COLOSSIANS 1:13

And having spoiled principalities and powers, he made a shew of them openly, triumphing over them in it.

COLOSSIANS 2:15

This same verse in *The Amplified Bible* says:

[God] disarmed the principalities and the powers that were ranged against us and made a bold display and public example of them, in triumphing over them in Him and in it [the cross].

Through the cross, the devil's powers were rendered useless. Now if that name has done that, and that name has been given to you and me, do you understand what awesome power you and I have when we use the name of Jesus? It's not just a thing that we add on at the end of a prayer, "in the name of Jesus." It's something that is going to cause everything we pray about to come to pass.

"Whatsoever you ask the Father in My name," Jesus said, "I'm going to do it for you. If I don't have it, I'll make it for you. I'll make a way where there is no way. I'm the way, the truth, and the life. I'm Alpha and Omega, the beginning and the end, the first and the last, who was and is and is to come. When you speak My name, I'm going to come. I'll back you up in an impossible situation. When your back's against the wall and you don't know which way to turn, mention My name, and I'm going to be right there." When you fully understand the power in the name of Jesus, it will change the way you pray.

Now, as I said, a name is only as powerful as that which backs it up. I heard Richard Roberts say that when he was a young man, he wanted to rebel against his father. He wanted nothing to do with his dad's name, so he left and went to the University of Kansas. But no one knew him there, and he couldn't even open a bank account. Eventually he got so mad he said, "Listen, I'm Richard Roberts. My dad's Oral Roberts."

Suddenly, people started responding to him. "Oh, you're the son of Oral Roberts! Okay." He just mentioned his father's name and things happened. Even though he didn't want the name, in the end it actually helped him.

Now people do that with the name of Jesus, too. They refuse to use the power in the name — how dumb can you get? When sickness and disease came knocking on your door today, did you use that name? No? Why not? When poverty tried to attach itself to you, did you use that name? No? Why not?

Do you understand that when you mention that name, all heaven stands at attention and moves right in to back you up? Boom! Just like that! It's the key that unlocks the door to the blessing, and it's yours.

People might say, "Well, you're just using it as a formula."

But Jesus told us, "Use My name; go into all the world in My name."

"By whose authority do you come here?"

"I come here by the name of Jesus Christ of Nazareth, the Son of the Living God."

"By whose authority do you lay hands on these sick people?"

"By the authority of the name that's above every name, the name of Jesus."

> When you realize the authority in the name of Jesus, you'll get bold.

When you realize the authority in the name of Jesus, you'll get bold. When I left South Africa, people said, "There goes Rodney to America with nobody but God behind him." But I didn't need anyone or anything else. I came and God blessed. Wherever we go in the world, whether by invitation or not, we go there in the name of Jesus and by His authority.

That name will give you supernatural, divine favor. That name will open the door for you into places where there is no door. That name will make a way where there is no way. That name will furnish a table in the wilderness. That name will make the crooked paths straight. That name will calm the worst storm in your life. That name will make things look like heaven.

I'll tell you, you'll think twice before using that name carelessly again. Think twice before you just say, "Blahblahblah, in Jesus' name, amen." That name is powerful! And it belongs to you! It's your possession!

Jesus says, "I'm going to give you eternal life, and you will come to live in heaven with Me, but while you're down here on earth, I'm going to give you My name."

I have His name! That's what Christian means: "Little anointed one, little Jesus." Religious people get upset when you talk like this.

"Well, who do you think you are?"

"I don't think I'm anything, but I know who He is."

I know who He is. He's given me His name. It's mine. It belongs to me and it belongs to you. It's yours at two o'clock in the morning. It's yours on Monday, Tuesday, Wednesday, Thursday, and Friday. That name is yours. You're His child. You just have to mention that name and a holy boldness comes upon you.

The late John Osteen was one of the boldest pastors I know. He was invited to a secular event with businessmen of different faiths. The coordinator of the dinner said, "Now listen, when you pray over the food, don't use the name of Jesus because you'll offend the people of other faiths."

Pastor Osteen didn't say anything until they called him up to pray. He said, "Father, in the name of Jesus, I thank You for this meal. I thank You for the name of Jesus, and for the food in Jesus' name. I pray that, in Jesus' name, You'll bless everybody here. Thank You Lord, in Jesus' name."

Another time, Pastor Osteen got on a hotel elevator and heard people on the elevator cussing up a storm, using the name of the Lord in vain, with the foulest language. So he boldly said, "Praise God! Oh, I love You, Jesus! I worship You. Oh, thank You Jesus, You're so awesome. Lord, I just worship You. I give You praise. I give You honor."

They all looked at him. Finally one of them said, "What are you doing?"

He said, "I'm just giving my God equal time."

Now some people get timid when it comes to using the name. They'll pray a prayer and then end it with, "For God's sake." Or, "Lord, bless this food for Jesus' sake." Well, Jesus is not eating the food, you are! "Lord, bless this food for Rodney's sake, in Jesus' name." Don't get to the end of the prayer and mumble, "inJesusname." Don't be ashamed of the name — be bold!

I'm not ashamed of the name. I've been in places where somebody was cussing and using name of Jesus. You know what I did? I said, "Oh, you know Him, too? Is He here? That's wonderful! He's my friend! You just mentioned my friend's name."

"What do you mean?"

"Well, you just mentioned Jesus. You know Him as well? You seem to know Him. You mention Him often."

The name of Jesus has authority in three worlds — in heaven before God and all of the angels, in earth over men, and under the earth, over the devil and all the demons of hell. That name carries power. That name has authority.

When the enemy sees you coming, he says, "Get out of the way, he's using that name! She's using that name, we can't go to that house! They use that name in that house! We can't go near these people. They use that name. They know what that name stands for, and they know what that name means. Leave them alone. They're using that name!"

Whenever the enemy comes your way, don't even think about it. Just say, "I'm going to use that name, I'm going to pull that name out and it's loaded, it's ready to be fired. Satan, you're messing with a believer, and I'm going to use that name!"

Wherefore God also hath highly exalted him, and given him
a name which is above every name:

That at the name of Jesus every knee should bow, of things in heaven, and things in earth, and things under the earth;

And that every tongue should confess that Jesus Christ is Lord, to the glory of God the Father.

PHILIPPIANS 2:9-11

Chapter 8

The Compassion of Jesus

*H*e shall feed his flock like a shepherd: he shall gather the
lambs with his arm, and carry them in his bosom, and
shall gently lead those that are with young.

ISAIAH 40:11

Hollywood once tried to portray Jesus as a confused, weak man who was battling with His own identity. He didn't know who He was and struggled with what He was called to do. But the gospels show clearly that Jesus knew exactly who He was. He was a person of very strong character and great compassion — and He was no wimp. He knew He came to the earth for a reason. He came to the earth with a purpose.

*For this purpose the Son of God was manifested, that he
might destroy the works of the devil.*

1 JOHN 3:8

Jesus came to destroy the works of the devil. Many try to make out that Jesus really wasn't interested in mankind, that He was just interested in Himself and that He formed a following for His own benefit. However, He came to pay the price for the sin of man and to give His life for the world. He laid down His life so that you and I could live free of the bondage of sin and overcome all the devil's attacks and schemes. He said, "I am come that you might have life, and that you might have it more abundantly." (See John 10:10.)

In Acts 10:38, Peter preached about **how God anointed Jesus of Nazareth with the Holy Ghost and with power: who went about doing good, and healing all that were oppressed of the devil; for God was with him.** The ministry of Jesus, the compassionate One, was to do good, to bless people, to touch people, and to change lives. Everywhere He went, He healed the sick and He cast out devils.

When we look at Jesus, we see not only was He *able* to do what He did, but because of His compassion, He was *willing*. If you ask many people in the world today, "Is God able?" they would say, "Yes, He's able." But they're not sure if He would be willing. Jesus is not only able, but He's willing. He wants to touch mankind more than mankind wants to be touched.

We've had people who have been bedridden whom God has raised up, and people bound by incurable disease whom God has healed. Why? Because Jesus' whole purpose and His whole desire is to touch and to change people's lives. His desire is not to offer you a home in heaven, yet let you live in hell until you get there. The prayer that He taught the disciples was, **Thy will be done in earth, as it is in heaven** (Matthew 6:10). God's will is that you be touched, changed, set free, and delivered right here on earth.

Now in order to see how willing Jesus was, let's look at Him in operation. Matthew 8:1 says, **When he was come down from the mountain, great multitudes followed him.**

Why do you think they followed Him? They followed Him because He had something special. You know, in the middle of summer, everybody wants to follow the ice cream truck. Now I am not calling Jesus an ice cream truck, but when people realize that you have what they need, they come and get it. Jesus had something people really needed and wanted. He had the words of life and His words brought about change in their lives. He could come into their lives and calm the storm.

Jesus never talked to people like the religious world does today. He never tried to put them down or condemn them. You've got to realize that Jesus loves people, and He loves sinners. He can't stand religion and He can't stand tradition. The people He was always bumping into and knocking heads with were the religious people of the day. They hated Him because He loved people and had the power to change lives. By his words and actions He showed them to be the prideful hypocrites they were.

The people He fought with the most were the Pharisees, the Sadducees — the "wouldn't sees" and the "couldn't sees." He really had problems with them on the Sabbath. On the Sabbath, they came out ready to kill. I don't know if this happened, but I've just got a feeling that when Jesus woke up on Sabbath mornings, He rubbed His hands together and said, "Oh, boy! Sabbath day! Let's cause some trouble today! Let's find some sick people to heal, because you know it's gonna irritate those religious people."

Religious people also have a problem accepting the fact that God is *always* willing and desiring to heal people. One day, a leper came to Him, worshipping and saying, "Lord, if You will, You can make me clean." (See Mark 1:40.)

Did Jesus say, "I don't want to right now, be sick for another two years"? Did He say, "Nope, I've put this sickness on you to teach you a lesson"? Or did He say, "I don't want to heal you, I've put this sickness on you to bring you closer to Me"?

No! He said, "I will! I want to! Be clean." Jesus wanted to heal him, and He did heal him. Immediately the man's leprosy was cleansed.

Well, the leper told everybody about how Jesus healed him, and His fame spread throughout the region. They began bringing the sick and the demon-possessed, and He set them free. Matthew 8:16-17 says,

> *When the even was come, they brought unto him many that were possessed with devils: and he cast out the spirits with his word, and healed all that were sick:*
>
> *That it might be fulfilled which was spoken by Esaias, the prophet, saying, Himself took our infirmities, and bare our sicknesses.*

Let's compare the word "compassion" with the word "sympathy." Sometimes we think we have compassion, but we're actually having sympathy. They are two different things. Sympathy says, "I know how you feel," but compassion says, "I *feel* how you feel."

Jesus not only had *sympathy* for people, He went a step further. He had *compassion* for the people around Him. He *felt* how they felt. When He looked at people, He felt the burdens they had. He wept over the people of Jerusalem, even when He knew they would turn on Him and kill Him. Do we have that same compassion for the lost?

When the compassion of Jesus takes over the Church of the Lord Jesus Christ, we're not going to walk around with our noses up in the air, looking down at everybody, judging everybody. When we feel His compassion, we will be broken. We will begin to weep. I've driven through cities and found myself just beginning to weep over the lost. Do you weep over the lost?

One man of God told me that he was walking out of a hotel one day with another preacher, and a drunk was walking by them. The preacher he was with looked at the drunk, shook his head, and said, "That's just terrible, just sick."

The man of God turned to him and said, "That would be you and me without Jesus."

Religion looks at those who are lost, dying, and caught in the clutches of sin and turns up its nose with a "holier than thou" attitude. Religion wants to condemn. But Jesus never condemns. Jesus comes with compassion to forgive and heal and deliver.

But when he saw the multitudes, he was moved with compassion on them, because they fainted, and were scattered abroad, as sheep having no shepherd.

MATTHEW 9:36

Sympathy says, "I know how you feel," but sits and does not lift a hand to do a thing. Compassion says, "I feel exactly how you feel," and then compassion *acts*. Remember that: *Sympathy sits. Compassion acts.*

In Matthew 14:14, **Jesus went forth, and saw a great multitude, and was moved with compassion toward them, and he healed their sick.** He didn't just say, "Oh, look at all these sick people. It's just terrible how things are in the world, but there's nothing you can do about it." No. He acted. He moved out. He began to heal the sick and cast out devils.

> *Then Jesus called his disciples unto him, and said, I have compassion on the multitude, because they continue with me now three days, and have nothing to eat: and I will not send them away fasting, lest they faint in the way.*
>
> MATTHEW 15:32

These people were with Him for three days, and they weren't staying at the Hilton. So what did Jesus do? Compassion acted. In His compassion, He took a little boy's lunch of a few loaves and fishes, blessed it, multiplied it, and fed the multitude.

Look at Matthew 20:30-34:

> *And, behold, two blind men sitting by the way side, when they heard that Jesus passed by, cried out, saying, Have mercy on us, O Lord, thou son of David.*
>
> *And the multitude rebuked them, because they should hold their peace: but they cried the more, saying, Have mercy on us, O Lord, thou son of David.*
>
> *And Jesus stood still, and called them, and said, What will ye that I should do unto you?*
>
> *They say unto him, Lord, that our eyes may be opened.*
>
> *So Jesus had compassion on them, and touched their eyes: and immediately their eyes received sight, and they followed him.*

Now go to Luke 19:41-42:

> *And when he come near, he beheld the city [Jerusalem], and wept over it,*
>
> *Saying, If thou hadst known, even thou, at least in this thy day, the things which belong unto thy peace! but now they are hid from thine eyes.*

> When you see people who are bound by the chains of sin, the compassion of God rises up on the inside of you and breaks your heart, because you know Jesus wants to set them free.

Jesus wept over Jerusalem. He wanted to bring the people close to Him, but they would not come, and He wept. When you see people who are bound by the chains of sin, the compassion of God rises up on the inside of you and breaks your heart, because you know Jesus wants to set them free.

We must extend the compassion Jesus has had for us to others. Since He's set us free, He can set others free. If He broke the chains off us, He can break the chains off others. We need to extend the same mercy to others that He extended towards us. We need to extend the same forgiveness to others that He extended towards us. Let us *never* get religious! Let us never look down on people.

How can we have the compassion Jesus has? We can only have His compassion as we allow the Holy Spirit to do a work on the inside of us. So many people's hearts are hard and callous toward others. They're never moved by anything they see in the lives of other people. They're only moved when it directly touches them or their family. But Jesus knows exactly how people feel and what they're going through, and He is willing to do something about it.

For we have not an high priest which cannot be touched with the feeling of our infirmities; but was in all points tempted like as we are, yet without sin.

HEBREWS 4:15

There's nothing that you're going through that Jesus doesn't know about. Have you ever been in a situation or had a problem in your life, and you thought you were the only one in the whole universe to go through that problem? Well, you're not. Thousands upon thousands of people are facing the same situations you're facing every day.

And who knows better than Jesus Himself? Hebrews 4:16 goes on to say that we can come boldly to the throne of grace and we can obtain mercy and find grace to help in the time of need. Why? Because He suffered and He bore the curse for you and me. He knows the weight of sin and the condemnation, which He fought in the Garden of Gethsemane. The Bible says that He sweat great drops of blood when He was striving against sin. His flesh was not willing to go through with the suffering He knew He would endure over the next few days. He had to fight the temptation not to go through with it, and He prayed with His whole being as He strove to submit to the will of the Father. (See Luke 22:44.)

Jesus knows exactly what you're facing. He knows every temptation and every fault you're struggling with. He doesn't condemn you or judge you. He is moved with compassion towards you — to heal you, to touch you, to set you free, and to bring deliverance in your life.

And here's the bottom line: it's not like He has to do it in the future. It's already been done! Compassion acted two thousand years ago. All you have to do is to respond to it. You just have to say, "Lord, here I am. I surrender my life to You." Throw your hands up and just say, "Lord, I surrender." That's all it takes. Don't fight it!

When He looked at the woman caught in adultery, He said, "Where are your accusers?" She said, "I don't have any." He said, "Well, I don't condemn you either, so go and sin no more." (See John 8:3-11.) Just like that!

Peter, thinking he was going to impress Jesus with how spiritual he was, said, "Lord, if somebody wrongs us, how many times must we forgive them in a day? Seven times?" Peter thought Jesus would say, "Peter, calm down, seven's excessive. Three times will be enough, man!" But he underestimated the mercy and compassion that his Master brought. Jesus said, "Look, not seven times, *but seventy times seven!"* (See Matthew 18:21-22.)

Do you know how many times that is? Start out in the morning: "I forgive you, I forgive you, I forgive you, I forgive you, I forgive you, I forgive you, I forgive you, I forgive you, I forgive you, I forgive you, I forgive you, I forgive you, I forgive you, I forgive you, I forgive you, I forgive you some more."

Let's have some lunch. "I forgive you. I forgive you. I forgive you. I forgive you. I forgive you. I forgive you."

Time for supper. "I forgive you. I forgive you. I forgive you. I forgive you. I forgive you. Well, it's time to go to sleep. I think I still have a bunch of 'I forgive yous' in reserve." And then the next day you would start all over again!

If Jesus could give us one sentence to tell people of the world today, it would be, "Tell the world I love them and I'm not against them." Jesus would want to tell you, who are reading this book, that He loves you. He's not against you. He's for you. He loves you!

Before the Good Samaritan came and picked up the man who was lying bleeding and dying on the Jericho road, religion and tradition had passed by, and none of them did anything for him. They left him there. But the Good Samaritan came and, having compassion, picked him up, poured in the oil and the wine, and restored his soul. (See Luke 10:29-37.)

That's what Jesus wants to do to hurting humanity. His compassion is here, extended towards you. If you're sick in your body, His compassion is extended towards you. If you have pain in your body, His compassion is extended towards you. Maybe you have a broken heart, you've been hurt, you've been bruised, you've been lying by the highway of life. You've been beaten up by sin. If you've been beaten up by the Church or religious institutions, Jesus has compassion on you.

Jesus is extending His compassion to you right now, to touch the hearts of everyone — men and women, young and old. He is here to bind up the broken heart. He is here to set the captives free. He's come to deliver you from any form of addiction and bondage. Jesus has come to break the chains of sin and death and of hell.

The truth is, until we receive the compassion of Jesus for our own lives and allow Him to save, heal, and deliver *us*, we won't have a whole lot of compassion towards *others*. As we let the Holy Spirit move in our hearts and soften our hearts, our hearts will be moved with the compassion of Jesus towards others.

> *Heal the sick, cleanse the lepers, raise the dead, cast out devils: freely ye have received, freely give.*
>
> MATTHEW 10:8

Let Him touch you right now, and then go out and extend His compassion to others who are hurting.

Chapter 9

Jesus, the Joy of Our Salvation

In the end of the sabbath, as it began to dawn toward the first day of the week, came Mary Magdalene and the other Mary to see the sepulchre.

And, behold, there was a great earthquake: for the angel of the Lord descended from heaven, and came and rolled back the stone from the door and sat upon it.

His countenance was like lightning, and his raiment white as snow:

And for fear of him the keepers did shake, and become as dead men.

And the angel answered and said unto the woman, Fear not ye: for I know that ye seek Jesus, which was crucified.

He is not here: for he is risen, as he said. Come, see the place where the Lord lay.

And go quickly, and tell his disciples that he is risen from the dead; and, behold, he goeth before you into Galilee; there shall ye see him: lo, I have told you.

And they departed quickly from the sepulchre with fear and great joy.

MATTHEW 28:1-8

When you read this scripture, you may think, *How can you have fear and great joy at the same time?* It's talking about a reverential awe and a fear of God, something that needs to come back in the body of Christ. If you were to see Jesus in all of His glory and all of His splendor, you'd just stand there, your mouth open, not knowing what to say. You would stand in awe of Him because He is so awesome.

When the two women came to the tomb, I imagine they walked slowly up to the sepulchre because their hearts were heavy. When your heart is heavy, you walk slowly, with your head and hands hanging down. They hadn't understood what He had told them. They hadn't understood that He would rise again. The closest friend they'd had for three and a half years was dead, and they were walking up to His grave. They did not know what was about to take place. They had no clue. Had they known it, they would have run to the sepulchre.

But they left differently than they came. The Bible says that they departed quickly. They left with a glad heart and in reverential fear of the awesomeness of the power of God, because they had just witnessed something that nobody had ever seen before. They had just seen a stone being rolled away in an earthquake and the keepers of the tomb fall as dead men. And then the announcement was made: "He is not here."

"What do you mean He is not here?"

"He's not here. He was here, but He's not here now. He does not occupy this space any longer. He is risen. He's not dead. He's alive. He's not sleeping. He's awake. He's risen. Come, let me show you the place where He lay. Now go quickly and tell His disciples. Tell them that He's risen from the dead. *He is risen from the dead!*

"I'm going to go tell Peter and John. I just have to tell somebody! *He's alive!*"

Can you imagine the sadness with which they came to the tomb and then the joy they had when they left? They were totally dumbstruck, completely dumbfounded. There's a saying in England, "gobsmacked," which literally means "smacked in the mouth." The Bible says they left with fear and great joy. Oh, hallelujah!

The Amplified Bible says they left the tomb hastily with fear and great joy and *ran* to tell the disciples. And what was their message? It was a joyous message. It was a Good News message. And that Gospel message is still being proclaimed: everyone who comes to God comes through the power of the blood and the resurrection of Jesus Christ. They come into new life, into that same resurrection life made manifest on that resurrection morning. *When that new life comes to dwell on the inside of us, we experience the same joy that they experienced on that day.*

Even though we weren't there, we are now there by the Holy Ghost, because we are being quickened together in Christ. Two thousand years later that joy is still grabbing hold of us, and we stand in awe of the empty tomb. Then we run with joy to tell the world that He is alive and that He's risen. Hallelujah!

There are people who say, "We don't really have the same joy they had because they were right there — we were not." Listen, you *were* there in the Spirit. When you come to the cross and you surrender your life to Jesus, you realize that you were crucified with Him, that you died with Him, that you were buried with Him, and that you've been raised to a new life in Him. (See Galatians 2:20.)

It gives us great joy that because He lives, I can live also. Because He lives, death has no dominion over me. Sickness and disease have no dominion over me. Poverty has no dominion over me. Sin has no dominion over me because my life is hid with Christ in God. I can live today because He lives and He reigns. My heart rejoices and no man can take my joy from me! (See John 16:22.)

> *Whom having not seen, ye love; in whom, though now ye see him not, yet believing, ye rejoice with joy unspeakable and full of glory.*
>
> 1 PETER 1:8

The reason you and I can have that joy that's unspeakable and full of glory is because of that same resurrection life. That's what is happening in our Holy Ghost meetings — people are coming into contact with the power and the anointing of the Spirit of God. It's that resurrection life coming all over again. It's the same Spirit, who raised Jesus Christ from the dead, who dwells in you.

It's going to quicken your mortal body. (See Romans 8:11.) Have you ever been quickened by the Holy Ghost?

> When you look into their eyes and they begin to speak about the joy of their salvation, that same joyful realization of what took place two thousand years ago comes again.

Later on when Jesus walked with the disciples on the road to Emmaus, they didn't even know it was Him. (See Luke 24:13-33.) And when they discussed it among themselves later, they said, "Didn't our hearts burn within us when He spoke to us?"

Don't our hearts burn within us when He speaks to us? When you meet somebody who's been born again, who's been washed in the blood of Jesus, who knows what took place at the cross of Calvary, doesn't your heart burn within you? When you look into their eyes and they begin to speak about the joy of their salvation, that same joyful realization of what took place two thousand years ago comes again. That's how the joy of the Good News is communicated.

Some people say, "Well, that joy business is just an emotional experience, and you shouldn't have an experience-based Gospel."

What a bunch of garbage! You mean going up to the tomb was not an experience? You mean when the stone was rolled away, it wasn't an experience? Go talk to the keepers of the tomb. They'll tell you what an experience they had. Only the people who have never had an experience with Jesus want to run down having an experience with Him.

When you seek God's presence as your vital need, He will become real to you, as real as any other person you have met. You meet Him in His Word. When you get a revelation of your salvation and the joy of it manifests in you, I guarantee that you will respond to it, because it is real. You can experience anything that is real. God's love can be manifested through your emotions and so can joy or any other fruit of the Spirit.

Several years ago we were having a conference in Jerusalem. Now, I'm probably one of the least religious people to ever go to the Holy Land, so I told the tour guides not to take me to any of the shrines or any of the churches. Well, that canceled out many of the places you can go!

I did agree to see the Garden Tomb though, one of two sites said to be the tomb of Jesus. The guide at the Garden Tomb was, in his rather religious way, telling us about the resurrection of the Lord Jesus Christ that took place there. He actually got a little excited and even laughed when he announced to everyone that Jesus is risen, the stone was rolled away, and that He is alive.

When we had a break, he looked over at me. He recognized me and said, "You're that preacher who goes around with that joy stuff," and started verbally attacking me ten feet from where the stone was rolled away!

I'm thinking, *Hello? Something's wrong with this picture.*

I said, "Excuse me, sir, did you know that when this stone was rolled away, the people around this tomb fell as dead men? Did you know that when they heard that He was risen, they were filled with joy — and they weren't just smiling. And besides that, you just got through telling me the story, and you even got a little excited for yourself that the stone was rolled away and that He is risen. Yet you attack me for traveling around the world with 'that joy stuff.'"

I can't help it if I get excited about what He did two thousand years ago! It's not just something off the pages of a history book; it's something that is real. He is alive, He is risen and He's living in my heart. And I can't be quiet!

They can say we are radical. They can say we're overboard. But I will not be quiet, because He's alive and He lives on the inside of me. I've got something to shout about. I've got something to rejoice about. He is risen! The stone is rolled away! He's alive forevermore! Hallelujah!

Jesus, the *joy* of my salvation. It's not, "Jesus, the depression of my salvation." It's not, "Jesus, the sadness of my salvation."

If you watch the Easter services in churches all over the world on television, you'd think it was a mass funeral. They stand there, with a sad look on their faces, droning somberly, "And we are so thankful today that He died for us, that He arose again, and that He is Lord." Where's the joy?

The reality of the resurrection is more than just words. It's the joy of our salvation and it's emotional! I guarantee you, a month after the resurrection, those disciples were still excited about it. Somebody said, "Now, don't overdo it, we know He rose from the dead, but don't get too excited about it. We've heard the story before, but let's be more mature about this thing now."

I want to tell you, this is not something that we "psych" ourselves into. This is not just a temporary emotional high. You can wake me up at two o'clock in the morning and I'll feel the same way. It has nothing to do with emotions gone awry. Jesus has touched me. He's changed me. And I just have to tell somebody!

Have you ever had some good news in the natural, and you couldn't wait to run and tell your friends? They don't know what news you've got and you say, "You won't believe this! You've got to see it! Remember how sad we were because He was dead? Well, He's not dead anymore, buddy! I just came from the tomb!"

Our critics say the Christian walk is not to be based on experience. But I want you to know that the whole of life is experience. When a woman gives birth to a baby, it's an experience. She can't say, "Well, I want to give birth to this baby but I don't want to have an experience. I don't want this birth to be based on experience."

Your whole life is experience. You ride a roller coaster and you have an experience. If you plug your finger into a light socket, you will have an experience. When you get married, you have an experience. Everyone should have the opportunity to experience a mother-in-law! It's an experience. Everything in life is an experience. You go eat at certain restaurants because you like the dining experience.

"What are you going to eat?"

"Ah, it doesn't matter, as long as I eat something. It doesn't really have to be an experience. This restaurant will do — the food's not that good, the decor's terrible, and the service is bad — but I don't really want an experience-based restaurant."

Why do you go back to a certain restaurant? Experience! You go back because the last time you went, you had a good experience.

Jesus is my joy. He's my experience of that joy. Jesus is my life. He's my experience of that life. Jesus is my peace. He's my experience of that peace.

People say, "I want to meet Jesus, but I don't really want to have an experience with Him. I don't want that joy. I don't want that walking and leaping and praising God. I don't want that stomping-on-the-riser stuff. They're just having an experience, and I want none of that. I don't want that laughing-in-the-meeting stuff. I just want to listen to the message and have no experience."

Why? So you can leave the revival meeting and tell people that nothing happened? We can experience a roller coaster ride. We can experience a meal. We can experience the pleasure of friends and family. We can experience playing a sport. We can experience all those things. But then we come to church and say we don't want to experience joy because we don't want an experience-based Christianity.

Everything we believe should be based on the Word of God. Our experiences should be in line with the Word of God, but you cannot truly know Jesus without an experience with Him. *You have to have an experience with Him.*

When you have an experience with Jesus, it will result in a joy that is unspeakable and full of glory that will flow out of your innermost being. You will experience such joy that you won't be able to keep quiet about it. If you haven't experienced that, then *you've never met Him,* because Jesus is an experience! When you really experience Him, you will never be the same.

Chapter 10

Jesus, Our Righteousness

*B*ut seek (aim at and strive after) first of all His kingdom and His righteousness (His way of doing and being right), and then all these things taken together will be given you besides.

MATTHEW 6:33 AMP

Therefore put on God's complete armor, that you may be able to resist and stand your ground on the evil day [of danger], and, having done all [the crisis demands], to stand [firmly in your place].

Stand therefore [hold your ground], having tightened the belt of truth around your loins and having put on the breastplate of integrity and of moral rectitude and right standing with God.

And having shod your feet in preparation [to face the enemy with the firm-footed stability, the promptness, and the readiness produced by the good news] of the Gospel of peace.

Lift up over all the [covering] shield of saving faith, upon which you can quench all the flaming missiles of the wicked [one].

And take the helmet of salvation and the sword that the Spirit wields, which is the Word of God.

EPHESIANS 6:13-17 AMP

Do you know what Jesus did for you? One of the biggest problems in the Church is that many Christians don't know exactly what Jesus did for them at Calvary's cross two thousand years ago. They don't realize that Jesus came and took upon Himself the sin of the world *so that you could take upon yourself His righteousness.* Jesus *became* sin so that you and I could *become* righteous. (See 2 Corinthians 5:21.)

The Word of God tells us in Romans 8:1, **There is therefore now no condemnation to them which are in Christ Jesus, who walk not after the flesh, but after the Spirit.** So if you're born again and washed in the blood of Jesus, then there's no condemnation on you. And yet if you look in the Church world, you'll see that people are beating themselves and others up with guilty memories of what they did five, ten, fifteen, and twenty years ago. Some Christians go around with a guilt complex from this condemnation. I want you to know, the Bible says there's no condemnation if you are in Christ Jesus.

When Jesus comes, He makes you righteous. He comes and points His scepter of righteousness at you and declares that you are righteous. That means that you can now stand in the presence of God without any sense of guilt, inferiority, or condemnation, because Jesus has paid for your sin and God has forgiven you. He's washed you in the blood of Jesus. The Bible says He will take your sins from you as far as the east is from the west, and He will put them in the sea of forgetfulness.

Since your sins have been removed as far as the east is from the west and put in the sea of forgetfulness, what business do you have bringing them up again and again? In other words, you should not be talking about your past life. Stop talking about the days when you were in the world. They're dead and gone. You're a new person in Christ Jesus.

Sin goes with the sinner. Righteousness goes with the believer. Some people say, "Well, I'm just an old sinner saved by grace." Hold it! Which are you? Are you a sinner or are you saved by grace? Don't combine the two. You're trying to sound humble, but you don't realize you're being foolishly unscriptural. If I'm a child of God, how can I be a sinner?

Jesus came to deal with the sin problem by hanging on the cross for us, by becoming sin for us. *The Church needs to have a revelation of Jesus, our righteousness.*

For too long, the Church has focused on heaven. "Well, when we get to heaven there will be victory over sin. We'll be over-comers then. But while we're here, we're just little sinners saved by grace. We're so unworthy."

With that mind-set, we always come to God with guilt, with condemnation, with a feeling of unworthiness. People think that's being holy, but from that teaching comes the attitude that, this side of heaven, all we can expect is failure, misery, disap-pointment, and weakness. "Oh, we're just going to struggle through life, and one day Jesus will come and He's going to get us out of this mess. Rodney, pray for me that I can make it another week in my walk with Gawwwd."

But Jesus, your righteousness, has come to you. He's already forgiven you. If you're out of fellowship, then get into fellowship. If there are sins in your life that you've been allowing to stay, then get rid of those. But once you're rid of them, don't keep trying to beat yourself up every week to get yourself back to that place where He's already taken you. He's already forgiven you; He's already made you righteous. You've got to walk in the reality of that.

Being constantly aware of your right-standing with God also helps you resist further sin. When the devil comes with condem-nation and follows up with temptation, you say, "Sorry, you're knocking on the wrong door, baby. I'm free from that temptation because I'm no longer a slave to sin! I've been delivered! Sin will no longer have dominion over me, because I'm a child of the Living God. I've been washed in the blood of Jesus. I've been cleansed! He's taken out the stony heart and put in a heart of flesh. I have a new spirit within me! He has made me to be a new creature. I'm a new creature in Christ Jesus!"

Remember what we said about Paul in chapter five? Before the apostle Paul was saved, he worked to persecute, imprison, and kill Christians. But he is the one who wrote this to the church at Corinth: **Therefore if any man be in Christ, he is a new creature: old things are passed away; behold, all things are**

become new (2 Corinthians 5:17). The apostle Paul realized this truth. That's why he told people all the time, "Receive us, we've wronged nobody" (see 2 Corinthians 7:2), even though he had killed Christians for a living before he got saved. He understood that he had been made righteous through Jesus' blood.

When Jesus hung on the cross, He hung there in my sin. **God made him who had no sin to be sin for us, so that in him we might become the righteousness of God** (2 Corinthians 5:21 NIV). Jesus, He who knew no sin, was righteousness personified. He walked across the great divide and came and identified with you and me. He became sin so that we could become righteous.

Jesus took our place. He was our substitute. He became sin. He didn't have to do it, but He did it for you and me. We've been washed in His blood. We've been cleansed by His blood. We've been made whole. We've been set free. We are new creatures. That's why we can now come *boldly* to the throne of grace and obtain mercy and help in time of need. (See Hebrews 4:16.) Why? Because He has made a way for us and He's made that way plain.

But what happens if we *do* sin? The Bible says if we do sin **we have an advocate with the Father, Jesus Christ the righteous** (1 John 2:1). That's why John said in 1 John 1:9, **If we confess our sins, he is faithful and just to forgive us our sins, and to cleanse us from all unrighteousness.** The moment we sin and fall, we should ask Him to forgive us.

First John 1:9 is not giving people a license to sin. It's giving you a license to be righteous.

You might say, "Well, does that mean I have a license to sin?" No, you don't need a license. You'll sin without one. First John 1:9 is not giving people a license to sin. It's giving you a license to be righteous. When I love Him and see what He's done for me, I don't want to sin. If I even think about sinning, something rises up in me and says, "No, get away from me." I don't want to do anything that's going to offend Jesus, that's going to grieve the Lord Jesus Christ, because I love Him so much.

Why do so many people just put up with their sin situation? Coming to church is hard for them when they come slinking in the door expecting to get beat up from the pulpit. They think, *I've been bad this week. Beat me. If the preacher can really beat me, then I'm going to feel condemned and I'm really going to feel sorry for what I did. I'll leave here feeling like something happened in my life.* Do you want to keep living through that whole thing again and again?

Adam knew God intimately. He walked and talked with God. But Adam, after he sinned, hid from God because he was afraid of Him.

Are you that way? If you've done something wrong, do you go to God and say, "Lord, I've done something wrong, forgive me," or can you not worship like you really want to because you think He just might beat you?

God loves you and wants to forgive you. He's on your side. He's not against you. He wants to pull you to Himself, and say, "Come here, it's all right. There, there, it will be all right." That's what He wants to do. He wants to bless you.

You think He doesn't know what you're going through? He knows exactly what you're going through. Hebrews 4:15 says that Jesus was tempted in every way we are, but yet did not sin. In other words, He was tempted every way we are, but He always *decided* not to sin. You have to constantly make decisions not to sin. Temptation comes, you look at it, and you decide. Listen, I leave many a restaurant with great victory because I resist the temptation of the seven-layer chocolate cake. And I feel so good!

Sin comes along, but you resist it. Sin will work in different areas in different people. Sin comes in many packages. Some sins are outward, where everybody can see. But some sins are inward, such as pride, unforgiveness, bitterness, jealousy, and all the hidden sins of the heart. But you make the choice. You have to have the same attitude with every choice you face. Each time you make a decision: "No, I won't partake of that because that's of the nature of death, and I'm of the nature of life. That's of darkness. I'm of light. And darkness and light don't mix."

When you realize you're righteous, you can resist the devil and he will flee from you. (See James 4:7.) "Hey," you say, "what are you doing around my house? You don't belong here. I'm the righteousness of God in Christ Jesus. I don't have anything to do with this sin thing."

Jude 24 tells us He is able to keep us from falling. For too long Christians have gone around saying, "Well, I might fall this week. Rodney, pray for me that I don't fall." They act like a mountain climber who's going to climb a sheer 4,000-foot cliff and says, "Pray for me that I don't fall." You're on your way down already — I can already hear you screaming. Don't climb a mountain if you think you're going to fall!

Many preachers are running, afraid they're going to fail. They're afraid they're going to fall. I had a preacher friend who was always saying he didn't want his ministry to grow because he was afraid that if he got to a certain place he might blow it and cause reproach on the body of Christ.

I said, "So you're really planning to do it, aren't you? You're planning to fall, aren't you? You've been talking about it for years." And the sad thing is that he went on, the ministry grew, and he fell. It was just like he planned it; he strategized his own fall.

But I'm not running the race like I'm going to fall. When you want to run a race, you don't stand at the starting line saying, "I don't want to start because I'm afraid I'll get a hundred yards down the road and fall."

If you run in the race and suddenly you just fall, bless God, just get up, dust yourself off, and take off running again. You don't just lie down and cry, "Do you want to come join me at the First Church of the Fallen?"

"How you doing down there?"

"Oh, pray for me. I've fallen, Rodney. Pray for me."

"Well, *get up!* Get on your feet. What are you lying there in the mud for? Get up!"

"But what about all those other times I've fallen?"

There are no other times! You're a new creature in Christ. Jesus will never bring up your past. He will never bring up any failing you've had. He will never even bring up your shortcomings. Religion will do that to you, but Jesus won't do that to you. He's not going to come and bring up your past faults and your failings because your sins are forgiven.

When we realize that we *are* righteous in Jesus Christ, we realize that we're not slaves to sin anymore. We don't have to dance to sin's tune. We've been set free. We've been delivered. We've been washed in the blood. We've been cleansed. We've been made righteous. Without Him we're a nothing, but thank God, we're in Him. (see Acts 17:28.)

If you can get this, you will walk in victory.

> *And you, that were sometimes alienated and enemies in your mind by wicked works, yet now hath he reconciled*
>
> *In the body of his flesh through death, to present you holy and unblameable and unreproveable in his sight.*
>
> COLOSSIANS 1:21-22

Reconciliation has already been done for you in Christ. You stand complete in Him. Ephesians 5:27 says, **That he might present it to himself a glorious church, not having spot, or wrinkle, or any such thing; but that it should be holy and without blemish.** You stand righteous and holy in Him!

Now I'm going to share something with you, and if this doesn't cause a reaction, you really need revival! Romans 5:17-19 explains how sin and death came through one man, Adam. Then it explains how sin and death were defeated through one man, Jesus, so that many — that's us — could be made righteous.

If by one man's offence death reigned by one; much more they which receive abundance of grace and of the gift of righteousness shall reign in life by one, Jesus Christ.

Therefore as by the offence of one judgment came upon all men to condemnation; even so by the righteousness of one the free gift came upon all men unto justification of life.

For as by one man's disobedience many were made sinners, so by the obedience of one shall many be made righteous.

Everybody wants to talk about the fall, about when Adam sinned and sin came into the world, but that's not the end of the story. The Bible says there is a second Adam and His name is Jesus Christ of Nazareth, the Son of the Living God. He sped across time and space, took on human flesh, was obedient even unto death on the cross, paid the price of sin on the cross of Calvary, and spent three days and three nights in the heart of the earth. Then He rose from the dead, and having spoiled principalities and powers, He made a show of them openly, triumphing over them in it. (See Colossians 2:15.)

Now here's where you and I come in. Jesus took with Him the keys of death and hell and the grave and He said to us, "I've given you the keys of the kingdom. Whatever you bind on earth shall be bound in heaven. Whatever you loose on earth shall be loosed in heaven. Greater is He that is in you than he that is in the world. I've raised you up to sit with Me in heavenly places." (See Revelation 1:18, Matthew 16:19, 1 John 4:4, and Ephesians 2:6.)

And it's not just in heaven! Through Jesus, you reign as a king in this life, and if you reign as a king in this life, you have a kingdom, and you as king have dominion over it. Therefore you have dominion over sin. You have authority over sin because you reign as a king in this life through Jesus Christ.

That's something to get excited about! I'm seated in the heavenly places with Christ Jesus. He's my righteousness. The Gospel comes to the beggar, to the tramp, to the leper, walks down into the ditch full of muck and mire, and pulls him out, washes him, puts a robe and a ring and shoes on him, and says, "This is my friend." That's what Jesus does.

Jesus is your righteousness. It doesn't matter what you've done.

It's time to get rid of that old sin consciousness and those old sin rags you've been draping yourself in, worshipping every day at the altar of sin. It's time to lay that aside and come over into righteousness and realize what Jesus purchased for you at Calvary's cross. When guilt and condemnation come your way, you resist the enemy and say "No! That person doesn't live here anymore! Jesus is my righteousness and I'm free! Jesus has set me free!"

Chapter 11

Jesus, Our Great Physician

The Spirit of the Lord is upon me, because he hath anointed me to preach the gospel to the poor; he hath sent me to heal the brokenhearted, to preach deliverance to the captives, and recovering of sight to the blind, to set at liberty them that are bruised.

LUKE 4:18

I am the Lord that healeth thee.

EXODUS 15:26

No matter what the need, whether it was provision, forgiveness of sin, or healing of the body, Jesus always met it. And I want you to know that Jesus is the same today. He still heals as readily as He forgives sin. But often when folks accept Him as their Savior, they do not also accept Him as their Healer.

I remember when I first found out that Jesus was my Healer. When I was five years old, I noticed I had a lot of warts on my hands, so I went to my father and said, "Dad, I've got these warts."

He said, "Son, we can pray right now."

My dad prayed with me, and he cursed those warts. Within three or four days, every single one of them dried up and fell off my hands. Can you imagine the impression that left on a five-year-old? I knew that Jesus healed as a solid fact. I'd seen it.

When I was about thirteen, my pastor and I got into a theological argument about healing. He was telling me that God sometimes put sickness and disease on you to teach you a lesson, and I was telling him, "Pastor, that's not true."

He got kind of angry.

I said, "It's not true, Pastor. My Bible says, **Every good gift and every perfect gift is from above, and cometh down from** the Father of lights, with whom is no variableness, neither shadow of turning (James 1:17)!" He got mad and stormed out of the house.

The next morning I woke up covered in spots — measles. I was shocked. My pastor came around the house to gloat over my sickness. I was sick now, and obviously God was gonna teach me a lesson. He walked to the door and said, "How are the sick and the diseased?"

I said, "Oh, I'm not sick and diseased."

"Yes you are. You're covered in spots."

"No pastor," I said, "these spots are not here for me, they're here for you. The Bible says, **And for this cause God shall send them strong delusion, that they should believe a lie** (2 Thessalonians 2:11). These spots are for you. I'm healed by the stripes that Jesus bore for me at the cross of Calvary two thousand years ago!" (See 1 Peter 2:24.) Again, he got mad and left.

I went into my room, closed the door, took my Bible and spoke the Word of God out loud. I said, "Jesus, You're my Healer. I don't care what he says. I don't care if he thinks this is on me to teach me a lesson. You're my Healer." The next day the spots were gone. They had disappeared. When he came back that day and looked at me, he said, "What happened to the spots?"

I said, "I told you, they were just there for you."

You have to come to the place where you accept Him as your Healer. People here in America don't have to believe God for their healing because they know they've got the Blue Cross or the Red Cross or some other cross to run to — any "cross" except the cross of Calvary. But what happens if all the healthcare and health insurance fail and the doctors cannot help you?

"Well then, I'll have to start believing God." Is God your last resort? Too often we don't receive Jesus as our Healer all the time, and suddenly we come to a crisis and say, "Oh, I've got to believe God!" Well, if you can't exercise your faith over small illnesses, if you can't exercise your faith over a spider bite or the flu, then what are you going to do when they diagnose you with cancer? Then you're going to go to pieces. "I don't know what I'm gonna do!"

You have to exercise your faith, to build your faith in the fact that Jesus is your Healer. I'm not saying that you mustn't go to doctors or use medicine — there's nothing wrong with that. But they can't heal everything. You have to get it in your heart of hearts that Jesus is your Healer, because in the future, there could be some deadly incurable plague that sweeps through. What are you going to do? You better practice now. You better develop your faith in Jesus as your Healer now.

It's easier to believe God when you're healed and walking in divine health than to wait until you're in a mess and trying to believe God for your healing. You have to get up and tell your body to get in line every day. "Body, you're gonna get in line with the Word of God. Sickness and disease, you have to go. Jesus is my Healer!"

Once when my appendix was giving me tremendous pain, I told the Lord, "I need You to heal it now. I'm here on vacation, trying to rest. I don't have time to mess with this stupid thing, and I'm not going to go run to a doctor so he can stick a knife in me. You are my Doctor, You always have been my Doctor. You're my Healer and always have been. I need help! I need it right *now!*" I spoke God's Word over my body even as I lay there in pain on the bed.

When I woke up after two days of this, the pain was gone. I started weeping and said, "Yes, You always have been my Healer, haven't You?" Where do I go when I'm in trouble? Who do I turn to? Who do I run to? Jesus! Why? He's my Healer!

Far too many people base their faith on what happens to other people, and that's a big problem. "Well, I had an uncle once who believed God, and he died. And Aunt Minnie, she was believing God and she had a stroke. And Uncle Jack, he was believing God and got hit by a bus. So you see, we shouldn't really believe God."

Listen, you can't go around basing your faith on what happened to Aunt Minnie and Uncle Jack. You've got to base your faith on Jesus. He's the author and the finisher of your faith, not someone else's experience! The Word of God is true! You have to line up with the Word of God. You can't go basing the validity of the Word of God on what happens to me or anyone else.

But we still imagine that there are limits on what God can do.

"Can He forgive sin?"

"Oh yes."

"Can He forgive murder?"

"Yeah."

"So you're telling me that Jesus can forgive all manner of sin, but there are certain sicknesses that He cannot do anything about? And you'll just have to go see a doctor?"

Hold it. When we repent, He forgives all our sin. He washes us clean, and Jesus put sickness and sin in the same category.

And he entered into a ship, and passed over, and came into His own city.

And behold, they brought to him a man sick of the palsy, lying on a bed: and Jesus seeing their faith said unto the sick of the palsy; Son, be of good cheer; thy sins are forgiven thee.

And, behold, certain of the scribes said within themselves, This man blasphemeth.

And Jesus knowing their thoughts said, Wherefore think ye evil in your hearts?

For whether is easier, to say, Thy sins be forgiven thee; or to say, Arise, and walk?

But that ye may know that the Son of Man hath power on earth to forgive sins (then saith he to the sick of the palsy,) Arise, take up thy bed and go unto thine house.

And he arose, and departed to his house.

But when the multitudes saw it, they marvelled, and glorified God, which had given such power unto men.

MATTHEW 9:1-7

Jesus is saying, "I can forgive your sin and I can heal your body. Your sins are forgiven, so take up your bed and walk." Have you ever noticed what Jesus would always say to people when He had healed them? He'd say, "Go and sin no more, lest a worse thing comes on you." (See John 5:14, John 8:11.)

Why did Jesus forgive the man of his sin and then tell him to take up his bed and walk? Why did Jesus repeatedly connect sin to sickness? Because the *root cause* of sickness and disease in the earth is *sin.* Sickness and disease were not a part of the Garden of Eden before Adam sinned. Sickness does not come from heaven. It comes from the sin nature in man.

Now somebody is bound to say, "Are you trying to tell me that if I get sick then I'm full of sin?" *No!* I never said that. I'm just showing you that sickness has its root in sin, in the sin nature of man.

Of course, there are times when people do get sick because they're in sin. For example, if a person has a lot of unforgiveness and bitterness in their heart, it affects their body. If they have a violent temper and they're angry all the time, that's going to affect their body. The Bible says, **A merry heart doeth good like a medicine: but a broken spirit drieth the bones** (Proverbs 17:22). We've got people with broken spirits, and their bones are so dry you can hear them creak.

Because Jesus linked sickness and sin, it's easy for people to get upset, because they think we're saying that if somebody is sick they're in sin. I never said that. Again, I said sin and sickness go hand in hand, and sickness has its roots in sin. If you could get sin totally out of the way, you'd remove sickness completely. Sin and sickness are the foul offspring of the devil.

Jesus says, "I can do it all the same. It's not a problem to Me. I'll forgive your sin and heal your body." In our services, we see people come down to the altar in the healing lines and start asking God to forgive them. The moment they repent of their sins, the healing power of God just floods their whole body.

To see the true origin of sickness, we need only look at the ministry of Jesus described in Acts 10:38:

> *How God anointed Jesus of Nazareth with the Holy Ghost and with power: who went about doing good, and healing all that were oppressed of the devil; for God was with him.*

Jesus went about healing all those who were oppressed of the devil. So that means sickness is the oppression of the devil. That's what the Bible said! Sickness is not a blessing from heaven. Sickness is not God trying to teach us a lesson. What happens if you've been sick for forty years? Are you trying to tell me that you're too stupid to learn the lesson God's trying to teach you? That's theology gone crazy!

Hebrews 13:8 says that Jesus Christ is the same yesterday, today, and forever. That means He hasn't changed! That means if He did it in Bible days, He's going to do it today! If He was a Healer in Matthew, Mark, Luke, and John, then He's a Healer today!

Then Jesus went thence, and departed into the coasts of Tyre and Sidon.

> **Sickness is not a blessing from heaven. Sickness is not God trying to teach us a lesson. What happens if you've been sick for forty years? Are you trying to tell me that you're too stupid to learn the lesson God's trying to teach you? That's theology gone crazy!**

And, behold, a woman of Canaan came out of the same coasts and cried unto him, saying, Have mercy on me, oh Lord, thou Son of David; my daughter is grievously vexed with a devil.

But he answered her not a word. And his disciples came and besought him, saying, Send her away; for she crieth after us.

But he answered and said, I am not sent but unto the lost sheep of the house of Israel.

Then came she and worshipped him, saying, Lord, help me.

But he answered and said, It is not meet to take the children's bread, and cast it to dogs.

And she said, Truth, Lord: yet even the dogs eat of the crumbs which fall from their masters' table.

Then Jesus answered and said unto her, O woman, great is thy faith: be it unto thee even as thou wilt. And her daughter was made whole from that very hour.

MATTHEW 15:21-28

Don't get distracted by Jesus comparing the Canaanites, who were long-time enemies of the Jews, to dogs. What you have to realize is that He said healing is the children's bread! It's our birthright! It's not something that we have to beg for. Just as your children have the right to eat the food on your table, healing is your birthright from your heavenly Father! Healing belongs to us simply because we're in the family of God. We can come, sit down at the table of our Father, and we can eat the bread of healing.

Why did Jesus heal the sick? I'm going to give you five reasons why He healed the sick.

The first reason Jesus healed the sick was that it was promised in the Word of God. Jesus was fulfilling the Word of His Father.

When the even was come, they brought unto him many that were possessed with devils: and he cast out the spirits with his word, and healed all that were sick:

119

That it might be fulfilled which was spoken by Esaias the prophet, saying, Himself took our infirmities, and bare our sicknesses.

MATTHEW 8:16-17

Fear not; for thou shalt not be ashamed: neither be thou confounded; for thou shalt not be put to shame: for thou shalt forget the shame of thy youth, and shalt not remember the reproach of thy widowhood any more.

For thy Maker is thine husband; the LORD of hosts is his name; and thy Redeemer the Holy One of Israel; The God of the whole earth shall he be called.

ISAIAH 54:4-5

Second, Jesus healed the sick in order to reveal His will. We saw this in Mark 1:40-42. He was willing!

And there came a leper to him, beseeching him, and kneeling down to him, and saying unto him, If thou wilt, thou canst make me clean.

And Jesus, moved with compassion, put forth his hand, and touched him, and saith unto him, I will; be thou clean.

And as soon as he had spoken, immediately the leprosy departed from him, and he was cleansed.

Jesus never turned down anyone who asked Him for healing — even the Syrophenician woman. Jesus delivered her daughter because of her persistent faith.

Third, He healed the sick to manifest the works of God.

Jesus answered, Neither hath this man sinned, nor his parents: but that the works of God should be made manifest.

JOHN 9:3

Fourth, Jesus healed the sick because of His compassion.

And Jesus went forth, and saw a great multitude, and was moved with compassion toward them, and he healed their sick.

MATTHEW 14:14

And, behold, two blind men sitting by the way side, when they heard that Jesus passed by, cried out, saying, Have mercy on us, O Lord, thou son of David.

And the multitude rebuked them, because they should hold their peace: but they cried the more, saying, Have mercy on us, O Lord, thou son of David.

And Jesus stood still, and called them, and said, What will ye that I shall do unto you?

They say unto him, Lord, that our eyes may be opened.

So Jesus had compassion on them, and touched their eyes: and immediately their eyes received sight, and they followed him.

MATTHEW 20:30-34

Now when he came nigh to the gate of the city, behold, there was a dead man carried out, the only son of his mother, and she was a widow: and much people of the city was with her.

And when the Lord saw her, he had compassion on her, and said unto her, Weep not.

And he came and touched the bier: and they that bare him stood still. And he said, Young man, I say unto thee, Arise.

And he that was dead sat up, and began to speak. And he delivered him to his mother.

LUKE 7:12-15

And Jesus went about all the cities and villages, teaching in their synagogues, and preaching the gospel of the kingdom, and healing every sickness and every disease among the people.

But when he saw the multitudes, he was moved with compassion on them, because they fainted, and were scattered abroad, as sheep having no shepherd.

MATTHEW 9:35-36

And fifth, He healed people because of their faith. The centurion in Matthew 8:5-13 said, "Lord, You don't have to go anywhere, just speak the Word and my servant will be healed." Jesus marveled at the faith of this man who was not even an Israelite and declared that his servant was healed according to what he believed.

In Mark 5:25-34, the woman who had the issue of blood believed she would receive her healing if she could only touch Jesus' garment. Jesus did not notice her touching His garment until He felt the anointing flowing out of Him into her, drawn out by her faith. Jesus told her that it was her faith that had made her whole.

Is healing always the will of God?

And it came to pass, when he was in a certain city, behold a man full of leprosy: who seeing Jesus fell on his face, and besought him, saying, Lord, if thou wilt, thou canst make me clean.

And he put forth his hand, and touched him, saying, I will: be thou clean. And immediately the leprosy departed from him.

LUKE 5:12-13

Many people in the religious world pray, "Lord, if it be Thy will, heal Sister Bucketmouth. Lord, if it be Thy will, heal Brother Doodad." But we know from God's Word that healing *is* the will of God. We need to settle this issue in our hearts.

Yet some folks say, "If healing is God's will, why doesn't everybody get healed?" That's like saying, "Why doesn't everybody get saved?" Are we going to throw out salvation because not everybody gets saved? Even though people turn down salvation, it's not going to stop me from preaching salvation. Even though people might turn down healing, it's not going to stop me from preaching healing! Salvation and healing are set in the Gospel! They have been paid for and purchased by the blood of Jesus and by the stripes He bore at Calvary!

"I don't understand why some people receive their healing and some don't, Rodney." Well, there are a lot of things that we don't understand, and every case is different. There are reasons why you don't always see instantaneous miracles, but I'm not going to debate why one person is healed instantly and the next one isn't. That is an issue between them and God. I'm going to go for it like God *will* heal everybody, every single time that we pray for them! If I didn't believe that, I would never pray for the sick. We have to remember that God's Word is true, regardless of our personal experience.

"Well, what happens if we pray and they die?" If they're born again, they will go to heaven. Death for the child of God is not a problem. For the child of God, death is a blessing. The only ones who have a problem with death are the ones who are left behind, but if they are believers and the person who died is a believer, we do not mourn as those who have no hope. (See 1 Thessalonians 4:13.) We know we will be together for eternity.

Is healing God's will? There are several phrases that I want you to note from the ministry of Jesus. "He healed all that were sick." (See Matthew 8:16.) "He healed them all." (See Matthew 12:15.) "He healed their sick." (See Matthew 14:14.) "As many as touched Him were made perfectly whole." (See Matthew 14:36.)

Even though when Jesus went to Nazareth He could do no *mighty* work because of their *unbelief,* He still healed some people. In other places He usually healed every single sick person in the place.

> *And Jesus went about all Galilee, teaching in their synagogues, and preaching the gospel of the kingdom, and healing all manner of sickness and all manner of disease among the people.*
>
> *And his fame went throughout all Syria; and they brought unto him all sick people that were taken with divers diseases and torments, and those which were possessed with devils,*

and those that were lunatic, and those that had the palsy; and he healed them.

MATTHEW 4:23-24

When the even was come, they brought unto him many that were possessed with devils: and he cast out the spirits with his word, and he healed all that were sick.

MATTHEW 8:16

But when Jesus knew it, he withdrew himself from thence; and great multitudes followed him, and he healed them all.

MATTHEW 12:15

In Nazareth, Jesus healed a few sick people of minor ailments, but could do no mighty miracles because of their unbelief. In other places, mentioned above, He healed and delivered *everyone* who came to Him. What was the difference? It was not Jesus — He is the same yesterday, today, and forever. The difference between miracles and no miracles was the faith — or unbelief — of the *people*. So which do you want to believe God for?

I believe for God to heal *everybody*. If I didn't believe that, I wouldn't preach. I believe that the day is coming soon when people will come into the presence of God crippled, broken, bruised, tattered and torn, and *every single one will be healed.* Every single sinner in the house will get saved. Every single backslider in the house will come back to God. And everyone who is possessed or tormented by demons will be gloriously set free.

Need more? Look at Matthew 14:14:

Jesus went forth, and saw a great multitude, and was moved with compassion towards them, and he healed their sick.

And how about Matthew 14:34-36?

And when they were gone over, they came into the land of Gennesaret.

124

And when the men of that place had knowledge of him, they sent out into all that country round about, and brought unto him all that were diseased;

And besought him that they might only touch the hem of his garment: and as many as touched him were made perfectly whole.

I didn't write this, Matthew did! Now look a little farther at Matthew 15:30-31:

And great multitudes came unto him, having with them those that were lame, blind, dumb, maimed, and many others, and cast them down at Jesus' feet; and he healed them:

Insomuch that the multitude wondered, when they saw the dumb to speak, the maimed to be whole, the lame to walk, and the blind to see: and they glorified the God of Israel.

Now down to Matthew 19:2:

And great multitudes followed him; and he healed them there.

Go to Matthew 21:14:

And the blind and the lame came to him in the temple; and he healed them.

Here's the bottom line for healing: you have to believe the truth of the Word of God and hide it in your heart. You must have your faith built in God and established in the Lord Jesus Christ as your Healer.

Those who trust in the Lord are like Mount Zion, which cannot be shaken but endures forever.

As the mountains surround Jerusalem, so the Lord surrounds his people both now and forevermore.

PSALM 125:1-2 NIV

You've got to get it into your heart, "Jesus is my Healer." Even if those are the last words out of your mouth on your deathbed, it's better to go saying, "Jesus is my Healer," than just capitulating and going out filled with doubt and unbelief, saying, "Maybe He's not my Healer." You don't know that you won't be raised up from your so-called deathbed because you would not give up on God's promises.

"Okay," you say. "Jesus healed back then, and it's wonderful that He wants to heal today. It's also wonderful that He's the Great Physician, but how in the world does this relate to me?"

Friend, that's where you've got to grab hold of what I'm saying and realize that the Bible is not talking to anybody else. *God is talking to you.* His Word is for you. Are you born again? Are you washed in the blood? Is Jesus your Lord and Savior? Then healing is yours. Healing belongs to you. Healing is the children's bread, and you are God's child. Healing belongs to you! It's yours. It's your birthright. It's not something you have to pay for. It's not something you have to beg for. *It's yours.* You have a new physician today — Jesus, M.D.

Maybe you have already been healed, but you wonder, "How can I walk in God's healing power all the time?" This is an easy one: Start praying for the sick. When you pray for the sick, you activate God's healing power in your own life, and it becomes a living reality to you.

Make a point of finding somebody who's sick and lay hands on them. God's healing power, the same healing power that went through you to them, will start quickening your mortal body and become a living reality on the inside of you. I guarantee that if you make this a way of life, you will walk in the revelation that you are healed and Jesus is your Healer.

Chapter 12

Jesus, Our Protector

*H*e who dwells in the secret place of the Most High shall remain stable and fixed under the shadow of the Almighty [Whose power no foe can withstand].

I will say of the Lord, He is my Refuge and my Fortress, my God; on Him I lean and rely, and in Him I [confidently] trust!

For [then] He will deliver you from the snare of the fowler and from the deadly pestilence.

[Then] He will cover you with His pinions, and under His wings shall you trust and find refuge; His truth and His faithfulness are a shield and a buckler.

You shall not be afraid of the terror of the night, nor of the arrow (the evil plots and slanders of the wicked) that flies by day,

Nor of the pestilence that stalks in darkness, nor of the destruction and sudden death that surprise and lay waste at noonday.

A thousand may fall at your side, and ten thousand at your right hand, but it shall not come near you.

Only a spectator shall you be [yourself inaccessible in the secret place of the Most High] as you witness the reward of the wicked.

Because you have made the Lord your refuge, and the Most High your dwelling place,

There shall no evil befall you, not any plague or calamity come near your tent.

For He will give His angels [especial] charge over you to accompany and defend and preserve you in all your ways [of obedience and service].

They shall bear you up on their hands, lest you dash your foot against a stone.

You shall tread upon the lion and adder; the young lion and the serpent shall you trample underfoot.

Because he has set his love upon Me, therefore will I deliver him; I will set him on high, because he knows and understands My name [has a personal knowledge of My mercy, love, and kindness —trusts and relies on Me, knowing I will never forsake him, no, never].

He shall call upon Me, and I will answer him; I will be with him in trouble, I will deliver him and honor him.

With long life will I satisfy him and show him My salvation.

PSALM 91:1-16 AMP

The Bible tells us that in the last days men's hearts will fail them for fear of the things that are going to come upon the earth. (See Luke 21:26.) People are afraid of a lot of things. Some are afraid to get on an airplane. Some are afraid of the dark. Others are afraid of driving in the city. Fears grip the hearts of many of God's people for various reasons.

God, however, doesn't want His people fearful. God wants His people faithful. But you can't be faithful when you're fearful. We learned in an earlier chapter that the word "salvation" comes from the Greek word *sozo,* which means soundness, wholeness, healing, preservation, deliverance, provision, *and protection.* Jesus is not only our Savior, He's our protector. He's our all in all.

Jesus is your hiding place. He's your shelter in the time of storm. It doesn't matter where you are or what conditions of life surround you. You could be in the inner city in the middle of a drive-by shooting, you could be where bombs are going off or where planes are crashing. It doesn't matter — He's there to protect you and to shield you.

There's no more powerful description of God's protection than Psalm 91. As we just read in *The Amplified Bible,* verse 1 says, **He who dwells in the secret place of the Most High shall remain stable and fixed under the shadow of the Almighty**

[Whose power no foe can withstand]. You must realize that God is all-powerful. There is no other power greater than Him. You need to focus on His power and His ability to protect you, rather than those things that cause fear to rise up in you.

Now if you don't have these truths firmly fixed and established in your heart, you will live in fear. You'll drive down the road at night, and you'll be afraid. You won't even be able to go out. When you get on an airplane, you'll be sitting there holding onto the seat, your knuckles white. Have you been afraid of something recently? You need a revelation of Psalm 91! Fear comes knocking on every door. It even has the nerve to call on me! But God wants you to get to the place where you've become stable and your heart is fixed on the fact that He is your protector and no foe can withstand Him.

There's no enemy big enough to prevail over Almighty God. So guess where I'm going to hide? Psalm 20 says that some trust in chariots, and some trust in horses, but we will remember the name of our God. Proverbs 18:10 says that the name of the Lord is a strong and a mighty tower, and the righteous run into it and are saved.

When this becomes a revelation to you, you're going to be believing differently and speaking differently. Psalm 91:2 in *The Amplified Bible* says, **I will say of the Lord, He is my Refuge.** When trouble comes, you will find out what a person believes, because it will come out of their mouth. When some people get into a crisis situation in an airliner, for instance, the first thing they say is, "Awwww we're going to die!"

But when I get in an airplane, bless God, I don't care if there is a bomb on board. I know there will be ten angels holding that bomb so it cannot go off until we've landed and deplaned. I believe that with all my heart. God is our protector. I will say of the Lord, He is my refuge, my fortress, my God, on Him I lean and rely and in Him I confidently trust. This is our confidence; this is our hope. He will deliver us.

When you say He is your refuge, your protector, that's when you stand still and you see the salvation and deliverance of God. You don't have to lie awake at night worrying about your family members. His hand is upon your family. He will protect them. He will protect their rising up and their lying down, their coming in and their going out.

You won't have to pray, "Lord, please give us blessing on this journey." I'm not saying you shouldn't; I'm saying you won't have to pray it when you say it. You'll just say, "He's my refuge and my fortress." You acknowledge Him because you know He's right there in the automobile with you. He's right there in the plane with you. He's right there when you get up. He's right there when you lie down. He's right there when you come in and go out. He's your refuge, your strong tower, your fortress, your shield, your protector, your bomb shelter.

In addition, **He will deliver you from the snare of the fowler and from the deadly pestilence** (v. 3). All around the world there's turmoil and wars and rumors of wars, men against men and nation against nation. But as believers, as those that are washed in the blood of the Lamb, with Jesus on our side, we'll just see it. It's not going to come near us, for He is there to protect us. And when the enemy comes against us, there's that wall of fire about us.

Remember the exodus? When the children of Israel left Egypt, God gave them a pillar of cloud by day and a pillar of fire by night. But when they got to the edge of the sea and Pharaoh started coming behind them, the fire of God went between the children of Israel and the enemy so they couldn't get near them. He's still our pillar of fire today!

Then it says in Psalm 91:4: **He will cover you with His pinions, and under His wings shall you find trust and refuge; His truth and His faithfulness are a shield and a buckler.** This is not a tiny shield, it's a *giant* shield covering you. The enemy can't even find you. All he sees is God's shield.

That's why verse 5 says, **You shall not be afraid of the terror of the night, nor of the arrow (the evil plots and slanders of the wicked) that flies by day.** Don't be afraid today. He's with you. I don't care if you've been threatened. Don't be afraid. Do not walk in fear, but lift up your head. Keep your eye on Him. He's your protector.

Neither should we be afraid of **the pestilence that stalks in darkness** (v. 6). Some people are afraid of every germ and all kinds of diseases. They can't even enjoy eating at a restaurant. I'm not afraid of disease or sickness, because He is my protector.

A thousand may fall at your side, and ten thousand at your right hand, but it shall not come near you. In Rhodesia, during the long civil war before that country became Zimbabwe, a group of Rhodesian missionaries saw this scripture come true. A rebel military force had been killing white people on the farms all over the area, and this group of missionaries saw a large number of heavily armed soldiers coming toward them. They knew their lives were in grave danger. So these Rhodesian missionaries got down on their knees and began to pray, to call out to the name of the Lord as their protector.

Something phenomenal took place. When they looked out the window they saw the rebel army soldiers fleeing in terror. Men armed with guns and hand grenades were fleeing, running as fast as they could. When they were captured later, they were asked why they ran.

They said, "Well, we thought that there were just a few people staying in the farm house. But as we came toward the house to capture it, we saw this whole army dressed in white surrounding the house, and we were so afraid that we took off running."

Those missionaries saw Psalm 91 come true. **A thousand may fall at your side, and ten thousand at your right hand, but it shall not come near you** (v. 7). It will not come near you, either!

You will only be a spectator to catastrophe. Why? Psalm 91:8 says you'll be inaccessible in the secret place of the Most High. The enemy's trying to get you, but he can't find you. He's looking for you, but you're caught up in that mist, that cloud, that fog of the glory of God.

> Bullets fired at point blank range are not going to hit their target because there's a giant angel standing with his finger stuck up the barrel. Don't believe it? Well then, get ready for the bullet. But I believe it.
>
> For this to work in your life, you've got to take God's Word for it. You've got to accept it, believe it, and hide it in your heart.

That verse goes on to say, **as you witness the reward of the wicked.** I'll tell you right now, things are going to escalate! There are going to be horrors in these final hours that we've never ever witnessed. The hurricanes, earthquakes, famines, and wars and rumors of wars are not going to get better. I want you to understand that. I'm not telling you that everything's going to get better and everything's going to be wonderful. In the world, it's only going to get worse.

Nation will rise up against nation. We'll see diseases, the likes of which have never been heard before, as terrorist nations use chemical and biological warfare. They could drop a certain type of bomb right now on a city and kill everybody there without spoiling the cars, the houses, or anything else. That's the kind of thing that will be experienced in these last days.

And I want you to know, if you don't know how to trust God as your protector in these last days, I don't know how you and your family are going to make it. I don't want to frighten anybody, but you don't have to be a rocket scientist to see these things coming. However, if He's your shield and your protection, then that changes things a little bit, doesn't it! Bullets fired at point blank range are not going to hit their target because there's a giant angel standing with his finger stuck up the barrel. Don't believe it? Well then, get ready for the bullet. But I believe it.

For this to work in your life, you've got to take God's Word for it. You've got to accept it, believe it, and hide it in your heart. You've got to stand upon the Word of God. You've got to activate the Word of God in your life.

It's a cause and effect relationship that you can see in Psalm 91:9-10 (AMP):

> *Because you have made the Lord your refuge, and the Most High your dwelling place,*
>
> *There shall no evil befall you, nor any plague or calamity come near your tent.*

These verses mean you can sleep at night in total peace because He's there with you. We've heard testimonies from farmers who have been faithful to obey God, and when a freeze came, everybody else's farm froze up, but their farm didn't. Why? Because Jesus was their protector.

Do you know how many times I've heard testimonies of people who love God with all their heart who have a terrible car wreck and get out without one scratch on them? They should have been dead, but He was their protector.

Why will no evil nor any plague or calamity come near your tent? **For He will give His angels [especial] charge over you to accompany and defend and preserve you in all your ways [of obedience and service].** We've got angels looking after us, and I'm not talking about little babies with big diapers and a bow and arrow! I'm talking about ten- or twelve-foot angelic beings. Your enemies will be running around in total confusion when the angel of God encamps about you.

> *Are they not all ministering spirits, sent forth to minister for them who shall be heirs of salvation?*
>
> HEBREWS 1:14

Angels are out there working on your behalf. They're all ministering spirits sent forth to minister to those of us who are heirs of salvation. If you're an heir of salvation, then the angels of God have been sent forth to minister for you and in your behalf. They are protecting you. They're working in your behalf. They're going ahead of you to make the crooked way straight. They're going ahead of you to give you the supernatural, divine favor of God.

And when the servant of the man of God was risen early, and gone forth, behold, an host compassed the city both with horses

and chariots. And his servant said unto him, Alas, my master! how shall we do?

And he answered, Fear not: for they that be with us are more than they that be with them.

And Elisha prayed, and said, LORD, I pray thee, open his eyes, that he may see. And the LORD opened the eyes of the young man; and he saw: and, behold, the mountain was full of horses and chariots of fire round about Elisha.

2 KINGS 6:15-17

It doesn't matter what or who comes against you to destroy you if you trust God's Word. A whole army of the enemy is no match for the army of angels that surround you to protect you! You cannot see them (unless God supernaturally opens your eyes), but they are there nonetheless.

And there were four leprous men at the entering in of the gate: and they said one to another, Why sit we here until we die?

If we say, We will enter into the city, then the famine is in the city, and we shall die there: and if we sit still here, we die also. Now therefore come, and let us fall unto the host of the Syrians: if they save us alive, we shall live; and if they kill us, we shall but die.

And they rose up in the twilight, to go unto the camp of the Syrians: and when they were come to the uttermost part of the camp of Syria, behold, there was no man there.

For the Lord had made the host of the Syrians to hear a noise of chariots, and a noise of horses, even the noise of a great host: and they said one to another, Lo, the king of Israel hath hired against us the kings of the Hittites, and the kings of the Egyptians, to come upon us.

Wherefore they arose and fled in the twilight, and left their tents, and their horses, and their asses, even the camp as it was, and fled for their life.

2 KINGS 7:3-7

When God is on your side, armies will flee in terror before you. It doesn't make sense in the natural, but it is a reality. This is not going to happen for you if you do not believe God's Word. You must put your faith and trust in God's Word and angels will work on your behalf.

Notice the last part of verse 11 in *The Amplified Bible*. They will **defend and preserve you in all your ways [of obedience and service].** That's why you want to make sure that you're obeying Him and serving Him. The angels of the Lord are there, but they cannot defend you in your ways of disobedience. You can't be smoking crack and asking your angel to play lookout! Make sure that you're obeying God. Make sure that you're doing everything you know how to do to walk in the plan and the purpose of God for your life. When you obey God, the enemy cannot touch you, because the hand of God is upon your life.

This is crucial: God's protection is in His presence. You must stay in His presence in order to be under His protection. Sin removes you from His presence and His protection.

Now look to the next verses, Psalm 91:12-14 (AMP):

They shall bear you up on their hands, lest you dash your foot against a stone.

You shall tread upon the lion and adder; the young lion and the serpent shall you trample underfoot.

Because he has set his love upon Me, therefore, I will deliver him; I will set him on high, because he knows and understands My name [has a personal knowledge of My mercy,

love, and kindness — trusts and relies on Me, knowing I will
never forsake him, no, never].

God is with you constantly. He's with you in the dark hours, when the circumstances look bleak, when the storms rise up against you. When the wind's blowing and it looks like you're going down, He's there in the boat with you. "I'll never leave you nor forsake you," Jesus says. (See Hebrews 13:5.)

Now, look at verse 15: **He will call upon Me, and I will answer him; I will be with him in trouble, I will deliver him and honor him.** He's waiting for you to call on Him. Some people don't want to call on God because they're afraid to bother Him. They think He's too busy. But you're not bothering Him. He *wants* you to bother Him! You have not because you ask not. (See James 4:2.) Call unto Him!

Call unto me, and I will answer thee, and show thee great
and mighty things, which thou knowest not.

JEREMIAH 33:3

And it shall come to pass, that before they call, I will answer;
and while they are yet speaking, I will hear.

ISAIAH 65:24

I pray this word goes right into your heart and burns like a Holy Ghost firebrand on the inside of you!

Jesus is your shelter in the time of trouble. The Bible doesn't say you won't have any trouble, but God says, "I will be with you in trouble." He wants to remind you that while you're in trouble, He's there. Call upon Him. You could get into trouble and die, not knowing or else forgetting that He's right there with you. So call to Him. Cry out to Him.

If you find yourself in a problem and you call on the Lord and He doesn't deliver you, you come and tell me, and I'll quit the ministry and come and join you. That's a strong statement, but I want you to know that when you call out to Him with all of your heart, He's going to come. He didn't bring you this far to leave you. **I will deliver him and honor him** (v. 15). He not only wants to deliver you, He wants to honor you!

Look at the last verse: **With long life I will satisfy him and show him My salvation.** They put preservatives in most of the food we eat. In fact, I heard that a favorite snack of ours has a shelf life of twenty-seven years. If you want something to last long, you must preserve it. God says I will give you long life. That means He is going to preserve you.

With long life, will I satisfy him and show him My salvation (v. 16). There are people who have this passage of Scripture printed on a T-shirt, printed on a book mark, or printed on a wall hanging — yet they die young. They never experience the reality of this passage because they've never come to the place where they've said, "Yes, Jesus is my Savior, He's my Healer, He's my Deliverer, but He's also my Protector. He is my shelter. He is my rock. He's my tower. He's my wall of fire." They've never received it. They've never taken this word and made it personal and acted upon it and told it to their wife and told it to their children and told it to their loved ones. Have you?

God might be requiring you to do certain things that mean stepping out of your comfort zone, stepping out beyond the natural, carnal mind and into a place where you must confront your fear. That brings us to the life of Joshua, because if there was ever an individual who should have been afraid, it was Joshua.

Joshua was second in command to Moses, leading the children of Israel to the promised land. Then Moses died and God told Joshua, "I want you to take his place." I don't know about you, but if that were me, my knees would be having close fellowship one with the other!

"Moses is dead and I must take his place. God, are You sure?" Joshua was having the same argument with God that Moses had right at the beginning. When God called Moses, he was afraid the Israelites wouldn't accept his authority, so he said, "Who must I say sent me?"

God said, "Tell them I AM sent you."

Now God was coming to Joshua to tell him, "I'm the same I AM with you as I AM with Moses." God is coming to us by the power of His Word, saying, "I AM THAT I AM. I AM. As I was with Moses, as I was with Joshua, so I AM with you." It's not something you've got to try to get. It's already yours. Just walk in it.

Now look at God's promise to Joshua in Joshua 1:5: **There shall not any man be able to stand before thee all the days of thy life: as I was with Moses, so I will be with thee: I will not fail thee, nor forsake thee.** How can you be afraid of anybody when God is your Protector? No one's going to be able to stand against you, because God will not fail you.

Many times people say, "I know Jesus is my protector and I shouldn't be afraid, but you don't know my circumstances." No, you may know your circumstances, but you don't know God's promises like you say you do. If you really knew Jesus as your protector, you wouldn't go to pieces, working on your next nervous breakdown.

Can't you see Joshua getting braver and braver as God tells him:

I will not fail thee nor forsake you.

Be strong and of a good courage: for unto this people shalt thou divide for an inheritance the land, which I sware unto their fathers to give them.

Only be thou strong and very courageous, that thou mayest observe to do according to all the law, which Moses my servant commanded thee: turn not from it to the right hand or to the left, that thou mayest prosper whithersoever thou goest.

JOSHUA 1:5-7

It takes courage, but when you put your eyes on Jesus, keep them on Him and don't look to the left or to the right, you're going to be blessed in every area of your life — blessed coming in, blessed going out, blessed in the city, blessed in the field, blessed rising up, blessed lying down, blessed, blessed, blessed, blessed.

Joshua 1:8 says: **This book of the law shall not depart out of thy mouth; but thou shalt meditate therein day and night.** This is the secret to success: meditating continually on God's Word, speaking it and thinking it constantly. Do that with Psalm 91: I will say of the Lord, He's my refuge. Take these scriptures and carry them around with you and think about them. Meditate on the Word of God. To meditate on the Word of God, you learn it and you talk about it with your family. "He's our strong tower. He's our refuge. He's our fortress." You're excited about it, so you talk about it.

When you meditate that way, and when you speak that way, the Bible says you're going to make your way prosperous, and you're going to have good success. **Be strong,** He said, **and of a good courage; be not afraid; neither be thou dismayed: for the Lord thy God is with thee whithersoever thou goest** (v. 9). He is also with you!

Jesus is your Protector.

Chapter 13

Jesus, Our Provider

*The thief comes only in order to steal and kill and destroy.
I came that they might have and enjoy life, and have it
in abundance (to the full, till it overflows).*

*I am the Good Shepherd. The Good Shepherd risks and lays
down His [own] life for the sheep.*

JOHN 10:10-11 AMP

God knows what you need. He knows everything about you. He knows when you're rising up and when you're lying down, when you're coming in and when you're going out. He knows your dreams and your desires. But most important, He wants to meet your needs. He wants to see the dreams and desires He's placed in your heart fulfilled.

Jesus said He came to give us abundant life, but most Christians are having just-getting-by life. How does that happen?

People in the Church accept Jesus as their Savior, and some in the Church accept Him as their Healer, but they often have a hard time, accepting Him as their Provider. What's more, some of us accept Him as our Provider but we don't accept Him as our Provider in *every* area of our lives. When we not only accept Jesus as our Savior and Healer, but also our Provider, we're expecting His provision every day. We're believing Him to care for our every need.

Therefore I say unto you, Take no thought for your life, what ye shall eat, or what ye shall drink; nor yet for your body, what ye shall put on. Is not the life more than meat, and the body than raiment?

Behold the fowls of the air: for they sow not, neither do they reap, nor gather into barns; yet your heavenly Father feedeth them. Are ye not much better than they?

Which of you by taking thought can add one cubit unto his stature?

And why take ye thought for raiment? Consider the lilies of the field, how they grow; they toil not, neither do they spin:

And yet I say unto you, That even Solomon in all his glory was not arrayed like one of these.

Wherefore, if God so clothe the grass of the field, which to day is, and to morrow is cast into the oven, shall he not much more clothe you, O ye of little faith?

Therefore take no thought, saying, What shall we eat? or, What shall we drink? or, Wherewithal shall we be clothed?

(For after all these things do the Gentiles seek:) for your heavenly Father knoweth that ye have need of all these things.

But seek ye first the kingdom of God, and his righteousness; and all these things shall be added unto you.

Take therefore no thought for the morrow: for the morrow shall take thought for the things of itself. Sufficient unto the day is the evil thereof.

MATTHEW 6:25-34

According to Jesus, we should not even be thinking about our food, drink, and clothing, because our heavenly Father knows what we need and will take care of these things as we seek His kingdom and His righteousness. The problem is that most people — even Christians — spend most of their day worrying about small things that Jesus promised to take care of. We need to stop worrying and start expecting God's provision to be there for us as we serve Him.

When some people wake up in the morning, they're not expecting God's provision. They're expecting lack. They're not expecting God's favor; they're expecting to be attacked by ten o'clock! I don't live like that. I'm waking up looking for the blessing of heaven. I'm looking for the provision of the Lord. The

Bible says the blessing of the Lord makes one rich and He adds no sorrow with it. (See Proverbs 10:22.)

God wants you to have abundant life — good measure, pressed down, shaken together, and running over. (See Luke 6:38.) That's what you are to expect. What are you expecting from tomorrow? Good things. What are you expecting from this week? Good things. I'm not believing for bad things. I'm believing for good things. I'm believing for the provision of the Lord.

Sometimes, however, we slip and find ourselves worrying about the Lord's provision. This even happens to ministers. I remember a time when we were on the road, constantly, in crusades. I couldn't take a week off and believe that God was going to meet the needs of our ministry during my time off. I had a battle with that, and the Lord really had to speak to me about it, "You mean I can't meet the need if you take a holiday? Don't you work for Me?"

I said, "Yes, Lord, I work for You."

He said, "Well, can't you have a holiday on Me?"

I really had to come to a point of trusting God that even if I wasn't preaching, He still would provide for me. That's hard for a minister.

He's a Provider. His very presence, His very nature is that if He showed up at your house and there was no food, He would provide food. He said, "I am the way, the truth, and the life." (See John 14:6.) So when you're sitting there and you're saying to yourself, *There is no way,* you must realize that there *is* a way and His name is Jesus. He makes a way.

Somebody said, "I don't know what to do, I've got a brick wall behind me and I've got a brick wall in front of me." But Jesus will make a way. He'll open the door. If there's no door to open, He'll blow a hole in the wall!

In John, chapter 2, we find that the very first miracle Jesus did was a miracle of provision. He provided for a need. Jesus, His mother Mary, and the disciples were at a wedding in Cana of

Galilee. When the wine was all gone, Mary said to Jesus, "They have no more wine." Then she said to the servants. "Whatever He says to you, do it."

I believe that's the key to the provision of the Lord: *"Whatever He tells you to do, do it."* You may not know what to do, but the Word of the Lord will come to you — "Do this," or "Do that," and the door will open. God will make a way where there is no way, and the provision of the Lord will be there.

What was the result of this miracle? It wasn't just that the guests had something to drink that day. The purpose of Jesus' miracle is revealed in John 2:11 (AMP):

This, the first of His signs (miracles, wonderworks), Jesus performed in Cana of Galilee, and manifested His glory [by it He displayed His greatness and His power openly], and His disciples believed in Him [adhered to, trusted in, and relied on Him].

Because of His miracle of provision, His disciples believed in Him. When you have a need in your life and God, by His power, begins to supply your need, your whole life changes. Your trust in Him rises, so that you can believe Him for all kinds of things. "I saw Him do it last week," you say, "so I know He'll do it again today. I remember what He did ten years ago, so I know He's gonna do it again."

With that miracle, Jesus showed forth His glory and His goodness. I believe the reason He turned water into wine as His first miracle was because He wanted that to be a statement. Providing the wine is probably the least that He could have done. First of all, Jesus came to save from sin and heal sick bodies. The last thing down the line would be to provide wine for a friend's wedding. But I believe He's trying to say, "I do the least thing I can do first, because I want to show you that there's nothing in your life that I can't take care of. If you accept Me as your Savior and your Healer, I'll also be your Provider, so that when you have a need, you know I will supply everything that you need."

In John 15:7, Jesus says, **If ye abide in me, and my words abide in you, ye shall ask what ye will, and it shall be done unto you.** Whatever you need, ask, and He'll give it.

After this, Jesus went to the farther side of the sea of Galilee — that is, the Sea of Tiberias,

And a great crowd was following Him because they had seen the signs (miracles) which He [continually] performed upon those who were sick.

And Jesus walked up the mountainside and sat down there with His disciples.

Now the Passover, the feast of the Jews, was approaching.

Jesus looked up then, and seeing that a vast multitude was coming toward Him, He said to Philip, Where are we to buy bread, so that all these people may eat?

But he said this to prove (test) him, for He well knew what He was about to do.

Philip answered Him, Two hundred pennies' (forty dollars) worth of bread is not enough that everyone may receive even a little.

Another of His disciples, Andrew, Simon Peter's brother, said to Him,

There's a little boy here, who has [with him] five barley loaves, and two small fish; but what are they among so many people?

Jesus said, Make all the people recline (sit down). Now the ground (a pasture) was covered with thick grass at the spot, so that the men threw themselves down, about 5,000 in number.

Jesus took the loaves, and when He had given thanks, He distributed to the disciples and the disciples to the reclining people; so also [He did] with the fish, as much as they wanted.

When they all had enough, He said to His disciples, Gather up now the fragments (the broken pieces that are left over), so that nothing may be lost and wasted.

So accordingly they gathered them up, and they filled twelve [small hand] baskets with fragments left over by those who had eaten from the five barley loaves.

JOHN 6:1-13 AMP

This is a very powerful miracle of provision. People are hungry, so Jesus takes a little boy's lunch and then He multiplies it. Now it's one thing to hear that God provides food and drink in Bible times, but it happens now too. When my family was living in the Transkei region of South Africa, I heard of a miracle of provision among Baptist missionaries. About sixty people had gathered one night at the mission, and all they had was one chicken. But they prayed and God multiplied their one chicken. All sixty ate chicken and were filled!

God's provision is not just for Bible times — it's for right now. It's for you and me. If we just believe God, He'll make a way where there is no way. God wants His people to live in a higher realm of the supernatural. It's time to move up and live in a higher realm of the provision of God in our lives. We've got to quit looking at our own resources. If we're looking at our salary as our source of supply, we're going to be devastated if our company closes down tomorrow.

> When you lose your job, suddenly you find out how much you really believe in the Lord's provision.

This has got to become real in your daily life. It's easy to clap your hands and sing in church, "He's my Provider." But it's another thing to really trust in Him when you're in the middle of a problem. When you lose your job, suddenly you find out how much you really believe in the Lord's provision.

When you get into that position, you've got to truly believe that Jesus is a multiplier. You've got to believe that He doesn't look at how much you have, but takes what you have and multiplies it, stretches it, and makes it go further than it's ever gone before. You might look at your income as limited, but He will stretch it

Jesus, Our Provider

to do more than it's ever done before. When I look at what God does through this ministry with the income we receive, I'm amazed. Our income is not even a tenth of what some of the larger ministries in America receive, yet what God's doing through this ministry is so tremendous! God can stretch it. He can make it go further than ever before!

Of course, we realize that God blesses us also because we're good stewards of our resources, we tithe, and give offerings to honor Him. When we honor Him, He blesses us. My wife, Adonica, and I have seen that when we have limited resources available and God tells us to give, we give. We still end up doing everything we wanted to do with the limited resources — even minus what we've given — because God stretches it and multiplies it. Faithful tithers have long seen that the 90 percent they retain after tithing goes much farther than if they'd kept 100 percent.

God not only provides food, drink, and clothing, He provides open doors. He provides supernatural favor to meet our every need. I want to show you several more miracles of provision.

> *When they arrived in Capernaum, the collectors of the half shekel [the temple tax] went up to Peter and said, Does not your Teacher pay the half shekel?*
>
> *He answered, Yes. And when he came home, Jesus spoke to him [about it] first, saying, What do you think, Simon? From whom do earthly rulers collect duties or tribute — from their own sons or from others not of their own family?*
>
> *And when Peter said, From other people not of their own family, Jesus said, Then the sons are exempt.*
>
> *However, in order not to give offense and to cause them to stumble [that is, to cause them to judge unfavorably and unjustly] go down to the sea and throw in a hook. Take the first fish that comes up, and when you open its mouth you will find there a shekel. Take it and give it to them to pay the temple tax for Me and for yourself.*
>
> MATTHEW 17:24-27 AMP

147

Now Peter's a fisherman, and in all of Peter's years of fishing, he's never caught a fish with a coin in its mouth. But he never needed it until now. It's a relief to know that Jesus knows where the fish are and that He wants to take care of your needs!

When they were getting near to Jerusalem, to Bethphage and Bethany at the Mount of Olives, He sent ahead two of His disciples

And instructed them, Go into the village in front of you, and as soon as you enter it, you will find a colt tied, which has never been ridden by anyone; unfasten it and bring it [here].

If anyone asks you, Why are you doing this? answer, The Lord needs it, and He will send it back here presently.

So they went away and found a colt tied at the door out in the [winding] open street, and they loosed it.

And some who were standing there said to them, What are you doing, untying the colt?

And they replied as Jesus had directed them, and they allowed them to go.

And they brought the colt to Jesus and threw their outer garments upon it, and He sat on it.

MARK 11:1-7 AMP

Jesus needed a vehicle. If this happened today, He'd say, "Now go to the dealership down the road, and you'll see a car on the lot. Just get in it and bring it over here. If they ask what you're doing with the car, just say, "My Master has need of it. We'll bring it back." There was a need, and God provided for that need.

When they needed the upper room, the same thing happened. In Mark 14:12-16, the apostles said they needed a place to get together for the Passover meal. Jesus told them to look for a man with a big pot and to follow him home. "Go in there," Jesus said, "and tell them that we need their guest room. You'll find everything laid out for you."

God provides, no matter how impossible it looks. He furnishes a table in the wilderness. He makes the crooked paths straight. He'll provide for you. All He wants you to do is to trust Him. Will you trust Him? Maybe you want to go to Bible school, but you're worried about your tuition. Would you trust Him? If you can't believe God for your tuition, how are you ever going to believe God when it comes to funding your ministry or missions operation?

A lot of people have said, "Well, you know, it's great that you preach this message of provision and all that, but Jesus didn't have anything and Jesus even said it Himself, 'Foxes have holes, birds have nests, but the Son of man hath not where to lay His head.'" Jesus didn't have a home because He didn't need one. What He did need, He got. You don't really need anything when you're all you need. When you walk on water just as a hobby, do you think you're going to lose one night's sleep about a need?

Jesus knows what *you* have need of, though. He knows you have a family. He knows you need to work and earn money to provide for your family. He knows! That's why He tells you to seek first the kingdom of God and His righteousness and all these things will be added — not subtracted — unto you. He knows what *you* have need of!

For years my family didn't need a home either. We just traveled, lived in hotels, and kept our stuff in storage. For years we'd wanted to get a home, but we'd stopped talking about it, because every time we asked the Lord if we could get a home, He said no. I said, "Lord, I'd love to give my wife and kids a house. I don't want the kids growing up in a hotel room."

When the revival broke out in central Florida in 1993, the Lord spoke to me and said, "It's time for you to get a home, son. Go and get some property, and build a house for your family." So we soon found the piece of property and started building the house.

One day, as I was walking out on the foundation, I just lifted up my hands with tears rolling down my cheeks and said, "Lord, thank You so much for this house for my family." As I said that, the Lord spoke to me audibly and said, "Son, you've built My house for the last fourteen years. Now I'm going to build your house."

I said, "Lord, do You really mean that? You're going to build my house?"

He said, "Yes, you watch it, I'm building your house. I'll make a way for you."

Jesus knew my desire. It's such a pleasure just to come home, to have a place called "home."

When we moved into the house, I got my wife and the kids together and said, "This home is just a blessing from God, and if God tells us to give it away, we will." You see, everything we have belongs to Him — we're just stewards, managers, of what He blesses us with. As stewards, we need to do whatever He tells us to do with everything we have. So if He ever needs my house, He has it without a question.

Jesus can provide a home and transportation. We know He can provide you with a job. We know He can provide you with food. What else do you need? What are your needs today? Jesus meets them all.

The [uncompromisingly] righteous shall flourish like the palm tree [be long-lived, stately, upright, useful, and fruit-ful]; they shall grow like a cedar in Lebanon [majestic, stable, durable, and incorruptible].

Planted in the house of the Lord, they shall flourish in the courts of our God.

[Growing in grace] they shall still bring forth fruit in old age; they shall be full of sap [of spiritual vitality] and [rich in the] verdure [of trust, love, and contentment].

[They are living memorials] to show that the Lord is upright and faithful to His promises; He is my Rock, and there is no unrighteousness in Him.

PSALM 92:12-15 AMP

Some people are so worried about dying early, but God's Word says the uncompromisingly righteous will be **long-lived, stately, upright, useful, and fruitful.** *The King James Version* says that they shall be **fat and flourishing.** *The Amplified Bible* says, **they shall be full of sap.** Are you full of sap? Are you full of spiritual vitality? Are you rich in trust, love, and contentment?

We are living memorials! Our lives show the world that the Lord is upright and faithful to His promises. He is our rock, there's no unrighteousness in Him, and our lives exhibit this truth to a lost and dying world.

Psalm 23:1 AMP says, **The Lord is my Shepherd [to feed, guide, and shield me], I shall not lack.** To feed, guide, and shield me is everything I need. I shall not lack! I wake up in the morning with an air of expectancy, looking for the favor of God, looking for the blessing of God.

Have you come to that place where you just trust the Lord? Trust Him! You've got nothing to lose, so trust Him. He's there to help you. He's there to make the way for you. He's your Provider. He loves you. He'll walk into your house and multiply food. He knows how to pay the bills, and He knows how to pay tax money. He knows about transportation needs, and He knows about accommodation needs. And most of all, He can make a way where there is no way!

> *And you shall return and obey the voice of the Lord and do all His commandments which I command you today.*
>
> *And the Lord your God will make you abundantly prosperous in every work of your hand, in the fruit of your body, of your cattle, of your land, for good; for the Lord will again delight in prospering you, as He took delight in your fathers.*
>
> DEUTERONOMY 30:8-9 AMP

Your heavenly Father will make you *abundantly prosperous,* for He *delights* in prospering you because you obey His commandments.

God loves to bless His obedient children. Are you His child? Do you submit to His will and His Word? Then God will bless you and enjoy every moment of it. You don't have to run after blessing. Run after Jesus and blessing and provision will run after you!

Chapter 14

Jesus, the Baptizer in the Holy Spirit

Jesus answered and said unto her, Whosoever drinketh of this water shall thirst again:

But whosoever drinketh of the water that I shall give him shall never thirst; but the water that I shall give him shall be in him a well of water springing up into everlasting life.

JOHN 4:13-14

In the last day, that great day of the feast, Jesus stood and cried, saying, If any man thirst, let him come unto me, and drink.

He that believeth on me, as the scripture hath said, out of his belly shall flow rivers of living water.

(But this spake he of the Spirit, which they that believe on him should receive: for the Holy Ghost was not yet given; because that Jesus was not yet glorified.)

JOHN 7:37-39

In John 4:14, Jesus speaks about a well of water springing up into everlasting life. But in John 7:38, He says "out of your belly shall flow rivers of living water." So He's talking about two different things taking place in the life of every believer. Number one, there is a well of water springing up into everlasting life. Number two, there is a river coming out of their belly.

You could call salvation a *well anointing*. And what a well it is! The Bible says, **Therefore with joy shall ye draw water out of the wells of salvation** (Isaiah 12:3). Joy is the bucket that goes down and pulls up the water of life from the well of your salvation. Your salvation should be a source of life and joy, not a dry and heavy burden.

The water of the Spirit can also gush out like a mighty river. There are people who believe that there's just one experience: when you get saved, you are automatically baptized with the Holy Spirit at the same time. But that's not true. Otherwise, Jesus wouldn't have spoken about both the well and the river. You can get baptized in the Holy Spirit at the same time as you get saved, but they are two separate and distinct experiences.

John the Baptist, Jesus' cousin, was a forerunner to the ministry of the Lord Jesus Christ, and he announced what Jesus' ministry would be about.

I indeed baptize you with water unto repentance: but he that cometh after me is mightier than I, whose shoes I am not worthy to bear: he shall baptize you with the Holy Ghost, and with fire.

MATTHEW 3:11

John proclaimed how the ministry of Jesus would differ from his own. John was saying — and I mean no offense — "I'm a Baptist, but there's coming a Pentecostal after me and He will baptize you with the Holy Ghost and fire." This One is coming after him, he says in Matthew 3:12, **Whose fan is in his hand, and he will thoroughly purge his floor, and gather his wheat into the garner; but he will burn up the chaff with unquenchable fire.**

What does fire do? Fire purges. Fire purifies. If you want to refine gold, you've got to put it through the fire, and it will come out pure. As the molten gold liquefies, the impurities float to the top, where they can be scooped away. And that's what the Holy Ghost comes to do in our life. He comes to purify us by melting our hearts and scooping off the sin and impurities.

Now let's look at the words of Jesus once again in John 14. He's preparing His disciples for the time when He is going to leave. He says He's going to go away, but He's not going to leave them alone. He's going to send the Holy Ghost, the Comforter. He's going to send the *Paraclete* (the "One called alongside to help"), the Teacher, the Advocate, the Intercessor, to help every believer.

> *And I will pray the Father, and he shall give you another Comforter, that he may abide with you for ever.*

JOHN 14:16

Jesus prayed to the Father to send the Holy Ghost. The Bible says the Father sent the Son, then the Son sent the Spirit. The Father sent the Son and the Son sent the Spirit, but the Spirit never came until the Son left. Jesus goes on to say,

> *And I will pray the Father, and he shall give you another Comforter, that he may abide with you for ever;*
>
> *Even the Spirit of truth; whom the world cannot receive, because it seeth him not, neither knoweth him: but ye know him; for he dwelleth with you, and shall be in you.*
>
> *I will not leave you comfortless: I will come to you...*
>
> *But the Comforter, which is the Holy Ghost, whom the Father will send in my name, he will teach you all things, and bring all things to your remembrance, whatsoever I have said unto you.*

JOHN 14:16-18,26

No wonder we need the Holy Spirit! We need Him every day of our lives, every waking moment. He will teach us and bring all things to our remembrance, whatever Jesus has said unto us.

> *But when the Comforter is come, whom I will send unto you from the Father, even the Spirit of truth, which proceedeth from the Father, he shall testify of me.*

JOHN 15:26

The Holy Spirit will bear witness and will testify about Jesus. We have testimonies coming in from remote parts of the world — China, the mountains of Tibet and Nepal, India, and even Saudi Arabia. People there have watched video tapes of our revival services, and even though some of them couldn't speak a word of English, the power of the Holy Spirit put them on the floor.

Their testimony is that while they were on the floor, Jesus appeared to them and said, "When you get up, ask these missionaries to tell you about Me, because I love you." These people, who had never heard the Gospel, went to the missionaries and said, "Could you tell us about Jesus?"

The missionaries said, "What do you mean, tell you about Jesus? Who told you about Him?"

They said, "Well, we were lying on the floor just awhile ago and a man in a white robe stood before us and told us that He loved us, and that when we got up off the floor, we should come and ask you about Him."

The Holy Spirit will testify about Jesus just as Jesus was testifying about the coming of the Holy Ghost because He knew we needed the Holy Spirit. He knew that we needed to know Him intimately and that we needed to have a personal relationship with the Holy Spirit. He wanted us not just to be saved and have the *well* on the inside, but He wanted us also to have the overflowing *river* coming out of us, because He wanted us to be witnesses unto Him everywhere we go.

Now, let me show you this. There are a lot of people who have been filled with the Spirit of God but have never had the release of the Spirit in their life. Why? Because they never yielded to the Spirit of God in the area of speaking in other tongues. I've seen people who just shook until their false teeth rattled when the power of God came on them, yet they never had the release of their prayer language. From time to time the anointing of God would come on them so strongly, they didn't know what to do with themselves, but nobody was there to teach them how to yield to the Spirit of God.

> *Nevertheless I tell you the truth; It is expedient for you that I go away: for if I do not go away, the Comforter will not come unto you; but if I depart, I will send him unto you.*

JOHN 16:7

Can you imagine Peter, James, and John standing there, listening to Jesus say, "It's better for you that I go away"? Their minds must have struggled to grasp what He meant by that.

"We don't want You to go away. Stay around some more."

"But," He says, "it's better for you that I go away. If I don't go away, the Comforter will not come unto you. If I depart, I will send Him to you."

> *And when he is come, he will reprove the world of sin, and of righteousness, and of judgment.*
>
> *Of sin, because they believe not on me;*
>
> *Of righteousness, because I go to my Father, and ye see me no more;*
>
> *Of judgment, because the prince of this world is judged.*
>
> *I have yet many things to say unto you, but you cannot bear them now.*

JOHN 16:8-12

What did Jesus mean by that? They not only wouldn't be able to bear it, but they wouldn't be able to understand it just then. Why? Because the Holy Spirit is the one who gives you understanding and insight into the Word of God. That's why we have people in the earth who read the same Bible as we do and can't see what it's saying. They read the same Bible and can't even see it. They don't believe healing is for today, don't believe God wants to bless them, and can't see the powerful reality of the Gospel.

Howbeit when he, the Spirit of truth, is come, he will guide you into all truth.

JOHN 16:13

> Millions of Christians in China can't announce where their services will be the next week because the secret police might hear. Do you know how those people go to church? By the Holy Ghost.

Jesus said that the Holy Spirit will guide us. Let's take the underground Church in China, which has been undergoing tremendous persecution for decades, as an example. Millions of Christians in China can't announce where their services will be the next week because the secret police might hear. Do you know how those people go to church? By the Holy Ghost. They have to pray and get the mind of God. The Holy Spirit tells them where their next meeting is, and they show up on Sunday in the right place.

The people come into this little room and they pack in there with no comfy pews, no music, none of what we'd call praise and worship. They just sing with tears rolling down their cheeks as they worship.

But in America, we can definitely have church without the Holy Ghost! There are churches strewn all over the nation without the Holy Ghost. They don't need Him to move, because man has perfected the art of gathering people together. Just as Disney has perfected the art of moving masses of people through an amusement park, the Church has perfected the art of gathering people and just tickling their ears. That's the whole idea for many churches: "We want 'em to come back, so get 'em in and out. As long as they're putting their money in, we're happy."

We don't want you just to get in and out. We want you *in* and we want you *staying in* and we want you full of the Holy Ghost and full of the fire of God!

I've heard many stories of people who are truly led by the Holy Spirit. When I was in Norway, I heard about two brothers whose father had pioneered a church in a remote region of China at the turn of the century. The two brothers decided to go back to China to find the church their father had pioneered. They could still speak Chinese, as they had learned it while growing up in China. The Communists had changed the name of the town, but they finally got into the region and found someone to take them there. They arrived in the town at eleven o'clock at night.

As they got out of the car, a man walked towards them. He said, "Hello, I'm the pastor here. We've been waiting for you." There were several hundred Chinese Christians gathered at a house. The Norwegian men asked if somebody told them they were coming.

The Chinese said, "Oh, yes. Three nights ago the Word of the Lord came forth prophetically that 'The sons of the one who brought you the Good News will be here. Be ready for them. They will arrive at eleven o'clock.'"

Our brothers and sisters in China know far more about living in the realm of the Spirit of God than we do here. We're led by natural things and circumstances, but these people are led by the Holy Ghost. The church in China is growing at an incredible rate. More than forty thousand people are being saved into the church in China every single day. These people know how to hear the voice of God.

We totally underestimate the power of the Holy Ghost. Jesus knew these things when He walked the earth. How did *He* function all the time? By the Holy Ghost. He was led by the Spirit. He said, **The Son can do nothing of himself, but what he seeth the Father do** (John 5:19). He was watching the Holy Spirit morning, noon, and night, everywhere He went. He would follow the promptings and the leadings of the Spirit of God — nothing more, nothing less.

That's the cry of my heart: for the body of Christ to become more sensitive to the Spirit of God. We must be more sensitive to His promptings and leadings. The Church in America has gotten so comfortable that they don't need to hear the voice of

God. They don't need to listen to the promptings and leadings of the Spirit of God.

That's why we must strip away all of the things that would hold us back. We must strip away all the things that would block our ears and our hearts from being sensitive to the Spirit of grace. Stop looking for your comfort. Stop staying in your comfort zone. Press in and get to the point where you only do what the Holy Spirit wants you to do and go where He wants you to go.

You know, if the Holy Spirit tells you to do something, He will make a way for you. We just don't believe God enough. After the former Soviet Union opened up to the Gospel, American missionaries prophesied over a local pastor. The Holy Spirit said, "God's going to start using you in an unusual way." They left, and when they came back a year later and asked about his ministry, he said, "Well, I have three churches, but they're very far apart. They're eight hundred miles to a thousand miles apart. I preach at each every Sunday.

They said, "What are you talking about? How could you?"

He said, "Well, you know you prophesied that God would use me in an unusual way? He does. Each Sunday I preach at the one place, and I walk out and then I just suddenly find myself at the next place. Then I preach to them and then I walk out and I find myself instantly at the next church. And then I go home."

We badly underestimate the power of the Holy Ghost. Jesus felt we would need the Holy Spirit to lead us, to guide us, to teach us, to empower us, to enable us, to grace us, to anoint us, and to point us. That's why He sent the Holy Spirit. If Jesus felt we needed the Holy Ghost, then we need the Holy Ghost — not just in a meeting when we get touched, but when we walk out the door — and tomorrow and the next day and the next day and the next day!

I'm concerned about the Church in the western world. I'm concerned about America and our whole attitude toward the Spirit of God. The Holy Spirit has been relegated to a mere minor manifestation — somebody giving a tongue or an interpretation, a word of wisdom, or a word of knowledge — but He's far beyond that. He's more than that. He's greater than that. I'm talking about the Spirit of God indwelling you, rising up and then coming out of you like a mighty river, a mighty river of God!

God's wanting His people to learn to lean on the Holy Spirit and to trust the Holy Spirit. We've got to trust that God's going to make a way, so that even if you don't know where you're going two, three, four, or five days from now, the Holy Spirit already knows. He's already moving situations together. He's already bringing things together, preparing the way for you, going ahead of you, making the crooked paths straight.

The Bible says He will show you things to come. Jesus says, "He shall glorify Me, for He shall receive of Mine and show it unto you." (See John 16:14.)

> *And, being assembled together with them, commanded them that they should not depart from Jerusalem, but wait for the promise of the Father, which, saith he, ye have heard of me.*
>
> *For John truly baptized with water; but ye shall be baptized with the Holy Ghost not many days hence...*
>
> *But ye shall receive power, after that the Holy Ghost is come upon you: and you shall be witnesses unto me both in Jerusalem, and in all Judea, and in Samaria and unto the uttermost part of the earth.*
>
> ACTS 1:4-5,8

Well, then that's exactly what happened in Acts, chapter 2:

> *When the day of Pentecost was fully come, they were all with one accord in one place.*
>
> *And suddenly there came a sound from heaven as of a rushing mighty wind, and it filled all the house where they were sitting.*
>
> *And there appeared unto them cloven tongues like as of fire, and it sat upon each of them.*

And they were all filled with the Holy Ghost, and began to speak with other tongues, as the Spirit gave them utterance.

And there were dwelling at Jerusalem Jews, devout men, out of every nation under heaven.

Now when this was noised abroad, the multitude came together, and were confounded, because that every man heard them speak in his own language.

And they were all amazed and marvelled, saying one to another, Behold, are not all these which speak Galilaeans?

And how hear we every man in our own tongue, wherein we were born?

Parthians, and Medes, and Elamites, and the dwellers in Mesopotamia, and in Judea, and Cappadocia, and Pontus, and Asia,

Phrygia, and Pamphylia, in Egypt, and in the parts of Libya about Cyrene, and strangers of Rome, Jews and proselytes,

Cretes and Arabians, we do hear them speak in our tongues the wonderful works of God.

And they were all amazed, and were in doubt, saying one to another, What meaneth this?

Others mocking said, These men are full of new wine.

But Peter, standing up with the eleven, lifted up his voice, and said unto them, Ye men of Judea, and all ye that dwell at Jerusalem, be this known unto you, and hearken to my words:

For these are not drunken, as ye suppose, seeing it is but the third hour of the day.

But this is that which was spoken by the prophet Joel;

And it shall come to pass in the last days, saith God, I will pour out of my Spirit upon all flesh: and your sons and your daughters shall prophesy, and your young men shall see visions, and your old men shall dream dreams:

And on my servants and on my handmaidens I will pour out in those days of my Spirit; and they shall prophesy.

ACTS 2:1-18

Now let's go to Acts 2:38-39:

> *Then Peter said unto them, Repent, and be baptized every*
> *one of you in the name of Jesus Christ for the remission of sins,*
> *and ye shall receive the gift of the Holy Ghost.*
>
> *For the promise is unto you, and to your children, and to all*
> *that are afar off, even as many as the Lord our God shall call.*

Some people say that the gift of the Holy Spirit passed away, that it was only for that time. But this scripture says, **the promise is unto you, and to your children, and to all that are afar off, even as many as the Lord our God shall call.**

Is God still calling people now? If God's still calling people now, then the promise of the Holy Ghost is for you and your children, even those who are afar off, as many as the Lord shall call. And that means you and me. There is an experience subsequent to salvation, and it's known as the baptism in the Holy Ghost and fire.

> *Now when the apostles which were at Jerusalem heard that*
> *Samaria had received the word of God, they sent unto them*
> *Peter and John:*
>
> *Who, when they were come down, prayed for them, that they*
> *might receive the Holy Ghost:*
>
> *(For as yet he was fallen upon none of them: only they were*
> *baptized in the name of the Lord Jesus.)*
>
> *Then they laid their hands on them, and they received the*
> *Holy Ghost.*
>
> ACTS 8:14-17

They were saved, but they had not received the Holy Ghost. Peter and John had to go down there and lay hands upon them. Then they got the Holy Ghost.

Are you convinced of the necessity of allowing Jesus to baptize you in the Holy Spirit? If not, I can prove it to you again. Go to Acts 9, where Saul of Tarsus got saved on the road to Damascus. Look in Acts 9:17:

And Ananias went his way, and entered into the house; and putting his hands on him said, Brother Saul, the Lord, even Jesus, that appeared unto thee in the way as thou camest, hath sent me, that thou mightest receive thy sight, and be filled with the Holy Ghost.

Saul is born again, but he's not yet full of the Holy Ghost. God sent Ananias to come and lay hands upon Saul so that he could get the gift of the Holy Ghost.

Go to Acts 10:44. Peter is at the house of Cornelius, a Gentile, and he's preaching. The Bible says,

While Peter yet spake these words, the Holy Ghost fell on all them which heard the word.

And they of the circumcision which believed were astonished, as many as came with Peter, because that on the Gentiles also was poured out the gift of the Holy Ghost.

For they heard them speak with tongues, and magnify God. Then answered Peter,

Can any man forbid water, that these should not be baptized, which have received the Holy Ghost as well as we?

ACTS 10:44-47

Again we have people who get saved, but then they got something more — the gift of the Holy Ghost.

Now, one last passage of Scripture to see the necessity of the baptism of the Holy Spirit. Go with me to Acts 19:1-6:

And it came to pass, that, while Apollos was at Corinth, Paul having passed through the upper coasts came to Ephesus: and finding certain disciples,

He said unto them, Have ye received the Holy Ghost since ye believed? And they said unto him, We have not so much as heard whether there be any Holy Ghost.

And he said unto them, Unto what then were ye baptized? They said, Unto John's baptism.

Then said Paul, John verily baptized with the baptism of repentance, saying unto the people, that they should believe on him which should come after him, that is, on Christ Jesus.

When they heard this, they were baptized in the name of the Lord Jesus.

And when Paul laid his hands upon them, the Holy Ghost came on them; and they spake with tongues, and prophesied.

They were already disciples. Then Paul baptized them in water because they were only baptized under John's baptism. He laid hands upon them, the Holy Spirit came upon them, and they all spoke with tongues and prophesied.

Jesus is the baptizer in the Holy Ghost. If He felt that it was important, then it's important for every single one of us to be baptized in the Holy Ghost. And when we receive the Holy Spirit, we'll notice that our lives will be millions of times more powerful than ever before. Hallelujah!

The power of the Holy Spirit is power to overcome sin. Power to reject temptation will come upon you when you get baptized in the Holy Ghost. If you are trying to live a holy life, but you can't because your flesh, your carnal nature, always gets the better of you, then you need to get full of the Holy Ghost, and you won't yield to temptation like you used to. The Spirit of God will rise up big and strong on the inside of you and empower you to resist and overcome temptations!

If you haven't allowed Jesus to baptize you in the Holy Ghost, let Him do it right now! Don't live another second without all of God's power working in your life.

Chapter 15

Jesus, the Tradition Breaker

A *nd it came to pass on the second sabbath after the first, that he went through the corn fields; and his disciples plucked the ears of corn, and did eat, rubbing them in their hands.*

And certain of the Pharisees said unto them, Why do ye that which is not lawful to do on the sabbath days?

And Jesus answering them said, Have ye not read so much as this, what David did, when himself was an hungred, and they which were with him;

How he went into the house of God, and did take and eat the shewbread, and gave also to them that were with him; which it is not lawful to eat but for the priests alone?

And he said unto them, That the Son of man is Lord also of the sabbath.

LUKE 6:1-5

Sabbath days were the days when the Pharisees accelerated their persecution of Jesus. Matthew, Mark, Luke, and John reported what Jesus did on the Sabbath, because the religious leaders had established certain traditions regarding the Sabbath, and Jesus broke every one of them! He seemed to relish the opportunity to annoy the Pharisees every Sabbath by healing people right in front of them.

On one Sabbath, Jesus taught in the synagogue. That was acceptable to the Pharisees, but there was a man in the congregation whose right hand was withered. The scribes and Pharisees watched Jesus to see whether He would heal him on the Sabbath day. If He did, they could find an accusation against Him. (See Luke 6:6-10.) To their way of thinking, healing would be considered work, and it was against the Law to work on the Sabbath.

Can you believe that some religious people actually got their kicks by following Jesus to see if He broke tradition?

But he knew their thoughts, and said to the man which had the withered hand, Rise up, and stand forth in the midst. And he arose and stood forth.

Then Jesus said unto them, I will ask you one thing; Is it lawful on the sabbath days to do good, or to do evil? to save life, or to destroy it?

And looking round about upon them all, he said unto the man, Stretch forth thy hand. And he did so: and his hand was restored whole as the other.

And they were filled with madness; and communed one with the other what they might do to Jesus.

LUKE 6:8-11

"How dare you heal on the Sabbath day," the Pharisees said. They had every other day of the week to heal the man and could not and would not do so, but Jesus comes and heals on the Sabbath day, and they want to nail Him for it.

Now, when you look at Jesus' ministry closely, you'll see one thing that sticks out. Everywhere He went, He went head to head with religion and tradition. And the closer we get to Jesus, the more we're going to come head to head with religion and tradition. When that happens, we have a tendency to back off, to find the path of least resistance. We don't want to rock the boat. Well, most of us don't!

I go into churches and the pastors say they want me to have a revival, but they also say, "Rodney, please don't rock the boat. It's taken us fourteen years to build this dingy. Don't rock it."

And I have to tell them, "Oh, I didn't come to rock the boat. I came to turn the stupid thing over!"

These Pharisees were not concerned about setting people free. They didn't care to see people delivered, coming out of darkness into light. Their job, they felt, was to protect the Law to the very letter — every jot, every tittle, every line of the Law. Unfortunately, they had warped and perverted God's Law to the point where "the Law" meant all the rules and traditions they had devised — their self-serving, religious interpretations of the Law. The Bible tells is in Hebrews 4:15 that Jesus was without sin and Luke 24:44 tells us that Jesus fulfilled the *whole* law while He walked the earth. But when the Pharisees saw Jesus and the disciples picking grain on the Sabbath, the Pharisees considered that to be work. Religious people extend the "letter" of the law and have no understanding of the "spirit" of the law.

Religion and tradition will kill you, like a python that wraps its coils around you and slowly squeezes the life out of you until there is nothing left. Religion and tradition will rob you of your joy. They will rob you of your freedom. They will rob you of the joy of your salvation. You once may have been on fire for God, but it's slowly waned until there's nothing but a shell left.

Look at Christians who have been pulled into a religious attitude ten or fifteen years after salvation. They've been abused and bullied through the system of religious tradition and then discarded like empty shells along the highway of life. That's not why Jesus came! Jesus came to set us free. Jesus came to give us life, to give us life more abundantly.

Religion and the traditions of men will kill you, because religion and traditions are not interested in you, they're only interested in promoting themselves. When we started our church, people in other churches got upset and said, "We're going to lose some people to that church, and then we're going to lose their tithe." I suddenly realized that too many pastors are not interested in people, they're just interested in their money. Something's wrong somewhere.

More tradition: "You have to have a Sunday night service."

I said, "Why?"

"Well, if you don't have a Sunday night service, the people are going to go to other churches."

I said, "So?"

"Well, if they go to other churches, they might leave you."

I said, "Are we supposed to have a service just to keep people in our church?" That's not the purpose of this place. The purpose of this place is to get people free.

The experts say you can't have services over ninety minutes long if you expect your church to grow large. In other words, if we cut it down to forty-five minute services, we'll have a huge church. But at what price? A huge church full of lukewarm believers? Some churches have perfected a twenty-two minute Sunday morning service, from the first hymn to the benediction — including the offering. Why don't you just open up a drive-through window and call it McChurch — "You want Communion with that"?

The pastor of a great church in Shreveport, Louisiana, told me they've always been under pressure to have a short Sunday morning service — an hour and a half — quickly get people in, quickly get people out. He thought, *Lord, if only we could have longer Sunday morning services, where we could be free, not be pressured, and just worship You.*

The pastor told me, "You won't believe what we did. We dumped our Sunday night service. In our traditional mind-set, we always had to have the Sunday morning service quick so we could get the people to come back that night. So we dumped our Sunday night service, extended Sunday morning, and started a Saturday night service." Now their Saturday nights are as full as Sunday morning. Why? Because he's breaking tradition. If you want Jesus to show up, you have to break tradition.

Am I against *all* tradition? No. There are good traditions and bad traditions. There are good traditions based on the Word of God, and those we want to keep. Second Thessalonians 2:15 says, **Therefore, brethren, stand fast, and hold the traditions which you have been taught, whether by word, or our epistle.** Hold to the good traditions in God's Word, such as the laying on of hands, casting out devils, speaking in tongues, and worshipping and praising God. These are all good traditions which are in the Word and were practiced by the early Church. But we don't want to do them just because of tradition. We want to do them with substance, with our whole heart.

> *Now we command you, brethren, in the name of our Lord Jesus Christ, that ye withdraw yourself from every brother that walketh disorderly, and not after the tradition which he received of us.*
>
> 2 THESSALONIANS 3:6

There's good tradition and then there's bad tradition. What are bad traditions? The traditions of men.

> *Beware lest any man spoil you through philosophy and vain deceit, after the tradition of men, after the rudiments of the world, and not after Christ.*
>
> COLOSSIANS 2:8

Psalm 1:1 says, **Blessed is the man that walketh not in the counsel of the ungodly, nor standeth in the way of sinners, nor sitteth in the seat of the scornful.** That verse shows that there's a progression that happens to those who follow after the traditions of men. You first start to walk in the counsel of the ungodly. After awhile, you end up standing in the way of sinners. Pretty soon, you're sitting in the seat of the scornful, the mockers. Nobody goes straight to the seat of mockers. They first start walking in the counsel of the ungodly.

Be careful who you listen to. That's why you shouldn't allow your television to teach your children the standards they should adopt in their lives. Hollywood fathers all look and act like idiots. The children on television are the ones with all the answers, and they show no respect for their fathers. If I had ever spoken to my dad the way the kids talk to their fathers on television, I would have been the first kid in orbit!

> But the closer you get to Jesus, and the more time you spend in the gospels, the more you will find something rising up on the inside of you that is contrary to what people say. When people say, "It cannot be done this way," you will say, "It *can* be done this way, because all things are possible with God."

But those are the traditions of man, and in most homes, they are just accepted. Then we wonder why we have trouble with our children later in their lives. We allow the world's traditions into our homes, and those worldly traditions work to destroy the Christian home.

But the closer you get to Jesus, and the more time you spend in the gospels, the more you will find something rising up on the inside of you that is contrary to what people say. When people say, "It cannot be done this way," you will say, "It *can* be done this way, because all things are possible with God."

Forasmuch as ye know that ye were not redeemed with corruptible things, as silver and gold, from your vain conversation [manner of life] received by tradition from your fathers.

1 PETER 1:18

Jesus redeemed us from tradition. We were redeemed from the useless, vain way of living inherited from our forefathers. The fight that you're going to have is not just in your flesh or in your mind. The fight you're going to have walking the Spirit-filled life is against religious tradition. Tradition will try to stop the flow of the anointing of the Spirit of God.

You have to make a decision. Every time you feel like you're getting religious and traditional, go spend some time with Jesus in the gospels. I like hanging around Him.

Neither give heed to fables and endless genealogies, which minister questions, rather than godly edifying which is in faith: so do.

1 TIMOTHY 1:4

Religion and tradition minister questions and arguments, but God's Word and the Holy Spirit always bring the answers.

> *But refuse profane and old wives' fables, and exercise thyself rather unto godliness.*
>
> 1 TIMOTHY 4:7

Refuse these old wives' tales. The Church in America is bound by old wives' tales. In other words, people live in a fantasy world, detached from reality. For instance, you have people blaming the devil for disasters in their lives that were actually caused by their own stupidity and disobedience. They try to cast devils out of rebellious children when what they need to do is straighten up themselves. They need to set a good example, give the child a whole lot of love and understanding — and probably a good spanking — and they will be on their way to straightening things out. Now let's look at the traditions of the elders versus the commandments of God.

> *Then came to Jesus scribes and Pharisees, which were of Jerusalem, saying,*
>
> *Why do thy disciples transgress the tradition of the elders? for they wash not their hands when they eat bread.*
>
> *But he answered and said unto them, Why do ye also transgress the commandment of God by your tradition?*
>
> MATTHEW 15:1-3

It's one or the other. You can't have the traditions of the elders and the commandments of God. The two are diametrically opposed. The two will fight each other. You can't have a nice, dignified, staid, traditional religious church and the power of God at the same time. "All right, folks, this morning we have a diluted version of God and His power, and after the service, if you seek God in a deeper way, you can go in the back room where we have Him hidden away where He won't offend people."

In Matthew 15:8, Jesus quoted the prophet Isaiah's words from the heart of God: **This people draweth nigh unto me with their mouth, and honoureth me with their lips; but their heart is far from me.** In how many churches all over the world today do they draw near the Lord with their mouths, but keep their hearts far from Him? They're looking at their watch saying, "I wish the preacher would shut up. I need to get home. I've got a goose in the oven." But their goose was cooked a long time ago!

The Scripture goes on to say: **But in vain they do worship me, teaching for doctrines the commandments of men.** (Matthew 15:9) For too long, we've had the teachings of men taught in the Church as doctrines.

People say, "Well, this is the way it should be."

But I say, "Who said? Show me in the Bible." They can never show you in the Bible.

"Well, um, this is the ah, history of the ah, ah, well, we've kind of always done it ah, this way, ah, haven't we?" Tradition.

We don't do things the normal way in our church. When we have a water baptism, we line them up and have them lift their hands and pray, then the power of God knocks them under the water. And you know what I've come to realize? That is normal. God is normal and all this tradition is abnormal. So when they say, "Can't you do anything the normal way?" we say, "We are normal. This is normal."

Tradition is abnormal. Religion is abnormal.

For the Pharisees, and all the Jews, except they wash their hands oft, eat not, holding the tradition of the elders (Mark 7:3.) In other words, these poor guys are washing their hands every five minutes. Now there's nothing wrong with washing your hands. When I come out of a crusade and I've laid hands on everybody's head, the first thing I do is wash my hands. But the Pharisees can't eat because they haven't ceremonially washed their hands. There were so many rules and regulations about the washing of their cups, pots, brazen vessels, and tables. Everything had to be so clean on the outside, but they were rotten on the inside. They were like a rosy apple that has a big worm inside.

The Pharisees asked Jesus, "Why don't Your disciples walk according to the traditions of the elders? They eat bread with unwashed hands."

Jesus said to them:

> *Well hath Esaias prophesied of you hypocrites, as it is written, This people honoureth me with their lips, but their heart is far from me.*
>
> *Howbeit in vain do they worship me, teaching for doctrines the commandments of men.*
>
> *For laying aside the commandments of God, ye hold the tradition of men, as the washing of pots and cups: and many other such like things ye do.*
>
> *And he said unto them, Full well ye reject the commandment of God, that ye may keep your own tradition.*
>
> MARK 7:6-7

To religious tradition, it doesn't matter what God says. They will lay those commandments aside to hold the traditions of men.

Look at Matthew 15:6, the second part of the verse, **Thus have ye made the commandment of God of none effect by your tradition.** In other words, the Word of God is there, but it's been made powerless. The Word of God is there, but you're not going to get the benefit from it because your tradition has neutralized it.

If the devil cannot stop the Word of God from being preached, he will try to strip it of its power by introducing the tradition of man into it. Beware of the tradition of man — it refuses to acknowledge the power of God!

God cannot move within the framework of religious tradition. He's looking for a people who are hungry, who are thirsty, who are saying, "Oh God, move! God, I'm tired of the status quo!

Lord, I'm hungry for You. God, just come and touch me!" Then He touches them and the church explodes.

In many cases, a few years go by and these exploding churches become religious and traditional themselves. They develop the status quo, don't want to rock the boat, and God can't move anymore. Then He has to bring people from the outside again, raise people up from nothing, because He's always looking for a people who will run with the Spirit of God. You cannot please God while you try to please and satisfy people!

If Jesus was a tradition-buster, don't you want to be a tradition-buster? Well, the only thing that will burn tradition out of you is the fire of the Holy Ghost. When the fire of God comes, it's going to burn religion and tradition out of your life. You'll never be the same again.

The Lord wants to touch people first of all by His Word. The Word comes like a hammer and breaks the rock of tradition into pieces. And then He wants to come by His Spirit and begin a work deep down on the inside of your heart. The Spirit will bring about a change and put the fire of revival deep down on the inside of you, a fire that will burn through every fiber of your being.

For a tradition-buster, revival's not a meeting you have, revival is a way of life. You live it, you eat it, you sleep it, you walk it, you talk it, you drink it, you pray it. Everything is revival. You have revival when you go home. There's revival in your car driving down the road. *It is not a meeting. It is a way of life.*

I'm not talking about just doing something crazy on the outside. I'm talking about a whole attitude of heart. We've watched people come into crusades on a Tuesday night who look like death warmed over. But by Friday night, they're exuberantly worshipping God! There's a light in their eyes. The glory's on their face. Tradition is broken!

But you can't leave it up to a preacher or a service. You've got to do it every day. You've got to shake yourself loose from tradition every day. I know what God had to do in my own life to break me free from religious tradition. I was raised in a godly home, and I thank God for my mother and father, but we were part of a traditional church, and if it weren't for the grace of God, I'd be somewhere in the traditional church playing some traditional religious game. But I'm so grateful that Jesus came and set me free.

Let Him set you free too!

Chapter 16

The Healing and Miracle Ministry of Jesus

Jesus returned in the power of the Spirit into Galilee: and there went out a fame of him through all the region round about.

And he taught in the synagogues, being glorified of all.

And he came to Nazareth, where he had been brought up: and, as his custom was, he went in the synagogue on the sabbath day, and stood up for to read.

And there was delivered unto him the book of the prophet Esaias. And when he had opened the book, he found the place where it was written,

The Spirit of the Lord is upon me, because he hath anointed me, (empowered me, enabled me, graced me) *to preach the gospel to the poor; he hath sent me to heal the brokenhearted, to preach deliverance to the captives, and recovering of sight to the blind, to set at liberty them that are bruised,*

To preach the acceptable year of the Lord.

LUKE 4:14-19 (INSERT MINE)

But so much the more went there a fame abroad of him: and great multitudes came together to hear, and to be healed of their infirmities

And he withdrew himself into the wilderness, and prayed.

And it came to pass on a certain day, as he was teaching, that there were Pharisees and doctors of the law sitting by, which were come out of every town of Galilee, and Judea, and Jerusalem: and the power of the Lord was present to heal them.

LUKE 5:15-17

As we've studied the gospels of Matthew, Mark, Luke, and John, no matter what miracle Jesus was performing, whether it was a miracle of provision, whether He was casting devils out of somebody, whether He was healing them, or forgiving their sin, it was all the same for Him. Whether Jesus said, "Your sins are forgiven you. Take up your bed and walk," or "Fill the waterpots to the brim," it was all the same to Him, because He was operating by His heavenly Father's anointing, by the power of the Holy Spirit.

He hasn't changed yet, even two millennia later. The same anointing that brings healing and miracles is the same anointing that brings joy, freedom, liberty, and deliverance to *your* situation.

We simply need to be ready to apply the lessons we've learned from our study of Jesus' life. When you apply faith to what you're believing God for, you'll have miracles. You'll have miracles of provision if you'll release your faith in that area. You'll have creative miracles if you'll release your faith in that area. You'll get healing miracles if you release your faith in that area — it's all covered under the same anointing.

The anointing that raises the dead is the same anointing that heals a person of cancer. God shows up in the person of the Lord Jesus Christ and miracles start happening. Signs and wonders start happening and the impossible begins to take place. All it takes is people with the anointing who just believe and say, "Lord, I trust You, I believe You, I'm looking for a miracle."

If you need tax money, He'll tell you where the fish is. If you run out of wine at a wedding, He'll tell you what to do to get wine. Nothing is impossible with Him. We have to build our faith in His Word and the touch of the Lord Jesus Christ — not only that He performed miracles in Bible days, but He still does today. He's the same yesterday, today and forever. (See Hebrews 13:8.) We just have to activate the promises of God, because what God promises, He will perform. (See Romans 4:21.)

For the word of God is quick, and powerful, and sharper than any twoedged sword, piercing even to the dividing asunder of soul and spirit, and of the joints and marrow, and is a discerner of the thoughts and intents of the heart.

HEBREWS 4:12

Just one word from Jesus and the cripples will walk. Just one word from Jesus and the blind will see. Just one word from Jesus and the deaf will hear again. Just one word from Jesus and the dead will be raised.

If we have a problem with results, the problem is not with Jesus. The problem is with our ability to trust Him and to believe His Word. Down through the years, God has anointed different people to flow in healing and miracles and signs and wonders. We still need people who will believe God, who will stretch their faith and say, "I believe that Jesus is alive and I believe that He can perform miracles, signs, and wonders."

Although we've already studied it in depth, let's glance again at the very first miracle that Jesus did, which was one of provision in John 2:1. As you recall, there was a marriage in Cana of Galilee and Jesus, His mother, and His disciples were there. When their host ran out of wine, Mary said to Jesus, "They have no wine." And then she turned to the servants and told them to get ready to do whatever Jesus told them to do. If we want to get into the position where miracles and healing start flowing, we must get into the place where we do whatever Jesus tells us to do.

In a church we pioneered in Africa, a gentleman who suffered from a heart condition and high blood pressure was there for healing. Under the anointing of the Holy Spirit, I just pointed to him and said, "Run." He took off running right across the front of the church, across the back, then back up to the front, and just fell out under the power of God. He got up totally healed.

Why did I say run? God told me to tell him to run. When I spoke to the man later, he said, "I just felt like I needed to run, and then you said to run, and it was like confirmation to me." *Whatever He says unto you, do it.*

One Sunday, I went to the hospital to see a man who'd just had a car wreck. He was in a neck brace and in a lot of pain from a severe injury. As I began to pray, the power of God went into him. He said, "When you prayed, I felt this warmth go right up through my body and into my neck."

181

I said, "What do you feel like you want to do?"

He said, "I'd like to get up."

I said, "Take that brace off right now."

The man looked at me and his eyes got big. He grabbed the brace, pulled it off, moved his head around, then jumped out of bed and started running around the hospital ward, totally healed by the power of God. Then they took me from ward to ward, just praying for everybody. I don't know how many people were released from that place that night!

The message of the cross and the resurrection is a message of goodness. The Gospel is a message of miracles, signs, and wonders. When you preach it and proclaim it, there will be people who will be saved, healed, and delivered. Everywhere Jesus went, He not only preached and taught, but He demonstrated the power of God. Jesus did not preach just to hear the sound of His own voice. He preached His message to obtain an end result, to see the works of God manifested in the lives of men. That's what we should be doing.

But for you to live what Jesus said, these truths must be rooted and established in your heart once and for all. The enemy will come to challenge all of these truths, because he knows if he can shake you off of them, your walk will be wobbly. If you don't know what you believe, you will be double-minded and unstable in all your ways. But once the truth of God's Word is established in your heart, the devil cannot move you away from God's best.

These truths are like an oak tree when it is planted in the ground. The first time you hear the Word, it is like an acorn. The Word is the seed, planted in your heart. But as you reinforce the seed, water it, and fertilize it, it continues to grow and mature. As the tree grows up, the roots run broad and deep underneath. The enemy knows that, so once you become firmly fixed and established in the Word of God concerning the fact that He's your Savior, He's your Healer, He's your Provider — then that's it. You are like a mighty oak who cannot be uprooted, no matter how strong the wind.

I want to challenge you to establish the truth once and for all in your heart, because I really believe in these last days you're going to need deep roots. As things go haywire, different kinds of disasters will force you to rely fully on God for your healing, your provision, or your deliverance. What do you do when doctors can't help you anymore? What do you do when your bank can't help you anymore? If a crisis arose, many people would go to pieces because they don't believe the Word of God.

To see the power in the words spoken by Jesus, let's go to the second miracle He did:

> *So Jesus came again unto Cana of Galilee, where he made the water wine. And there was a certain nobleman, whose son was sick at Capernaum.*
>
> *When he heard that Jesus was come out of Judea into Galilee, he went unto him, and besought him that he would come down, and heal his son: for he was at the point of death.*
>
> *Then said Jesus unto him, Except ye see signs and wonders ye will not believe.*
>
> *The nobleman saith unto him, Sir, come down ere my child die.*
>
> *Jesus saith unto him, Go thy way; thy son liveth. And the man believed the word that Jesus had spoken unto him, and he went his way.*
>
> *And as he was now going down, his servants met him and told him, saying, Thy son liveth.*
>
> *Then inquired he of them the hour when he began to amend. And they said unto him, Yesterday at the seventh hour the fever left him.*
>
> *So the father knew that it was at the same hour, in the which Jesus said unto him, Thy son liveth: and himself believed, and his whole house.*
>
> JOHN 4:46-53

A nobleman, whose son was at the point of death, heard that Jesus was headed his way. So he came to Jesus and told Him what he needed. Rather than coming to touch the boy as the father had requested, Jesus just *spoke* the Word and said, "Your son lives." The father *accepted Jesus' word in faith,* then turned around and headed home. On the way home, his servants met him and said, "Hey, your boy's fine."

He said, "What time did it happen?"

They said, "The seventh hour." Then he realized it was the exact same time that Jesus had spoken the Word and he had believed.

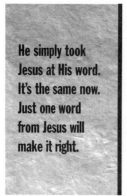

He simply took Jesus at His word. It's the same now. Just one word from Jesus will make it right.

This miracle shows us something powerful. This father didn't need to see a sign or watch Jesus touch his son. He simply took Jesus at His word. It's the same now. Just one word from Jesus will make it right. Just one word from Jesus will calm the storm. Just one word from Jesus will set the captives free. Just one word from Jesus will cause the blind to see. Just one word from Jesus will cause the deaf to hear. Just one word from Jesus will cause the lame to walk. *Just one word from Jesus!*

That's why, before I even pray for people, I get quiet. I wait in my spirit to see what the Lord would say. I know that one word from Jesus spoken over those circumstances will change everything. Sometimes they're healed instantly. Sometimes the Lord says, "Within the next thirty days." Some will see a total turnaround and a transformation within the next ninety days. With other people the Lord will say, "In the next twelve months, there will come a change."

We've seen that happen with couples who have been trying to have children without success. Couples all over the world have brought their babies to us to show us the fruit of our prayers. We laid hands on them to be fruitful and multiply and replenish the earth — and they did! Some people had been trying to have a baby for sixteen years without success, but God gave them the desire of their heart after we prayed. Some of these couples gave birth barely nine months later!

Sometimes we have to believe the words of Jesus when they don't make sense at all in the natural. Luke 5:1-5 describes Simon Peter's reaction to Jesus' words:

> *And it came to pass, that, as the people pressed upon him to hear the word of God, he stood by the lake of Gennesaret,*
>
> *And saw two ships standing by the lake; but the fishermen were gone out of them, and were washing their nets.*
>
> *And he entered one of the ships, which was Simon's, and prayed him that he would thrust out a little from the land. And he sat down, and taught the people out of the ship.*
>
> *Now when he had left speaking, he said unto Simon, Launch out into the deep, and let down your nets for a draught.*
>
> *And Simon answering said unto him, Master, we have toiled all the night and have taken nothing; nevertheless at thy word I will let down the net.*

Simon Peter was a career fisherman and Jesus wasn't, but Peter showed us the kind of faith we need when he said, **Nevertheless at thy word I will let down the net.** Many times a miracle will come when the natural circumstances look totally bleak. The word of the Lord may come and be totally opposite to the circumstances. The doctors may have told you you're going to die, and in the natural that's the way it looks. But when Jesus comes, He will speak a word that will override your circumstances.

Why? Because He can make a way where there is no way. Nothing's impossible with Him, and He illustrated that point with Simon Peter. Peter said, **Nevertheless at thy word I will let down the net.** And he did.

And when they had this done, they inclosed a great multitude of fishes: and their net brake.

And they beckoned unto their partners, which were in the other ship, that they should come and help them. And they came, and filled both ships, so that they began to sink.

When Simon Peter saw it, he fell down at Jesus' knees, saying, Depart from me; for I am a sinful man, O Lord.

For he was astonished, and all that were with him, at the draught of the fishes which they had taken:

And so was also James, and John, the son of Zebedee, which were partners with Simon. And Jesus said unto Simon, "Fear not; from henceforth thou shall catch men.

And when they had brought their ships to land, they forsook all, and followed Him.

LUKE 5:6-11

After Peter, James, and John saw what happened, they dropped their nets and walked away from their boats to follow Jesus. Who wants to just keep fishing after seeing Jesus do an incredible miracle? When people see what miracles occur in their lives as they act on God's Word, they'll make life-changing decisions too.

As you go forth with faith in His Word and in His miracle-working power, God will use you in a place where there's lack and work a miracle of provision through you. Some friends of ours, a pastor and his wife, needed to cook several hundred turkeys to feed the needy one Thanksgiving. A family in the church who owned a restaurant volunteered to cook the turkeys. They cooked the turkeys morning, noon, and night.

While they were cooking, the restaurant owners mentioned to the pastor and his wife that their business was really struggling, but they didn't want to accept anything for cooking the turkeys. They just wanted to do it to help the homeless and those who were in need for Thanksgiving. Well, later the pastor and his wife went back there for lunch, and they had to wait outside because the place was so packed. They asked the owners, "What happened to your business?"

They said, "Well, we don't understand what happened, but from the moment we started cooking your turkeys, business just took off."

When you act on the Word of God, things change in your life. Not only that, when you walk with Jesus and act on His words, your own words take on new power.

> *And there was in their synagogue a man with an unclean spirit; and he cried out,*
>
> *Saying, Let us alone; what have we to do with thee, thou Jesus of Nazareth? art thou come to destroy us? I know thee who thou art, the Holy One of God.*
>
> *And Jesus rebuked him, saying, Hold thy peace, and come out of him.*
>
> *And when the unclean spirit had torn him, and cried with a loud voice, he came out of him.*
>
> *And they were all amazed, insomuch that they questioned among themselves, saying, What thing is this? What new doctrine is this? for with authority commandeth he even the unclean spirits, and they do obey him.*
>
> MARK 1:23-27

Jesus walked in the anointing, so His words carried authority. When He walked in the place, the devils in the person began to cry out. When light comes, darkness has to flee. And so when *you* are walking in the power and anointing of the Spirit of God and *you* walk into a place where people are bound by devils, they'll begin to cry out.

These devils knew who Jesus was and started blabbing. Jesus said, in effect, "Shut up and come out." Those nearby were amazed. **What thing is this?** When we walk in God's Word and the power of His Spirit, we can speak with that authority too.

When we were in Bangor, Maine, there was a gentleman who would cause a disturbance at every revival meeting in town. He'd come in and start cussing, and preachers would go over and start binding and rebuking. They'd spend an hour or two focusing on him without results, and he'd just wreck the whole service.

When I walked out to preach one night, he was sitting up front, staring at me. So I felt led to just pick on him. When I preached, I looked right in his eyes. My words were provoking words, and after I'd preached forty-five minutes or so, I leaned over and put my hand on his head. When I did, he stuck his hand right up in my face and made a very rude sign and started spewing profanities at me. I immediately burst out laughing because I was shocked.

As I had my hand on his head, I just said, "Shut up!" and he collapsed in the seat and didn't move. The wind went right out of his sails. He just collapsed in the seat.

You've just got to get ready. You never know what's going to happen. But when you know your authority, it doesn't matter. Whether it's a devil or just a rebellious individual, you can take authority over them. However, you have to know what you're dealing with, because devils obey the name of Jesus, but the flesh doesn't necessarily do so.

Another time, back in 1990, I was ministering and there was a man who was glaring daggers at me. As another minister was walking up the aisle, he lost his balance and put his hand on the man's shoulder. I heard the man say to him, "I'm going to kill you," and he started following him to the back of the church.

It was right at the end of the service, so I went to the back and the guy stood there and said to me, "I've killed eight people. I'm going to kill you." Now I'd just come out of the meeting and I was under a heavy anointing of the power of God, so I just burst out laughing. He said, "You don't understand. I'm going to...." And he went on with a whole string of profanity.

I looked at him straight in the eye and said, "You can't kill me, I'm already dead. Anytime you want to try, go ahead and start. But I love you, man."

"Don't you come with that stuff," he said.

I said, "Man, I love you. Jesus loves you. You can't kill me."

He said, "I'll be back tomorrow. I'll know if you're a man of God or not."

He disappeared out the back door and I started praying. I mean I *really* prayed. I said, "God, we've got twenty-four hours. We need a miracle. I need You to visit this guy in the night, send an angel, do whatever it takes. The guy's a psychopath. He's going to blow me away. He told me he would know if I was a man of God or not, and God, You know I am a man of God, but if ever I need confirmation, I need it tonight. If he comes back tomorrow and blows me away, then everybody will believe I'm not a man of God."

The next night there he was, sitting and glaring at me. I thought, *This is my final service on planet earth. So, since it's my last night on the earth, I'm just going to preach right in his face. I mean just preach!* "Jesus loves you and He wants to save you, sir." I'm preaching for my life!

Then I gave the altar call. The first person to move was this man. He came running down the aisle, fell on his knees, tears rolling down his cheeks, crying out to God, "Save me, save me." And then he fell to the floor and, for about twenty minutes, he just lay there and quoted whole chapters of the Bible.

It turned out that he was called by God to be a minister when he backslid. He'd joined the military, become a mercenary, and had killed many people. He was tormented by the devil.

After the service, I asked him what changed his mind.

He said, "Well, I know you're a man of God."

I said, "How do you know?"

He said, "Last night I tried to run my truck into a wall, but I couldn't do it. So I went home, loaded a gun, and tried to shoot myself, but I was unable to do that either. Eventually, I just started trembling and shaking. I knew that you'd been praying for me."

The Lord saved this man, filled him with the Holy Ghost, and I believe today he's in the ministry. Today he's serving God.

As powerful as the spoken word is, it's not the only way Jesus applied the power of God. There's a miracle that gets mentioned in Matthew, Mark, and Luke, where Jesus heals Peter's mother-in-law. Read it in Matthew 8:14-15:

And when Jesus was come into Peter's house, he saw his wife's mother laid, and sick of a fever.

And he touched her hand, and the fever left her: and she arose, and ministered unto them.

We've been talking about speaking the Word and receiving a miracle, but here we see something different. Jesus just *touched* her hand and the fever left her. Here Jesus never even said one word — all He did was touch her, and the fever left.

So many times people make a big production of healing. They pray a big, long prayer like, "Ohhhhhh, God, as we're gathered in this place, Lord, we thank Thee that Thou seest Sister Jones, Lord, and how that she has a need. And God we just pray that Thou wouldst reach down and touch her, Lord...." And they go on and on. But in the gospels you never find Jesus actually praying for anybody when he ministered to them. He spoke the Word, and they were healed. He touched people, and they were healed.

Right now, Jesus has spoken His Word to you: "Be healed!" Right now, Jesus has His nail-scarred hand on your body, on your broken heart. Be made whole!

Right now, Jesus wants to meet your needs, open doors of opportunity, and give you the blessings of heaven. All you need to do is believe His Word, and His healing miracle ministry will flow into your life.

The Healings and Miracles of Jesus

1. Converts water into wine
   John 2:1-11

2. Heals the nobleman's son
   John 4:46-54

3. Heals the demoniac
   Mark 1:23-26
   Luke 4:33-36

4. Heals Peter's mother-in-law
   Matthew 8:14-15
   Mark 1:29-31
   Luke 4:38-39

5. Cleanses the leper
   Matthew 8:1-4
   Mark 1:40-44
   Luke 5:12-14

6. Heals the paralyzed man
   Matthew 9:1-8
   Mark 2:1-12
   Luke 5:17-26

7. Heals the impotent man
   John 5:1-16

8. Restores the withered hand
   Matthew 12:9-13
   Mark 3:1-5
   Luke 6:6-11

9. Restores the centurion's servant
   Matthew 8:5-13
   Luke 7:1-10

10. Raises the widow's son to life at the village of Nain
    Luke 7:11-16

11. Heals a demoniac
    Matthew 12:22-33

Mark 3:11
Luke 11:14-15

12. **Stills the storm**
Matthew 8:23-27
Matthew 14:32
Mark 4:35-41
Luke 8:22-25

13. **Casts demons out of the man from Gadara**
Matthew 8:28-34
Mark 5:1-20
Luke 8:26-39

14. **Raises the daughter of Jairus from the dead**
Matthew 9:18-19,23-26
Mark 5:22-24,35-43
Luke 8:41-42,49-56

15. **Heals the woman with the issue of blood**
Matthew 9:20-22
Mark 5:25-34
Luke 8:43-48

16. **Restores the sight of two blind men**
Matthew 9:27-31

17. **Heals a demoniac**
Matthew 9:32-33

18. **Walks upon the sea of Galilee**
Matthew 14:22-33
Mark 6:45-51
John 6:16-21

19. **Heals the daughter of the Syrophenician woman**
Matthew 15:21-28
Mark 7:24-30

20. **Feeds more than four-thousand people**
Matthew 15:32-39
Mark 8:1-9

21. Restores hearing to the deaf-mute man
    Mark 7:31-37

22. Restores sight to a blind man
    Mark 8:22-26

23. Heals the epileptic boy
    Matthew 17:14-21
    Mark 9:14-29
    Luke 9:37-43

24. Obtains tax money from a fish's mouth
    Matthew 17:24-27

25. Heals ten lepers — only one of them returns to thank Jesus
    Luke 17:11-19

26. Restores sight to a man born blind
    John, chapter 9

27. Raises Lazarus from the dead
    John 11:1-46

28. Heals the woman with a spirit of infirmity
    Luke 13:10-17

29. Heals a man with dropsy
    Luke 14:1-6

30. Restores sight to the blind
    Matthew 20:29-34
    Mark 10:46-52
    Luke 18:35-43

31. Curses the fig tree
    Matthew 21:17-22
    Mark 11:12-14,20-24

32. Heals the ear of Malchus
    Luke 22:49-51

33. The second catch of fish
    John 21:6

Chapter 17

Called To Do the Works of Jesus

Verily, verily, I say unto you, He that believeth on me, the works that I do shall he do also; and greater works than these shall he do; because I go unto my Father.

JOHN 14:12

You and I are called to do the works of Jesus, but to do them we have to know what works Jesus did and how we can follow His example.

How God anointed Jesus of Nazareth with the Holy Ghost and with power: who went about doing good, and healing all that were oppressed of the devil; for God was with him.

ACTS 10:38

The Spirit of the Lord is upon me, because he hath anointed me to preach the gospel to the poor; he hath sent me to heal the brokenhearted, to preach deliverance to the captives, and recovering of sight to the blind, to set at liberty them that are bruised,

To preach the acceptable year of the Lord.

LUKE 4:18-19

Jesus was led by the Holy Spirit at all times, and He was empowered by the Holy Spirit at all times. He didn't say or do anything without the Holy Ghost. He came to the poor to tell them, "You don't have to be poor anymore."

He came to those who were brokenhearted to tell them, "You don't have to be brokenhearted anymore."

He came to those who were bound to tell them, "'You don't have to be bound anymore."

He came to those who were oppressed to tell them, "You don't have to be oppressed anymore. I've come that you might have life and have it more abundantly. (See John 10:10.) I have come to set you free."

Do we really understand what it means to do the works of Jesus?

Jesus came to let mankind out of prison. He's already unlocked the prison door, but people are sitting there, not moving — and many of them are believers. We need to let them know that they are free to go. We've got to tell people what Jesus did, because they're sitting in the jail while the doors are wide open, thinking that they're bound, not knowing that He's set them free.

Jesus has already forgiven. Jesus has already healed. Jesus has already delivered. All they have to do is repent of their sins and accept it.

Everything that you and I need to live and walk in victory has already been done at the cross of Calvary by the blood of Jesus! Through the blood of Jesus and by the name of Jesus we have all authority over the enemy.

For this purpose the Son of God was manifested, that he might destroy the works of the devil.

1 JOHN 3:8

And having spoiled principalities and powers, he (Jesus) *made a show of them openly, triumphing over them in it* (the finished work of the cross).

COLOSSIANS 2:15 (INSERT MINE)

Jesus destroyed the power of the devil, so the devil has no power over you. The only power that the devil has is the power that *you* give him. That's why the Bible tells you not to give place to the devil. (See Ephesians 4:27.)

People make out like the devil has all this power. He might be big in their eyes, but there's no one as big as my God. God is a big God, a mighty God, a great God, a righteous God. There's no other god like Him. When He speaks, the heavens shake, the earth trembles, the mountains are brought low, and the valleys are made straight. Nothing is impossible with Him.

You have to realize this, because the Bible says that those who know their God will do exploits in His name. (See Daniel 11:32.) If you and I are called to do the works of Jesus, then how in the world are we going to do the works of Jesus if we think we've got a small God and a big devil? Some Christians act like God and the devil are in the wrestling ring together and the devil's beating up God, who's saying, "Help Me, Church, pray for Me, I need help, I need more strength!"

I want you to know that's a lie from the pit of hell! God and the devil are not even in the same category. The devil is a creation, but God is the Creator. The devil has a beginning and an end, but God *is* the beginning and the ending! Besides that, I read the back of the Book and it tells us *God wins!* That's why 1 John 4:4 says that greater is He who is in you than he who is in the world.

All this means that you and the devil aren't in the same category either! The first two chapters of Ephesians say that God has raised you up together with Christ and He's put you together with Him, seated in heavenly places with all things are under your feet. Matthew 28:18-20 says that He's given you all His power and authority in heaven and earth, to go into all the world and preach the Gospel.

Remember, two-thirds of God's name is "go." The other two-thirds of His name is "do." Go into all the world and preach the Gospel. The Bible says that one of the signs that will follow a believer in Jesus is that they will cast out devils. When you are doing the works of Jesus, then you are casting out devils — devils are not casting you out! (See Mark 16:15-18.)

When you *know* your God, you can do exploits in His name. He says to you what He said to Joshua, "Just like I was with Moses, so shall I be with you. Nothing shall stand before you, all the days of your life. Every place in which the sole of your foot shall tread, I have given it unto you. Lift up your eyes and look from the place where you now stand, to the North, to the South, to the East, and the West, I've given you all the land, go in and possess it, it's yours. I have delivered the enemy into your hand. Go in and take the cities, there'll not be one city too big." (See Joshua 1:1-18.)

> **When you *know* your God, you can do exploits in His name.**

God says to the Church now, "I have placed My power and My anointing on the inside of you and you're called to do the works of Jesus — every one of you."

"Oh Rodney, please pray for me, nothing seems to be working." Nothing's working because you're not working! You need to work. Jesus said, **I must work the works of him that sent me** (John 9:4), and just as Jesus must do the works, you have to do the works. You must make a decision every morning to work the works of Jesus.

"Well, I don't feel like praying for the sick today. I barely feel like getting out of bed!" You've got to get out of bed and go do the works of Jesus, no matter how you feel. If I went by how I feel sometimes, I wouldn't get out of bed myself. You just have to make a decision that it doesn't matter how you feel. It doesn't matter what's going on around you. You must decide that circumstances are not going to stop you from doing the works of Jesus.

You see, too many people are in a position where they're just waiting on God. "Oh, I'm waiting on God. Whatever He wants. I just believe in the Doris Day doctrine, 'Que sera, sera. Whatever will be will be.' You know God's ways are past finding out, His ways are higher than our ways, His thoughts are higher than our thoughts. So I'm just waiting on God."

Well, it's time you get hooked up with the Holy Ghost to find out what His ways are and what His thoughts are! When you do that, you'll get the same message Jesus gave: "Greater works shall ye do." (See John 14:12.) But He's waiting for you. You say you're waiting for Him, but He's waiting for you. You just have to make a decision! You just have to get off your blessed assurance, shake yourself, and say "I'm going to do the works of Jesus."

Now let me make this clear. If you do the works of Jesus, you're going to have opposition. Opposition will be a truck with your name written on it, coming down the road looking for you. Conflict will come, but that just means you're in the right company. Every time Jesus spoke in public, some folks picked up rocks to stone Him. So when they say you're of the devil, remember that they said Jesus cast out devils by the devil. It doesn't matter what people say, just make sure you are right with God and keep doing the works of Jesus. It doesn't matter how you feel, just keep doing the works of Jesus. It doesn't matter what the circumstances around you look like, keep doing the works of Jesus.

He that believeth on me, the works that I do shall he do also. What were these works? Jesus walked on water, fed five thousand, raised Lazarus from the dead, raised the widow's boy from the dead outside the city of Nain, raised Jairus' daughter from the dead, opened the eyes of the blind, opened the ears of the deaf, cleansed the leper, and much more. **And greater works than these shall he do; because I go unto my Father.** *God has invested His power, His name, His blood, and His Spirit to enable and empower you to do the works of Jesus.* I'm telling you, we're living in the day and age where we will see some of those greater works. When the Church realizes this, they will shake nations for Jesus!

The time to do the works of Jesus is now, not just on Sunday morning. Sunday morning is a time to celebrate the works that He's been doing on Monday, Tuesday, Wednesday, Thursday, Friday, and Saturday! You must *always* be doing the works of Jesus.

So what's keeping us from doing the works of Jesus? Folks have a variety of excuses. Some people say, "You know I'm fighting this sickness in my body. If I can just get healed of it, then I'll go get somebody else healed."

I'm telling you, if you'll just get out there and do the works of Jesus and lay hands on the sick, you'll look again for the symptoms and they'll be gone. While you were doing the works of Jesus, your own body was healed.

Somebody else said, "I just have this great financial need, and when it gets sorted out, then I'll be able to go and do the works of Jesus."

No, just start right where you are. If you go out of your way to be a blessing to other people, your own needs will be supernaturally met by the power of the Holy Ghost.

People are always waiting for a time that never comes. They're like a donkey chasing a carrot on a stick. They're looking for the pot of gold at the end of the rainbow. To do the works of Jesus, you've just got to start where you are — as bad as you feel, as tired as you feel, as messed up as you feel. *We shouldn't go by how we feel!*

Don't even go by the way you look. "Rodney, if I can just lose a little bit more weight, then I'll be used of God. Maybe if I was prettier or more handsome, I could have a successful ministry." I've seen plenty of preachers who dress so nice and look so wonderful, but they're not doing the works of Jesus. It doesn't matter how you look. God uses people of all different shapes and sizes to do the works of Jesus.

So what are other things we think hold us back?

"Well, I don't really speak that well." Moses didn't think he was a good speaker either, but he stood up to Pharaoh and led the children of Israel out of bondage. (See Exodus 4:10.) When you're doing the works of Jesus, the Holy Spirit will give you the words to say. You'll be amazed at the wonderful things that come out of your mouth!

"Well, I don't really have the education." It's not so much education that you need to do the works of Jesus, as it is the anointing. There are a lot of Bible seminaries that make their students ineffective, so that they never produce anything for the kingdom of God. By instilling the students with religion and tradition rather than the anointing of the Holy Spirit, they instill death in them. Many Bible students, who go into seminary believers, come out doubters! We want to instill life into people.

I do believe that a Bible education is important, but make sure that you get educated in the commandments of God and not the traditions of man. As long as you have a revelation of the *love* of God and you believe in the *power* of the Word of God and you have the *anointing* on your life, you will be an able minister of the Gospel!

Don't let excuses keep you from working the works of Jesus. Allow the reality of the anointing of the Holy Spirit to empower you to overcome any obstacle. God is looking for a Church that is so full of the anointing of the Spirit of God, it just splashes out of us everywhere we go. The famous British man of God, Smith Wigglesworth, once walked into a train passenger car and two ministers fell out of their seats onto their faces. They said, "Pray for us. You convict us of sin." Wigglesworth never said one word. His very presence convicted them of their sins. Why? Because he did the works of Jesus every day. The anointing was with him wherever he went.

If you realize that Jesus Christ of Nazareth, the Son of the Living God, lives on the inside of you, has come to make His home on the inside of you, and is empowering you by His anointing, what more do you need? All you need to do the works of Jesus is the anointing of the Holy Ghost and the determination to use what's been given you.

Some folks think you need to be an ordained minister to do the works of Jesus. When I started out in the ministry, pastors said to me, "Where are your ordination papers? Where are your credentials?"

I had to say, "I don't have any." They didn't check to see if I had the anointing or if I was doing the works of Jesus. As if they expected me to take ordination papers and put them on a man's head and say, "Rise in Jesus' name." As if I were going to use those papers to cast out devils. I have never heard the devil say, "Oh, no! I'm getting out of here. He's got them papers!"

But one day I was praying and I said, "Lord, if I could just have an ordination certificate, then I would be welcome in more churches." In the spirit, the Lord showed me an ordination certificate which said, "This is to certify that Rodney Howard-Browne has been ordained to the Gospel ministry," and there were three signatures: the Father, the Son, and the Holy Ghost. I didn't worry about papers anymore.

About 18 months later, I did get my ordination papers. I even carried my card with me. When I walked into the next church and showed them my papers, can you believe it, they told me, "Oh, don't worry about the papers. Put them away. We don't need those."

Listen, if you want ordination papers, these are your papers: **These works shall ye do and greater works than these shall ye do because I go to my Father.** Your papers came on the day of Pentecost when, with a mighty rushing wind, there appeared cloven tongues like as of fire, and they were all filled with the Holy Ghost and began to speak with other tongues. (See Acts 2:1-4.) Remember this, man did not call you to the ministry — God did.

This is something to get excited about! You've got marching orders from the Son of the Living God! He said these works shall you do and greater works shall you do. You are called to do the works of Jesus, and it's not about you, your abilities, your liabilities, or your inabilities. If you will yield to His Spirit, He will use you in a mighty way. Please understand that! God's not looking for qualified people. God's not looking for educated people. God's looking for *available* people.

Will you respond to His call today?

Chapter 18

Jesus, Our Good Shepherd

*T*he Lord is my Shepherd [to feed, guide, and shield me], I shall not lack.

He makes me lie down in [fresh, tender] green pastures; He leads me beside still and restful waters.

He refreshes and restores my life (my self); He leads me in the paths of righteousness [uprightness and right standing with Him — not for my earning it, but] for His name's sake.

Yes, though I walk through the [deep, sunless] valley of the shadow of death, I will fear or dread no evil, for You are with me; Your rod [to protect] and Your staff [to guide], they comfort me.

You prepare a table before me in the presence of my enemies. You anoint my head with oil; my [brimming] cup runs over.

Surely or only goodness and mercy and unfailing love shall follow me all the days of my life, and through the length of my days the house of the Lord [and His presence] shall be my dwelling place.

PSALM 23:1-6 AMP

Most likely, Psalms 23 and 91 are the two most published psalms. Everybody's praying for God's provision and protection. Christians will have it in their cars, on T-shirts, on coffee mugs, and yet they never seem to live by it. Why would people have something on a card or a coffee mug or a T-shirt and not live by it?

"Well, 'The Lord is my Shepherd' is nice. It looks good on a wall. It looks good on a bookmark. It looks good on the dashboard."

But it's got to come off your dashboard, off your T-shirt, off your coffee mug, and it's got to go *into* your heart. The fact that Jesus is your Shepherd has to become a living reality.

He's the *Good* Shepherd! So many people today gather in churches all over the world thinking that Jesus is against them. They think of Him as a bad shepherd, sitting there with a big club, waiting to beat them in the head for all their sin. Jesus is not the beater of the sheep!

I heard one preacher say that sheep are dumb. Sheep are not dumb. They know where the grass and the water are, and they're going to find them. They also know how to find safety. If you see them jumping the fence, it's for a reason. If they're jumping the fence, it's because they're saying, "I ain't gonna take this beating anymore."

Look what Jesus says in John 10:1-5:

Verily, verily, I say unto you, He that entereth not by the door into the sheepfold, but climbeth up some other way, the same is a thief and a robber.

But he that entereth in by the door is the shepherd of the sheep.

To him the porter openeth; and the sheep hear his voice: and he calleth his own sheep by name, and leadeth them out.

And when he putteth forth his own sheep, he goeth before them, and the sheep follow him: for they know his voice.

And a stranger will they not follow, but will flee from him: for they know not the voice of strangers.

Now, not all sheep know the voice of their shepherd, and not all shepherds treat their sheep well. I come from South Africa, born in the city of Port Elizabeth, and lived most of my life in the Transkei. The local indigenous tribe, the Xhosa, had large herds of sheep. But unlike the shepherds of the Middle East Jesus was familiar with, the Xhosa people use dozens of their youngest children to herd the sheep.

When these kids, just three to five years old, look after the sheep, they act like kids. They'll run home at the sight of an animal threatening the flock, and because there's a frequent change of shepherds, the sheep don't get to know who the shepherd is. It could be one little guy or his brother or his cousin. They don't know their shepherd. So when he speaks, they don't listen. When he shouts at them, they don't pay attention. Since the sheep won't listen to their directions, the little shepherd boys whip them with sticks and beat them to drive them from camp to camp.

But if you go to the Middle East, you see a very different picture of what it means to be a shepherd. The shepherds are grown men who *live* with the sheep. The sheep lie down to sleep, they lie down to sleep. After awhile, they smell like the sheep and even look like their sheep. There's never a time that they're not with their sheep. When the shepherd gets up, the sheep get up. When the shepherd moves out ahead, all the sheep just come in behind and follow the shepherd, because they know him and they trust him.

From the time they're little lambs, the sheep hear that same shepherd's voice, so they know his voice very well. When he speaks, his sheep follow his voice, so that even if two flocks get tangled up together, each will follow the right shepherd by following the voice they know.

What a contrast that is from the little African shepherds I saw as a kid. And I see the same contrast between shepherds in the Church. I see the shepherds who try to beat the sheep and corral everybody, pushing them around and forcing them into places. "Get over here, you dumb sheep!" And, "Grab him! He's going over the fence!"

If you're a bad shepherd, herding your sheep takes all your time and effort. You have these hundred sheep and you can't sleep at night. You're trying to keep them in the pen. They're jumping out. They don't know who you are. They're constantly trying to run away.

On the other hand, Jesus said, "My sheep know My voice. The voice of a stranger they're not going to follow." When the pastor, the undershepherd, follows the example of Jesus, the Chief Shepherd, then people can come into church and relax, because there's no coercion, no force. If you have to force people to stay, it's not God.

Did you ever wonder why the Psalm talks about "leading me beside still waters"? It's a picture of how a good shepherd provides a relaxing place for his flock to drink. Sheep can't drink in fast running water. The way their nostrils are situated, the water would splash in and they would drown while trying to drink. So the shepherd — the good shepherd — digs a u-shaped hollow in the bank. Then the water can flow into the little hollow and become still. When he calls the sheep in to drink, they come because they know he's prepared a safe place for them.

Jesus said, "My sheep know My voice. They know My voice! The voice of a stranger *they will not follow.*" I believe that in these last days, Jesus is calling His sheep. He's calling them from all different regions. He's telling them, "It's time to come now. It's time." The Shepherd is giving a clarion call: "Come in! Come in from the cold! Come in from a life of self and sin! Come in to My provision and My safety!" He's calling those who are lost. He's calling those who are dying.

Jesus is calling them to come in and they're hearing His voice. I have never seen so many backsliders coming back to God as in this day and this hour. It's awesome! The Shepherd is calling! The Shepherd is calling for His sheep, "Come! Come! Come! **Come unto me, all ye that labour and are heavy laden, and I will give you rest** (Matthew 11:28).

There's a vital difference between a shepherd and a hireling. The shepherd is constantly concerned with the safety of his sheep. The hireling is going to run the moment trouble comes. The shepherd is going to stay. The shepherd will be the calming factor. The shepherd will say, "It's all right. The wolf is coming, but I'll take care of it. Don't worry about a thing."

And there are times when a good shepherd, a good pastor, is going to have to protect his flock from "wolves." We don't want to be suspicious of everybody who comes into revival, into the sheepfold, but we've got to know that it's safe for the rest of the sheep to come and drink at the river. That means that if somebody's out of line in their worship or their manner, we're going stop them. It's not that we're running around like policemen — we're happy and free in our worship, and we love the move of God — but when someone gets out of line, we're going to set them straight.

This has really been a problem in the revival around the world. Pastors who never flowed in revival now suddenly have revival hitting their churches, and because they're afraid to stop the move of God, they're allowing everything. They're afraid to stop all kinds of crazy things that are happening, like people making animal noises, barking like dogs, and roaring like lions — and then calling it revival! If you bark like a dog in our church, you're in the doghouse with us! We thank God for the joy and all the manifestations of the Spirit, but we're not going to allow anything like that.

I know that's my job as the pastor, as shepherd of my flock. When pastors don't stop things as they get out of line, their sheep get concerned. They feel in their heart, *There's something wrong here.* But since the pastor's not doing anything about it, they think it must be right. Nevertheless, they still feel uneasy in their spirit and can't drink at the river and feel safe.

Their shepherd needs to come down and say, "Now stop that. You're out of line. You're in the flesh." As a good shepherd of my flock, I want you to come and drink and feel safe when you come and drink. My flock knows that if there is anything spiritually amiss, we'll be on it like ugly on a monkey!

You might be asking how we can know who is in the Spirit and who is in the flesh when two people are sitting next to each other and they are both making a noise. We stop one person, but we don't stop the other. How do we know which one is in the Spirit?

It's the same way the apostle Paul knew when the woman cried out and said, "These men are servants of the Most High God, which show unto us the way of salvation." (See Acts 16:16-18.) In the natural, there was no way of knowing that what she was saying was out of line, because it was the truth. But Paul discerned that it was a spirit of divination, and one day he really got irritated about it and said, "Come out of her!"

> When a pastor allows carnality in services, it's like a restaurant owner allowing total strangers to walk in and start adding mystery ingredients to the food after his chef has prepared it.

People probably attacked Paul, saying things like, "Did you see the apostle Paul cast the devil out of the woman who was affirming his ministry? Don't ever go to Paul's meetings and affirm his ministry — you never know what's gonna happen."

When a pastor allows carnality in services, it's like a restaurant owner allowing total strangers to walk in and start adding mystery ingredients to the food after his chef has prepared it. No! Any restaurant owner would walk in and say to the stranger, "Who are you?"

"Well, I just feel called of God to be here today."

"And what's that you're putting in our pot?"

"I'm not telling you," they say, while they're putting in all kinds of stuff.

So you might go to a revival meeting and sit there, tasting strange stuff in your food, but saying, "This is God. Oh, praise God! Hallelujah! Oh, glory! Terrible stuff, but hallelujah anyway! Oh, glory to God. Just keep chewing, it's gonna get better, brother! Praise God! Amen! Hallelujah!" No! We don't want to eat the imitation food, the fake food, we want the good stuff — directly from heaven's table!

He shall feed his flock like a shepherd: he shall gather the lambs with his arm, and carry them in his bosom, and shall gently lead those that are with young.

ISAIAH 40:11

Good shepherds have to follow Jesus closely. Jesus, as the head of the Church, goes out ahead of us, saying, "Come on." I'm listening for Him, and I'm saying to you, "Come on. I hear Jesus say, 'Let's go.' I hear Jesus saying, 'It's time to move.' I hear Jesus saying, 'It's time to run.'" I'm listening just like you are.

Some pastors think that because they're the pastor, everything they say is of God. "Well I'm the pastor, so when I say it, it's GOD." No, it's not. I'm not God. Never will be God. I'm just here to feed the flock of God. But if I feel God's telling us to do something, then it's up to the people to follow me. They should know the voice of the Good Shepherd and know in their hearts whether the pastor is leading in the right direction or not.

Problems arise when the pastor doesn't know God's voice and the congregation has no clue either. When people are lead astray, it is their own fault, because they should build their own relationship with God and not rely completely on another person for God's wisdom and direction. But when God gives us a godly pastor and we keep ourselves sensitive to God's Spirit, we will stay on the right track with God.

Don't ever believe someone who tells you that they have all the answers for the direction of your life. Whatever anyone tells you should already have been told to you by the Holy Spirit. Otherwise, put it on the shelf — lay it aside. If it *is* God, it *will* happen. *Listen to your spirit!*

Psalm 23 goes on to describe what life is like when we follow our Good Shepherd:

> *You prepare a table before me in the presence of my enemies. You anoint my head with oil; my [brimming] cup runs over.*
>
> *Surely or only goodness and mercy and unfailing love shall follow me all the days of my life, and through the length of my days the house of the Lord [and His presence] shall be my dwelling place.*
>
> PSALM 23:5-6 AMP

This table is not set for you in heaven — you have no enemies in heaven. This table is set for you here and now.

Now, you're sitting at the table with all your enemies around you. They don't like you; they hate you. They're gnashing their teeth at you. But you're protected by your Shepherd, so you can just ignore them and sit there and eat, pray, and have a fun time! Your head is being anointed with oil by your loving Shepherd. And when you get up from the table, guess who's following you? Goodness and mercy!

Your enemy says, "I was gonna attack you, but I can't."

"Why?"

"It's them two big fellows with you! Goodness and mercy. We can't touch you!"

And it says that they follow you *all the days of your life.*

He feeds us. He leads us. He guides us. He fills us. He protects us. He's with us! We're never alone! He's with us! He's at our side! He loves us!

Even if you run off and leave the ninety-nine, He knows you by name and He'll seek you out. "I'll go fetch him. Come here, you. Don't you just love this sheep? He just needs special attention."

Jesus is our *Good Shepherd!* And He loves us so very much. Hallelujah!

Chapter 19

The Sweet Presence of Jesus

*Thou wilt show me the path of life: in thy presence is
fulness of joy; at thy right hand there are pleasures for
evermore.*

PSALM 16:11

The Church needs to have the sweet revelation of Jesus. So
many times when they're trying this and they're trying that, the
only thing they really need is His presence. While the world is
crying out for the presence of Jesus, because it's only in the presence of Jesus that they're going to find true satisfaction, the
Church is often running away from His presence. And if the
Church doesn't walk in His presence, how will people meet Jesus?

What separates us from His presence? For the unbeliever, it's
sin. It's not big sin or little sin. It's just plain, flat-out, ornery,
stinking sin. For the believer, it can be a little more subtle than
that. It's still sin, but you don't recognize it as sin, because it's
hidden in your heart; it takes place on the inside. But if you really
look at your attitude, you will know it is sin. The only ones who
know it is wrong are you and God.

It's what I call the *hidden sins of the heart*. That's what separates the believer from God's presence. The blood of Jesus brings
a believer into fellowship with God at the new birth, but later he
feels like the presence of God is far from him. Why? Because of
his hidden sins: pride, bitterness, jealousy, unforgiveness, a critical and judgmental attitude — we can go on and on.

Now don't misunderstand me. A believer can also be separated from the presence of God by outward sin — lying, stealing,
adultery, and so on. But most believers have stopped doing those
things, so it's easy for them to think everything's okay. If they are
not in the presence of God and feel far from Him, they wonder

why. It's probably because they are not allowing the Spirit of God to deal with the sins of their heart.

To get into the presence of God and stay there, we've got to *stop* what we're doing. We've got to make a decision to repent. We've got to turn around and make a 180-degree turn. We've got to flee from the very thing that keeps us from His presence.

You know what it's like. You've gone along in the presence of God, but suddenly you start doing something that you know you shouldn't be doing. His presence starts to leave us. You would think we would learn after one or two or three trips to the Land of No Presence. Even an old dog, when he goes down to a water trough to drink and a brick falls on his head every time, starts to think to himself, "Water, drink, brick, pain." So he quits what he's doing to stop the pain.

We need to be as smart as that old dog. You know perfectly well when you're sinning, when you're stepping outside of God's presence. You know when you're going to do it. You decide to sin, so don't be surprised to find yourself out of His presence.

Don't come tell me, "Well, Rodney, I just don't know how it happened. It just happened. I was serving God and praying in tongues and the next thing I knew I went and I robbed a bank. I don't understand how it happened."

"Rodney, I was just serving the Lord and singing some of the worship tapes and suddenly I found that I had some other woman in my arms. I don't know how it happened. The devil made me do it."

You know the moment you've missed the mark! You've sinned and departed from God's presence. Do you also know that you keep missing it by doing the same thing? Isn't that a form of insanity — to do the same thing over and over and expect a different result?

"Well, the last time I did this, I got out of His presence. But let's just do it again, anyway."

Surely an alarm needs to go off. "Bwaaahhh, bwaaahhh, bwaaahhh, *You are now leaving the presence of the Lord! You are stepping into the Land of No Presence! Repent! Back up! This is your final warning."* And then, when you back up and repent, "You are now in the safe zone."

Well, we have that alarm — He's the Holy Spirit. We simply have to respond when the alarm goes off in our hearts. We must not harden our hearts to the alarm of the Holy Spirit. We've got to allow Him to continually do a softening work in our hearts, because over a period of time our hearts can become hardened. We allow people to get to us. We allow hurts and disobedience to come in, and our hearts become hard and calloused. We need to allow the Spirit of God to come and do a softening work. We must get back into His presence.

Get hungry for more of Jesus.

Get thirsty for more of Jesus.

If you hunger and thirst after righteousness you will be filled. God said, if you draw nigh to Me, I will draw nigh to you. We must stay in His presence *and not come out!*

We have to make the decision on a daily, hourly, minute-by-minute basis: "I will stay in His presence, and I'm not going to allow anything — the deceitfulness of riches, the cares of this world, the lust of other things — to come in and pull me away from the presence of the Lord Jesus."

Someone said, "Well, I just feel like having an argument. I think I'm going to phone up that individual and just give them a piece of my mind."

You'd better not do that. You might be giving away the last little piece of your mind! You may need it sometime. That's why some people are walking around with no mind. They've given it all away!

You have to consistently make the decision to stay in God's presence. Every time the temptation comes up, you're going to choose not to be drawn away from Him. Now notice that I'm not looking for a manifestation. I'm looking for His presence. I'm seeking His face and not His hand. You may need a healing miracle, but more than anything, you need His presence.

When you wake up in the morning, say, "This is the day the Lord has made! I will rejoice and be glad in it! I'm going to worship Him! I'm going to praise Him! I'm going to praise Him in the morning! I'm going to praise Him in the noontime! I'm going to praise Him in the evening. As long as I have breath I'm going to praise Him!"

This revival is about people deciding to get into God's presence, and then deciding to stay there — no matter what.

People are not going to get the presence of Jesus from some religious institution, because religion promotes religion, not Jesus. He wants to be there more than we want Him and more than we allow Him. We've got to open the door. We've got to say, "Come, Lord. Come by Your power. Come by Your anointing and touch the lives of hungry people."

Most people think revival means big meetings and lots of souls being saved, but that is the *result* of revival. Revival is when God's people get hungry for His presence, and He literally takes over their lives and their meetings. Once the church is revived, then it is time for sinners to get saved — which is an awakening. Sinners can't have revival, because they have not yet had "vival"! People come to Jesus — because Jesus is there, they sense His presence, and everything they need is in His presence.

God's presence is everything we need to live and walk in victory. If you look at some of the songs that were written out of revival, you'll see that they had the presence of Jesus, such as that old hymn, "In the Garden," that has the line, *and the joy we share as we tarry there, none other has ever known.* Those songs were all written out of encounters with the Lord Jesus Christ in great revival.

If in His presence there is fullness of joy, then I want you to know that in His presence there is healing. In His presence there is provision. In His presence is everything that you and I need. When Jesus walks in the door, something is going to happen. When Jesus walks in the door, the very atmosphere is going to change.

We must never become blasé about the presence of the Lord. We must never come to the place where we say, "Well, we've been there. We've seen that. We've done that. Now we want something else." God doesn't want us to be like the children of Israel when they wandered in the desert. They complained and grumbled over the manna that came from heaven. When they didn't have it, they complained. When they had it, they complained.

What do *you* want? People don't have the presence of Jesus, and they complain. Then they have the presence of Jesus and they complain. What do you want? I know what I want. I want His presence more than anything that this world has to offer. I want the continuous presence of Jesus.

I don't just want His presence on a Sunday morning. I want His presence on a Monday morning, on a Tuesday, on a Wednesday, on a Thursday, on a Friday, on a Saturday. I want to live and dwell in His presence, because I've found out that His presence is the hiding place for the believer. When the storms of life are raging, where do I go? I go to His presence. I go to the cleft of the rock. I go to the secret place. Psalm 31:19-20 says,

> I want to live and dwell in His presence, because I've found out that His presence is the hiding place for the believer. When the storms of life are raging, where do I go? I go to His presence.

Oh, how great is thy goodness, which thou hast laid up for them that fear thee; which thou hast wrought for them that trust in thee before the sons of men!

Thou shalt hide them in the secret of thy presence from the pride of man: thou shalt keep them secretly in a pavilion from the strife of tongues.

If you're getting arrogant, I know what the cure is. You've just got to get in His presence. The more you're in His presence, the smaller you become and the bigger He becomes. The reason some people are puffed up with their own importance, a legend in their own minds, is because they've been outside of the presence of Jesus. When you come into the presence of Jesus, you realize that you are nothing and He is everything.

When we started our church a preacher called me and he was angry. He said, "I just want to tell you right now, you're not an apostle."

I said, "Okay. That's fine."

He said, "You're not a prophet."

I said, "That's fine, whatever you say."

He said, "You're not an evangelist. You're not a pastor. You're not a teacher."

I started to laugh on the telephone. I was laughing so much, tears were rolling down my cheeks. I said, "You're a very funny man."

He said, "Why?"

I said, "You have blessed me with this phone call."

"What do you mean?"

I said, "For years I've been praying, 'Lord, I'm nothing. You're everything.' And now you've phoned me to confirm that my prayer has finally been answered!"

Everybody's worried about titles, but I'm not. You can call me what you like — I just want the presence of Jesus. In His presence, there's fullness of joy. In His presence is everything we need. And I want His presence all the time. Someone said, "You can't have it all the time." But I want His presence all the time. Every day. When I lie on my bed, when I wake up in the morning, and when I drive down the road.

People will notice when you're in the presence of Jesus. Look at Acts 4:13. The people of Jerusalem looked at Peter and John and perceived that they were unlearned and ignorant men, but they marveled and they took knowledge of the fact that they'd been with Jesus. Do people take knowledge that *you've* been with Jesus?

It's the presence of Jesus that's going to make the difference in your life. It's the presence of Jesus that's going to put you over. It's the presence of Jesus that's going to cause you to rise above the storms of life, to rise above the circumstances of life. And you can have it every day! You can make the decision: "Today I'm not going to hang around Sister Bucketmouth or Brother Doodad. I'm going to hang around Jesus."

"Well, Rodney, what will people say?" Who cares? They've already said it! It doesn't matter!

I just want Jesus — Jesus in the morning, Jesus in the noon-time, Jesus in the evening. Jesus, Jesus, Jesus. It's hard to stay arrogant when you're in the presence of Jesus. When He comes, He overwhelms you. He's so big.

It's hard to grumble when you're in the presence of Jesus. It's hard to gripe when you're in the presence of Jesus. It's hard to complain when you're in the presence of Jesus. It's hard to criticize when you're in the presence of Jesus. It's hard to judge when you're in the presence of Jesus. And it's nearly impossible to sin when you're in the presence of Jesus. To me, it looks like the only place you'd want to be is in the presence of Jesus!

When people enter revival, the things that used to get them down stop getting them down. Why? Because they get into the presence of the Lord Jesus Christ. If you can get into the presence of the Lord for a day, then you can stay there for a week, or you can stay there for a month, or you can stay there for six months. Then, bless God, you can stay there permanently and you can live there no matter what. Don't let the enemy draw you out! Don't let him take you out of the presence of Jesus. Just say, "No, I'm not going to argue, I'm doing a good work for God. I'm staying in the presence of Jesus. I'm going to do the work of the Lord."

You have to *make a decision to stay* in the presence of the Lord. I hold revival services in some places and the ministers are so busy they can't even come to the service. "Well, Rodney, I've got to take care of business."

I say, "Lord, have mercy! Shut the shop down! We're having revival. Don't you believe what's happening is important? You were running around last week and you're going to be running around next week. Just shut it down."

"Well, there's business to take care of."

"Forget the business. This is bigger business."

You have to make a decision. When you're dealing with the presence of Jesus, you can choose to either be like Mary or you can choose to be like Martha. (See Luke 10:38-42.) You can be like Martha, encumbered about with her serving duties, running here and running there. Or you can decide to be like Mary and come and sit at His feet.

Your choice depends on how desperate you are, how hungry you are, and how thirsty you are. Jesus is not going to come and force His presence on you. You've got to come to Him and say, "Lord, I want to be in Your presence. I want to be in Your presence daily. I just want to live there, right on Glory Boulevard, in Presence Place."

It's a hiding place. It's a secret place. When we have revival meetings week after week, sometimes the hardest section of the meeting to break through is the ministers' section. Why? Because half of them are outside handing out their business cards. Or they're sitting there trying to work out what in the world is happening. *How is he doing that?* they're thinking. *And what is he saying that causes this to happen?*

When we worship, many ministers just sit there. They don't even know how to worship. I've said, "Lord, why is that? Shouldn't preachers be the ones worshipping more than anybody else?"

The Lord told me one time, "They can't worship because they're too used to being worshipped."

When we come into a church or meeting, it doesn't matter who we are and where we're from. The only individual that matters here is Jesus, King of kings, and Lord of lords. That's why revival has a way of equalizing everybody. When everybody is flat on the floor under the power of God, it doesn't really matter who is what! Have you noticed that when you're on the floor, everyone is on the same level?

Remember Psalm 31:20, which says the presence of the Lord will hide you from the pride of men. If I want to be hidden from the pride of men, I must daily seek to live in His presence. It also says that the hiding place will be a secret place that will keep you from the strife of tongues. Tongues will be wagging and gossiping, but it will not affect you because you're in His presence.

I can always tell the moment that I'm starting to get out of His presence. It's when the critical things people say against my ministry start to affect me. Then, the moment I get back in God's presence, what they say doesn't matter. In fact, the effect of His presence is very funny.

Somebody asked me, "Did you read the book attacking you?"

I said, "Yeah, I read the book; it was a good book. I laughed my way through the whole thing. Thank God, He used a critic to verify that this is a genuine revival. It's documented in history and there's nothing they can do to take it out now!"

But that was only because of the anointing of God. If I'd have read the book in the flesh, I'd have gotten mad. But when I read it under the anointing, it was a funny book, because whether my critics agreed with the revival or not, they had documented it. So it will go down in history now. When you live in God's presence, He will protect you. People will say critical things, but their words will run off you like water off a duck's back.

The Lord has laid on my heart that people are coming to revival meetings desperate to hear from God, to be in His presence. In our meetings last year, we had people from forty-nine states and forty foreign countries. People are coming to hear from God. And the only way they're going to hear from God is to get into His presence.

Even if I'm not preaching the precise message a person needs to hear, while I'm preaching God will speak to them directly because they're in His presence. God's presence will go right through the human intellect and touch the heart. God doesn't want to touch heads — there are too many fat heads. He wants to touch, change, and transform hearts.

In my meetings, the power of God is all over the place. And I pray that as you read this, you feel the power of God falling like rain on you.

Fill Your child to overflowing with Your presence, Lord!

It's in His presence that times of refreshing come. Do you need refreshing? Be refreshed. What are you waiting for? Acts 3:19 says,

> *Repent ye therefore, and be converted, that your sins may be blotted out, when the times of refreshing shall come from the presence of the Lord.*

I believe you can be healed while reading this book. I believe you can be delivered from oppression and depression; from fear and the control, manipulation, and doctrines of men. You're set free by the power of the Holy Ghost!

Chapter 20

Living in the Presence of Jesus

*N*ow *when they saw the boldness of Peter and John, and perceived that they were unlearned and ignorant men, they marvelled; and they took knowledge of them, that they had been with Jesus.*

ACTS 4:13

We often read the gospels and say to ourselves, "Wouldn't it have been wonderful to have lived in Bible days!" When I was a kid growing up, I thought it would be the neatest thing if I could have lived back then. Just imagine hanging around Jesus all the time. I would never have left His side!

It must have been the greatest fun in the world to be around Jesus, because there was never a dull moment. The gospels tell of all the miracles He did, but the end of the book of John says that if all the other miracles He did were written down, all the books in the world couldn't contain them.

Miracles in the morning, miracles at noon, miracles in the evening. Miracles of provision, forgiving people of their sin, healing the sick, casting out devils. What fun! Walking on the water, feeding multitudes, waking up in the morning and saying, "I wonder what He's going to do today! Did you see what He did yesterday? *What is He going to do today?*"

But I've got news! We never have to wonder how it might have been to live with Jesus. Why? Because we, the blood-washed, blood-bought Church of the Lord Jesus Christ, *are* living in the days of Jesus! No, we're not in Israel, and Jesus is not actually walking around physically so we can run up and touch Him, but He has come to live on the inside of each and every one of us.

Jesus really is here today, but He's having to wait to stand up on the inside of many people, because they won't give Him first place in their life. They won't allow the life of Christ to come forth.

Jesus said that we would do the works He did and even greater works, because He was going to His Father. (See John 14:12.) He promised the Holy Ghost would come to empower us after He was gone, and the Holy Ghost indeed came on the day of Pentecost. (See Acts 2:1-4.) The Bible tells us, **In him we live, and move, and have our being** (Acts 17:28) and **Out of your belly shall flow rivers of living water** (John 7:38). What Jesus was saying was that out of our innermost being will flow His presence. So when we think about living in the presence of Jesus, we don't have to think about going to heaven, going to Israel, or getting a time machine and going back in time. We don't have to go back in time because He has come to us here in the future!

Jesus has come to indwell man, to empower man, to anoint man, to equip man, to grace man, to enable man. Where you go, Jesus goes. He is living on the inside of you. He wants to look through your eyes, He wants to touch through your hands. He wants to speak out of your mouth!

Sometimes people are waiting on the lightning to strike and the water to part and a loud voice to say, "Yea, lift thy hand and say, 'Be healed.'" But it's not going to be that way! It's just going to be you, stepping out in faith because the Greater One lives in you. That which is impossible with man is possible with God. He is the God of the impossible. He can make a way where there is no way.

Why don't you just make a decision right now? Decide that you're going to live in the presence of God twenty-four hours a day, seven days a week, fifty-two weeks a year, living and dwelling in the presence of God, because if the same Spirit that raised Christ from the dead dwells in you, it's going to quicken or make alive your mortal body. (See Romans 8:11.)

John G. Lake, that great apostle of faith, was very aware of that power in him. He went to South Africa and pioneered 550 churches in five years. While he was in Africa, the bubonic plague broke out, but he went right in amongst the people, praying for them and ministering to them. When plague victims died, they would foam at the mouth, and if you came in contact with that foam, you would catch the plague too. It was very contagious.

Doctors and scientists couldn't understand why Dr. Lake had survived several years of ministry to these people, so they asked to examine him. He told them to scrape some of the plague foam off a patient and put it under the microscope. They put it under the microscope and saw that it had living disease germs. Then he said, "Put it on my hands." They put it on his hands, and he said "Now scrape it off and look at it again."

They put it back under the microscope and saw that the plague germs were all dead! They asked him how this was possible. He said, "The law of the spirit of life in Christ Jesus has made me free from the law of sin and death." (See Romans 8:2.)

So why doesn't every Christian walk in divine healing? Some people don't realize what Jesus did for them at the cross of Calvary. Many times believers beg God to do what He has already done.

> *Who his own self bare our sins in his own body on the tree, that we, being dead to sins, should live unto righteousness: by whose stripes ye were healed.*
>
> I PETER 2:24

John G. Lake knew what Jesus had done, that the work of the cross was complete and provided divine health. But Lake also made the daily decision to *live* in God's presence.

God comes to live in us and He wants to do mighty works through us. If you grab hold of this, it'll change your life. We've got to let Jesus rise up big on the inside of us and make a decision *every day* to live in His presence.

The best way I know to live in His presence is just to worship Him. It's not that you have to cry, "Oh God, I pray that this day

I would live in Thy presence." Simply worship Him. Talk to Him, praise Him, and thank Him.

This is why the Church needs revival, because revival brings people back into the presence of Jesus. Hosea 6:2 (NIV) says: **After two days he will revive us; on the third day he will restore us, that we may live in his presence.** That is what revival is all about: living in His presence.

People say, "Rodney, if you lived happy and free all the time, it just wouldn't be right. You're going to have some bondage and oppression in life. You can't be free and happy all the time. It's not normal. Jesus didn't promise us that life would be easy. He promised us that the way would be *haaarrrddd*." I've heard preachers tell the people as they come to the altar, "Now it's going to be really hard for you now that you've given your life to Jesus." The guy has been serving the devil all of his life, and now they're telling him it's going to be hard? *Give me a break!*

Jesus said, "Take My yoke upon you, learn of Me, My yoke is easy, My burden is light." (See Matthew 11:29-30.) What's this "heavy burden" part? The Bible says, "the way of the transgressor is hard." (See Proverbs 13:15.) What's really hard is to try to serve Jesus with one foot in the world and one foot in the kingdom! You have one foot in hell and one foot in heaven, and you're miserable. Just make the decision to cut your ties with hell and you'll have heaven on earth.

The Bible tells us, "Let God arise and His enemies be scattered." (See Psalm 68:1.) When God arises — when we praise Him — our enemies are scattered. The Bible says in Deuteronomy 28:7 that He will cause our enemies to run from us in seven different directions. I don't know why people have a problem grasping this. It's not complicated.

If Jesus walked into our houses right now, we'd never have another problem that could

> If Jesus walked into our houses right now, we'd never have another problem that could overcome us. Well, the truth of the matter is that He has already walked in our houses! He lives in us, but we don't even realize it!

overcome us. Well, the truth of the matter is that He has already walked in our houses! He lives in us, but we don't even realize it! We're so busy looking at our circumstances, talking about our problems, and watching television. We listen to all the lies of the devil. We should be taking our eyes off the wind and waves and putting our eyes on Jesus, the living Word of God:

> *Come unto me, all ye that labour and are heavy laden, and I will give you rest.*
>
> MATTHEW 11:28

> *Then he uttered his oracle: "Arise, Balak, and listen; hear me, son of Zippor.*
>
> *God is not a man, that he should lie, nor a son of man, that he should change his mind. Does he speak and then not act? Does he promise and not fulfill?*
>
> *I have received a command to bless; he has blessed, and I cannot change it.*
>
> *No misfortune is seen in Jacob, no misery observed in Israel. The Lord their God is with them; the shout of the King is among them.*
>
> NUMBERS 23:18-21 NIV

When the shout of the King is among you, when the Lord is with you, and when you live in the presence of God, no misfortune in your life will faze you. There will be no misery in your life when you're living in the presence of God.

The moment you get outside the presence of God, you get hit. The safest place is the cleft of the rock, the secret place of the Most High. If you don't believe what I'm telling you, then you don't believe Psalm 91:

> *He that dwelleth in the secret place of the most High shall abide under the shadow of the Almighty. I will say of the*

225

Lord, He is my refuge and my fortress: my God; in him will I trust. Surely he shall deliver thee from the snare of the fowler, and from the noisome pestilence...

A thousand shall fall at thy side, and ten thousand at thy right hand; but it shall not come nigh thee...

There shall no evil befall thee, neither shall any plague come nigh thy dwelling. For he shall give his angels charge over thee, to keep thee in all thy ways.

PSALM 91:1-3,7,10-11

In *The Amplified Bible,* it says those angels will **preserve you in all your ways [of obedience and service].** In other words, the angels will not keep you in the ways of disobedience and disservice, but they will keep you when you walk in obedience.

God brought them out of Egypt; they have the strength of a wild ox.

There is no sorcery against Jacob, no divination against Israel. It will now be said of Jacob and of Israel, "See what God has done!"

NUMBERS 23:22-23 NIV

You have to catch it. We're living in the presence of Jesus. God is with us. Emmanuel, "God with us." That's His presence. And when you live in the presence of God, nobody can put a curse on you. Any curse will ricochet and go all the way back to them.

God is not a man, that he should lie; neither the son of man, that he should repent: hath he said, and shall he not do it? or hath he spoken, and shall he not make it good?

Behold, I have received commandment to bless: and he hath blessed; and I cannot reverse it.

NUMBERS 23:19-20

No man can curse what God has blessed. Has God pronounced His blessing over you? Then no man can curse you! Whoever curses you will be cursed, and whoever blesses you will be blessed. (See Numbers 24:9.)

> *The Lord said, "I have indeed seen the misery of my people in Egypt. I have heard them crying out because of their slave drivers, and I am concerned about their suffering.*
>
> *"So I have come down to rescue them from the hand of the Egyptians to bring them up out of that land into a good and spacious land, a land flowing with milk and honey — the home of the Canaanites, Hitttites, Amorites, Perizzites, Hivites and Jebusites.*
>
> EXODUS 3:7-8 NIV

That's what God has done for you and for me! He has brought us into His blessings. This is not something that is *going to* happen. This has already transpired, and it took place at the cross of Calvary. On the cross! That is where our victory was won: on the cross! The cross is final!

If you look at the Church in America today, you would think we had to pray and ask Jesus to come back and finish up. But He finished it! To live in the presence of God, you've got to grab hold of that fact. You've got to see it. You've got to come up higher. You've got to come above the clouds. You've got to come up above the storm of the world. You've got to come up and see where the eagles soar. You've got to come up and see all that heaven has for you!

> *The Lord your God is with you, he is mighty to save. He will take great delight in you, he will quiet you with his love, he will rejoice over you with singing.*
>
> ZEPHANIAH 3:17 NIV

God is rejoicing over you today. He is walking up and down in your house rejoicing over you with singing and with gladness. The Lord your God is mighty in your midst: mighty to save, mighty to heal, mighty to deliver!

Here are some points that will help you. These are principles that I apply in my life on a regular basis as I try to live in the presence of God.

First, never forget that God is your source. The moment you think *you* have to do it, you replace God as the source and you become dependent upon yourself. When you become dependent upon yourself, you're also dependent on your own limitations. Suddenly you find out you can't do anything — you question your qualifications or your education. You realize you don't have the answers, so suddenly you don't know what to do.

But as long as you keep God as your source, you know that He knows the end from the beginning. You know that He makes a way where there is no way. Even if you don't know what's going on right now, you know God's going to help you.

James 1:5 says, **If any of you lack wisdom, let him ask of God, that giveth to all men liberally, and upbraideth not; and it shall be given him.** God's going to give you wisdom; all you've got to do is ask. Just say, "Lord I don't know what to do, but Your Word says if I lack wisdom and I ask of You, You're going to give me wisdom. Lord, I need wisdom." God will tell you the way. Then all you have to do is walk in that wisdom and He'll make a way where there is no way.

I always remember that God is my source. I have never, ever, in all these years, thought I was bringing revival or working miracles. I have always known it was God. I have always known it was His power. All I am is a messenger boy.

Second, act on God's Word as a way of life. Do what He tells you to do! Don't call Him, "Lord, Lord," and then refuse or neglect to do the things He tells you to do. For instance, you can't live in the presence of God and have unforgiveness in your heart. You can't live in the presence of God if you're living in sin. It's impossible to be with Him if you're practicing sin. You have to make a decision to put those things behind you. Act on His Word, walk in the love of God, and obey Him.

And don't say that you don't know when you missed it. You knew before you sinned that you were going to sin. You planned to. You didn't just walk down the road and end up robbing a bank.

"Rodney, I don't understand! I woke up this morning on fire for God. I was serving God, praising God, and the next thing I knew I went to deposit my check, but instead of saying, 'Will you deposit it,' I said 'Stick 'em up!' and pulled out a gun! I don't understand how it happened."

Backsliding does not come overnight. You don't go to sleep on fire for God and wake up cold, not serving God, wanting nothing to do with God. There is a gradual cooling-off process. That's why the Bible says to protect your heart with all diligence, for out of it flow the issues of life. (See Proverbs 4:23.) Protect your heart daily with the Word of God. You're even going to have to protect yourself from some of the people you hang around, because they'll come and quench the fire in your life.

Third, don't lose the excitement of living for Jesus. Get excited and stay excited. Expect God to move every day, even on an off day, on a day of rest. God never sleeps. That's why I don't like to go to sleep — I might miss some excitement. Since I want to hang around Him and I know He doesn't sleep, I'm concerned that if I go to sleep I might miss something!

Get excited about serving Jesus. If you get excited about living for Jesus and serving Jesus, there'll never be a morning that you don't want to get out of bed and live life to the fullest. You'll get up with a spring in your step and you'll face every obstacle with joy, because you know that He's with you and that He's going to help you.

Fourth, always give Jesus the glory. For every little thing, give Him the glory. I give Him glory just because I am able to walk outside and see a sunny day. I give Him glory for the palm trees and the grass and the privilege to be alive. When you do this, the presence of God comes on you.

"Well, I've got nothing to be excited about, Rodney. Will you please pray for me? The air conditioner's not working in my house, the TV broke down, and my computer won't work anymore."

Well, are you breathing? Give God the glory! "Lord, thank You for the ability to breath air. Thank You that I'm alive today. Thank You for the privilege of being alive in this day and this time." When you start doing that, the presence of God just comes in.

Have a thankful heart for the tiniest little things: the water you drink, the air you breathe, the ability to use your hands. There are some people who can't use their hands today. There are some people who can't walk normally, or who are confined to a wheelchair, paralyzed for the rest of their lives. Some of these people have more of a thankful attitude than people who have the use of all their limbs.

We've got young people thirteen years of age wanting to kill themselves because life isn't worth living. Who sold them that lie? As long as you're breathing, as long as you have life on the inside of you, as long as you can depend upon Jesus, there's no problem too great!

God will move the mountains for you, but in order for Him to move the mountains, you've got to thank Him for each little shovelful. You can't just give Him glory when a mountain gets moved. You've got to thank Him when a molehill gets moved. Thank Him for every little molehill, keep a heart that is thankful all the time, and when a mountain gets in your way, the presence of God will blow it away!

Under the old covenant, God inhabited the praises of His people, but under the new covenant God inhabits the people of praise. So when you praise and thank Him, God comes and makes you His sanctuary.

Fifth, think back on your past victories. Think about where He's brought you from and where you could have been. Reflect briefly on your life, then think about the day He saved you. Think about the family He's blessed you with — your spouse, your children. Think about all the failures God turned around. Think about the times it looked like you were never going to make it. You even thought to yourself, *I don't know how I'm going to get through*. Then remember how God brought you through every one of those things!

Well, He's not going to drop you now! He didn't bring you this far to leave you. He didn't teach you to swim to let you drown, either. The Bible says that He who began a good work in you is able to complete it. (See Philippians 1:6.) And Hebrews 12:2 tells us that He's the author and the finisher of our faith. That means if He authored it, He started it, so He'll complete it.

Sixth, always testify. Always talk about God's goodness. Talk about His goodness to your children every day when you sit around the table to eat. Talk about the goodness of Jesus, His greatness, and His wondrous works. That's how His presence comes. When you talk about how the Lord first touched you, it just comes afresh to you again. Just try to tell somebody each day, "I want to tell you what happened to me." When you start telling, it comes alive on the inside of you again. You bring His presence.

You know what a lot of Christians are doing? The moment they get together, they say, "Let me tell you what the devil did to me last week. Now Monday he attacked me here, and Tuesday, that happened, then Wednesday...."

What happens? The presence of God is gone — and I'm gone too! I don't want to hang around that mess. I'd rather be with those who talk about the Lord — His goodness, His grace, His glory, His mercy, His faithfulness, His lovingkindness, and all of the blessings that He's so freely and lavishly bestowed upon you.

Can you think of things to testify about? You could have been in a straight jacket in a mental institution today, but here you are sitting clothed in your right mind. You've got something to shout about! You could still be bound by religious tradition today, but He has delivered you and set you free. You could be sick, dying of a terminal disease, but Jesus has set you free. That's something to shout about! That's something to testify about!

Think about what could have been and think about how God delivered you. If He delivered you once, He'll deliver you again and again! Hallelujah!

Remember, you can consistently live in the presence of Jesus if you:

- Never forget that God is your source.
- Act on God's Word as a way of life.
- Don't lose the excitement of living for Jesus.
- Always give Jesus the glory.
- Think back on your past victories.
- And always testify of His goodness.

Chapter 21

Pressing in to Jesus

*A*nd, *behold, there was a man named Zacchaeus, which was the chief among the publicans, and he was rich.*

And he sought to see Jesus who he was; and could not for the press, because he was little of stature.

And he ran before, and climbed up into a sycamore tree to see him: for he was to pass that way.

And when Jesus came to the place, he looked up, and saw him, and said unto him, Zacchaeus, make haste, and come down; for to day I must abide at thy house.

And he made haste, and came down, and received him joyfully.

LUKE 19:2-6

"You need to press in to Jesus."

That's a statement I make all the time, and people often come to me and say, "What do you mean by 'press in to Jesus'?"

What does it mean to press in? How do you press in, and what is there to press into? Let's look at the story of Zacchaeus in the gospel of Luke. First of all, Zacchaeus was a wealthy tax collector who wanted to see Jesus, but he was too short to see over the crowd. So he devised this plan: "I've got to see Jesus, so I'm going to climb up in this tree. Then, when He passes by, I'll be able to see Him."

Just picture a wealthy man climbing up and sitting in a tree, waiting for Jesus to come by. He wanted to see Jesus so much, he didn't care what anybody thought of him.

"Well, isn't that old Zach? Hey Zacchaeus, what are you doing up a tree?"

Imagine how Zacchaeus felt when Jesus told Him to come down. He knew his life would never be the same.

When you're desperate, you'll do anything. We've got an individual attending our Bible school right now who drove eight days to get to Florida from Alaska. When you're desperate, you're going to do anything you can to get to the place where you can see Jesus. When you are desperate to see Him, nothing else matters.

A lot of people are facing dire circumstances today because they're just putting up with a situation. "Well, I guess this is my lot in life," they say. "I'm just going to have to put up with this sickness and disease. I'm just going to have to put up with this circumstance at my work. I'm just going to have to put up with this problem in my marriage."

Well, it's time to get up off of your blessed assurance and stop putting up with it! It's time to say, "No more! I'm not going to tolerate this sickness and disease another day in my life. I'm not going to tolerate this lack another day in my life. I'm going to do something! I don't care what it takes! Even if I have to get out of the house and climb a tree, I'm going to get close to Jesus!"

How desperate are you?

I remember going to pray for a person who had emphysema. They could barely breathe, even on an oxygen machine, but they were sitting there smoking a cigarette. They said, "Pastor Rodney, would you pray for me?"

I said, "What's wrong?"

"I've got emphysema."

"Well, how desperate are you to get healed?"

"I need a miracle. Can I get some new lungs?"

This person wasn't desperate enough to live to even quit smoking! How desperate are you?

And again he entered into Capernaum after some days; and it was noised that he was in the house.

And straightway many were gathered together, insomuch that there was no room to receive them, no, not so much as about the door: and he preached the word unto them.

MARK 2:1-2

Jesus came into this house, and then everybody started telling the neighbors, "Hey, you know who's in that house? It's Jesus!" People were stuck all over that house — in the living room, in the basement, in the bathroom, in the kitchen! But when you're desperate, the crowd doesn't matter.

And they came unto him, bringing one sick of the palsy, which was borne of four.

And when they could not come nigh unto him for the press, they uncovered the roof where he was: and when they had broken it up, they let down the bed wherein the sick of the palsy lay.

When Jesus saw their faith, he said unto the sick of the palsy, Son, thy sins be forgiven thee.

But there were certain of the scribes sitting there, and reasoning in their hearts,

Why doth this man thus speak blasphemies? who can forgive sins but God only?

And immediately when Jesus perceived in his spirit that they so reasoned within themselves, he said unto them, Why reason ye these things in your hearts?

Whether is it easier to say to the sick of the palsy, Thy sins be forgiven thee; or to say, Arise, and take up thy bed, and walk?

But that ye may know that the Son of man hath power on earth to forgive sins, (he saith to the sick of the palsy,)

I say unto thee, Arise, and take up thy bed, and go thy way into thine house.

And immediately he arose, took up the bed, and went forth before them all; insomuch that they were all amazed, and glorified God, saying, We never saw it on this fashion.

MARK 2:3-12

When you get desperate, you don't care. These four were thinking, "We've got to get in that house! Our friend is sick and there's only one way in — through the roof. So let's climb on top of the house, rip up the roof, and let him down from the top. *We have to get hold of Jesus.*"

Somebody said, "You can't do that, He's preaching!"

"I don't care what He's doing. I'm going to get hold of Jesus."

Somebody said, "But you can't rip up the roof, they'll arrest you. You'll get thrown in prison for vandalism."

"I don't care! I've got to get hold of Jesus. I'm desperate."

How desperate are you?

When people get into desperate situations, they do the most amazing things. I heard about a lady who arrived on the scene of an automobile wreck. Someone was trapped under the automobile and this little lady picked the automobile up and pulled the person out from under it. She did something that she could not do physically. In a moment of desperation, she did something beyond her natural abilities.

That reminds me of a funny story. A drunk decided to take a shortcut home through the graveyard one night. Unfortunately for him, the gravedigger had dug a new grave that day, and it was directly in his path. He fell headlong into the grave, and it was so deep he couldn't get out of it. After an hour of trying, he realized there was no way to get out, so he decided just to sit there and spend the night.

At midnight, a second drunk man staggered out of the bar and decided to also cut through the graveyard. Boom! He fell into the same open grave. He tried to jump out, but to no avail. It was far too deep. The first drunk, who had fallen asleep, was awakened by the noise. He said to the second drunk, who was unaware of his presence in the grave, "You're not gonna get out of this grave tonight!"

But he did!

When you're desperate you can find a way!

How desperate are you? Are you desperate enough to press in to Jesus?

So many of us are living with situations that we're just putting up with — in our job, in our finances, in our marriage, in our physical body. Are we desperate enough to say, "I've had it now! Devil, you've come this far and you can't come any farther!"

> **How desperate are you? Are you desperate enough to press in to Jesus?**

Zacchaeus was desperate, and he pressed into Jesus. The way that he pressed in was by climbing a tree. The four men were desperate to help their friend, and they pressed in to Jesus by ripping up a roof. The way you press in might be totally different from anybody else.

Look at this familiar story in Mark 5:25-34:

> *And a certain woman, which had an issue of blood twelve years,*
>
> *And had suffered many things of many physicians, and had spent all that she had, and was nothing bettered, but rather grew worse,*
>
> *When she had heard of Jesus, came in the press behind, and touched his garment.*
>
> *For she said, If I may touch but his clothes, I shall be whole.*
>
> *And straightway the fountain of her blood was dried up; and she felt in her body that she was healed of that plague.*
>
> *And Jesus, immediately knowing in himself that virtue had gone out of him, turned him about in the press, and said, Who touched my clothes?*
>
> *And his disciples said unto him, Thou seest the multitude thronging thee, and sayest thou, Who touched me?*
>
> *And he looked round about to see her that had done this thing.*
>
> *But the woman fearing and trembling, knowing what was done in her, came and fell down before him, and told him all the truth.*

And he said unto her, Daughter, thy faith hath made thee
whole; go in peace, and be whole of thy plague.

This woman had desperate faith, so she pressed in through the crowd to touch the hem of Jesus' garment. You've got to have that same kind of desperate faith. Desperate faith will cause you to rise up and grab hold of your miracle.

Desperate faith is when you cry, "That's it!" You need to get mad at the right thing. You've been getting mad at the preacher, at your brother, at your sister. But you need to get mad at the *devil* and rise up and do something in Jesus' name.

If you're unhappy and desperate enough about the way things are, you can change them. How desperate are you?

Speaking of desperate people, look at the story of Bartimaeus in Mark 10:46-50:

And they came to Jericho: and as he went out of Jericho with
his disciples and a great number of people, blind Bartimaeus,
the son of Timaeus, sat by the highway side begging.

And when he heard that it was Jesus of Nazareth, he began to
cry out, and say, Jesus, thou son of David, have mercy on me.

And many charged him that he should hold his peace: but he
cried the more a great deal, Thou son of David, have mercy
on me.

And Jesus stood still, and commanded him to be called. And
they call the blind man, saying unto him, Be of good comfort,
rise; he calleth thee.

And he, casting away his garment, rose, and came to Jesus.

That last verse is very important. The garment Bartimaeus was wearing signified that he was a blind man, just as blind people today might use a white cane or a guide dog. Bartimaeus cast away the garment that signified he was blind. What was he doing? In his desperation, he was taking off the clothes that attached him to his blindness, saying, "I'm leaving the past behind and I'm going forward. I'm pressing in to Jesus. Doesn't matter what the past has been like. I'm pressing in to Jesus. I'm desperate."

> *And Jesus answered and said unto him, What wilt thou that I should do unto thee? The blind man said unto him, Lord, that I might receive my sight.*
>
> *And Jesus said unto him, Go thy way; thy faith hath made thee whole. And immediately he received his sight, and followed Jesus in the way.*
>
> MARK 10:51-52

When you're pressing in to Jesus, like Bartimaeus, you've got to leave that old garment behind. Leave that old garment of doubt and unbelief, that old garment of "you're never going to make it," that old garment of "you're going to fail." Take off that old garment of sickness and disease, that old garment of poverty and lack. Cast off those old garments of depression, oppression, fear, bondage, religious tradition, doctrines of men, and doctrines of devils. When you press in to Jesus, you're going to leave them behind and go on, because Jesus has got great things prepared for you.

Listen to what the apostle Paul wrote to the Philippian church.

> *Not as though I had already attained, either were already perfect: but I follow after, if that I may apprehend that for which also I am apprehended of Christ Jesus.*
>
> *Brethren, I count not myself to have apprehended: but this one thing I do, forgetting those things which are behind, and reaching forth unto those things which are before,*
>
> *I press toward the mark for the prize of the high calling of God in Christ Jesus.*
>
> PHILIPPIANS 3:12-14

I don't know about you, but I made a decision: I'm pressing in to Jesus. Sometimes "casting off the old" might mean getting rid of some of the friends you've had because they're holding you back. They're hold you in bondage. They are the ones who are telling you that you can't make it. They want you living in the past, on yesterday's bread, eating yesterday's manna. But it's a new day, and you just have to say, "I'm forgetting those things which are behind and reaching forth unto the things which are before."

Do you realize what is before you? History books are waiting to be written about the man and woman of God who will totally, 100 percent, yield themselves to the Spirit of God, forgetting the past and saying, "Those days are over." Will that be you?

Make this day the day you cast off the old garment and press in to Jesus!

Conclusion

In Revelation 1:8, Jesus tells us that He is the Alpha and Omega, the beginning and the end. In this book, I believe I have only scratched the surface of all He was, is, and will be to those of us who love Him.

To be perfectly honest, I didn't know how or where to end this book, because the more I study, preach, and write about Jesus, the more I see and the more I want to tell you. Finally, to get the book published, I had to stop somewhere!

If there is one thing I would like you to remember always, it is that Jesus loves you and He is for you. No matter where you are or what you've done, no matter how bad you have messed up – as a believer or an unbeliever – you can come to Him at any time and He will not condemn you. He will forgive you and set you free.

Not only is Jesus the only one who can give you eternal life, but Jesus is the only one who can give purpose and meaning to your life. He is the only one who can tell you who you are and what you are created to be and do. He is the only one who can give you true joy, peace, and love.

Jesus wants to bless you beyond your wildest dreams! He will challenge you to grow up and mature along the way, but He will never push you. He is a gentleman and He respects your will. It's up to you to seek Him – in the Word of God, as you pray, in church, on the job, and as you fellowship with other believers. He will go as far with you as you will allow Him to go. And I can tell you from personal experience that He can take you a long, long way!

Begin this adventure right now, if you haven't already, and see if your life doesn't turn out to be more than you could ever have imagined!

Prayer to accept Jesus as your personal Lord and Savior:

Father, I come to you in the precious name of Your Son, Jesus. You said in Your Word that if I confess with my mouth that Jesus Christ is my Lord and my Savior and I believe in my heart that God has raised Him from the dead, I will be saved. I make the decision today to surrender every area of my life to the lordship of Jesus.

Jesus, come into my heart. Take out the stony heart and put in a heart of flesh. I turn my back on the world and on sin. I repent and I put my trust in You. I acknowledge that I am a sinner. I would like to thank You for dying on the cross for my sin and shedding Your blood for me so that I might be forgiven of my sin. Thank You that You rose from the dead and that one day, You are coming back for me.

I confess that Jesus Christ has come in the flesh and that He is my personal Lord and Savior. Thank You, Lord Jesus, for saving me. I accept by faith the free gift of salvation. Amen (so be it).

Dear Friend, if you just prayed this prayer, I would like to welcome you into the family of God! Your sins are forgiven! This is the good news of the Gospel of the Lord Jesus Christ. You are now a child of God and you will live with Him forever. I encourage you to do several things to get to know Him. Read your Bible and pray every day (talk to Jesus about every thing in your life). Find a Bible-believing church that believes in the lordship of Jesus Christ. Be around strong believers who will encourage you and lift you up in your walk with God. Tell someone about your new-found faith and joy that only Jesus can bring. Use this book and my other books and tapes to help you in your new walk with God.

A Note from Pastor Rodney About the Four Gospels

There is no better way to meet the real Jesus than through the gospels of Matthew, Mark, Luke, and John. I have done my best in the previous pages to introduce Him to you, but in the following pages you will meet Him first hand. You will see Him cleanse the lepers, cast out demons, and raise the dead. You will feel His great love and experience His sacrifice, burial, and resurrection. You will get to know Jesus as He really is for yourself.

I have placed the following symbols in the four gospels to note the traits of Jesus we have discussed in the previous chapters. I have chosen twelve major themes from Jesus' life and ministry, and each theme has its own symbol. Below you will find a brief description of these.

Jesus, our Authority

I have used a throne to symbolize the authority we have in Jesus, because Ephesians 2:6 tells us that we are raised us up and sit together in heavenly places in Christ Jesus.

Jesus, the Baptizer in the Holy Spirit

I have used a dove to symbolize Jesus as our baptizer in the Holy Ghost, because it was in the form of a dove that the Holy Spirit came upon Jesus in Matthew 3:16.

Jesus, the Compassionate

I have used the shepherd's crook to represent the compassion of Jesus as our Good Shepherd. In His compassion you will see

Jesus heal and forgive, but you will also see Him correct and teach in the same way a shepherd in the Middle East will use his crook to rescue and direct his sheep.

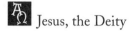 Jesus, the Deity

Jesus is the Son of God, and in Revelation 1:11 He is introduced to us as the "alpha and omega, the first and the last," the beginning and the end. This symbol contains the Greek letters alpha and omega, which point out Jesus' divinity.

Jesus, Who Calls Us to Do His Works

The bread and the wine are used in communion to remind us of Jesus' crucifixion and resurrection, which paid for our salvation and healing. I use these symbols to remind us that true communion is doing the will and works of the Father as Jesus did: preaching and teaching about the good news of salvation, healing the sick, and feeding the hungry.

Jesus, our Great Physician

Jesus is our healer and His prescriptions always work. I have used the prescription symbol to show the places we can see Jesus as our Great Physician.

Jesus, our Savior

Luke 4:18-19 tells us the mission Jesus accomplished as our Savior and what He paid for by His sacrifice on the cross. I have used the cross to mark the places where we see Jesus as the Lamb of God, who was sacrificed so we might know God personally.

Jesus, Our Protector

Psalm 91 tells us that God has a plan of protection for us. The shield shows the places where Jesus acts out or promises protection through faith in and fellowship with Him.

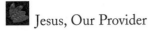 Jesus, Our Provider

When Jesus faced five thousand hungry people, He did not turn His back on them, but fed them by multiplying a little boy's lunch. I have used the loaves and fishes as a symbol of where we see Jesus as our Provider or where He teaches on the provision of God.

Jesus, our Righteousness

Isaiah 61:10 declares that the Messiah, Jesus, will dress us in a robe of righteousness. Through His new covenant, Jesus made us right with God. I have used the symbol of the robe to illustrate the righteousness in which Jesus has dressed us.

Jesus, the Tradition-Breaker

Jesus never accepted that man could make customs and traditions that would limit our relationship with God and all that He wants for us. Again and again we see Jesus defy the legalists, cut through their red tape of religion, and get people into the good things God has for them. In Matthew 21:12-13 we see Jesus turn over the moneychangers' tables in the temple, because they perverted God's law to cheat His people. I have used the symbol of coins being spilled to show where Jesus breaks tradition to show us the true heart of God.

Jesus, in Whose Presence is Fullness of Joy

Jesus is the Joy of our Salvation. He was not quiet and reserved in the presence of God, nor did He expect His disciples to be. In Luke 19:37-40 Jesus tells the Pharisees that if the people couldn't express their joy at who God was, then the very stones of the ground would cry out His praises. I have used the symbol of a person with upraised hands and a happy heart to show that in the presence of Jesus all our needs are met.

Matthew

1 The book of the generation of Jesus Christ, the son of David, the son of Abraham.

2 Abraham begat Isaac; and Isaac begat Jacob; and Jacob begat Judas and his brethren;

3 And Judas begat Phares and Zara of Thamar; and Phares begat Esrom; and Esrom begat Aram;

4 And Aram begat Aminadab; and Aminadab begat Naasson; and Naasson begat Salmon;

5 And Salmon begat Booz of Rachab; and Booz begat Obed of Ruth; and Obed begat Jesse;

6 And Jesse begat David the king; and David the king begat Solomon of her *that had been the wife* of Urias;

7 And Solomon begat Roboam; and Roboam begat Abia; and Abia begat Asa;

8 And Asa begat Josaphat; and Josaphat begat Joram; and Joram begat Ozias;

9 And Ozias begat Joatham; and Joatham begat Achaz; and Achaz begat Ezekias;

10 And Ezekias begat Manasses; and Manasses begat Amon; and Amon begat Josias;

11 And Josias begat Jechonias and his brethren, about the time they were carried away to Babylon:

12 And after they were brought to Babylon, Jechonias begat Salathiel; and Salathiel begat Zorobabel;

13 And Zorobabel begat Abiud; and Abiud begat Eliakim; and Eliakim begat Azor;

14 And Azor begat Sadoc; and Sadoc begat Achim; and Achim begat Eliud;

15 And Eliud begat Eleazar; and Eleazar begat Matthan; and Matthan begat Jacob;

16 And Jacob begat Joseph the husband of Mary, of whom was born Jesus, who is called Christ.

17 So all the generations from Abraham to David *are* fourteen generations; and from David until the carrying away into Babylon *are* fourteen generations; and from the carrying away into Babylon unto Christ *are* fourteen generations.

18 Now the birth of Jesus Christ was on this wise: When as his mother Mary was espoused to Joseph, before they came together, she was found with child of the Holy Ghost.

19 Then Joseph her husband, being a just *man,* and not willing to make her a publick example, was minded to put her away privily.

20 But while he thought on these things, behold, the angel of the Lord appeared unto him in a dream, saying, Joseph, thou son of David, fear not to take unto thee Mary thy wife: for that which is conceived in her is of the Holy Ghost.

21 And she shall bring forth a son, and thou shalt call his name JESUS: for he shall save his people from their sins.

22 Now all this was done, that it might be fulfilled which was spoken of the Lord by the prophet, saying,

23 Behold, a virgin shall be with child, and shall bring forth a son, and they shall call his name Emmanuel, which being interpreted is, God with us.

24 Then Joseph being raised from sleep did as the angel of the Lord had bidden him, and took unto him his wife:

25 And knew her not till she had brought forth her firstborn son: and he called his name JESUS.

2 Now when Jesus was born in Bethlehem of Judaea in the days of Herod the king, behold, there came wise men from the east to Jerusalem,

2 Saying, Where is he that is born King of the Jews? for we have seen his star in the east, and are come to worship him.

3 When Herod the king had heard *these things,* he was troubled, and all Jerusalem with him.

4 And when he had gathered all the chief priests and scribes of the people together, he demanded of them where Christ should be born.

5 And they said unto him, In Bethlehem of Judaea: for thus it is written by the prophet,

6 And thou Bethlehem, in the land of Juda, art

not the least among the princes of Juda: for out of thee shall come a Governor, that shall rule my people Israel.

7 Then Herod, when he had privily called the wise men, enquired of them diligently what time the star appeared.

8 And he sent them to Bethlehem, and said, Go and search diligently for the young child; and when ye have found *him*, bring me word again, that I may come and worship him also.

9 When they had heard the king, they departed; and, lo, the star, which they saw in the east, went before them, till it came and stood over where the young child was.

10 When they saw the star, they rejoiced with exceeding great joy.

11 And when they were come into the house, they saw the young child with Mary his mother, and fell down, and worshipped him: and when they had opened their treasures, they presented unto him gifts; gold, and frankincense, and myrrh.

12 And being warned of God in a dream that they should not return to Herod, they departed into their own country another way.

13 And when they were departed, behold, the angel of the Lord appeareth to Joseph in a dream, saying, Arise, and take the young child and his mother, and flee into Egypt, and be thou there until I bring thee word: for Herod will seek the young child to destroy him.

14 When he arose, he took the young child and his mother by night, and departed into Egypt:

15 And was there until the death of Herod: that it might be fulfilled which was spoken of the Lord by the prophet, saying, Out of Egypt have I called my son.

16 Then Herod, when he saw that he was mocked of the wise men, was exceeding wroth, and sent forth, and slew all the children that were in Bethlehem, and in all the coasts thereof, from two years old and under, according to the time which he had diligently enquired of the wise men.

17 Then was fulfilled that which was spoken by Jeremy the prophet, saying,

18 In Rama was there a voice heard, lamentation, and weeping, and great mourning, Rachel weeping *for* her children, and would not be comforted, because they are not.

19 But when Herod was dead, behold, an angel of the Lord appeareth in a dream to Joseph in Egypt,

20 Saying, Arise, and take the young child and his mother, and go into the land of Israel: for they are dead which sought the young child's life.

21 And he arose, and took the young child and his mother, and came into the land of Israel.

22 But when he heard that Archelaus did reign in Judaea in the room of his father Herod, he was afraid to go thither: notwithstanding, being warned of God in a dream, he turned aside into the parts of Galilee:

23 And he came and dwelt in a city called Nazareth: that it might be fulfilled which was spoken by the prophets, He shall be called a Nazarene.

3 In those days came John the Baptist, preaching in the wilderness of Judaea,

2 And saying, Repent ye: for the kingdom of heaven is at hand.

3 For this is he that was spoken of by the prophet Esaias, saying, The voice of one crying in the wilderness, Prepare ye the way of the Lord, make his paths straight.

4 And the same John had his raiment of camel's hair, and a leathern girdle about his loins; and his meat was locusts and wild honey.

5 Then went out to him Jerusalem, and all Judaea, and all the region round about Jordan,

6 And were baptized of him in Jordan, confessing their sins.

7 But when he saw many of the Pharisees and Sadducees come to his baptism, he said unto them, O generation of vipers, who hath warned you to flee from the wrath to come?

8 Bring forth therefore fruits meet for repentance:

9 And think not to say within yourselves, We have Abraham to *our* father: for I say unto you, that God is able of these stones to raise up children unto Abraham.

10 And now also the axe is laid unto the root of the trees: therefore every tree which bringeth not forth good fruit is hewn down, and cast into the fire.

11 I indeed baptize you with water unto repentance: but he that cometh after me is mightier than I, whose shoes I am not worthy to bear: he shall baptize you with the Holy Ghost, and *with* fire:

12 Whose fan *is* in his hand, and he will throughly purge his floor, and gather his wheat into the garner; but he will burn up the chaff with unquenchable fire.

13 Then cometh Jesus from Galilee to Jordan unto John, to be baptized of him.

14 But John forbad him, saying, I have need to be baptized of thee, and comest thou to me? 15 And Jesus answering said unto him, Suffer *it to be so* now: for thus it becometh us to fulfil all righteousness. Then he suffered him. 16 And Jesus, when he was baptized, went up straightway out of the water: and, lo, the heavens were opened unto him, and he saw the Spirit of God descending like a dove, and lighting upon him: 17 And lo a voice from heaven, saying, This is my beloved Son, in whom I am well pleased.

4 Then was Jesus led up of the Spirit into the wilderness to be tempted of the devil. 2 And when he had fasted forty days and forty nights, he was afterward an hungred. 3 And when the tempter came to him, he said, If thou be the Son of God, command that these stones be made bread. 4 But he answered and said, It is written, Man shall not live by bread alone, but by every word that proceedeth out of the mouth of God. 5 Then the devil taketh him up into the holy city, and setteth him on a pinnacle of the temple, 6 And saith unto him, If thou be the Son of God, cast thyself down: for it is written, He shall give his angels charge concerning thee: and in *their* hands they shall bear thee up, lest at any time thou dash thy foot against a stone. 7 Jesus said unto him, It is written again, Thou shalt not tempt the Lord thy God. 8 Again, the devil taketh him up into an exceeding high mountain, and sheweth him all the kingdoms of the world, and the glory of them; 9 And saith unto him, All these things will I give thee, if thou wilt fall down and worship me. 10 Then saith Jesus unto him, Get thee hence, Satan: for it is written, Thou shalt worship the Lord thy God, and him only shalt thou serve. 11 Then the devil leaveth him, and, behold, angels came and ministered unto him. 12 Now when Jesus had heard that John was cast into prison, he departed into Galilee; 13 And leaving Nazareth, he came and dwelt in Capernaum, which is upon the sea coast, in the borders of Zabulon and Nephthalim: 14 That it might be fulfilled which was spoken by Esaias the prophet, saying, 15 The land of Zabulon, and the land of Neph-

thalim, *by* the way of the sea, beyond Jordan, Galilee of the Gentiles; 16 The people which sat in darkness saw great light; and to them which sat in the region and shadow of death light is sprung up. 17 From that time Jesus began to preach, and to say, Repent: for the kingdom of heaven is at hand. 18 And Jesus, walking by the sea of Galilee, saw two brethren, Simon called Peter, and Andrew his brother, casting a net into the sea: for they were fishers. 19 And he saith unto them, Follow me, and I will make you fishers of men. 20 And they straightway left *their* nets, and followed him. 21 And going on from thence, he saw other two brethren, James *the son* of Zebedee, and John his brother, in a ship with Zebedee their father, mending their nets; and he called them. 22 And they immediately left the ship and their father, and followed him. 23 And Jesus went about all Galilee, teaching in their synagogues, and preaching the gospel of the kingdom, and healing all manner of sickness and all manner of disease among the people. 24 And his fame went throughout all Syria: and they brought unto him all sick people that were taken with divers diseases and torments, and those which were possessed with devils, and those which were lunatick, and those that had the palsy; and he healed them. 25 And there followed him great multitudes of people from Galilee, and *from* Decapolis, and *from* Jerusalem, and *from* Judaea, and *from* beyond Jordan.

5 And seeing the multitudes, he went up into a mountain: and when he was set, his disciples came unto him: 2 And he opened his mouth, and taught them, saying, 3 Blessed *are* the poor in spirit: for theirs is the kingdom of heaven. 4 Blessed *are* they that mourn: for they shall be comforted. 5 Blessed *are* the meek: for they shall inherit the earth. 6 Blessed *are* they which do hunger and thirst after righteousness: for they shall be filled. 7 Blessed *are* the merciful: for they shall obtain mercy. 8 Blessed *are* the pure in heart: for they shall see God.

251

⁹ Blessed *are* the peacemakers: for they shall be called the children of God.

¹⁰ Blessed *are* they which are persecuted for righteousness' sake: for theirs is the kingdom of heaven.

¹¹ Blessed are ye, when *men* shall revile you, and persecute *you,* and shall say all manner of evil against you falsely, for my sake.

¹² Rejoice, and be exceeding glad: for great *is* your reward in heaven: for so persecuted they the prophets which were before you.

¹³ Ye are the salt of the earth: but if the salt have lost his savour, wherewith shall it be salted? it is thenceforth good for nothing, but to be cast out, and to be trodden under foot of men.

¹⁴ Ye are the light of the world. A city that is set on an hill cannot be hid.

¹⁵ Neither do men light a candle, and put it under a bushel, but on a candlestick; and it giveth light unto all that are in the house.

¹⁶ Let your light so shine before men, that they may see your good works, and glorify your Father which is in heaven.

¹⁷ Think not that I am come to destroy the law, or the prophets: I am not come to destroy, but to fulfil.

¹⁸ For verily I say unto you, Till heaven and earth pass, one jot or one tittle shall in no wise pass from the law, till all be fulfilled.

¹⁹ Whosoever therefore shall break one of these least commandments, and shall teach men so, he shall be called the least in the kingdom of heaven: but whosoever shall do and teach *them,* the same shall be called great in the kingdom of heaven.

²⁰ For I say unto you, That except your righteousness shall exceed *the righteousness* of the scribes and Pharisees, ye shall in no case enter into the kingdom of heaven.

²¹ Ye have heard that it was said by them of old time, Thou shalt not kill; and whosoever shall kill shall be in danger of the judgment:

²² But I say unto you, That whosoever is angry with his brother without a cause shall be in danger of the judgment: and whosoever shall say to his brother, Raca, shall be in danger of the council: but whosoever shall say, Thou fool, shall be in danger of hell fire.

²³ Therefore if thou bring thy gift to the altar, and there rememberest that thy brother hath ought against thee;

²⁴ Leave there thy gift before the altar, and go thy way; first be reconciled to thy brother, and then come and offer thy gift.

²⁵ Agree with thine adversary quickly, whiles thou art in the way with him; lest at any time the adversary deliver thee to the judge, and the judge deliver thee to the officer, and thou be cast into prison.

²⁶ Verily I say unto thee, Thou shalt by no means come out thence, till thou hast paid the uttermost farthing.

²⁷ Ye have heard that it was said by them of old time, Thou shalt not commit adultery:

²⁸ But I say unto you, That whosoever looketh on a woman to lust after her hath committed adultery with her already in his heart.

²⁹ And if thy right eye offend thee, pluck it out, and cast *it* from thee: for it is profitable for thee that one of thy members should perish, and not *that* thy whole body should be cast into hell.

³⁰ And if thy right hand offend thee, cut if off, and cast it from thee: for it is profitable for thee that one of thy members should perish, and not *that* thy whole body should be cast into hell.

³¹ It hath been said, Whosoever shall put away his wife, let him give her a writing of divorcement:

³² But I say unto you, That whosoever shall put away his wife, saving for the cause of fornication, causeth her to commit adultery: and whosoever shall marry her that is divorced committeth adultery.

³³ Again, ye have heard that it hath been said by them of old time, Thou shalt not forswear thyself, but shalt perform unto the Lord thine oaths:

³⁴ But I say unto you, Swear not at all; neither by heaven; for it is God's throne:

³⁵ Nor by the earth; for it is his footstool: neither by Jerusalem; for it is the city of the great King.

³⁶ Neither shalt thou swear by thy head, because thou canst not make one hair white or black.

³⁷ But let your communication be, Yea, yea; Nay, nay: for whatsoever is more than these cometh of evil.

³⁸ Ye have heard that it hath been said, An eye for an eye, and a tooth for a tooth:

³⁹ But I say unto you, That ye resist not evil: but whosoever shall smite thee on thy right cheek, turn to him the other also.

⁴⁰ And if any man will sue thee at the law, and take away thy coat, let him have *thy* cloke also.

⁴¹ And whosoever shall compel thee to go a mile, go with him twain.

⁴² Give to him that asketh thee, and from him that would borrow of thee turn not thou away.
⁴³ Ye have heard that it hath been said, Thou shalt love thy neighbour, and hate thine enemy.
⁴⁴ But I say unto you, Love your enemies, bless them that curse you, do good to them that hate you, and pray for them which despitefully use you, and persecute you;
⁴⁵ That ye may be the children of your Father which is in heaven: for he maketh his sun to rise on the evil and on the good, and sendeth rain on the just and on the unjust.
⁴⁶ For if ye love them which love you, what reward have ye? do not even the publicans the same?
⁴⁷ And if ye salute your brethren only, what do ye more *than others?* do not even the publicans so?
⁴⁸ Be ye therefore perfect, even as your Father which is in heaven is perfect.

6 Take heed that ye do not your alms before men, to be seen of them: otherwise ye have no reward of your Father which is in heaven.
² Therefore when thou doest *thine* alms, do not sound a trumpet before thee, as the hypocrites do in the synagogues and in the streets, that they may have glory of men. Verily I say unto you, They have their reward.
³ But when thou doest alms, let not thy left hand know what thy right hand doeth:
⁴ That thine alms may be in secret: and thy Father which seeth in secret himself shall reward thee openly.
⁵And when thou prayest, thou shalt not be as the hypocrites *are:* for they love to pray standing in the synagogues and in the corners of the streets, that they may be seen of men. Verily I say unto you, They have their reward.
⁶ But thou, when thou prayest, enter into thy closet, and when thou hast shut thy door, pray to thy Father which is in secret; and thy Father which seeth in secret shall reward thee openly.
⁷ But when ye pray, use not vain repetitions, as the heathen *do:* for they think that they shall be heard for their much speaking.
⁸ Be not ye therefore like unto them: for your Father knoweth what things ye have need of, before ye ask him.
⁹ After this manner therefore pray ye: Our Father which art in heaven, Hallowed be thy name.
¹⁰ Thy kingdom come. Thy will be done in earth, as *it is* in heaven.
¹¹ Give us this day our daily bread.

¹² And forgive us our debts, as we forgive our debtors.
¹³ And lead us not into temptation, but deliver us from evil: For thine is the kingdom, and the power, and the glory, for ever. Amen.
¹⁴ For if ye forgive men their trespasses, your heavenly Father will also forgive you:
¹⁵ But if ye forgive not men their trespasses, neither will your Father forgive your trespasses.
¹⁶ Moreover when ye fast, be not, as the hypocrites, of a sad countenance: for they disfigure their faces, that they may appear unto men to fast. Verily I say unto you, They have their reward.
¹⁷ But thou, when thou fastest, anoint thine head, and wash thy face;
¹⁸ That thou appear not unto men to fast, but unto thy Father which is in secret: and thy Father, which seeth in secret, shall reward thee openly.
¹⁹ Lay not up for yourselves treasures upon earth, where moth and rust doth corrupt, and where thieves break through and steal:
²⁰ But lay up for yourselves treasures in heaven, where neither moth nor rust doth corrupt, and where thieves do not break through nor steal:
²¹ For where your treasure is, there will your heart be also.
²² The light of the body is the eye: if therefore thine eye be single, thy whole body shall be full of light.
²³ But if thine eye be evil, thy whole body shall be full of darkness. If therefore the light that is in thee be darkness, how great *is* that darkness!
²⁴ No man can serve two masters: for either he will hate the one, and love the other; or else he will hold to the one, and despise the other. Ye cannot serve God and mammon.
²⁵ Therefore I say unto you, Take no thought for your life, what ye shall eat, or what ye shall drink; nor yet for your body, what ye shall put on. Is not the life more than meat, and the body than raiment?
²⁶ Behold the fowls of the air: for they sow not, neither do they reap, nor gather into barns; yet your heavenly Father feedeth them. Are ye not much better than they?
²⁷ Which of you by taking thought can add one cubit unto his stature?
²⁸ And why take ye thought for raiment? Consider the lilies of the field, how they grow; they toil not, neither do they spin:

²⁹ And yet I say unto you, That even Solomon in all his glory was not arrayed like one of these.

³⁰ Wherefore, if God so clothe the grass of the field, which to day is, and to morrow is cast into the oven, *shall he* not much more *clothe* you, O ye of little faith?

³¹ Therefore take no thought, saying, What shall we eat? or, What shall we drink? or, Wherewithal shall we be clothed?

³² (For after all these things do the Gentiles seek:) for your heavenly Father knoweth that ye have need of all these things.

³³ But seek ye first the kingdom of God, and his righteousness; and all these things shall be added unto you.

³⁴ Take therefore no thought for the morrow: for the morrow shall take thought for the things of itself. Sufficient unto the day *is* the evil thereof.

7 Judge not, that ye be not judged.
² For with what judgment ye judge, ye shall be judged: and with what measure ye mete, it shall be measured to you again.

³ And why beholdest thou the mote that is in thy brother's eye, but considerest not the beam that is in thine own eye?

⁴ Or how wilt thou say to thy brother, Let me pull out the mote out of thine eye; and, behold, a beam *is* in thine own eye?

⁵ Thou hypocrite, first cast out the beam out of thine own eye; and then shalt thou see clearly to cast out the mote out of thy brother's eye.

⁶Give not that which is holy unto the dogs, neither cast ye your pearls before swine, lest they trample them under their feet, and turn again and rend you.

⁷Ask, and it shall be given you; seek, and ye shall find; knock, and it shall be opened unto you:

⁸ For every one that asketh receiveth; and he that seeketh findeth; and to him that knocketh it shall be opened.

⁹ Or what man is there of you, whom if his son ask bread, will he give him a stone?

¹⁰ Or if he ask a fish, will he give him a serpent?

¹¹ If ye then, being evil, know how to give good gifts unto your children, how much more shall your Father which is in heaven give good things to them that ask him?

¹² Therefore all things whatsoever ye would that men should do to you, do ye even so to them: for this is the law and the prophets.

¹³ Enter ye in at the strait gate: for wide *is* the gate, and broad *is* the way, that leadeth to destruction, and many there be which go in thereat:

¹⁴ Because strait *is* the gate, and narrow *is* the way, which leadeth unto life, and few there be that find it.

¹⁵ Beware of false prophets, which come to you in sheep's clothing, but inwardly they are ravening wolves.

¹⁶ Ye shall know them by their fruits. Do men gather grapes of thorns, or figs of thistles?

¹⁷ Even so every good tree bringeth forth good fruit; but a corrupt tree bringeth forth evil fruit.

¹⁸ A good tree cannot bring forth evil fruit, neither *can* a corrupt tree bring forth good fruit.

¹⁹ Every tree that bringeth not forth good fruit is hewn down, and cast into the fire.

²⁰ Wherefore by their fruits ye shall know them.

²¹ Not every one that saith unto me, Lord, Lord, shall enter into the kingdom of heaven; but he that doeth the will of my Father which is in heaven.

²² Many will say to me in that day, Lord, Lord, have we not prophesied in thy name? and in thy name have cast out devils? and in thy name done many wonderful works?

²³ And then will I profess unto them, I never knew you: depart from me, ye that work iniquity.

²⁴ Therefore whosoever heareth these sayings of mine, and doeth them, I will liken him unto a wise man, which built his house upon a rock:

²⁵ And the rain descended, and the floods came, and the winds blew, and beat upon that house; and it fell not: for it was founded upon a rock.

²⁶ And every one that heareth these sayings of mine, and doeth them not, shall be likened unto a foolish man, which built his house upon the sand:

²⁷ And the rain descended, and the floods came, and the winds blew, and beat upon that house; and it fell: and great was the fall of it.

²⁸ And it came to pass, when Jesus had ended these sayings, the people were astonished at his doctrine:

²⁹ For he taught them as *one* having authority, and not as the scribes.

8 When he was come down from the mountain, great multitudes followed him.

² And, behold, there came a leper and wor-

shipped him, saying, Lord, if thou wilt, thou canst make me clean.

³ And Jesus put forth *his* hand, and touched him, saying, I will; be thou clean. And immediately his leprosy was cleansed.

⁴ And Jesus saith unto him, See thou tell no man; but go thy way, shew thyself to the priest, and offer the gift that Moses commanded, for a testimony unto them.

⁵And when Jesus was entered into Capernaum, there came unto him a centurion, beseeching him,

⁶ And saying, Lord, my servant lieth at home sick of the palsy, grievously tormented.

⁷ And Jesus saith unto him, I will come and heal him.

⁸ The centurion answered and said, Lord, I am not worthy that thou shouldest come under my roof: but speak the word only, and my servant shall be healed.

⁹ For I am a man under authority, having soldiers under me: and I say to this *man*, Go, and he goeth; and to another, Come, and he cometh; and to my servant, Do this, and he doeth *it*.

¹⁰ When Jesus heard *it*, he marvelled, and said to them that followed, Verily I say unto you, I have not found so great faith, no, not in Israel.

¹¹ And I say unto you, That many shall come from the east and west, and shall sit down with Abraham, and Isaac, and Jacob, in the kingdom of heaven.

¹² But the children of the kingdom shall be cast out into outer darkness: there shall be weeping and gnashing of teeth.

¹³ And Jesus said unto the centurion, Go thy way; and as thou hast believed, so be it done unto thee. And his servant was healed in the selfsame hour.

¹⁴ And when Jesus was come into Peter's house, he saw his wife's mother laid, and sick of a fever.

¹⁵ And he touched her hand, and the fever left her: and she arose, and ministered unto them.

¹⁶ When the even was come, they brought unto him many that were possessed with devils: and he cast out the spirits with *his* word, and healed all that were sick:

¹⁷ That it might be fulfilled which was spoken by Esaias the prophet, saying, Himself took our infirmities, and bare *our* sicknesses.

¹⁸ Now when Jesus saw great multitudes about him, he gave commandment to depart unto the other side.

¹⁹ And a certain scribe came, and said unto him, Master, I will follow thee whithersoever thou goest.

²⁰ And Jesus saith unto him, The foxes have holes, and the birds of the air *have* nests; but the Son of man hath not where to lay *his* head.

²¹ And another of his disciples said unto him, Lord, suffer me first to go and bury my father.

²² But Jesus said unto him, Follow me; and let the dead bury their dead.

²³ And when he was entered into a ship, his disciples followed him.

²⁴ And, behold, there arose a great tempest in the sea, insomuch that the ship was covered with the waves: but he was asleep.

²⁵ And his disciples came to *him,* and awoke him, saying, Lord, save us: we perish.

²⁶ And he saith unto them, Why are ye fearful, O ye of little faith? Then he arose, and rebuked the winds and the sea; and there was a great calm.

²⁷ But the men marvelled, saying, What manner of man is this, that even the winds and the sea obey him!

²⁸ And when he was come to the other side into the country of the Gergesenes, there met him two possessed with devils, coming out of the tombs, exceeding fierce, so that no man might pass by that way.

²⁹ And, behold, they cried out, saying, What have we to do with thee, Jesus, thou Son of God? art thou come hither to torment us before the time?

³⁰ And there was a good way off from them an herd of many swine feeding.

³¹ So the devils besought him, saying, If thou cast us out, suffer us to go away into the herd of swine.

³² And he said unto them, Go. And when they were come out, they went into the herd of swine: and, behold, the whole herd of swine ran violently down a steep place into the sea, and perished in the waters.

³³ And they that kept them fled, and went their ways into the city, and told every thing, and what was befallen to the possessed of the devils.

³⁴ And, behold, the whole city came out to meet Jesus: and when they saw him, they besought *him* that he would depart out of their coasts.

9 And he entered into a ship, and passed over, and came into his own city. ℞

2 And, behold, they brought to him a man sick of the palsy, lying on a bed: and Jesus seeing their faith said unto the sick of the palsy; Son, be of good cheer; thy sins be forgiven thee.

3 And, behold, certain of the scribes said within themselves, This *man* blasphemeth.

4 And Jesus knowing their thoughts said, Wherefore think ye evil in your hearts?

5 For whether is easier, to say, *Thy* sins be forgiven thee; or to say, Arise, and walk?

6 But that ye may know that the Son of man hath power on earth to forgive sins, (then saith he to the sick of the palsy,) Arise, take up thy bed, and go unto thine house.

7 And he arose, and departed to his house.

8 But when the multitudes saw *it,* they marvelled, and glorified God, which had given such power unto men.

9 And as Jesus passed forth from thence, he saw a man, named Matthew, sitting at the receipt of custom: and he saith unto him, Follow me. And he arose, and followed him.

10 And it came to pass, as Jesus sat at meat in the house, behold, many publicans and sinners came and sat down with him and his disciples.

11 And when the Pharisees saw *it,* they said unto his disciples, Why eateth your Master with publicans and sinners?

12 But when Jesus heard *that,* he said unto them, They that be whole need not a physician, but they that are sick.

13 But go ye and learn what *that* meaneth, I will have mercy, and not sacrifice: for I am not come to call the righteous, but sinners to repentance.

14 Then came to him the disciples of John, saying, Why do we and the Pharisees fast oft, but thy disciples fast not?

15 And Jesus said unto them, Can the children of the bridechamber mourn, as long as the bridegroom is with them? but the days will come, when the bridegroom shall be taken from them, and then shall they fast.

16 No man putteth a piece of new cloth unto an old garment, for that which is put in to fill it up taketh from the garment, and the rent is made worse.

17 Neither do men put new wine into old bottles: else the bottles break, and the wine runneth out, and the bottles perish: but they put new wine into new bottles, and both are preserved.

18 While he spake these things unto them, behold, there came a certain ruler, and worshipped him, saying, My daughter is even now dead: but come and lay thy hand upon her, and she shall live. ℞

19 And Jesus arose, and followed him, and *so did* his disciples.

20 And, behold, a woman, which was diseased with an issue of blood twelve years, came behind *him,* and touched the hem of his garment: ℞

21 For she said within herself, If I may but touch his garment, I shall be whole.

22 But Jesus turned him about, and when he saw her, he said, Daughter, be of good comfort; thy faith hath made thee whole. And the woman was made whole from that hour.

23 And when Jesus came into the ruler's house, and saw the minstrels and the people making a noise, ℞

24 He said unto them, Give place: for the maid is not dead, but sleepeth. And they laughed him to scorn.

25 But when the people were put forth, he went in, and took her by the hand, and the maid arose.

26 And the fame hereof went abroad into all that land.

27 And when Jesus departed thence, two blind men followed him, crying, and saying, *Thou* Son of David, have mercy on us. ℞

28 And when he was come into the house, the blind men came to him: and Jesus saith unto them, Believe ye that I am able to do this? They said unto him, Yea, Lord.

29 Then touched he their eyes, saying, According to your faith be it unto you.

30 And their eyes were opened; and Jesus straitly charged them, saying, See *that* no man know *it.*

31 But they, when they were departed, spread abroad his fame in all that country.

32 As they went out, behold, they brought to him a dumb man possessed with a devil.

33 And when the devil was cast out, the dumb spake: and the multitudes marvelled, saying, It was never so seen in Israel.

34 But the Pharisees said, He casteth out devils through the prince of the devils.

35 And Jesus went about all the cities and villages, teaching in their synagogues, and preaching the gospel of the kingdom, and ℞

healing every sickness and every disease among the people.

36 But when he saw the multitudes, he was moved with compassion on them, because they fainted, and were scattered abroad, as sheep having no shepherd.

37 Then saith he unto his disciples, The harvest truly *is* plenteous, but the labourers *are* few;

38 Pray ye therefore the Lord of the harvest, that he will send forth labourers into his harvest.

10 And when he had called unto *him* his twelve disciples, he gave them power *against* unclean spirits, to cast them out, and to heal all manner of sickness and all manner of disease.

2 Now the names of the twelve apostles are these; The first, Simon, who is called Peter, and Andrew his brother; James *the son* of Zebedee, and John his brother;

3 Philip, and Bartholomew; Thomas, and Matthew the publican; James *the son* of Alphaeus, and Lebbaeus, whose surname was Thaddaeus;

4 Simon the Canaanite, and Judas Iscariot, who also betrayed him.

5 These twelve Jesus sent forth, and commanded them, saying, Go not into the way of the Gentiles, and into *any* city of the Samaritans enter ye not:

6 But go rather to the lost sheep of the house of Israel.

7 And as ye go, preach, saying, The kingdom of heaven is at hand.

8 Heal the sick, cleanse the lepers, raise the dead, cast out devils: freely ye have received, freely give.

9 Provide neither gold, nor silver, nor brass in your purses,

10 Nor scrip for *your* journey, neither two coats, neither shoes, nor yet staves: for the workman is worthy of his meat.

11 And into whatsoever city or town ye shall enter, enquire who in it is worthy; and there abide till ye go thence.

12 And when ye come into an house, salute it.

13 And if the house be worthy, let your peace come upon it: but if it be not worthy, let your peace return to you.

14 And whosoever shall not receive you, nor hear your words, when ye depart out of that house or city, shake off the dust of your feet.

15 Verily I say unto you, It shall be more tolerable for the land of Sodom and Gomorrha in the day of judgment, than for that city.

16 Behold, I send you forth as sheep in the midst of wolves: be ye therefore wise as serpents, and harmless as doves.

17 But beware of men: for they will deliver you up to the councils, and they will scourge you in their synagogues;

18 And ye shall be brought before governors and kings for my sake, for a testimony against them and the Gentiles.

19 But when they deliver you up, take no thought how or what ye shall speak: for it shall be given you in that same hour what ye shall speak.

20 For it is not ye that speak, but the Spirit of your Father which speaketh in you.

21 And the brother shall deliver up the brother to death, and the father the child: and the children shall rise up against *their* parents, and cause them to be put to death.

22 And ye shall be hated of all *men* for my name's sake: but he that endureth to the end shall be saved.

23 But when they persecute you in this city, flee ye into another: for verily I say unto you, Ye shall not have gone over the cities of Israel, till the Son of man be come.

24 The disciple is not above *his* master, nor the servant above his lord.

25 It is enough for the disciple that he be as his master, and the servant as his lord. If they have called the master of the house Beelzebub, how much more *shall they call* them of his household?

26 Fear them not therefore: for there is nothing covered, that shall not be revealed; and hid, that shall not be known.

27 What I tell you in darkness, *that* speak ye in light: and what ye hear in the ear, *that* preach ye upon the housetops.

28 And fear not them which kill the body, but are not able to kill the soul: but rather fear him which is able to destroy both soul and body in hell.

29 Are not two sparrows sold for a farthing? and one of them shall not fall on the ground without your Father.

30 But the very hairs of your head are all numbered.

31 Fear ye not therefore, ye are of more value than many sparrows.

32 Whosoever therefore shall confess me before men, him will I confess also before my Father which is in heaven.

33 But whosoever shall deny me before men,

him will I also deny before my Father which is in heaven.

³⁴ Think not that I am come to send peace on earth: I came not to send peace, but a sword.

³⁵ For I am come to set a man at variance against his father, and the daughter against her mother, and the daughter in law against her mother in law.

³⁶ And a man's foes *shall be* they of his own household.

³⁷ He that loveth father or mother more than me is not worthy of me: and he that loveth son or daughter more than me is not worthy of me.

³⁸ And he that taketh not his cross, and followeth after me, is not worthy of me.

³⁹ He that findeth his life shall lose it: and he that loseth his life for my sake shall find it.

⁴⁰ He that receiveth you receiveth me, and he that receiveth me receiveth him that sent me.

⁴¹ He that receiveth a prophet in the name of a prophet shall receive a prophet's reward; and he that receiveth a righteous man in the name of a righteous man shall receive a righteous man's reward.

⁴² And whosoever shall give to drink unto one of these little ones a cup of cold *water* only in the name of a disciple, verily I say unto you, he shall in no wise lose his reward.

11 And it came to pass, when Jesus had made an end of commanding his twelve disciples, he departed thence to teach and to preach in their cities.

² Now when John had heard in the prison the works of Christ, he sent two of his disciples,

³ And said unto him, Art thou he that should come, or do we look for another?

⁴ Jesus answered and said unto them, Go and shew John again those things which ye do hear and see:

⁵ The blind receive their sight, and the lame walk, the lepers are cleansed, and the deaf hear, the dead are raised up, and the poor have the gospel preached to them.

⁶ And blessed is *he,* whosoever shall not be offended in me.

⁷And as they departed, Jesus began to say unto the multitudes concerning John, What went ye out into the wilderness to see? A reed shaken with the wind?

⁸ But what went ye out for to see? A man clothed in soft raiment? behold, they that wear soft *clothing* are in kings' houses.

⁹ But what went ye out for to see? A prophet? yea, I say unto you, and more than a prophet.

¹⁰ For this is *he,* of whom it is written, Behold, I send my messenger before thy face, which shall prepare thy way before thee.

¹¹ Verily I say unto you, Among them that are born of women there hath not risen a greater than John the Baptist: notwithstanding he that is least in the kingdom of heaven is greater than he.

¹² And from the days of John the Baptist until now the kingdom of heaven suffereth violence, and the violent take it by force.

¹³ For all the prophets and the law prophesied until John.

¹⁴ And if ye will receive *it,* this is Elias, which was for to come.

¹⁵ He that hath ears to hear, let him hear.

¹⁶ But whereunto shall I liken this generation? It is like unto children sitting in the markets, and calling unto their fellows,

¹⁷ And saying, We have piped unto you, and ye have not danced; we have mourned unto you, and ye have not lamented.

¹⁸ For John came neither eating nor drinking, and they say, He hath a devil.

¹⁹ The Son of man came eating and drinking, and they say, Behold a man gluttonous, and a winebibber, a friend of publicans and sinners. But wisdom is justified of her children.

²⁰ Then began he to upbraid the cities wherein most of his mighty works were done, because they repented not:

²¹ Woe unto thee, Chorazin! woe unto thee, Bethsaida! for if the mighty works, which were done in you, had been done in Tyre and Sidon, they would have repented long ago in sackcloth and ashes.

²² But I say unto you, It shall be more tolerable for Tyre and Sidon at the day of judgment, than for you.

²³ And thou, Capernaum, which art exalted unto heaven, shalt be brought down to hell: for if the mighty works, which have been done in thee, had been done in Sodom, it would have remained until this day.

²⁴ But I say unto you, That it shall be more tolerable for the land of Sodom in the day of judgment, than for thee.

²⁵ At that time Jesus answered and said, I thank thee, O Father, Lord of heaven and earth, because thou hast hid these things from the wise and prudent, and hast revealed them unto babes.

26 Even so, Father: for so it seemed good in thy sight.

27 All things are delivered unto me of my Father: and no man knoweth the Son, but the Father; neither knoweth any man the Father, save the Son, and *he* to whomsoever the Son will reveal *him*.

28 Come unto me, all *ye* that labour and are heavy laden, and I will give you rest.

29 Take my yoke upon you, and learn of me; for I am meek and lowly in heart: and ye shall find rest unto your souls.

30 For my yoke *is* easy, and my burden is light.

12 At that time Jesus went on the sabbath day through the corn; and his disciples were an hungred, and began to pluck the ears of corn, and to eat.

2 But when the Pharisees saw *it,* they said unto him, Behold, thy disciples do that which is not lawful to do upon the sabbath day.

3 But he said unto them, Have ye not read what David did, when he was an hungred, and they that were with him;

4 How he entered into the house of God, and did eat the shewbread, which was not lawful for him to eat, neither for them which were with him, but only for the priests?

5 Or have ye not read in the law, how that on the sabbath days the priests in the temple profane the sabbath, and are blameless?

6 But I say unto you, That in this place is *one* greater than the temple.

7 But if ye had known what *this* meaneth, I will have mercy, and not sacrifice, ye would not have condemned the guiltless.

8 For the Son of man is Lord even of the sabbath day.

9 And when he was departed thence, he went into their synagogue:

10 And, behold, there was a man which had *his* hand withered. And they asked him, saying, Is it lawful to heal on the sabbath days? that they might accuse him.

11 And he said unto them, What man shall there be among you, that shall have one sheep, and if it fall into a pit on the sabbath day, will he not lay hold on it, and lift *it* out?

12 How much then is a man better than a sheep? Wherefore it is lawful to do well on the sabbath days.

13 Then saith he to the man, Stretch forth thine hand. And he stretched *it* forth; and it was restored whole, like as the other.

14 Then the Pharisees went out, and held a council against him, how they might destroy him.

15 But when Jesus knew *it,* he withdrew himself from thence: and great multitudes followed him, and he healed them all;

16 And charged them that they should not make him known:

17 That it might be fulfilled which was spoken by Esaias the prophet, saying,

18 Behold my servant, whom I have chosen; my beloved, in whom my soul is well pleased: I will put my spirit upon him, and he shall shew judgment to the Gentiles.

19 He shall not strive, nor cry; neither shall any man hear his voice in the streets.

20 A bruised reed shall he not break, and smoking flax shall he not quench, till he send forth judgment unto victory.

21 And in his name shall the Gentiles trust.

22 Then was brought unto him one possessed with a devil, blind, and dumb: and he healed him, insomuch that the blind and dumb both spake and saw.

23 And all the people were amazed, and said, Is not this the son of David?

24 But when the Pharisees heard *it,* they said, This *fellow* doth not cast out devils, but by Beelzebub the prince of the devils.

25 And Jesus knew their thoughts, and said unto them, Every kingdom divided against itself is brought to desolation; and every city or house divided against itself shall not stand:

26 And if Satan cast out Satan, he is divided against himself; how shall then his kingdom stand?

27 And if I by Beelzebub cast out devils, by whom do your children cast *them* out? therefore they shall be your judges.

28 But if I cast out devils by the Spirit of God, then the kingdom of God is come unto you.

29 Or else how can one enter into a strong man's house, and spoil his goods, except he first bind the strong man? and then he will spoil his house.

30 He that is not with me is against me; and he that gathereth not with me scattereth abroad.

31 Wherefore I say unto you, All manner of sin and blasphemy shall be forgiven unto men: but the blasphemy *against* the *Holy* Ghost shall not be forgiven unto men.

32 And whosoever speaketh a word against the Son of man, it shall be forgiven him: but whosoever speaketh against the Holy Ghost, it shall

not be forgiven him, neither in this world, neither in the *world* to come.

³³ Either make the tree good, and his fruit good; or else make the tree corrupt, and his fruit corrupt: for the tree is known by *his* fruit.
³⁴ O generation of vipers, how can ye, being evil, speak good things? for out of the abundance of the heart the mouth speaketh.
³⁵ A good man out of the good treasure of the heart bringeth forth good things: and an evil man out of the evil treasure bringeth forth evil things.
³⁶ But I say unto you, That every idle word that men shall speak, they shall give account thereof in the day of judgment.
³⁷ For by thy words thou shalt be justified, and by thy words thou shalt be condemned.
³⁸ Then certain of the scribes and of the Pharisees answered, saying, Master, we would see a sign from thee.
³⁹ But he answered and said unto them, An evil and adulterous generation seeketh after a sign; and there shall no sign be given to it, but the sign of the prophet Jonas:
⁴⁰ For as Jonas was three days and three nights in the whale's belly; so shall the Son of man be three days and three nights in the heart of the earth.
⁴¹ The men of Nineveh shall rise in judgment with this generation, and shall condemn it: because they repented at the preaching of Jonas; and, behold, a greater than Jonas *is* here.
⁴² The queen of the south shall rise up in the judgment with this generation, and shall condemn it: for she came from the uttermost parts of the earth to hear the wisdom of Solomon; and, behold, a greater than Solomon *is* here.
⁴³ When the unclean spirit is gone out of a man, he walketh through dry places, seeking rest, and findeth none.
⁴⁴ Then he saith, I will return into my house from whence I came out; and when he is come, he findeth *it* empty, swept, and garnished.
⁴⁵ Then goeth he, and taketh with himself seven other spirits more wicked than himself, and they enter in and dwell there: and the last *state* of that man is worse than the first. Even so shall it be also unto this wicked generation.
⁴⁶ While he yet talked to the people, behold, *his* mother and his brethren stood without, desiring to speak with him.
⁴⁷ Then one said unto him, Behold, thy mother and thy brethren stand without, desiring to speak with thee.

⁴⁸ But he answered and said unto him that told him, Who is my mother? and who are my brethren?
⁴⁹ And he stretched forth his hand toward his disciples, and said, Behold my mother and my brethren!
⁵⁰ For whosoever shall do the will of my Father which is in heaven, the same is my brother, and sister, and mother.

13 The same day went Jesus out of the house, and sat by the sea side.
² And great multitudes were gathered together unto him, so that he went into a ship, and sat; and the whole multitude stood on the shore.
³ And he spake many things unto them in parables, saying, Behold, a sower went forth to sow;
⁴ And when he sowed, some *seeds* fell by the way side, and the fowls came and devoured them up:
⁵ Some fell upon stony places, where they had not much earth: and forthwith they sprung up, because they had no deepness of earth:
⁶ And when the sun was up, they were scorched; and because they had no root, they withered away.
⁷ And some fell among thorns; and the thorns sprung up, and choked them:
⁸ But other fell into good ground, and brought forth fruit, some an hundredfold, some sixtyfold, some thirtyfold.
⁹ Who hath ears to hear, let him hear.
¹⁰ And the disciples came, and said unto him, Why speakest thou unto them in parables?
¹¹ He answered and said unto them, Because it is given unto you to know the mysteries of the kingdom of heaven, but to them it is not given.
¹² For whosoever hath, to him shall be given, and he shall have more abundance: but whosoever hath not, from him shall be taken away even that he hath.
¹³ Therefore speak I to them in parables: because they seeing see not; and hearing they hear not, neither do they understand.
¹⁴ And in them is fulfilled the prophecy of Esaias, which saith, By hearing ye shall hear, and shall not understand; and seeing ye shall see, and shall not perceive:
¹⁵ For this people's heart is waxed gross, and *their* ears are dull of hearing, and their eyes they have closed; lest at any time they should see with *their* eyes, and hear with *their* ears, and

should understand with *their* heart, and should be converted, and I should heal them.
¹⁶ But blessed *are* your eyes, for they see: and your ears, for they hear.
¹⁷ For verily I say unto you, That many prophets and righteous *men* have desired to see *those things* which ye see, and have not seen *them;* and to hear *those things* which ye hear, and have not heard *them.*
¹⁸ Hear ye therefore the parable of the sower.
¹⁹ When any one heareth the word of the kingdom, and understandeth *it* not, then cometh the wicked *one,* and catcheth away that which was sown in his heart. This is he which received seed by the way side.
²⁰ But he that received the seed into stony places, the same is he that heareth the word, and anon with joy receiveth it;
²¹ Yet hath he not root in himself, but dureth for a while: for when tribulation or persecution ariseth because of the word, by and by he is offended.
²² He also that received seed among the thorns is he that heareth the word; and the care of this world, and the deceitfulness of riches, choke the word, and he becometh unfruitful.
²³ But he that received seed into the good ground is he that heareth the word, and understandeth *it;* which also beareth fruit, and bringeth forth, some an hundredfold, some sixty, some thirty.
²⁴ Another parable put he forth unto them, saying, The kingdom of heaven is likened unto a man which sowed good seed in his field:
²⁵ But while men slept, his enemy came and sowed tares among the wheat, and went his way.
²⁶ But when the blade was sprung up, and brought forth fruit, then appeared the tares also.
²⁷ So the servants of the householder came and said unto him, Sir, didst not thou sow good seed in thy field? from whence then hath it tares?
²⁸ He said unto them, An enemy hath done this. The servants said unto him, Wilt thou then that we go and gather them up?
²⁹ But he said, Nay; lest while ye gather up the tares, ye root up also the wheat with them.
³⁰ Let both grow together until the harvest: and in the time of harvest I will say to the reapers, Gather ye together first the tares, and bind them in bundles to burn them: but gather the wheat into my barn.
³¹ Another parable put he forth unto them,

saying, The kingdom of heaven is like to a grain of mustard seed, which a man took, and sowed in his field:
³² Which indeed is the least of all seeds: but when it is grown, it is the greatest among herbs, and becometh a tree, so that the birds of the air come and lodge in the branches thereof.
³³ Another parable spake he unto them; The kingdom of heaven is like unto leaven, which a woman took, and hid in three measures of meal, till the whole was leavened.
³⁴ All these things spake Jesus unto the multitude in parables; and without a parable spake he not unto them:
³⁵ That it might be fulfilled which was spoken by the prophet, saying, I will open my mouth in parables; I will utter things which have been kept secret from the foundation of the world.
³⁶ Then Jesus sent the multitude away, and went into the house: and his disciples came unto him, saying, Declare unto us the parable of the tares of the field.
³⁷ He answered and said unto them, He that soweth the good seed is the Son of man;
³⁸ The field is the world; the good seed are the children of the kingdom; but the tares are the children of the wicked *one;*
³⁹ The enemy that sowed them is the devil; the harvest is the end of the world; and the reapers are the angels.
⁴⁰ As therefore the tares are gathered and burned in the fire; so shall it be in the end of this world.
⁴¹ The Son of man shall send forth his angels, and they shall gather out of his kingdom all things that offend, and them which do iniquity;
⁴² And shall cast them into a furnace of fire: there shall be wailing and gnashing of teeth.
⁴³ Then shall the righteous shine forth as the sun in the kingdom of their Father. Who hath ears to hear, let him hear.
⁴⁴ Again, the kingdom of heaven is like unto treasure hid in a field; the which when a man hath found, he hideth, and for joy thereof goeth and selleth all that he hath, and buyeth that field.
⁴⁵ Again, the kingdom of heaven is like unto a merchant man, seeking goodly pearls:
⁴⁶ Who, when he had found one pearl of great price, went and sold all that he had, and bought it.
⁴⁷ Again, the kingdom of heaven is like unto a

net, that was cast into the sea, and gathered of every kind:

⁴⁸ Which, when it was full, they drew to shore, and sat down, and gathered the good into vessels, but cast the bad away.

⁴⁹ So shall it be at the end of the world: the angels shall come forth, and sever the wicked from among the just,

⁵⁰ And shall cast them into the furnace of fire: there shall be wailing and gnashing of teeth.

⁵¹ Jesus saith unto them, Have ye understood all these things? They say unto him, Yea, Lord.

⁵² Then said he unto them, Therefore every scribe *which is* instructed unto the kingdom of heaven is like unto a man *that is* an householder, which bringeth forth out of his treasure *things* new and old.

⁵³ And it came to pass, *that* when Jesus had finished these parables, he departed thence.

⁵⁴ And when he was come into his own country, he taught them in their synagogue, insomuch that they were astonished, and said, Whence hath this *man* this wisdom, and *these* mighty works?

⁵⁵ Is not this the carpenter's son? is not his mother called Mary? and his brethren, James, and Joses, and Simon, and Judas?

⁵⁶ And his sisters, are they not all with us? Whence then hath this *man* all these things?

⁵⁷ And they were offended in him. But Jesus said unto them, A prophet is not without honour, save in his own country, and in his own house.

⁵⁸ And he did not many mighty works there because of their unbelief.

14 At that time Herod the tetrarch heard of the fame of Jesus,

² And said unto his servants, This is John the Baptist; he is risen from the dead; and therefore mighty works do shew forth themselves in him.

³For Herod had laid hold on John, and bound him, and put *him* in prison for Herodias' sake, his brother Philip's wife.

⁴ For John said unto him, It is not lawful for thee to have her.

⁵ And when he would have put him to death, he feared the multitude, because they counted him as a prophet.

⁶ But when Herod's birthday was kept, the daughter of Herodias danced before them, and pleased Herod.

⁷ Whereupon he promised with an oath to give her whatsoever she would ask.

⁸ And she, being before instructed of her mother, said, Give me here John Baptist's head in a charger.

⁹ And the king was sorry: nevertheless for the oath's sake, and them which sat with him at meat, he commanded *it* to be given *her.*

¹⁰ And he sent, and beheaded John in the prison.

¹¹ And his head was brought in a charger, and given to the damsel: and she brought *it* to her mother.

¹² And his disciples came, and took up the body, and buried it, and went and told Jesus.

¹³ When Jesus heard *of it,* he departed thence by ship into a desert place apart: and when the people had heard *thereof,* they followed him on foot out of the cities.

¹⁴ And Jesus went forth, and saw a great multitude, and was moved with compassion toward them, and he healed their sick.

¹⁵ And when it was evening, his disciples came to him, saying, This is a desert place, and the time is now past; send the multitude away, that they may go into the villages, and buy themselves victuals.

¹⁶ But Jesus said unto them, They need not depart; give ye them to eat.

¹⁷ And they say unto him, We have here but five loaves, and two fishes.

¹⁸ He said, Bring them hither to me.

¹⁹ And he commanded the multitude to sit down on the grass, and took the five loaves, and the two fishes, and looking up to heaven, he blessed, and brake, and gave the loaves to *his* disciples, and the disciples to the multitude.

²⁰ And they did all eat, and were filled: and they took up of the fragments that remained twelve baskets full.

²¹ And they that had eaten were about five thousand men, beside women and children.

²² And straightway Jesus constrained his disciples to get into a ship, and to go before him unto the other side, while he sent the multitudes away.

²³ And when he had sent the multitudes away, he went up into a mountain apart to pray: and when the evening was come, he was there alone.

²⁴ But the ship was now in the midst of the sea, tossed with waves: for the wind was contrary.

²⁵ And in the fourth watch of the night Jesus went unto them, walking on the sea.

26 And when the disciples saw him walking on the sea, they were troubled, saying, It is a spirit; and they cried out for fear.

27 But straightway Jesus spake unto them, saying, Be of good cheer; it is I; be not afraid.

28 And Peter answered him and said, Lord, if it be thou, bid me come unto thee on the water.

29 And he said, Come. And when Peter was come down out of the ship, he walked on the water, to go to Jesus.

30 But when he saw the wind boisterous, he was afraid; and beginning to sink, he cried, saying, Lord, save me.

31 And immediately Jesus stretched forth *his* hand, and caught him, and said unto him, O thou of little faith, wherefore didst thou doubt?

32 And when they were come into the ship, the wind ceased.

33 Then they that were in the ship came and worshipped him, saying, Of a truth thou art the Son of God.

34 And when they were gone over, they came into the land of Gennesaret.

35 And when the men of that place had knowledge of him, they sent out into all that country round about, and brought unto him all that were diseased;

36 And besought him that they might only touch the hem of his garment: and as many as touched were made perfectly whole.

15 Then came to Jesus scribes and Pharisees, which were of Jerusalem, saying,

2 Why do thy disciples transgress the tradition of the elders? for they wash not their hands when they eat bread.

3 But he answered and said unto them, Why do ye also transgress the commandment of God by your tradition?

4 For God commanded, saying, Honour thy father and mother: and, He that curseth father or mother, let him die the death.

5 But ye say, Whosoever shall say to *his* father or *his* mother, *It is* a gift, by whatsoever thou mightest be profited by me;

6 And honour not his father or his mother, *he shall be free.* Thus have ye made the commandment of God of none effect by your tradition.

7 *Ye* hypocrites, well did Esaias prophesy of you, saying,

8 This people draweth nigh unto me with their mouth, and honoureth me with *their* lips; but their heart is far from me.

9 But in vain they do worship me, teaching *for* doctrines the commandments of men.

10 And he called the multitude, and said unto them, Hear, and understand:

11 Not that which goeth into the mouth defileth a man; but that which cometh out of the mouth, this defileth a man.

12 Then came his disciples, and said unto him, Knowest thou that the Pharisees were offended, after they heard this saying?

13 But he answered and said, Every plant, which my heavenly Father hath not planted, shall be rooted up.

14 Let them alone: they be blind leaders of the blind. And if the blind lead the blind, both shall fall into the ditch.

15 Then answered Peter and said unto him, Declare unto us this parable.

16 And Jesus said, Are ye also yet without understanding?

17 Do not ye yet understand, that whatsoever entereth in at the mouth goeth into the belly, and is cast out into the draught?

18 But those things which proceed out of the mouth come forth from the heart; and they defile the man.

19 For out of the heart proceed evil thoughts, murders, adulteries, fornications, thefts, false witness, blasphemies:

20 These are *the things* which defile a man: but to eat with unwashen hands defileth not a man.

21 Then Jesus went thence, and departed into the coasts of Tyre and Sidon.

22 And, behold, a woman of Canaan came out of the same coasts, and cried unto him, saying, Have mercy on me, O Lord, *thou* Son of David; my daughter is grievously vexed with a devil.

23 But he answered her not a word. And his disciples came and besought him, saying, Send her away; for she crieth after us.

24 But he answered and said, I am not sent but unto the lost sheep of the house of Israel.

25 Then came she and worshipped him, saying, Lord, help me.

26 But he answered and said, It is not meet to take the children's bread, and to cast *it* to dogs.

27 And she said, Truth, Lord: yet the dogs eat of the crumbs which fall from their masters' table.

28 Then Jesus answered and said unto her, O woman, great *is* thy faith: be it unto thee even as thou wilt. And her daughter was made whole from that very hour.

29 And Jesus departed from thence, and came nigh unto the sea of Galilee; and went up into a mountain, and sat down there.

30 And great multitudes came unto him, having with them *those that were* lame, blind, dumb, maimed, and many others, and cast them down at Jesus' feet; and he healed them:

31 Insomuch that the multitude wondered, when they saw the dumb to speak, the maimed to be whole, the lame to walk, and the blind to see: and they glorified the God of Israel.

32 Then Jesus called his disciples *unto him,* and said, I have compassion on the multitude, because they continue with me now three days, and have nothing to eat: and I will not send them away fasting, lest they faint in the way.

33 And his disciples say unto him, Whence should we have so much bread in the wilderness, as to fill so great a multitude?

34 And Jesus saith unto them, How many loaves have ye? And they said, Seven, and a few little fishes.

35 And he commanded the multitude to sit down on the ground.

36 And he took the seven loaves and the fishes, and gave thanks, and brake *them,* and gave to his disciples, and the disciples to the multitude.

37 And they did all eat, and were filled: and they took up of the broken *meat* that was left seven baskets full.

38 And they that did eat were four thousand men, beside women and children.

39 And he sent away the multitude, and took ship, and came into the coasts of Magdala,

16 The Pharisees also with the Sadducees came, and tempting desired him that he would shew them a sign from heaven.

2 He answered and said unto them, When it is evening, ye say, *It will be* fair weather: for the sky is red.

3 And in the morning, *It will be* foul weather to day: for the sky is red and lowring. O *ye* hypocrites, ye can discern the face of the sky; but can ye not *discern* the signs of the times?

4 A wicked and adulterous generation seeketh after a sign; and there shall no sign be given unto it, but the sign of the prophet Jonas. And he left them, and departed.

5 And when his disciples were come to the other side, they had forgotten to take bread.

6 Then Jesus said unto them, Take heed and beware of the leaven of the Pharisees and of the Sadducees.

7 And they reasoned among themselves, saying, *It is* because we have taken no bread.

8 *Which* when Jesus perceived, he said unto them, O ye of little faith, why reason ye among yourselves, because ye have brought no bread?

9 Do ye not yet understand, neither remember the five loaves of the five thousand, and how many baskets ye took up?

10 Neither the seven loaves of the four thousand, and how many baskets ye took up?

11 How is it that ye do not understand that I spake *it* not to you concerning bread, that ye should beware of the leaven of the Pharisees and of the Sadducees?

12 Then understood they how that he bade *them* not beware of the leaven of bread, but of the doctrine of the Pharisees and of the Sadducees.

13 When Jesus came into the coasts of Caesarea Philippi, he asked his disciples, saying, Whom do men say that I the Son of man am?

14 And they said, Some *say that thou art* John the Baptist: some, Elias; and others, Jeremias, or one of the prophets.

15 He saith unto them, But whom say ye that I am?

16 And Simon Peter answered and said, Thou art the Christ, the Son of the living God.

17 And Jesus answered and said unto him, Blessed art thou, Simon Barjona: for flesh and blood hath not revealed *it* unto thee, but my Father which is in heaven.

18 And I say also unto thee, That thou art Peter, and upon this rock I will build my church; and the gates of hell shall not prevail against it.

19 And I will give unto thee the keys of the kingdom of heaven: and whatsoever thou shalt bind on earth shall be bound in heaven: and whatsoever thou shalt loose on earth shall be loosed in heaven.

20 Then charged he his disciples that they should tell no man that he was Jesus the Christ.

21 From that time forth began Jesus to shew unto his disciples, how that he must go unto Jerusalem, and suffer many things of the elders and chief priests and scribes, and be killed, and be raised again the third day.

22 Then Peter took him, and began to rebuke him, saying, Be it far from thee, Lord: this shall not be unto thee.

23 But he turned, and said unto Peter, Get thee behind me, Satan: thou art an offence unto me: for thou savourest not the things that be of God, but those that be of men.

24 Then said Jesus unto his disciples, If any *man* will come after me, let him deny himself, and take up his cross, and follow me.

25 For whosoever will save his life shall lose it: and whosoever will lose his life for my sake shall find it.

26 For what is a man profited, if he shall gain the whole world, and lose his own soul? or what shall a man give in exchange for his soul?

27 For the Son of man shall come in the glory of his Father with his angels; and then he shall reward every man according to his works.

28 Verily I say unto you, There be some standing here, which shall not taste of death, till they see the Son of man coming in his kingdom.

17 And after six days Jesus taketh Peter, James, and John his brother, and bringeth them up into an high mountain apart,

2 And was transfigured before them: and his face did shine as the sun, and his raiment was white as the light.

3 And, behold, there appeared unto them Moses and Elias talking with him.

4 Then answered Peter, and said unto Jesus, Lord, it is good for us to be here: if thou wilt, let us make here three tabernacles; one for thee, and one for Moses, and one for Elias.

5 While he yet spake, behold, a bright cloud overshadowed them: and behold a voice out of the cloud, which said, This is my beloved Son, in whom I am well pleased; hear ye him.

6 And when the disciples heard *it*, they fell on their face, and were sore afraid.

7 And Jesus came and touched them, and said, Arise, and be not afraid.

8 And when they had lifted up their eyes, they saw no man, save Jesus only.

9 And as they came down from the mountain, Jesus charged them, saying, Tell the vision to no man, until the Son of man be risen again from the dead.

10 And his disciples asked him, saying, Why then say the scribes that Elias must first come?

11 And Jesus answered and said unto them, Elias truly shall first come, and restore all things.

12 But I say unto you, That Elias is come already, and they knew him not, but have done unto him whatsoever they listed. Likewise shall also the Son of man suffer of them.

13 Then the disciples understood that he spake unto them of John the Baptist.

14 And when they were come to the multitude, there came to him a *certain* man, kneeling down to him, and saying,

15 Lord, have mercy on my son: for he is lunatick, and sore vexed: for ofttimes he falleth into the fire, and oft into the water.

16 And I brought him to thy disciples, and they could not cure him.

17 Then Jesus answered and said, O faithless and perverse generation, how long shall I be with you? how long shall I suffer you? bring him hither to me.

18 And Jesus rebuked the devil; and he departed out of him: and the child was cured from that very hour.

19 Then came the disciples to Jesus apart, and said, Why could not we cast him out?

20 And Jesus said unto them, Because of your unbelief: for verily I say unto you, If ye have faith as a grain of mustard seed, ye shall say unto this mountain, Remove hence to yonder place; and it shall remove; and nothing shall be impossible unto you.

21 Howbeit this kind goeth not out but by prayer and fasting.

22 And while they abode in Galilee, Jesus said unto them, The Son of man shall be betrayed into the hands of men:

23 And they shall kill him, and the third day he shall be raised again. And they were exceeding sorry.

24 And when they were come to Capernaum, they that received tribute *money* came to Peter, and said, Doth not your master pay tribute?

25 He saith, Yes. And when he was come into the house, Jesus prevented him, saying, What thinkest thou, Simon? of whom do the kings of the earth take custom or tribute? of their own children, or of strangers?

26 Peter saith unto him, Of strangers. Jesus saith unto him, Then are the children free.

27 Notwithstanding, lest we should offend them, go thou to the sea, and cast an hook, and take up the fish that first cometh up; and when thou hast opened his mouth, thou shalt find a piece of money: that take, and give unto them for me and thee.

18 At the same time came the disciples unto Jesus, saying, Who is the greatest in the kingdom of heaven?

2 And Jesus called a little child unto him, and set him in the midst of them,

3 And said, Verily I say unto you, Except ye be converted, and become as little children, ye shall not enter into the kingdom of heaven.

4 Whosoever therefore shall humble himself as this little child, the same is greatest in the kingdom of heaven.

5 And whoso shall receive one such little child in my name receiveth me.

6 But whoso shall offend one of these little ones which believe in me, it were better for him that a millstone were hanged about his neck, and *that* he were drowned in the depth of the sea.

7 Woe unto the world because of offences! for it must needs be that offences come; but woe to that man by whom the offence cometh!

8 Wherefore if thy hand or thy foot offend thee, cut them off, and cast *them* from thee: it is better for thee to enter into life halt or maimed, rather than having two hands or two feet to be cast into everlasting fire.

9 And if thine eye offend thee, pluck it out, and cast *it* from thee: it is better for thee to enter into life with one eye, rather than having two eyes to be cast into hell fire.

10 Take heed that ye despise not one of these little ones; for I say unto you, That in heaven their angels do always behold the face of my Father which is in heaven.

11 For the Son of man is come to save that which was lost.

12 How think ye? if a man have an hundred sheep, and one of them be gone astray, doth he not leave the ninety and nine, and goeth into the mountains, and seeketh that which is gone astray?

13 And if so be that he find it, verily I say unto you, he rejoiceth more of that *sheep*, than of the ninety and nine which went not astray.

14 Even so it is not the will of your Father which is in heaven, that one of these little ones should perish.

15 Moreover if thy brother shall trespass against thee, go and tell him his fault between thee and him alone: if he shall hear thee, thou hast gained thy brother.

16 But if he will not hear *thee, then* take with thee one or two more, that in the mouth of two or three witnesses every word may be established.

17 And if he shall neglect to hear them, tell *it* unto the church: but if he neglect to hear the church, let him be unto thee as an heathen man and a publican.

18 Verily I say unto you, Whatsoever ye shall bind on earth shall be bound in heaven: and whatsoever ye shall loose on earth shall be loosed in heaven.

19 Again I say unto you, That if two of you shall agree on earth as touching any thing that they shall ask, it shall be done for them of my Father which is in heaven.

20 For where two or three are gathered together in my name, there am I in the midst of them.

21 Then came Peter to him, and said, Lord, how oft shall my brother sin against me, and I forgive him? till seven times?

22 Jesus saith unto him, I say not unto thee, Until seven times: but, Until seventy times seven.

23 Therefore is the kingdom of heaven likened unto a certain king, which would take account of his servants.

24 And when he had begun to reckon, one was brought unto him, which owed him ten thousand talents.

25 But forasmuch as he had not to pay, his lord commanded him to be sold, and his wife, and children, and all that he had, and payment to be made.

26 The servant therefore fell down, and worshipped him, saying, Lord, have patience with me, and I will pay thee all.

27 Then the lord of that servant was moved with compassion, and loosed him, and forgave him the debt.

28 But the same servant went out, and found one of his fellowservants, which owed him an hundred pence: and he laid hands on him, and took *him* by the throat, saying, Pay me that thou owest.

29 And his fellowservant fell down at his feet, and besought him, saying, Have patience with me, and I will pay thee all.

30 And he would not: but went and cast him into prison, till he should pay the debt.

31 So when his fellowservants saw what was done, they were very sorry, and came and told unto their lord all that was done.

32 Then his lord, after that he had called him, said unto him, O thou wicked servant, I

forgave thee all that debt, because thou desiredst me:

³³ Shouldest not thou also have had compassion on thy fellowservant, even as I had pity on thee?

³⁴ And his lord was wroth, and delivered him to the tormentors, till he should pay all that was due unto him.

³⁵ So likewise shall my heavenly Father do also unto you, if ye from your hearts forgive not every one his brother their trespasses.

19 And it came to pass, *that* when Jesus had finished these sayings, he departed from Galilee, and came into the coasts of Judaea beyond Jordan;

² And great multitudes followed him; and he healed them there.

³The Pharisees also came unto him, tempting him, and saying unto him, Is it lawful for a man to put away his wife for every cause?

⁴ And he answered and said unto them, Have ye not read, that he which made *them* at the beginning made them male and female,

⁵ And said, For this cause shall a man leave father and mother, and shall cleave to his wife: and they twain shall be one flesh?

⁶ Wherefore they are no more twain, but one flesh. What therefore God hath joined together, let not man put asunder.

⁷ They say unto him, Why did Moses then command to give a writing of divorcement, and to put her away?

⁸ He saith unto them, Moses because of the hardness of your hearts suffered you to put away your wives: but from the beginning it was not so.

⁹ And I say unto you, Whosoever shall put away his wife, except *it be* for fornication, and shall marry another, committeth adultery: and whoso marrieth her which is put away doth commit adultery.

¹⁰ His disciples say unto him, If the case of the man be so with *his* wife, it is not good to marry.

¹¹ But he said unto them, All *men* cannot receive this saying, save *they* to whom it is given.

¹² For there are some eunuchs, which were so born from *their* mother's womb: and there are some eunuchs, which were made eunuchs of men: and there be eunuchs, which have made themselves eunuchs for the kingdom of heaven's sake. He that is able to receive *it*, let him receive *it*.

¹³ Then were there brought unto him little children, that he should put *his* hands on them, and pray: and the disciples rebuked them.

¹⁴ But Jesus said, Suffer little children, and forbid them not, to come unto me: for of such is the kingdom of heaven.

¹⁵ And he laid *his* hands on them, and departed thence.

¹⁶ And, behold, one came and said unto him, Good Master, what good thing shall I do, that I may have eternal life?

¹⁷ And he said unto him, Why callest thou me good? *there is* none good but one, *that is*, God: but if thou wilt enter into life, keep the commandments.

¹⁸ He saith unto him, Which? Jesus said, Thou shalt do no murder, Thou shalt not commit adultery, Thou shalt not steal, Thou shalt not bear false witness,

¹⁹ Honour thy father and *thy* mother: and, Thou shalt love thy neighbour as thyself.

²⁰ The young man saith unto him, All these things have I kept from my youth up: what lack I yet?

²¹ Jesus said unto him, If thou wilt be perfect, go *and* sell that thou hast, and give to the poor, and thou shalt have treasure in heaven: and come *and* follow me.

²² But when the young man heard that saying, he went away sorrowful: for he had great possessions.

²³ Then said Jesus unto his disciples, Verily I say unto you, That a rich man shall hardly enter into the kingdom of heaven.

²⁴ And again I say unto you, It is easier for a camel to go through the eye of a needle, than for a rich man to enter into the kingdom of God.

²⁵ When his disciples heard *it*, they were exceedingly amazed, saying, Who then can be saved?

²⁶ But Jesus beheld *them*, and said unto them, With men this is impossible; but with God all things are possible.

²⁷ Then answered Peter and said unto him, Behold, we have forsaken all, and followed thee; what shall we have therefore?

²⁸ And Jesus said unto them, Verily I say unto you, That ye which have followed me, in the regeneration when the Son of man shall sit in the throne of his glory, ye also shall sit upon twelve thrones, judging the twelve tribes of Israel.

²⁹ And every one that hath forsaken houses, or brethren, or sisters, or father, or mother, or

wife, or children, or lands, for my name's sake, shall receive an hundredfold, and shall inherit everlasting life.

30 But many *that are* first shall be last; and the last *shall be* first.

20 For the kingdom of heaven is like unto a man *that is* an householder, which went out early in the morning to hire labourers into his vineyard.

2 And when he had agreed with the labourers for a penny a day, he sent them into his vineyard.

3 And he went out about the third hour, and saw others standing idle in the marketplace,

4 And said unto them; Go ye also into the vineyard, and whatsoever is right I will give you. And they went their way.

5 Again he went out about the sixth and ninth hour, and did likewise.

6 And about the eleventh hour he went out, and found others standing idle, and saith unto them, Why stand ye here all the day idle?

7 They say unto him, Because no man hath hired us. He saith unto them, Go ye also into the vineyard; and whatsoever is right, *that* shall ye receive.

8 So when even was come, the lord of the vineyard saith unto his steward, Call the labourers, and give them *their* hire, beginning from the last unto the first.

9 And when they came that *were hired* about the eleventh hour, they received every man a penny.

10 But when the first came, they supposed that they should have received more; and they likewise received every man a penny.

11 And when they had received it, they murmured against the goodman of the house,

12 Saying, These last have wrought *but* one hour, and thou hast made them equal unto us, which have borne the burden and heat of the day.

13 But he answered one of them, and said, Friend, I do thee no wrong: didst not thou agree with me for a penny?

14 Take *that* thine *is*, and go thy way: I will give unto this last, even as unto thee.

15 Is it not lawful for me to do what I will with mine own? Is thine eye evil, because I am good?

16 So the last shall be first, and the first last: for many be called, but few chosen.

17 And Jesus going up to Jerusalem took the twelve disciples apart in the way, and said unto them,

18 Behold, we go up to Jerusalem; and the Son of man shall be betrayed unto the chief priests and unto the scribes, and they shall condemn him to death,

19 And shall deliver him to the Gentiles to mock, and to scourge, and to crucify *him:* and the third day he shall rise again.

20 Then came to him the mother of Zebedee's children with her sons, worshipping *him,* and desiring a certain thing of him.

21 And he said unto her, What wilt thou? She saith unto him, Grant that these my two sons may sit, the one on thy right hand, and the other on the left, in thy kingdom.

22 But Jesus answered and said, Ye know not what ye ask. Are ye able to drink of the cup that I shall drink of, and to be baptized with the baptism that I am baptized with? They say unto him, We are able.

23 And he saith unto them, Ye shall drink indeed of my cup, and be baptized with the baptism that I am baptized with: but to sit on my right hand, and on my left, is not mine to give, but *it shall be given to them* for whom it is prepared of my Father.

24 And when the ten heard *it,* they were moved with indignation against the two brethren.

25 But Jesus called them *unto him,* and said, Ye know that the princes of the Gentiles exercise dominion over them, and they that are great exercise authority upon them.

26 But it shall not be so among you: but whosoever will be great among you, let him be your minister;

27 And whosoever will be chief among you, let him be your servant:

28 Even as the Son of man came not to be ministered unto, but to minister, and to give his life a ransom for many.

29 And as they departed from Jericho, a great multitude followed him.

30 And, behold, two blind men sitting by the way side, when they heard that Jesus passed by, cried out, saying, Have mercy on us, O☐Lord, *thou* Son of David.

31 And the multitude rebuked them, because they should hold their peace: but they cried the more, saying, Have mercy on us, O Lord, *thou* Son of David.

32 And Jesus stood still, and called them, and said, What will ye that I shall do unto you?

33 They say unto him, Lord, that our eyes may be opened.

34 So Jesus had compassion *on them,* and

touched their eyes: and immediately their eyes received sight, and they followed him.

21 And when they drew nigh unto Jerusalem, and were come to Bethphage, unto the mount of Olives, then sent Jesus two disciples,

2 Saying unto them, Go into the village over against you, and straightway ye shall find an ass tied, and a colt with her: loose *them*, and bring *them* unto me.

3 And if any *man* say ought unto you, ye shall say, The Lord hath need of them; and straightway he will send them.

4 All this was done, that it might be fulfilled which was spoken by the prophet, saying,

5 Tell ye the daughter of Sion, Behold, thy King cometh unto thee, meek, and sitting upon an ass, and a colt the foal of an ass.

6 And the disciples went, and did as Jesus commanded them,

7 And brought the ass, and the colt, and put on them their clothes, and they set *him* thereon.

8 And a very great multitude spread their garments in the way; others cut down branches from the trees, and strawed *them* in the way.

9 And the multitudes that went before, and that followed, cried, saying, Hosanna to the Son of David: Blessed *is* he that cometh in the name of the Lord; Hosanna in the highest.

10 And when he was come into Jerusalem, all the city was moved, saying, Who is this?

11 And the multitude said, This is Jesus the prophet of Nazareth of Galilee.

12 And Jesus went into the temple of God, and cast out all them that sold and bought in the temple, and overthrew the tables of the moneychangers, and the seats of them that sold doves,

13 And said unto them, It is written, My house shall be called the house of prayer; but ye have made it a den of thieves.

14 And the blind and the lame came to him in the temple; and he healed them.

15 And when the chief priests and scribes saw the wonderful things that he did, and the children crying in the temple, and saying, Hosanna to the Son of David; they were sore displeased,

16 And said unto him, Hearest thou what these say? And Jesus saith unto them, Yea; have ye never read, Out of the mouth of babes and sucklings thou hast perfected praise?

17 And he left them, and went out of the city into Bethany; and he lodged there.

18 Now in the morning as he returned into the city, he hungered.

19 And when he saw a fig tree in the way, he came to it, and found nothing thereon, but leaves only, and said unto it, Let no fruit grow on thee henceforward for ever. And presently the fig tree withered away.

20 And when the disciples saw *it*, they marvelled, saying, How soon is the fig tree withered away!

21 Jesus answered and said unto them, Verily I say unto you, If ye have faith, and doubt not, ye shall not only do this *which is done* to the fig tree, but also if ye shall say unto this mountain, Be thou removed, and be thou cast into the sea; it shall be done.

22 And all things, whatsoever ye shall ask in prayer, believing, ye shall receive.

23 And when he was come into the temple, the chief priests and the elders of the people came unto him as he was teaching, and said, By what authority doest thou these things? and who gave thee this authority?

24 And Jesus answered and said unto them, I also will ask you one thing, which if ye tell me, I in like wise will tell you by what authority I do these things.

25 The baptism of John, whence was it? from heaven, or of men? And they reasoned with themselves, saying, If we shall say, From heaven; he will say unto us, Why did ye not then believe him?

26 But if we shall say, Of men; we fear the people; for all hold John as a prophet.

27 And they answered Jesus, and said, We cannot tell. And he said unto them, Neither tell I you by what authority I do these things.

28 But what think ye? A *certain* man had two sons; and he came to the first, and said, Son, go work to day in my vineyard.

29 He answered and said, I will not: but afterward he repented, and went.

30 And he came to the second, and said likewise. And he answered and said, I *go*, sir: and went not.

31 Whether of them twain did the will of *his* father? They say unto him, The first. Jesus saith unto them, Verily I say unto you, That the publicans and the harlots go into the kingdom of God before you.

32 For John came unto you in the way of righteousness, and ye believed him not: but the publicans and the harlots believed him: and ye, when ye had seen *it*, repented not afterward, that ye might believe him.

33 Hear another parable: There was a certain householder, which planted a vineyard, and hedged it round about, and digged a winepress in it, and built a tower, and let it out to husbandmen, and went into a far country:

34 And when the time of the fruit drew near, he sent his servants to the husbandmen, that they might receive the fruits of it.

35 And the husbandmen took his servants, and beat one, and killed another, and stoned another.

36 Again, he sent other servants more than the first: and they did unto them likewise.

37 But last of all he sent unto them his son, saying, They will reverence my son.

38 But when the husbandmen saw the son, they said among themselves, This is the heir; come, let us kill him, and let us seize on his inheritance.

39 And they caught him, and cast *him* out of the vineyard, and slew *him.*

40 When the lord therefore of the vineyard cometh, what will he do unto those husbandmen?

41 They say unto him, He will miserably destroy those wicked men, and will let out *his* vineyard unto other husbandmen, which shall render him the fruits in their seasons.

42 Jesus saith unto them, Did ye never read in the scriptures, The stone which the builders rejected, the same is become the head of the corner: this is the Lord's doing, and it is marvellous in our eyes?

43 Therefore say I unto you, The kingdom of God shall be taken from you, and given to a nation bringing forth the fruits thereof.

44 And whosoever shall fall on this stone shall be broken: but on whomsoever it shall fall, it will grind him to powder.

45 And when the chief priests and Pharisees had heard his parables, they perceived that he spake of them.

46 But when they sought to lay hands on him, they feared the multitude, because they took him for a prophet.

22 And Jesus answered and spake unto them again by parables, and said,

2 The kingdom of heaven is like unto a certain king, which made a marriage for his son,

3 And sent forth his servants to call them that were bidden to the wedding: and they would not come.

4 Again, he sent forth other servants, saying, Tell them which are bidden, Behold, I have pre-

pared my dinner: my oxen and *my* fatlings *are* killed, and all things *are* ready: come unto the marriage.

5 But they made light of *it,* and went their ways, one to his farm, another to his merchandise:

6 And the remnant took his servants, and entreated *them* spitefully, and slew *them.*

7 But when the king heard *thereof,* he was wroth: and he sent forth his armies, and destroyed those murderers, and burned up their city.

8 Then saith he to his servants, The wedding is ready, but they which were bidden were not worthy.

9 Go ye therefore into the highways, and as many as ye shall find, bid to the marriage.

10 So those servants went out into the highways, and gathered together all as many as they found, both bad and good: and the wedding was furnished with guests.

11 And when the king came in to see the guests, he saw there a man which had not on a wedding garment:

12 And he saith unto him, Friend, how camest thou in hither not having a wedding garment? And he was speechless.

13 Then said the king to the servants, Bind him hand and foot, and take him away, and cast *him* into outer darkness; there shall be weeping and gnashing of teeth.

14 For many are called, but few *are* chosen.

15 Then went the Pharisees, and took counsel how they might entangle him in *his* talk.

16 And they sent out unto him their disciples with the Herodians, saying, Master, we know that thou art true, and teachest the way of God in truth, neither carest thou for any *man:* for thou regardest not the person of men.

17 Tell us therefore, What thinkest thou? Is it lawful to give tribute unto Caesar, or not?

18 But Jesus perceived their wickedness, and said, Why tempt ye me, *ye* hypocrites?

19 Shew me the tribute money. And they brought unto him a penny.

20 And he saith unto them, Whose *is* this image and superscription?

21 They say unto him, Caesar's. Then saith he unto them, Render therefore unto Caesar the things which are Caesar's; and unto God the things that are God's.

22 When they had heard *these words,* they marvelled, and left him, and went their way.

23 The same day came to him the Sadducees,

which say that there is no resurrection, and asked him,

²⁴ Saying, Master, Moses said, If a man die, having no children, his brother shall marry his wife, and raise up seed unto his brother.

²⁵ Now there were with us seven brethren: and the first, when he had married a wife, deceased, and, having no issue, left his wife unto his brother:

²⁶ Likewise the second also, and the third, unto the seventh.

²⁷ And last of all the woman died also.

²⁸ Therefore in the resurrection whose wife shall she be of the seven? for they all had her.

²⁹ Jesus answered and said unto them, Ye do err, not knowing the scriptures, nor the power of God.

³⁰ For in the resurrection they neither marry, nor are given in marriage, but are as the angels of God in heaven.

³¹ But as touching the resurrection of the dead, have ye not read that which was spoken unto you by God, saying,

³² I am the God of Abraham, and the God of Isaac, and the God of Jacob? God is not the God of the dead, but of the living.

³³ And when the multitude heard *this*, they were astonished at his doctrine.

³⁴ But when the Pharisees had heard that he had put the Sadducees to silence, they were gathered together.

³⁵ Then one of them, *which was* a lawyer, asked *him a question*, tempting him, and saying,

³⁶ Master, which *is* the great commandment in the law?

³⁷ Jesus said unto him, Thou shalt love the Lord thy God with all thy heart, and with all thy soul, and with all thy mind.

³⁸ This is the first and great commandment.

³⁹ And the second *is* like unto it, Thou shalt love thy neighbour as thyself.

⁴⁰ On these two commandments hang all the law and the prophets.

⁴¹ While the Pharisees were gathered together, Jesus asked them,

⁴² Saying, What think ye of Christ? whose son is he? They say unto him, *The Son* of David.

⁴³ He saith unto them, How then doth David in spirit call him Lord, saying,

⁴⁴ The LORD said unto my Lord, Sit thou on my right hand, till I make thine enemies thy footstool?

⁴⁵ If David then call him Lord, how is he his son?

⁴⁶ And no man was able to answer him a word, neither durst any *man* from that day forth ask him any more *questions*.

23 Then spake Jesus to the multitude, and to his disciples,

² Saying, The scribes and the Pharisees sit in Moses' seat:

³ All therefore whatsoever they bid you observe, *that* observe and do; but do not ye after their works: for they say, and do not.

⁴ For they bind heavy burdens and grievous to be borne, and lay *them* on men's shoulders; but they *themselves* will not move them with one of their fingers.

⁵ But all their works they do for to be seen of men: they make broad their phylacteries, and enlarge the borders of their garments,

⁶ And love the uppermost rooms at feasts, and the chief seats in the synagogues,

⁷ And greetings in the markets, and to be called of men, Rabbi, Rabbi.

⁸ But be not ye called Rabbi: for one is your Master, *even* Christ; and all ye are brethren.

⁹ And call no *man* your father upon the earth: for one is your Father, which is in heaven.

¹⁰ Neither be ye called masters: for one is your Master, *even* Christ.

¹¹ But he that is greatest among you shall be your servant.

¹² And whosoever shall exalt himself shall be abased; and he that shall humble himself shall be exalted.

¹³ But woe unto you, scribes and Pharisees, hypocrites! for ye shut up the kingdom of heaven against men: for ye neither go in *yourselves*, neither suffer ye them that are entering to go in.

¹⁴ Woe unto you, scribes and Pharisees, hypocrites! for ye devour widows' houses, and for a pretence make long prayer: therefore ye shall receive the greater damnation.

¹⁵ Woe unto you, scribes and Pharisees, hypocrites! for ye compass sea and land to make one proselyte, and when he is made, ye make him twofold more the child of hell than yourselves.

¹⁶ Woe unto you, *ye* blind guides, which say, Whosoever shall swear by the temple, it is nothing; but whosoever shall swear by the gold of the temple, he is a debtor!

¹⁷ *Ye* fools and blind: for whether is greater, the gold, or the temple that sanctifieth the gold?

¹⁸ And, Whosoever shall swear by the altar, it is nothing; but whosoever sweareth by the gift that is upon it, he is guilty.

¹⁹ *Ye* fools and blind: for whether *is* greater, the gift, or the altar that sanctifieth the gift?

²⁰ Whoso therefore shall swear by the altar, sweareth by it, and by all things thereon.

²¹ And whoso shall swear by the temple, sweareth by it, and by him that dwelleth therein.

²² And he that shall swear by heaven, sweareth by the throne of God, and by him that sitteth thereon.

²³ Woe unto you, scribes and Pharisees, hypocrites! for ye pay tithe of mint and anise and cummin, and have omitted the weightier *matters* of the law, judgment, mercy, and faith: these ought ye to have done, and not to leave the other undone.

²⁴ *Ye* blind guides, which strain at a gnat, and swallow a camel.

²⁵ Woe unto you, scribes and Pharisees, hypocrites! for ye make clean the outside of the cup and of the platter, but within they are full of extortion and excess.

²⁶ *Thou* blind Pharisee, cleanse first that *which is* within the cup and platter, that the outside of them may be clean also.

²⁷ Woe unto you, scribes and Pharisees, hypocrites! for ye are like unto whited sepulchres, which indeed appear beautiful outward, but are within full of dead *men's* bones, and of all uncleanness.

²⁸ Even so ye also outwardly appear righteous unto men, but within ye are full of hypocrisy and iniquity.

²⁹ Woe unto you, scribes and Pharisees, hypocrites! because ye build the tombs of the prophets, and garnish the sepulchres of the righteous,

³⁰ And say, If we had been in the days of our fathers, we would not have been partakers with them in the blood of the prophets.

³¹ Wherefore ye be witnesses unto yourselves, that ye are the children of them which killed the prophets.

³² Fill ye up then the measure of your fathers.

³³ *Ye* serpents, *ye* generation of vipers, how can ye escape the damnation of hell?

³⁴ Wherefore, behold, I send unto you prophets, and wise men, and scribes: and *some* of them ye shall kill and crucify; and *some* of them shall ye scourge in your synagogues, and persecute *them* from city to city:

³⁵ That upon you may come all the righteous blood shed upon the earth, from the blood of righteous Abel unto the blood of Zacharias son of Barachias, whom ye slew between the temple and the altar.

³⁶ Verily I say unto you, All these things shall come upon this generation.

³⁷ O Jerusalem, Jerusalem, *thou* that killest the prophets, and stonest them which are sent unto thee, how often would I have gathered thy children together, even as a hen gathereth her chickens under *her* wings, and ye would not!

³⁸ Behold, your house is left unto you desolate.

³⁹ For I say unto you, Ye shall not see me henceforth, till ye shall say, Blessed *is* he that cometh in the name of the Lord.

24 And Jesus went out, and departed from the temple: and his disciples came to *him* for to shew him the buildings of the temple.

² And Jesus said unto them, See ye not all these things? verily I say unto you, There shall not be left here one stone upon another, that shall not be thrown down.

³And as he sat upon the mount of Olives, the disciples came unto him privately, saying, Tell us, when shall these things be? and what *shall be* the sign of thy coming, and of the end of the world?

⁴ And Jesus answered and said unto them, Take heed that no man deceive you.

⁵ For many shall come in my name, saying, I am Christ; and shall deceive many.

⁶ And ye shall hear of wars and rumours of wars: see that ye be not troubled: for all *these things* must come to pass, but the end is not yet.

⁷ For nation shall rise against nation, and kingdom against kingdom: and there shall be famines, and pestilences, and earthquakes, in divers places.

⁸ All these *are* the beginning of sorrows.

⁹ Then shall they deliver you up to be afflicted, and shall kill you: and ye shall be hated of all nations for my name's sake.

¹⁰ And then shall many be offended, and shall betray one another, and shall hate one another.

¹¹ And many false prophets shall rise, and shall deceive many.

¹² And because iniquity shall abound, the love of many shall wax cold.

¹³ But he that shall endure unto the end, the same shall be saved.

¹⁴ And this gospel of the kingdom shall be preached in all the world for a witness unto all nations; and then shall the end come.

15 When ye therefore shall see the abomination of desolation, spoken of by Daniel the prophet, stand in the holy place, (whoso readeth, let him understand:)

16 Then let them which be in Judaea flee into the mountains:

17 Let him which is on the housetop not come down to take any thing out of his house:

18 Neither let him which is in the field return back to take his clothes.

19 And woe unto them that are with child, and to them that give suck in those days!

20 But pray ye that your flight be not in the winter, neither on the sabbath day:

21 For then shall be great tribulation, such as was not since the beginning of the world to this time, no, nor ever shall be.

22 And except those days should be shortened, there should no flesh be saved: but for the elect's sake those days shall be shortened.

23 Then if any man shall say unto you, Lo, here *is* Christ, or there; believe *it* not.

24 For there shall arise false Christs, and false prophets, and shall shew great signs and wonders; insomuch that, if *it were* possible, they shall deceive the very elect.

25 Behold, I have told you before.

26 Wherefore if they shall say unto you, Behold, *he is* in the desert; go not forth: behold, he is in the secret chambers; believe *it* not.

27 For as the lightning cometh out of the east, and shineth even unto the west; so shall also the coming of the Son of man be.

28 For wheresoever the carcase is, there will the eagles be gathered together.

29 Immediately after the tribulation of those days shall the sun be darkened, and the moon shall not give her light, and the stars shall fall from heaven, and the powers of the heavens shall be shaken:

30 And then shall appear the sign of the Son of man in heaven: and then shall all the tribes of the earth mourn, and they shall see the Son of man coming in the clouds of heaven with power and great glory.

31 And he shall send his angels with a great sound of a trumpet, and they shall gather together his elect from the four winds, from one end of heaven to the other.

32 Now learn a parable of the fig tree; When his branch is yet tender, and putteth forth leaves, ye know that summer is nigh:

33 So likewise ye, when ye shall see all these things, know that it is near, *even* at the doors.

34 Verily I say unto you, This generation shall not pass, till all these things be fulfilled.

35 Heaven and earth shall pass away, but my words shall not pass away.

36 But of that day and hour knoweth no *man*, no, not the angels of heaven, but my Father only.

37 But as the days of Noe *were*, so shall also the coming of the Son of man be.

38 For as in the days that were before the flood they were eating and drinking, marrying and giving in marriage, until the day that Noe entered into the ark,

39 And knew not until the flood came, and took them all away; so shall also the coming of the Son of man be.

40 Then shall two be in the field; the one shall be taken, and the other left.

41 Two *women shall be* grinding at the mill; the one shall be taken, and the other left.

42 Watch therefore: for ye know not what hour your Lord doth come.

43 But know this, that if the goodman of the house had known in what watch the thief would come, he would have watched, and would not have suffered his house to be broken up.

44 Therefore be ye also ready: for in such an hour as ye think not the Son of man cometh.

45 Who then is a faithful and wise servant, whom his lord hath made ruler over his household, to give them meat in due season?

46 Blessed *is* that servant, whom his lord when he cometh shall find so doing.

47 Verily I say unto you, That he shall make him ruler over all his goods.

48 But and if that evil servant shall say in his heart, My lord delayeth his coming;

49 And shall begin to smite *his* fellowservants, and to eat and drink with the drunken;

50 The lord of that servant shall come in a day when he looketh not for *him*, and in an hour that he is not aware of,

51 And shall cut him asunder, and appoint *him* his portion with the hypocrites: there shall be weeping and gnashing of teeth.

25 Then shall the kingdom of heaven be likened unto ten virgins, which took their lamps, and went forth to meet the bridegroom.

2 And five of them were wise, and five *were* foolish.

3 They that *were* foolish took their lamps, and took no oil with them:

4 But the wise took oil in their vessels with their lamps.

5 While the bridegroom tarried, they all slumbered and slept.

6 And at midnight there was a cry made, Behold, the bridegroom cometh; go ye out to meet him.

7 Then all those virgins arose, and trimmed their lamps.

8 And the foolish said unto the wise, Give us of your oil; for our lamps are gone out.

9 But the wise answered, saying, *Not so;* lest there be not enough for us and you: but go ye rather to them that sell, and buy for yourselves.

10 And while they went to buy, the bridegroom came; and they that were ready went in with him to the marriage: and the door was shut.

11 Afterward came also the other virgins, saying, Lord, Lord, open to us.

12 But he answered and said, Verily I say unto you, I know you not.

13 Watch therefore, for ye know neither the day nor the hour wherein the Son of man cometh.

14 For *the kingdom of heaven is* as a man travelling into a far country, *who* called his own servants, and delivered unto them his goods.

15 And unto one he gave five talents, to another two, and to another one; to every man according to his several ability; and straightway took his journey.

16 Then he that had received the five talents went and traded with the same, and made *them* other five talents.

17 And likewise he that *had received* two, he also gained other two.

18 But he that had received one went and digged in the earth, and hid his lord's money.

19 After a long time the lord of those servants cometh, and reckoneth with them.

20 And so he that had received five talents came and brought other five talents, saying, Lord, thou deliveredst unto me five talents: behold, I have gained beside them five talents more.

21 His lord said unto him, Well done, *thou* good and faithful servant: thou hast been faithful over a few things, I will make thee ruler over many things: enter thou into the joy of thy lord.

22 He also that had received two talents came and said, Lord, thou deliveredst unto me two talents: behold, I have gained two other talents beside them.

23 His lord said unto him, Well done, good and faithful servant; thou hast been faithful over a

few things, I will make thee ruler over many things: enter thou into the joy of thy lord.

24 Then he which had received the one talent came and said, Lord, I knew thee that thou art an hard man, reaping where thou hast not sown, and gathering where thou hast not strawed:

25 And I was afraid, and went and hid thy talent in the earth: lo, *there* thou hast *that is* thine.

26 His lord answered and said unto him, *Thou* wicked and slothful servant, thou knewest that I reap where I sowed not, and gather where I have not strawed:

27 Thou oughtest therefore to have put my money to the exchangers, and *then* at my coming I should have received mine own with usury.

28 Take therefore the talent from him, and give *it* unto him which hath ten talents.

29 For unto every one that hath shall be given, and he shall have abundance: but from him that hath not shall be taken away even that which he hath.

30 And cast ye the unprofitable servant into outer darkness: there shall be weeping and gnashing of teeth.

31 When the Son of man shall come in his glory, and all the holy angels with him, then shall he sit upon the throne of his glory:

32 And before him shall be gathered all nations: and he shall separate them one from another, as a shepherd divideth *his* sheep from the goats:

33 And he shall set the sheep on his right hand, but the goats on the left.

34 Then shall the King say unto them on his right hand, Come, ye blessed of my Father, inherit the kingdom prepared for you from the foundation of the world:

35 For I was an hungred, and ye gave me meat: I was thirsty, and ye gave me drink: I was a stranger, and ye took me in:

36 Naked, and ye clothed me: I was sick, and ye visited me: I was in prison, and ye came unto me.

37 Then shall the righteous answer him, saying, Lord, when saw we thee an hungred, and fed *thee?* or thirsty, and gave *thee* drink?

38 When saw we thee a stranger, and took *thee* in? or naked, and clothed *thee?*

39 Or when saw we thee sick, or in prison, and came unto thee?

40 And the King shall answer and say unto them, Verily I say unto you, Inasmuch as ye have done *it* unto one of the least of these my brethren, ye have done *it* unto me.

41 Then shall he say also unto them on the left hand, Depart from me, ye cursed, into everlasting fire, prepared for the devil and his angels:
42 For I was an hungred, and ye gave me no meat: I was thirsty, and ye gave me no drink:
43 I was a stranger, and ye took me not in: naked, and ye clothed me not: sick, and in prison, and ye visited me not.
44 Then shall they also answer him, saying, Lord, when saw we thee an hungred, or athirst, or a stranger, or naked, or sick, or in prison, and did not minister unto thee?
45 Then shall he answer them, saying, Verily I say unto you, Inasmuch as ye did *it* not to one of the least of these, ye did *it* not to me.
46 And these shall go away into everlasting punishment: but the righteous into life eternal.

26 And it came to pass, when Jesus had finished all these sayings, he said unto his disciples,
2 Ye know that after two days is *the feast of* the passover, and the Son of man is betrayed to be crucified.
3 Then assembled together the chief priests, and the scribes, and the elders of the people, unto the palace of the high priest, who was called Caiaphas,
4 And consulted that they might take Jesus by subtilty, and kill *him*.
5 But they said, Not on the feast *day*, lest there be an uproar among the people.
6 Now when Jesus was in Bethany, in the house of Simon the leper,
7 There came unto him a woman having an alabaster box of very precious ointment, and poured it on his head, as he sat *at meat*.
8 But when his disciples saw *it*, they had indignation, saying, To what purpose *is* this waste?
9 For this ointment might have been sold for much, and given to the poor.
10 When Jesus understood *it*, he said unto them, Why trouble ye the woman? for she hath wrought a good work upon me.
11 For ye have the poor always with you; but me ye have not always.
12 For in that she hath poured this ointment on my body, she did *it* for my burial.
13 Verily I say unto you, Wheresoever this gospel shall be preached in the whole world, *there* shall also this, that this woman hath done, be told for a memorial of her.
14 Then one of the twelve, called Judas Iscariot, went unto the chief priests,

15 And said *unto them*, What will ye give me, and I will deliver him unto you? And they covenanted with him for thirty pieces of silver.
16 And from that time he sought opportunity to betray him.
17 Now the first *day* of the *feast of* unleavened bread the disciples came to Jesus, saying unto him, Where wilt thou that we prepare for thee to eat the passover?
18 And he said, Go into the city to such a man, and say unto him, The Master saith, My time is at hand; I will keep the passover at thy house with my disciples.
19 And the disciples did as Jesus had appointed them; and they made ready the passover.
20 Now when the even was come, he sat down with the twelve.
21 And as they did eat, he said, Verily I say unto you, that one of you shall betray me.
22 And they were exceeding sorrowful, and began every one of them to say unto him, Lord, is it I?
23 And he answered and said, He that dippeth *his* hand with me in the dish, the same shall betray me.
24 The Son of man goeth as it is written of him: but woe unto that man by whom the Son of man is betrayed! it had been good for that man if he had not been born.
25 Then Judas, which betrayed him, answered and said, Master, is it I? He said unto him, Thou hast said.
26 And as they were eating, Jesus took bread, and blessed *it*, and brake *it*, and gave *it* to the disciples, and said, Take, eat; this is my body.
27 And he took the cup, and gave thanks, and gave *it* to them, saying, Drink ye all of it;
28 For this is my blood of the new testament, which is shed for many for the remission of sins.
29 But I say unto you, I will not drink henceforth of this fruit of the vine, until that day when I drink it new with you in my Father's kingdom.
30 And when they had sung an hymn, they went out into the mount of Olives.
31 Then saith Jesus unto them, All ye shall be offended because of me this night: for it is written, I will smite the shepherd, and the sheep of the flock shall be scattered abroad.
32 But after I am risen again, I will go before you into Galilee.
33 Peter answered and said unto him, Though

all *men* shall be offended because of thee, *yet* will I never be offended.

³⁴ Jesus said unto him, Verily I say unto thee, That this night, before the cock crow, thou shalt deny me thrice.

³⁵ Peter said unto him, Though I should die with thee, yet will I not deny thee. Likewise also said all the disciples.

³⁶ Then cometh Jesus with them unto a place called Gethsemane, and saith unto the disciples, Sit ye here, while I go and pray yonder.

³⁷ And he took with him Peter and the two sons of Zebedee, and began to be sorrowful and very heavy.

³⁸ Then saith he unto them, My soul is exceeding sorrowful, even unto death: tarry ye here, and watch with me.

³⁹ And he went a little farther, and fell on his face, and prayed, saying, O my Father, if it be possible, let this cup pass from me: nevertheless not as I will, but as thou *wilt.*

⁴⁰ And he cometh unto the disciples, and findeth them asleep, and saith unto Peter, What, could ye not watch with me one hour?

⁴¹ Watch and pray, that ye enter not into temptation: the spirit indeed *is* willing, but the flesh *is* weak.

⁴² He went away again the second time, and prayed, saying, O my Father, if this cup may not pass away from me, except I drink it, thy will be done.

⁴³ And he came and found them asleep again: for their eyes were heavy.

⁴⁴ And he left them, and went away again, and prayed the third time, saying the same words.

⁴⁵ Then cometh he to his disciples, and saith unto them, Sleep on now, and take *your* rest: behold, the hour is at hand, and the Son of man is betrayed into the hands of sinners.

⁴⁶ Rise, let us be going: behold, he is at hand that doth betray me.

⁴⁷ And while he yet spake, lo, Judas, one of the twelve, came, and with him a great multitude with swords and staves, from the chief priests and elders of the people.

⁴⁸ Now he that betrayed him gave them a sign, saying, Whomsoever I shall kiss, that same is he: hold him fast.

⁴⁹ And forthwith he came to Jesus, and said, Hail, master; and kissed him.

⁵⁰ And Jesus said unto him, Friend, wherefore art thou come? Then came they, and laid hands on Jesus, and took him.

⁵¹ And, behold, one of them which were with Jesus stretched out *his* hand, and drew his sword, and struck a servant of the high priest's, and smote off his ear.

⁵² Then said Jesus unto him, Put up again thy sword into his place: for all they that take the sword shall perish with the sword.

⁵³ Thinkest thou that I cannot now pray to my Father, and he shall presently give me more than twelve legions of angels?

⁵⁴ But how then shall the scriptures be fulfilled, that thus it must be?

⁵⁵ In that same hour said Jesus to the multitudes, Are ye come out as against a thief with swords and staves for to take me? I sat daily with you teaching in the temple, and ye laid no hold on me.

⁵⁶ But all this was done, that the scriptures of the prophets might be fulfilled. Then all the disciples forsook him, and fled.

⁵⁷ And they that had laid hold on Jesus led *him* away to Caiaphas the high priest, where the scribes and the elders were assembled.

⁵⁸ But Peter followed him afar off unto the high priest's palace, and went in, and sat with the servants, to see the end.

⁵⁹ Now the chief priests, and elders, and all the council, sought false witness against Jesus, to put him to death;

⁶⁰ But found none: yea, though many false witnesses came, *yet* found they none. At the last came two false witnesses,

⁶¹ And said, This *fellow* said, I am able to destroy the temple of God, and to build it in three days.

⁶² And the high priest arose, and said unto him, Answerest thou nothing? what *is it which* these witness against thee?

⁶³ But Jesus held his peace. And the high priest answered and said unto him, I adjure thee by the living God, that thou tell us whether thou be the Christ, the Son of God.

⁶⁴ Jesus saith unto him, Thou hast said: nevertheless I say unto you, Hereafter shall ye see the Son of man sitting on the right hand of power, and coming in the clouds of heaven.

⁶⁵ Then the high priest rent his clothes, saying, He hath spoken blasphemy; what further need have we of witnesses? behold, now ye have heard his blasphemy.

⁶⁶ What think ye? They answered and said, He is guilty of death.

⁶⁷ Then did they spit in his face, and buffeted him; and others smote *him* with the palms of their hands,

68 Saying, Prophesy unto us, thou Christ, Who is he that smote thee?

69 Now Peter sat without in the palace: and a damsel came unto him, saying, Thou also wast with Jesus of Galilee.

70 But he denied before *them* all, saying, I know not what thou sayest.

71 And when he was gone out into the porch, another *maid* saw him, and said unto them that were there, This *fellow* was also with Jesus of Nazareth.

72 And again he denied with an oath, I do not know the man.

73 And after a while came unto *him* they that stood by, and said to Peter, Surely thou also art *one* of them; for thy speech bewrayeth thee.

74 Then began he to curse and to swear, *saying,* I know not the man. And immediately the cock crew.

75 And Peter remembered the word of Jesus, which said unto him, Before the cock crow, thou shalt deny me thrice. And he went out, and wept bitterly.

27 When the morning was come, all the chief priests and elders of the people took counsel against Jesus to put him to death:

2 And when they had bound him, they led *him* away, and delivered him to Pontius Pilate the governor.

3 Then Judas, which had betrayeth him, when he saw that he was condemned, repented himself, and brought again the thirty pieces of silver to the chief priests and elders,

4 Saying, I have sinned in that I have betrayed the innocent blood. And they said, What *is that* to us? see thou *to that.*

5 And he cast down the pieces of silver in the temple, and departed, and went and hanged himself.

6 And the chief priests took the silver pieces, and said, It is not lawful for to put them into the treasury, because it is the price of blood.

7 And they took counsel, and bought with them the potter's field, to bury strangers in.

8 Wherefore that field was called, The field of blood, unto this day.

9 Then was fulfilled that which was spoken by Jeremy the prophet, saying, And they took the thirty pieces of silver, the price of him that was valued, whom they of the children of Israel did value;

10 And gave them for the potter's field, as the Lord appointed me.

11 And Jesus stood before the governor: and the governor asked him, saying, Art thou the King of the Jews? And Jesus said unto him, Thou sayest.

12 And when he was accused of the chief priests and elders, he answered nothing.

13 Then said Pilate unto him, Hearest thou not how many things they witness against thee?

14 And he answered him to never a word; insomuch that the governor marvelled greatly.

15 Now at *that* feast the governor was wont to release unto the people a prisoner, whom they would.

16 And they had then a notable prisoner, called Barabbas.

17 Therefore when they were gathered together, Pilate said unto them, Whom will ye that I release unto you? Barabbas, or Jesus which is called Christ?

18 For he knew that for envy they had delivered him.

19 When he was set down on the judgment seat, his wife sent unto him, saying, Have thou nothing to do with that just man: for I have suffered many things this day in a dream because of him.

20 But the chief priests and elders persuaded the multitude that they should ask Barabbas, and destroy Jesus.

21 The governor answered and said unto them, Whether of the twain will ye that I release unto you? They said, Barabbas.

22 Pilate saith unto them, What shall I do then with Jesus which is called Christ? *They* all say unto him, Let him be crucified.

23 And the governor said, Why, what evil hath he done? But they cried out the more, saying, Let him be crucified.

24 When Pilate saw that he could prevail nothing, but *that* rather a tumult was made, he took water, and washed *his* hands before the multitude, saying, I am innocent of the blood of this just person: see ye *to it.*

25 Then answered all the people, and said, His blood *be* on us, and on our children.

26 Then released he Barabbas unto them: and when he had scourged Jesus, he delivered *him* to be crucified.

27 Then the soldiers of the governor took Jesus into the common hall, and gathered unto him the whole band *of soldiers.*

28 And they stripped him, and put on him a scarlet robe.

29 And when they had platted a crown of

thorns, they put *it* upon his head, and a reed in his right hand: and they bowed the knee before him, and mocked him, saying, Hail, King of the Jews!

30 And they spit upon him, and took the reed, and smote him on the head.

31 And after that they had mocked him, they took the robe off from him, and put his own raiment on him, and led him away to crucify *him*.

32 And as they came out, they found a man of Cyrene, Simon by name: him they compelled to bear his cross.

33 And when they were come unto a place called Golgotha, that is to say, a place of a skull,

34 They gave him vinegar to drink mingled with gall: and when he had tasted *thereof*, he would not drink.

35 And they crucified him, and parted his garments, casting lots: that it might be fulfilled which was spoken by the prophet, They parted my garments among them, and upon my vesture did they cast lots.

36 And sitting down they watched him there;

37 And set up over his head his accusation written, THIS IS JESUS THE KING OF THE JEWS.

38 Then were there two thieves crucified with him, one on the right hand, and another on the left.

39 And they that passed by reviled him, wagging their heads,

40 And saying, Thou that destroyest the temple, and buildest *it* in three days, save thyself. If thou be the Son of God, come down from the cross.

41 Likewise also the chief priests mocking *him*, with the scribes and elders, said,

42 He saved others; himself he cannot save. If he be the King of Israel, let him now come down from the cross, and we will believe him.

43 He trusted in God; let him deliver him now, if he will have him: for he said, I am the Son of God.

44 The thieves also, which were crucified with him, cast the same in his teeth.

45 Now from the sixth hour there was darkness over all the land unto the ninth hour.

46 And about the ninth hour Jesus cried with a loud voice, saying, Eli, Eli, lama sabachthani? that is to say, My God, my God, why hast thou forsaken me?

47 Some of them that stood there, when they heard *that*, said, This *man* calleth for Elias.

48 And straightway one of them ran, and took a spunge, and filled *it* with vinegar, and put *it* on a reed, and gave him to drink.

49 The rest said, Let be, let us see whether Elias will come to save him.

50 Jesus, when he had cried again with a loud voice, yielded up the ghost.

51 And, behold, the veil of the temple was rent in twain from the top to the bottom; and the earth did quake, and the rocks rent;

52 And the graves were opened; and many bodies of the saints which slept arose,

53 And came out of the graves after his resurrection, and went into the holy city, and appeared unto many.

54 Now when the centurion, and they that were with him, watching Jesus, saw the earthquake, and those things that were done, they feared greatly, saying, Truly this was the Son of God.

55 And many women were there beholding afar off, which followed Jesus from Galilee, ministering unto him:

56 Among which was Mary Magdalene, and Mary the mother of James and Joses, and the mother of Zebedee's children.

57 When the even was come, there came a rich man of Arimathaea, named Joseph, who also himself was Jesus' disciple:

58 He went to Pilate, and begged the body of Jesus. Then Pilate commanded the body to be delivered.

59 And when Joseph had taken the body, he wrapped it in a clean linen cloth,

60 And laid it in his own new tomb, which he had hewn out in the rock: and he rolled a great stone to the door of the sepulchre, and departed.

61 And there was Mary Magdalene, and the other Mary, sitting over against the sepulchre.

62 Now the next day, that followed the day of the preparation, the chief priests and Pharisees came together unto Pilate,

63 Saying, Sir, we remember that that deceiver said, while he was yet alive, After three days I will rise again.

64 Command therefore that the sepulchre be made sure until the third day, lest his disciples come by night, and steal him away, and say unto the people, He is risen from the dead: so the last error shall be worse than the first.

65 Pilate said unto them, Ye have a watch: go your way, make *it* as sure as ye can.

66 So they went, and made the sepulchre sure, sealing the stone, and setting a watch.

28 In the end of the sabbath, as it began to dawn toward the first *day* of the week, came Mary Magdalene and the other Mary to see the sepulchre.

2 And, behold, there was a great earthquake: for the angel of the Lord descended from heaven, and came and rolled back the stone from the door, and sat upon it.

3 His countenance was like lightning, and his raiment white as snow:

4 And for fear of him the keepers did shake, and became as dead *men*.

5 And the angel answered and said unto the women, Fear not ye: for I know that ye seek Jesus, which was crucified.

6 He is not here: for he is risen, as he said. Come, see the place where the Lord lay.

7 And go quickly, and tell his disciples that he is risen from the dead; and, behold, he goeth before you into Galilee; there shall ye see him: lo, I have told you.

8 And they departed quickly from the sepulchre with fear and great joy; and did run to bring his disciples word.

9 And as they went to tell his disciples, behold, Jesus met them, saying, All hail. And they came and held him by the feet, and worshipped him.

10 Then said Jesus unto them, Be not afraid: go tell my brethren that they go into Galilee, and there shall they see me.

11 Now when they were going, behold, some of the watch came into the city, and shewed unto the chief priests all the things that were done.

12 And when they were assembled with the elders, and had taken counsel, they gave large money unto the soldiers,

13 Saying, Say ye, His disciples came by night, and stole him *away* while we slept.

14 And if this come to the governor's ears, we will persuade him, and secure you.

15 So they took the money, and did as they were taught: and this saying is commonly reported among the Jews until this day.

16 Then the eleven disciples went away into Galilee, into a mountain where Jesus had appointed them.

17 And when they saw him, they worshipped him: but some doubted.

18 And Jesus came and spake unto them, saying, All power is given unto me in heaven and in earth.

19 Go ye therefore, and teach all nations, baptizing them in the name of the Father, and of the Son, and of the Holy Ghost:

20 Teaching them to observe all things whatsoever I have commanded you: and, lo, I am with you alway, *even* unto the end of the world. Amen.

Mark

1 The beginning of the gospel of Jesus Christ, the Son of God;

2 As it is written in the prophets, Behold, I send my messenger before thy face, which shall prepare thy way before thee.

3 The voice of one crying in the wilderness, Prepare ye the way of the Lord, make his paths straight.

4 John did baptize in the wilderness, and preach the baptism of repentance for the remission of sins.

5 And there went out unto him all the land of Judaea, and they of Jerusalem, and were all baptized of him in the river of Jordan, confessing their sins.

6 And John was clothed with camel's hair, and with a girdle of a skin about his loins; and he did eat locusts and wild honey;

7 And preached, saying, There cometh one mightier than I after me, the latchet of whose shoes I am not worthy to stoop down and unloose.

8 I indeed have baptized you with water: but he shall baptize you with the Holy Ghost.

9 And it came to pass in those days, that Jesus came from Nazareth of Galilee, and was baptized of John in Jordan.

10 And straightway coming up out of the water, he saw the heavens opened, and the Spirit like a dove descending upon him:

11 And there came a voice from heaven, *saying*, Thou art my beloved Son, in whom I am well pleased.

12 And immediately the Spirit driveth him into the wilderness.

13 And he was there in the wilderness forty days, tempted of Satan; and was with the wild beasts; and the angels ministered unto him.

14 Now after that John was put in prison, Jesus came into Galilee, preaching the gospel of the kingdom of God,

15 And saying, The time is fulfilled, and the kingdom of God is at hand: repent ye, and believe the gospel.

16 Now as he walked by the sea of Galilee, he saw Simon and Andrew his brother casting a net into the sea: for they were fishers.

17 And Jesus said unto them, Come ye after me, and I will make you to become fishers of men.

18 And straightway they forsook their nets, and followed him.

19 And when he had gone a little farther thence, he saw James the *son* of Zebedee, and John his brother, who also were in the ship mending their nets.

20 And straightway he called them: and they left their father Zebedee in the ship with the hired servants, and went after him.

21 And they went into Capernaum; and straightway on the sabbath day he entered into the synagogue, and taught.

22 And they were astonished at his doctrine: for he taught them as one that had authority, and not as the scribes.

23 And there was in their synagogue a man with an unclean spirit; and he cried out,

24 Saying, Let *us* alone; what have we to do with thee, thou Jesus of Nazareth? art thou come to destroy us? I know thee who thou art, the Holy One of God.

25 And Jesus rebuked him, saying, Hold thy peace, and come out of him.

26 And when the unclean spirit had torn him, and cried with a loud voice, he came out of him.

27 And they were all amazed, insomuch that they questioned among themselves, saying, What thing is this? what new doctrine *is* this? for with authority commandeth he even the unclean spirits, and they do obey him.

28 And immediately his fame spread abroad throughout all the region round about Galilee.

29 And forthwith, when they were come out of the synagogue, they entered into the house of Simon and Andrew, with James and John.

30 But Simon's wife's mother lay sick of a fever, and anon they tell him of her.

31 And he came and took her by the hand, and lifted her up; and immediately the fever left her, and she ministered unto them.

32 And at even, when the sun did set, they brought unto him all that were diseased, and them that were possessed with devils.

33 And all the city was gathered together at the door.

34 And he healed many that were sick of divers diseases, and cast out many devils; and suffered not the devils to speak, because they knew him.

35 And in the morning, rising up a great while before day, he went out, and departed into a solitary place, and there prayed.

36 And Simon and they that were with him followed after him.

37 And when they had found him, they said unto him, All *men* seek for thee.

38 And he said unto them, Let us go into the next towns, that I may preach there also: for therefore came I forth.

39 And he preached in their synagogues throughout all Galilee, and cast out devils.

40 And there came a leper to him, beseeching him, and kneeling down to him, and saying unto him, If thou wilt, thou canst make me clean.

41 And Jesus, moved with compassion, put forth *his* hand, and touched him, and saith unto him, I will; be thou clean.

42 And as soon as he had spoken, immediately the leprosy departed from him, and he was cleansed.

43 And he straitly charged him, and forthwith sent him away;

44 And saith unto him, See thou say nothing to any man: but go thy way, shew thyself to the priest, and offer for thy cleansing those things which Moses commanded, for a testimony unto them.

45 But he went out, and began to publish *it* much, and to blaze abroad the matter, insomuch that Jesus could no more openly enter into the city, but was without in desert places: and they came to him from every quarter.

2 And again he entered into Capernaum, after *some* days; and it was noised that he was in the house.

2 And straightway many were gathered together, insomuch that there was no room to receive *them*, no, not so much as about the door: and he preached the word unto them.

3 And they come unto him, bringing one sick of the palsy, which was borne of four.

4 And when they could not come nigh unto him for the press, they uncovered the roof where he was: and when they had broken *it* up, they let down the bed wherein the sick of the palsy lay.

5 When Jesus saw their faith, he said unto the sick of the palsy, Son, thy sins be forgiven thee.

6 But there were certain of the scribes sitting there, and reasoning in their hearts,

7 Why doth this *man* thus speak blasphemies? who can forgive sins but God only?

8 And immediately when Jesus perceived in his spirit that they so reasoned within themselves, he said unto them, Why reason ye these things in your hearts?

9 Whether is it easier to say to the sick of the palsy, *Thy* sins be forgiven thee; or to say, Arise, and take up thy bed, and walk?

10 But that ye may know that the Son of man hath power on earth to forgive sins, (he saith to the sick of the palsy,)

11 I say unto thee, Arise, and take up thy bed, and go thy way into thine house.

12 And immediately he arose, took up the bed, and went forth before them all; insomuch that they were all amazed, and glorified God, saying, We never saw it on this fashion.

13 And he went forth again by the sea side; and all the multitude resorted unto him, and he taught them.

14 And as he passed by, he saw Levi the *son* of Alphaeus sitting at the receipt of custom, and said unto him, Follow me. And he arose and followed him.

15 And it came to pass, that, as Jesus sat at meat in his house, many publicans and sinners sat also together with Jesus and his disciples: for there were many, and they followed him.

16 And when the scribes and Pharisees saw him eat with publicans and sinners, they said unto his disciples, How is it that he eateth and drinketh with publicans and sinners?

17 When Jesus heard *it*, he saith unto them, They that are whole have no need of the physician, but they that are sick: I came not to call the righteous, but sinners to repentance.

18 And the disciples of John and of the Pharisees used to fast: and they come and say unto him, Why do the disciples of John and of the Pharisees fast, but thy disciples fast not?

19 And Jesus said unto them, Can the children

of the bridechamber fast, while the bridegroom is with them? as long as they have the bridegroom with them, they cannot fast.

20 But the days will come, when the bridegroom shall be taken away from them, and then shall they fast in those days.

21 No man also seweth a piece of new cloth on an old garment: else the new piece that filled it up taketh away from the old, and the rent is made worse.

22 And no man putteth new wine into old bottles: else the new wine doth burst the bottles, and the wine is spilled, and the bottles will be marred: but new wine must be put into new bottles.

23 And it came to pass, that he went through the corn fields on the sabbath day; and his disciples began, as they went, to pluck the ears of corn.

24 And the Pharisees said unto him, Behold, why do they on the sabbath day that which is not lawful?

25 And he said unto them, Have ye never read what David did, when he had need, and was an hungred, he, and they that were with him?

26 How he went into the house of God in the days of Abiathar the high priest, and did eat the shewbread, which is not lawful to eat but for the priests, and gave also to them which were with him?

27 And he said unto them, The sabbath was made for man, and not man for the sabbath:

28 Therefore the Son of man is Lord also of the sabbath.

3 And he entered again into the synagogue; and there was a man there which had a withered hand.

2 And they watched him, whether he would heal him on the sabbath day; that they might accuse him.

3 And he saith unto the man which had the withered hand, Stand forth.

4 And he saith unto them, Is it lawful to do good on the sabbath days, or to do evil? to save life, or to kill? But they held their peace.

5 And when he had looked round about on them with anger, being grieved for the hardness of their hearts, he saith unto the man, Stretch forth thine hand. And he stretched *it* out: and his hand was restored whole as the other.

6 And the Pharisees went forth, and straightway took counsel with the Herodians against him, how they might destroy him.

7 But Jesus withdrew himself with his disciples to the sea: and a great multitude from Galilee followed him, and from Judaea,

8 And from Jerusalem, and from Idumaea, and *from* beyond Jordan; and they about Tyre and Sidon, a great multitude, when they had heard what great things he did, came unto him.

9 And he spake to his disciples, that a small ship should wait on him because of the multitude, lest they should throng him.

10 For he had healed many; insomuch that they pressed upon him for to touch him, as many as had plagues.

11 And unclean spirits, when they saw him, fell down before him, and cried, saying, Thou art the Son of God.

12 And he straitly charged them that they should not make him known.

13 And he goeth up into a mountain, and calleth *unto him* whom he would: and they came unto him.

14 And he ordained twelve, that they should be with him, and that he might send them forth to preach,

15 And to have power to heal sicknesses, and to cast out devils:

16 And Simon he surnamed Peter;

17 And James the *son* of Zebedee, and John the brother of James; and he surnamed them Boanerges, which is, The sons of thunder:

18 And Andrew, and Philip, and Bartholomew, and Matthew, and Thomas, and James the *son* of Alphaeus, and Thaddaeus, and Simon the Canaanite,

19 And Judas Iscariot, which also betrayed him: and they went into an house.

20 And the multitude cometh together again, so that they could not so much as eat bread.

21 And when his friends heard *of it*, they went out to lay hold on him: for they said, He is beside himself.

22 And the scribes which came down from Jerusalem said, He hath Beelzebub, and by the prince of the devils casteth he out devils.

23 And he called them *unto him*, and said unto them in parables, How can Satan cast out Satan?

24 And if a kingdom be divided against itself, that kingdom cannot stand.

25 And if a house be divided against itself, that house cannot stand.

26 And if Satan rise up against himself, and be divided, he cannot stand, but hath an end.

27 No man can enter into a strong man's house, and spoil his goods, except he will first bind the strong man; and then he will spoil his house.

28 Verily I say unto you, All sins shall be forgiven unto the sons of men, and blasphemies wherewith soever they shall blaspheme:

29 But he that shall blaspheme against the Holy Ghost hath never forgiveness, but is in danger of eternal damnation:

30 Because they said, He hath an unclean spirit.

31 There came then his brethren and his mother, and, standing without, sent unto him, calling him.

32 And the multitude sat about him, and they said unto him, Behold, thy mother and thy brethren without seek for thee.

33 And he answered them, saying, Who is my mother, or my brethren?

34 And he looked round about on them which sat about him, and said, Behold my mother and my brethren!

35 For whosoever shall do the will of God, the same is my brother, and my sister, and mother.

4 And he began again to teach by the sea side: and there was gathered unto him a great multitude, so that he entered into a ship, and sat in the sea; and the whole multitude was by the sea on the land.

2 And he taught them many things by parables, and said unto them in his doctrine,

3 Hearken; Behold, there went out a sower to sow:

4 And it came to pass, as he sowed, some fell by the way side, and the fowls of the air came and devoured it up.

5 And some fell on stony ground, where it had not much earth; and immediately it sprang up, because it had no depth of earth:

6 But when the sun was up, it was scorched; and because it had no root, it withered away.

7 And some fell among thorns, and the thorns grew up, and choked it, and it yielded no fruit.

8 And other fell on good ground, and did yield fruit that sprang up and increased; and brought forth, some thirty, and some sixty, and some an hundred.

9 And he said unto them, He that hath ears to hear, let him hear.

10 And when he was alone, they that were about him with the twelve asked of him the parable.

11 And he said unto them, Unto you it is given to know the mystery of the kingdom of God: but unto them that are without, all these *things* are done in parables:

12 That seeing they may see, and not perceive; and hearing they may hear, and not understand; lest at any time they should be converted, and *their* sins should be forgiven them.

13 And he said unto them, Know ye not this parable? and how then will ye know all parables?

14 The sower soweth the word.

15 And these are they by the way side, where the word is sown; but when they have heard, Satan cometh immediately, and taketh away the word that was sown in their hearts.

16 And these are they likewise which are sown on stony ground; who, when they have heard the word, immediately receive it with gladness;

17 And have no root in themselves, and so endure but for a time: afterward, when affliction or persecution ariseth for the word's sake, immediately they are offended.

18 And these are they which are sown among thorns; such as hear the word,

19 And the cares of this world, and the deceitfulness of riches, and the lusts of other things entering in, choke the word, and it becometh unfruitful.

20 And these are they which are sown on good ground; such as hear the word, and receive *it,* and bring forth fruit, some thirtyfold, some sixty, and some an hundred.

21 And he said unto them, Is a candle brought to be put under a bushel, or under a bed? and not to be set on a candlestick?

22 For there is nothing hid, which shall not be manifested; neither was any thing kept secret, but that it should come abroad.

23 If any man have ears to hear, let him hear.

24 And he said unto them, Take heed what ye hear: with what measure ye mete, it shall be measured to you: and unto you that hear shall more be given.

25 For he that hath, to him shall be given: and he that hath not, from him shall be taken even that which he hath.

26 And he said, So is the kingdom of God, as if a man should cast seed into the ground;

27 And should sleep, and rise night and day, and the seed should spring and grow up, he knoweth not how.

28 For the earth bringeth forth fruit of herself;

first the blade, then the ear, after that the full corn in the ear.

²⁹ But when the fruit is brought forth, immediately he putteth in the sickle, because the harvest is come.

³⁰ And he said, Whereunto shall we liken the kingdom of God? or with what comparison shall we compare it?

³¹ *It is* like a grain of mustard seed, which, when it is sown in the earth, is less than all the seeds that be in the earth:

³² But when it is sown, it groweth up, and becometh greater than all herbs, and shooteth out great branches; so that the fowls of the air may lodge under the shadow of it.

³³ And with many such parables spake he the word unto them, as they were able to hear *it.*

³⁴ But without a parable spake he not unto them: and when they were alone, he expounded all things to his disciples.

³⁵ And the same day, when the even was come, he saith unto them, Let us pass over unto the other side.

³⁶ And when they had sent away the multitude, they took him even as he was in the ship. And there were also with him other little ships.

³⁷ And there arose a great storm of wind, and the waves beat into the ship, so that it was now full.

³⁸ And he was in the hinder part of the ship, asleep on a pillow: and they awake him, and say unto him, Master, carest thou not that we perish?

³⁹ And he arose, and rebuked the wind, and said unto the sea, Peace, be still. And the wind ceased, and there was a great calm.

⁴⁰ And he said unto them, Why are ye so fearful? how is it that ye have no faith?

⁴¹ And they feared exceedingly, and said one to another, What manner of man is this, that even the wind and the sea obey him?

5 And they came over unto the other side of the sea, into the country of the Gadarenes.

² And when he was come out of the ship, immediately there met him out of the tombs a man with an unclean spirit,

³ Who had *his* dwelling among the tombs; and no man could bind him, no, not with chains:

⁴ Because that he had been often bound with fetters and chains, and the chains had been plucked asunder by him, and the fetters broken in pieces: neither could any *man* tame him.

⁵ And always, night and day, he was in the mountains, and in the tombs, crying, and cutting himself with stones.

⁶ But when he saw Jesus afar off, he ran and worshipped him,

⁷ And cried with a loud voice, and said, What have I to do with thee, Jesus, *thou* Son of the most high God? I adjure thee by God, that thou torment me not.

⁸ For he said unto him, Come out of the man, *thou* unclean spirit.

⁹ And he asked him, What *is* thy name? And he answered, saying, My name *is* Legion: for we are many.

¹⁰ And he besought him much that he would not send them away out of the country.

¹¹ Now there was there nigh unto the mountains a great herd of swine feeding.

¹² And all the devils besought him, saying, Send us into the swine, that we may enter into them.

¹³ And forthwith Jesus gave them leave. And the unclean spirits went out, and entered into the swine: and the herd ran violently down a steep place into the sea, (they were about two thousand;) and were choked in the sea.

¹⁴ And they that fed the swine fled, and told *it* in the city, and in the country. And they went out to see what it was that was done.

¹⁵ And they come to Jesus, and see him that was possessed with the devil, and had the legion, sitting, and clothed, and in his right mind: and they were afraid.

¹⁶ And they that saw *it* told them how it befell to him that was possessed with the devil, and *also* concerning the swine.

¹⁷ And they began to pray him to depart out of their coasts.

¹⁸ And when he was come into the ship, he that had been possessed with the devil prayed him that he might be with him.

¹⁹ Howbeit Jesus suffered him not, but saith unto him, Go home to thy friends, and tell them how great things the Lord hath done for thee, and hath had compassion on thee.

²⁰ And he departed, and began to publish in Decapolis how great things Jesus had done for him: and all *men* did marvel.

²¹ And when Jesus was passed over again by ship unto the other side, much people gathered unto him: and he was nigh unto the sea.

²² And, behold, there cometh one of the rulers of the synagogue, Jairus by name; and when he saw him, he fell at his feet,

23 And besought him greatly, saying, My little daughter lieth at the point of death: *I pray thee,* come and lay thy hands on her, that she may be healed; and she shall live.

24 And *Jesus* went with him; and much people followed him, and thronged him.

25 And a certain woman, which had an issue of blood twelve years, ℞

26 And had suffered many things of many physicians, and had spent all that she had, and was nothing bettered, but rather grew worse,

27 When she had heard of Jesus, came in the press behind, and touched his garment.

28 For she said, If I may touch but his clothes, I shall be whole.

29 And straightway the fountain of her blood was dried up; and she felt in *her* body that she was healed of that plague.

30 And Jesus, immediately knowing in himself that virtue had gone out of him, turned him about in the press, and said, Who touched my clothes?

31 And his disciples said unto him, Thou seest the multitude thronging thee, and sayest thou, Who touched me?

32 And he looked round about to see her that had done this thing.

33 But the woman fearing and trembling, knowing what was done in her, came and fell down before him, and told him all the truth.

34 And he said unto her, Daughter, thy faith hath made thee whole; go in peace, and be whole of thy plague.

35 While he yet spake, there came from the ruler of the synagogue's *house certain* ℞ which said, Thy daughter is dead: why troublest thou the Master any further?

36 As soon as Jesus heard the word that was spoken, he saith unto the ruler of the synagogue, Be not afraid, only believe.

37 And he suffered no man to follow him, save Peter, and James, and John the brother of James.

38 And he cometh to the house of the ruler of the synagogue, and seeth the tumult, and them that wept and wailed greatly.

39 And when he was come in, he saith unto them, Why make ye this ado, and weep? the damsel is not dead, but sleepeth.

40 And they laughed him to scorn. But when he had put them all out, he taketh the father and the mother of the damsel, and them that were with him, and entereth in where the damsel was lying.

41 And he took the damsel by the hand, and said unto her, Talitha cumi; which is, being interpreted, Damsel, I say unto thee, arise.

42 And straightway the damsel arose, and walked; for she was *of the age* of twelve years. And they were astonished with a great astonishment.

43 And he charged them straitly that no man should know it; and commanded that something should be given her to eat.

6 And he went out from thence, and came into his own country; and his disciples follow him.

2 And when the sabbath day was come, he began to teach in the synagogue: and many hearing *him* were astonished, saying, From whence hath this *man* these things? and what wisdom *is* this which is given unto him, that even such mighty works are wrought by his hands?

3 Is not this the carpenter, the son of Mary, the brother of James, and Joses, and of Juda, and Simon? and are not his sisters here with us? And they were offended at him.

4 But Jesus said unto them, A prophet is not without honour, but in his own country, and among his own kin, and in his own house.

5 And he could there do no mighty work, save that he laid his hands upon a few sick folk, and healed *them.*

6 And he marvelled because of their unbelief. And he went round about the villages, teaching.

7 And he called *unto him* the twelve, and began to send them forth by two and two; and gave them power over unclean spirits;

8 And commanded them that they should take nothing for *their* journey, save a staff only; no scrip, no bread, no money in *their* purse:

9 But *be* shod with sandals; and not put on two coats.

10 And he said unto them, In what place soever ye enter into an house, there abide till ye depart from that place.

11 And whosoever shall not receive you, nor hear you, when ye depart thence, shake off the dust under your feet for a testimony against them. Verily I say unto you, It shall be more tolerable for Sodom and Gomorrha in the day of judgment, than for that city.

12 And they went out, and preached that men should repent.

13 And they cast out many devils, and anointed

with oil many that were sick, and healed *them.*

¹⁴ And king Herod heard *of him;* (for his name was spread abroad:) and he said, That John the Baptist was risen from the dead, and therefore mighty works do shew forth themselves in him.

¹⁵ Others said, That it is Elias. And others said, That it is a prophet, or as one of the prophets.

¹⁶ But when Herod heard *thereof,* he said, It is John, whom I beheaded: he is risen from the dead.

¹⁷ For Herod himself had sent forth and laid hold upon John, and bound him in prison for Herodias' sake, his brother Philip's wife: for he had married her.

¹⁸ For John had said unto Herod, It is not lawful for thee to have thy brother's wife.

¹⁹ Therefore Herodias had a quarrel against him, and would have killed him; but she could not:

²⁰ For Herod feared John, knowing that he was a just man and an holy, and observed him; and when he heard him, he did many things, and heard him gladly.

²¹ And when a convenient day was come, that Herod on his birthday made a supper to his lords, high captains, and chief *estates* of Galilee;

²² And when the daughter of the said Herodias came in, and danced, and pleased Herod and them that sat with him, the king said unto the damsel, Ask of me whatsoever thou wilt, and I will give *it* thee.

²³ And he sware unto her, Whatsoever thou shalt ask of me, I will give *it* thee, unto the half of my kingdom.

²⁴ And she went forth, and said unto her mother, What shall I ask? And she said, The head of John the Baptist.

²⁵ And she came in straightway with haste unto the king, and asked, saying, I will that thou give me by and by in a charger the head of John the Baptist.

²⁶ And the king was exceeding sorry; *yet* for his oath's sake, and for their sakes which sat with him, he would not reject her.

²⁷ And immediately the king sent an executioner, and commanded his head to be brought: and he went and beheaded him in the prison,

²⁸ And brought his head in a charger, and gave it to the damsel: and the damsel gave it to her mother.

²⁹ And when his disciples heard *of it,* they came and took up his corpse, and laid it in a tomb.

³⁰ And the apostles gathered themselves together unto Jesus, and told him all things, both what they had done, and what they had taught.

³¹ And he said unto them, Come ye yourselves apart into a desert place, and rest a while: for there were many coming and going, and they had no leisure so much as to eat.

³² And they departed into a desert place by ship privately.

³³ And the people saw them departing, and many knew him, and ran afoot thither out of all cities, and outwent them, and came together unto him.

³⁴ And Jesus, when he came out, saw much people, and was moved with compassion toward them, because they were as sheep not having a shepherd: and he began to teach them many things.

³⁵ And when the day was now far spent, his disciples came unto him, and said, This is a desert place, and now the time *is* far passed:

³⁶ Send them away, that they may go into the country round about, and into the villages, and buy themselves bread: for they have nothing to eat.

³⁷ He answered and said unto them, Give ye them to eat. And they say unto him, Shall we go and buy two hundred pennyworth of bread, and give them to eat?

³⁸ He saith unto them, How many loaves have ye? go and see. And when they knew, they say, Five, and two fishes.

³⁹ And he commanded them to make all sit down by companies upon the green grass.

⁴⁰ And they sat down in ranks, by hundreds, and by fifties.

⁴¹ And when he had taken the five loaves and the two fishes, he looked up to heaven, and blessed, and brake the loaves, and gave *them* to his disciples to set before them; and the two fishes divided he among them all.

⁴² And they did all eat, and were filled.

⁴³ And they took up twelve baskets full of the fragments, and of the fishes.

⁴⁴ And they that did eat of the loaves were about five thousand men.

⁴⁵ And straightway he constrained his disciples to get into the ship, and to go to the other side before unto Bethsaida, while he sent away the people.

⁴⁶ And when he had sent them away, he departed into a mountain to pray.
⁴⁷ And when even was come, the ship was in the midst of the sea, and he alone on the land.
⁴⁸ And he saw them toiling in rowing; for the wind was contrary unto them: and about the fourth watch of the night he cometh unto them, walking upon the sea, and would have passed by them.
⁴⁹ But when they saw him walking upon the sea, they supposed it had been a spirit, and cried out:
⁵⁰ For they all saw him, and were troubled. And immediately he talked with them, and saith unto them, Be of good cheer: it is I; be not afraid.
⁵¹ And he went up unto them into the ship; and the wind ceased: and they were sore amazed in themselves beyond measure, and wondered.
⁵² For they considered not *the miracle* of the loaves: for their heart was hardened.
⁵³ And when they had passed over, they came into the land of Gennesaret, and drew to the shore.
⁵⁴ And when they were come out of the ship, straightway they knew him,
⁵⁵ And ran through that whole region round about, and began to carry about in beds those that were sick, where they heard he was.
⁵⁶ And whithersoever he entered, into villages, or cities, or country, they laid the sick in the streets, and besought him that they might touch if it were but the border of his garment: and as many as touched him were made whole.

7 Then came together unto him the Pharisees, and certain of the scribes, which came from Jerusalem.
² And when they saw some of his disciples eat bread with defiled, that is to say, with unwashen, hands, they found fault.
³ For the Pharisees, and all the Jews, except they wash *their* hands oft, eat not, holding the tradition of the elders.
⁴ And *when they come* from the market, except they wash, they eat not. And many other things there be, which they have received to hold, *as* the washing of cups, and pots, brasen vessels, and of tables.
⁵ Then the Pharisees and scribes asked him, Why walk not thy disciples according to the tradition of the elders, but eat bread with unwashen hands?

⁶ He answered and said unto them, Well hath Esaias prophesied of you hypocrites, as it is written, This people honoureth me with *their* lips, but their heart is far from me.
⁷ Howbeit in vain do they worship me, teaching *for* doctrines the commandments of men.
⁸ For laying aside the commandment of God, ye hold the tradition of men, *as* the washing of pots and cups: and many other such like things ye do.
⁹ And he said unto them, Full well ye reject the commandment of God, that ye may keep your own tradition.
¹⁰ For Moses said, Honour thy father and thy mother; and, Whoso curseth father or mother, let him die the death:
¹¹ But ye say, If a man shall say to his father or mother, *It is* Corban, that is to say, a gift, by whatsoever thou mightest be profited by me; *he shall be free.*
¹² And ye suffer him no more to do ought for his father or his mother;
¹³ Making the word of God of none effect through your tradition, which ye have delivered: and many such like things do ye.
¹⁴ And when he had called all the people *unto him,* he said unto them, Hearken unto me every one *of you,* and understand:
¹⁵ There is nothing from without a man, that entering into him can defile him: but the things which come out of him, those are they that defile the man.
¹⁶ If any man have ears to hear, let him hear.
¹⁷ And when he was entered into the house from the people, his disciples asked him concerning the parable.
¹⁸ And he saith unto them, Are ye so without understanding also? Do ye not perceive, that whatsoever thing from without entereth into the man, *it* cannot defile him;
¹⁹ Because it entereth not into his heart, but into the belly, and goeth out into the draught, purging all meats?
²⁰ And he said, That which cometh out of the man, that defileth the man.
²¹ For from within, out of the heart of men, proceed evil thoughts, adulteries, fornications, murders,
²² Thefts, covetousness, wickedness, deceit, lasciviousness, an evil eye, blasphemy, pride, foolishness:
²³ All these evil things come from within, and defile the man.

24 And from thence he arose, and went into the borders of Tyre and Sidon, and entered into an house, and would have no man know *it:* but he could not be hid.

25 For a *certain* woman, whose young daughter had an unclean spirit, heard of him, and came and fell at his feet:

26 The woman was a Greek, a Syrophenician by nation; and she besought him that he would cast forth the devil out of her daughter.

27 But Jesus said unto her, Let the children first be filled: for it is not meet to take the children's bread, and to cast *it* unto the dogs.

28 And she answered and said unto him, Yes, Lord: yet the dogs under the table eat of the children's crumbs.

29 And he said unto her, For this saying go thy way; the devil is gone out of thy daughter.

30 And when she was come to her house, she found the devil gone out, and her daughter laid upon the bed.

31 And again, departing from the coasts of Tyre and Sidon, he came unto the sea of Galilee, through the midst of the coasts of Decapolis.

32 And they bring unto him one that was deaf, and had an impediment in his speech; and they beseech him to put his hand upon him.

33 And he took him aside from the multitude, and put his fingers into his ears, and he spit, and touched his tongue;

34 And looking up to heaven, he sighed, and saith unto him, Ephphatha, that is, Be opened.

35 And straightway his ears were opened, and the string of his tongue was loosed, and he spake plain.

36 And he charged them that they should tell no man: but the more he charged them, so much the more a great deal they published *it;*

37 And were beyond measure astonished, saying, He hath done all things well: he maketh both the deaf to hear, and the dumb to speak.

8 In those days the multitude being very great, and having nothing to eat, Jesus called his disciples *unto him,* and saith unto them,

2 I have compassion on the multitude, because they have now been with me three days, and have nothing to eat:

3 And if I send them away fasting to their own houses, they will faint by the way: for divers of them came from far.

4 And his disciples answered him, From whence can a man satisfy these *men* with bread here in the wilderness?

5 And he asked them, How many loaves have ye? And they said, Seven.

6 And he commanded the people to sit down on the ground: and he took the seven loaves, and gave thanks, and brake, and gave to his disciples to set before *them;* and they did set *them* before the people.

7 And they had a few small fishes: and he blessed, and commanded to set them also before *them.*

8 So they did eat, and were filled: and they took up of the broken *meat* that was left seven baskets.

9 And they that had eaten were about four thousand: and he sent them away.

10 And straightway he entered into a ship with his disciples, and came into the parts of Dalmanutha.

11 And the Pharisees came forth, and began to question with him, seeking of him a sign from heaven, tempting him.

12 And he sighed deeply in his spirit, and saith, Why doth this generation seek after a sign? verily I say unto you, There shall no sign be given unto this generation.

13 And he left them, and entering into the ship again departed to the other side.

14 Now *the disciples* had forgotten to take bread, neither had they in the ship with them more than one loaf.

15 And he charged them, saying, Take heed, beware of the leaven of the Pharisees, and *of* the leaven of Herod.

16 And they reasoned among themselves, saying, *It is* because we have no bread.

17 And when Jesus knew *it,* he saith unto them, Why reason ye, because ye have no bread? perceive ye not yet, neither understand? have ye your heart yet hardened?

18 Having eyes, see ye not? and having ears, hear ye not? and do ye not remember?

19 When I brake the five loaves among five thousand, how many baskets full of fragments took ye up? They say unto him, Twelve.

20 And when the seven among four thousand, how many baskets full of fragments took ye up? And they said, Seven.

21 And he said unto them, How is it that ye do not understand?

22 And he cometh to Bethsaida; and they bring a blind man unto him, and besought him to touch him.

23 And he took the blind man by the hand, and led him out of the town; and when he had spit on his eyes, and put his hands upon him, he asked him if he saw ought.

24 And he looked up, and said, I see men as trees, walking.

25 After that he put *his* hands again upon his eyes, and made him look up: and he was restored, and saw every man clearly.

26 And he sent him away to his house, saying, Neither go into the town, nor tell *it* to any in the town.

27 And Jesus went out, and his disciples, into the towns of Caesarea Philippi: and by the way he asked his disciples, saying unto them, Whom do men say that I am?

28 And they answered, John the Baptist: but some *say*, Elias; and others, One of the prophets.

29 And he saith unto them, But whom say ye that I am? And Peter answereth and saith unto him, Thou art the Christ.

30 And he charged them that they should tell no man of him.

31 And he began to teach them, that the Son of man must suffer many things, and be rejected of the elders, and *of* the chief priests, and scribes, and be killed, and after three days rise again.

32 And he spake that saying openly. And Peter took him, and began to rebuke him.

33 But when he had turned about and looked on his disciples, he rebuked Peter, saying, Get thee behind me, Satan: for thou savourest not the things that be of God, but the things that be of men.

34 And when he had called the people *unto him* with his disciples also, he said unto them, Whosoever will come after me, let him deny himself, and take up his cross, and follow me.

35 For whosoever will save his life shall lose it; but whosoever shall lose his life for my sake and the gospel's, the same shall save it.

36 For what shall it profit a man, if he shall gain the whole world, and lose his own soul?

37 Or what shall a man give in exchange for his soul?

38 Whosoever therefore shall be ashamed of me and of my words in this adulterous and sinful generation; of him also shall the Son of man be ashamed, when he cometh in the glory of his Father with the holy angels.

9 And he said unto them, Verily I say unto you, That there be some of them that stand here, which shall not taste of death, till they have seen the kingdom of God come with power.

2 And after six days Jesus taketh *with him* Peter, and James, and John, and leadeth them up into an high mountain apart by themselves: and he was transfigured before them.

3 And his raiment became shining, exceeding white as snow; so as no fuller on earth can white them.

4 And there appeared unto them Elias with Moses: and they were talking with Jesus.

5 And Peter answered and said to Jesus, Master, it is good for us to be here: and let us make three tabernacles; one for thee, and one for Moses, and one for Elias.

6 For he wist not what to say; for they were sore afraid.

7 And there was a cloud that overshadowed them: and a voice came out of the cloud, saying, This is my beloved Son: hear him.

8 And suddenly, when they had looked round about, they saw no man any more, save Jesus only with themselves.

9 And as they came down from the mountain, he charged them that they should tell no man what things they had seen, till the Son of man were risen from the dead.

10 And they kept that saying with themselves, questioning one with another what the rising from the dead should mean.

11 And they asked him, saying, Why say the scribes that Elias must first come?

12 And he answered and told them, Elias verily cometh first, and restoreth all things; and how it is written of the Son of man, that he must suffer many things, and be set at nought.

13 But I say unto you, That Elias is indeed come, and they have done unto him whatsoever they listed, as it is written of him.

14 And when he came to *his* disciples, he saw a great multitude about them, and the scribes questioning with them.

15 And straightway all the people, when they beheld him, were greatly amazed, and running to *him* saluted him.

16 And he asked the scribes, What question ye with them?

17 And one of the multitude answered and said, Master, I have brought unto thee my son, which hath a dumb spirit;

18 And wheresoever he taketh him, he teareth him: and he foameth, and gnasheth with his

teeth, and pineth away: and I spake to thy disciples that they should cast him out; and they could not.

¹⁹ He answereth him, and saith, O☐faithless generation, how long shall I be with you? how long shall I suffer you? bring him unto me.

²⁰ And they brought him unto him: and when he saw him, straightway the spirit tare him; and he fell on the ground, and wallowed foaming.

²¹ And he asked his father, How long is it ago since this came unto him? And he said, Of a child.

²² And ofttimes it hath cast him into the fire, and into the waters, to destroy him: but if thou canst do any thing, have compassion on us, and help us.

²³ Jesus said unto him, If thou canst believe, all things *are* possible to him that believeth.

²⁴ And straightway the father of the child cried out, and said with tears, Lord, I believe; help thou mine unbelief.

²⁵ When Jesus saw that the people came running together, he rebuked the foul spirit, saying unto him, *Thou* dumb and deaf spirit, I charge thee, come out of him, and enter no more into him.

²⁶ And *the spirit* cried, and rent him sore, and came out of him: and he was as one dead; insomuch that many said, He is dead.

²⁷ But Jesus took him by the hand, and lifted him up; and he arose.

²⁸ And when he was come into the house, his disciples asked him privately, Why could not we cast him out?

²⁹ And he said unto them, This kind can come forth by nothing, but by prayer and fasting.

³⁰ And they departed thence, and passed through Galilee; and he would not that any man should know *it*.

³¹ For he taught his disciples, and said unto them, The Son of man is delivered into the hands of men, and they shall kill him; and after that he is killed, he shall rise the third day.

³² But they understood not that saying, and were afraid to ask him.

³³ And he came to Capernaum: and being in the house he asked them, What was it that ye disputed among yourselves by the way?

³⁴ But they held their peace: for by the way they had disputed among themselves, who *should be* the greatest.

³⁵ And he sat down, and called the twelve, and saith unto them, If any man desire to be first, *the same* shall be last of all, and servant of all.

³⁶ And he took a child, and set him in the midst of them: and when he had taken him in his arms, he said unto them,

³⁷ Whosoever shall receive one of such children in my name, receiveth me: and whosoever shall receive me, receiveth not me, but him that sent me.

³⁸ And John answered him, saying, Master, we saw one casting out devils in thy name, and he followeth not us: and we forbad him, because he followeth not us.

³⁹ But Jesus said, Forbid him not: for there is no man which shall do a miracle in my name, that can lightly speak evil of me.

⁴⁰ For he that is not against us is on our part.

⁴¹ For whosoever shall give you a cup of water to drink in my name, because ye belong to Christ, verily I say unto you, he shall not lose his reward.

⁴² And whosoever shall offend one of *these* little ones that believe in me, it is better for him that a millstone were hanged about his neck, and he were cast into the sea.

⁴³ And if thy hand offend thee, cut it off: it is better for thee to enter into life maimed, than having two hands to go into hell, into the fire that never shall be quenched:

⁴⁴ Where their worm dieth not, and the fire is not quenched.

⁴⁵ And if thy foot offend thee, cut it off: it is better for thee to enter halt into life, than having two feet to be cast into hell, into the fire that never shall be quenched:

⁴⁶ Where their worm dieth not, and the fire is not quenched.

⁴⁷ And if thine eye offend thee, pluck it out: it is better for thee to enter into the kingdom of God with one eye, than having two eyes to be cast into hell fire:

⁴⁸ Where their worm dieth not, and the fire is not quenched.

⁴⁹ For every one shall be salted with fire, and every sacrifice shall be salted with salt.

⁵⁰ Salt *is* good: but if the salt have lost his saltness, wherewith will ye season it? Have salt in yourselves, and have peace one with another.

10 And he arose from thence, and cometh into the coasts of Judaea by the farther side of Jordan: and the people resort unto him again; and, as he was wont, he taught them again.

² And the Pharisees came to him, and asked

him, Is it lawful for a man to put away *his* wife? tempting him.

3 And he answered and said unto them, What did Moses command you?

4 And they said, Moses suffered to write a bill of divorcement, and to put *her* away.

5 And Jesus answered and said unto them, For the hardness of your heart he wrote you this precept.

6 But from the beginning of the creation God made them male and female.

7 For this cause shall a man leave his father and mother, and cleave to his wife;

8 And they twain shall be one flesh: so then they are no more twain, but one flesh.

9 What therefore God hath joined together, let not man put asunder.

10 And in the house his disciples asked him again of the same *matter.*

11 And he saith unto them, Whosoever shall put away his wife, and marry another, committeth adultery against her.

12 And if a woman shall put away her husband, and be married to another, she committeth adultery.

13 And they brought young children to him, that he should touch them: and *his* disciples rebuked those that brought *them.*

14 But when Jesus saw *it,* he was much displeased, and said unto them, Suffer the little children to come unto me, and forbid them not: for of such is the kingdom of God.

15 Verily I say unto you, Whosoever shall not receive the kingdom of God as a little child, he shall not enter therein.

16 And he took them up in his arms, put *his* hands upon them, and blessed them.

17 And when he was gone forth into the way, there came one running, and kneeled to him, and asked him, Good Master, what shall I do that I may inherit eternal life?

18 And Jesus said unto him, Why callest thou me good? *there is* none good but one, *that is,* God.

19 Thou knowest the commandments, Do not commit adultery, Do not kill, Do not steal, Do not bear false witness, Defraud not, Honour thy father and mother.

20 And he answered and said unto him, Master, all these have I observed from my youth.

21 Then Jesus beholding him loved him, and said unto him, One thing thou lackest: go thy way, sell whatsoever thou hast, and give to the poor, and thou shalt have treasure in heaven: and come, take up the cross, and follow me.

22 And he was sad at that saying, and went away grieved: for he had great possessions.

23 And Jesus looked round about, and saith unto his disciples, How hardly shall they that have riches enter into the kingdom of God!

24 And the disciples were astonished at his words. But Jesus answereth again, and saith unto them, Children, how hard is it for them that trust in riches to enter into the kingdom of God!

25 It is easier for a camel to go through the eye of a needle, than for a rich man to enter into the kingdom of God.

26 And they were astonished out of measure, saying among themselves, Who then can be saved?

27 And Jesus looking upon them saith, With men *it is* impossible, but not with God: for with God all things are possible.

28 Then Peter began to say unto him, Lo, we have left all, and have followed thee.

29 And Jesus answered and said, Verily I say unto you, There is no man that hath left house, or brethren, or sisters, or father, or mother, or wife, or children, or lands, for my sake, and the gospel's,

30 But he shall receive an hundredfold now in this time, houses, and brethren, and sisters, and mothers, and children, and lands, with persecutions; and in the world to come eternal life.

31 But many *that are* first shall be last; and the last first.

32 And they were in the way going up to Jerusalem; and Jesus went before them: and they were amazed; and as they followed, they were afraid. And he took again the twelve, and began to tell them what things should happen unto him,

33 *Saying,* Behold, we go up to Jerusalem; and the Son of man shall be delivered unto the chief priests, and unto the scribes; and they shall condemn him to death, and shall deliver him to the Gentiles:

34 And they shall mock him, and shall scourge him, and shall spit upon him, and shall kill him: and the third day he shall rise again.

35 And James and John, the sons of Zebedee, come unto him, saying, Master, we would that thou shouldest do for us whatsoever we shall desire.

36 And he said unto them, What would ye that I should do for you?

37 They said unto him, Grant unto us that we may sit, one on thy right hand, and the other on thy left hand, in thy glory.

38 But Jesus said unto them, Ye know not what ye ask: can ye drink of the cup that I drink of? and be baptized with the baptism that I am baptized with?

39 And they said unto him, We can. And Jesus said unto them, Ye shall indeed drink of the cup that I drink of; and with the baptism that I am baptized withal shall ye be baptized:

40 But to sit on my right hand and on my left hand is not mine to give; but *it shall be given to them* for whom it is prepared.

41 And when the ten heard *it*, they began to be much displeased with James and John.

42 But Jesus called them *to him*, and saith unto them, Ye know that they which are accounted to rule over the Gentiles exercise lordship over them; and their great ones exercise authority upon them.

43 But so shall it not be among you: but whosoever will be great among you, shall be your minister:

44 And whosoever of you will be the chiefest, shall be servant of all.

45 For even the Son of man came not to be ministered unto, but to minister, and to give his life a ransom for many.

46 And they came to Jericho: and as he went out of Jericho with his disciples and a great number of people, blind Bartimaeus, the son of Timaeus, sat by the highway side begging.

47 And when he heard that it was Jesus of Nazareth, he began to cry out, and say, Jesus, *thou* Son of David, have mercy on me.

48 And many charged him that he should hold his peace: but he cried the more a great deal, *Thou* Son of David, have mercy on me.

49 And Jesus stood still, and commanded him to be called. And they call the blind man, saying unto him, Be of good comfort, rise; he calleth thee.

50 And he, casting away his garment, rose, and came to Jesus.

51 And Jesus answered and said unto him, What wilt thou that I should do unto thee? The blind man said unto him, Lord, that I might receive my sight.

52 And Jesus said unto him, Go thy way; thy faith hath made thee whole. And immediately he received his sight, and followed Jesus in the way.

11 And when they came nigh to Jerusalem, unto Bethphage and Bethany, at the mount of Olives, he sendeth forth two of his disciples,

2 And saith unto them, Go your way into the village over against you: and as soon as ye be entered into it, ye shall find a colt tied, whereon never man sat; loose him, and bring *him*.

3 And if any man say unto you, Why do ye this? say ye that the Lord hath need of him; and straightway he will send him hither.

4 And they went their way, and found the colt tied by the door without in a place where two ways met; and they loose him.

5 And certain of them that stood there said unto them, What do ye, loosing the colt?

6 And they said unto them even as Jesus had commanded: and they let them go.

7 And they brought the colt to Jesus, and cast their garments on him; and he sat upon him.

8 And many spread their garments in the way: and others cut down branches off the trees, and strawed *them* in the way.

9 And they that went before, and they that followed, cried, saying, Hosanna; Blessed *is* he that cometh in the name of the Lord:

10 Blessed *be* the kingdom of our father David, that cometh in the name of the Lord: Hosanna in the highest.

11 And Jesus entered into Jerusalem, and into the temple: and when he had looked round about upon all things, and now the eventide was come, he went out unto Bethany with the twelve.

12 And on the morrow, when they were come from Bethany, he was hungry:

13 And seeing a fig tree afar off having leaves, he came, if haply he might find any thing thereon: and when he came to it, he found nothing but leaves; for the time of figs was not *yet*.

14 And Jesus answered and said unto it, No man eat fruit of thee hereafter for ever. And his disciples heard *it*.

15 And they come to Jerusalem: and Jesus went into the temple, and began to cast out them that sold and bought in the temple, and overthrew the tables of the moneychangers, and the seats of them that sold doves;

16 And would not suffer that any man should carry *any* vessel through the temple.

17 And he taught, saying unto them, Is it not written, My house shall be called of all nations the house of prayer? but ye have made it a den of thieves.

¹⁸ And the scribes and chief priests heard *it,* and sought how they might destroy him: for they feared him, because all the people was astonished at his doctrine.

¹⁹ And when even was come, he went out of the city.

²⁰ And in the morning, as they passed by, they saw the fig tree dried up from the roots.

²¹ And Peter calling to remembrance saith unto him, Master, behold, the fig tree which thou cursedst is withered away.

²² And Jesus answering saith unto them, Have faith in God.

²³ For verily I say unto you, That whosoever shall say unto this mountain, Be thou removed, and be thou cast into the sea; and shall not doubt in his heart, but shall believe that those things which he saith shall come to pass; he shall have whatsoever he saith.

²⁴ Therefore I say unto you, What things soever ye desire, when ye pray, believe that ye receive *them,* and ye shall have *them.*

²⁵ And when ye stand praying, forgive, if ye have ought against any: that your Father also which is in heaven may forgive you your trespasses.

²⁶ But if ye do not forgive, neither will your Father which is in heaven forgive your trespasses.

²⁷ And they come again to Jerusalem: and as he was walking in the temple, there come to him the chief priests, and the scribes, and the elders,

²⁸ And say unto him, By what authority doest thou these things? and who gave thee this authority to do these things?

²⁹ And Jesus answered and said unto them, I will also ask of you one question, and answer me, and I will tell you by what authority I do these things.

³⁰ The baptism of John, was *it* from heaven, or of men? answer me.

³¹ And they reasoned with themselves, saying, If we shall say, From heaven; he will say, Why then did ye not believe him?

³² But if we shall say, Of men; they feared the people: for all *men* counted John, that he was a prophet indeed.

³³ And they answered and said unto Jesus, We cannot tell. And Jesus answering saith unto them, Neither do I tell you by what authority I do these things.

12 And he began to speak unto them by parables. A *certain* man planted a vine-yard, and set an hedge about *it,* and digged *a place for* the winefat, and built a tower, and let it out to husbandmen, and went into a far country.

² And at the season he sent to the husbandmen a servant, that he might receive from the husbandmen of the fruit of the vineyard.

³ And they caught *him,* and beat him, and sent *him* away empty.

⁴ And again he sent unto them another servant; and at him they cast stones, and wounded *him* in the head, and sent *him* away shamefully handled.

⁵ And again he sent another; and him they killed, and many others; beating some, and killing some.

⁶ Having yet therefore one son, his wellbeloved, he sent him also last unto them, saying, They will reverence my son.

⁷ But those husbandmen said among themselves, This is the heir; come, let us kill him, and the inheritance shall be ours.

⁸ And they took him, and killed *him,* and cast *him* out of the vineyard.

⁹ What shall therefore the lord of the vineyard do? he will come and destroy the husbandmen, and will give the vineyard unto others.

¹⁰ And have ye not read this scripture; The stone which the builders rejected is become the head of the corner:

¹¹ This was the Lord's doing, and it is marvellous in our eyes?

¹² And they sought to lay hold on him, but feared the people: for they knew that he had spoken the parable against them: and they left him, and went their way.

¹³ And they send unto him certain of the Pharisees and of the Herodians, to catch him in *his* words.

¹⁴ And when they were come, they say unto him, Master, we know that thou art true, and carest for no man: for thou regardest not the person of men, but teachest the way of God in truth: Is it lawful to give tribute to Caesar, or not?

¹⁵ Shall we give, or shall we not give? But he, knowing their hypocrisy, said unto them, Why tempt ye me? bring me a penny, that I may see *it.*

¹⁶ And they brought *it.* And he saith unto them, Whose *is* this image and superscription? And they said unto him, Caesar's.

¹⁷ And Jesus answering said unto them, Render to Caesar the things that are Caesar's, and

MARK 12

to God the things that are God's. And they marvelled at him.

¹⁸ Then come unto him the Sadducees, which say there is no resurrection; and they asked him, saying,

¹⁹ Master, Moses wrote unto us, If a man's brother die, and leave *his* wife *behind him,* and leave no children, that his brother should take his wife, and raise up seed unto his brother.

²⁰ Now there were seven brethren: and the first took a wife, and dying left no seed.

²¹ And the second took her, and died, neither left he any seed: and the third likewise.

²² And the seven had her, and left no seed: last of all the woman died also.

²³ In the resurrection therefore, when they shall rise, whose wife shall she be of them? for the seven had her to wife.

²⁴ And Jesus answering said unto them, Do ye not therefore err, because ye know not the scriptures, neither the power of God?

²⁵ For when they shall rise from the dead, they neither marry, nor are given in marriage; but are as the angels which are in heaven.

²⁶ And as touching the dead, that they rise: have ye not read in the book of Moses, how in the bush God spake unto him, saying, I *am* the God of Abraham, and the God of Isaac, and the God of Jacob?

²⁷ He is not the God of the dead, but the God of the living: ye therefore do greatly err.

²⁸ And one of the scribes came, and having heard them reasoning together, and perceiving that he had answered them well, asked him, Which is the first commandment of all?

²⁹ And Jesus answered him, The first of all the commandments *is,* Hear, O Israel; The Lord our God is one Lord:

³⁰ And thou shalt love the Lord thy God with all thy heart, and with all thy soul, and with all thy mind, and with all thy strength: this is the first commandment.

³¹ And the second *is* like, *namely* this, Thou shalt love thy neighbour as thyself. There is none other commandment greater than these.

³² And the scribe said unto him, Well, Master, thou hast said the truth: for there is one God; and there is none other but he:

³³ And to love him with all the heart, and with all the understanding, and with all the soul, and with all the strength, and to love *his* neighbour as himself, is more than all whole burnt offerings and sacrifices.

³⁴ And when Jesus saw that he answered discreetly, he said unto him, Thou art not far from the kingdom of God. And no man after that durst ask him *any question.*

³⁵ And Jesus answered and said, while he taught in the temple, How say the scribes that Christ is the Son of David?

³⁶ For David himself said by the Holy Ghost, The Lord said to my Lord, Sit thou on my right hand, till I make thine enemies thy footstool.

³⁷ David therefore himself calleth him Lord; and whence is he *then* his son? And the common people heard him gladly.

³⁸ And he said unto them in his doctrine, Beware of the scribes, which love to go in long clothing, and *love* salutations in the marketplaces,

³⁹ And the chief seats in the synagogues, and the uppermost rooms at feasts:

⁴⁰ Which devour widows' houses, and for a pretence make long prayers: these shall receive greater damnation.

⁴¹ And Jesus sat over against the treasury, and beheld how the people cast money into the treasury: and many that were rich cast in much.

⁴² And there came a certain poor widow, and she threw in two mites, which make a farthing.

⁴³ And he called *unto him* his disciples, and saith unto them, Verily I say unto you, That this poor widow hath cast more in, than all they which have cast into the treasury:

⁴⁴ For all *they* did cast in of their abundance; but she of her want did cast in all that she had, *even* all her living.

13 And as he went out of the temple, one of his disciples saith unto him, Master, see what manner of stones and what buildings *are here!*

² And Jesus answering said unto him, Seest thou these great buildings? there shall not be left one stone upon another, that shall not be thrown down.

³ And as he sat upon the mount of Olives over against the temple, Peter and James and John and Andrew asked him privately,

⁴ Tell us, when shall these things be? and what *shall be* the sign when all these things shall be fulfilled?

⁵ And Jesus answering them began to say, Take heed lest any *man* deceive you:

⁶ For many shall come in my name, saying, I am *Christ;* and shall deceive many.

⁷ And when ye shall hear of wars and

rumours of wars, be ye not troubled: for *such things* must needs be; but the end *shall* not *be* yet.

8 For nation shall rise against nation, and kingdom against kingdom: and there shall be earthquakes in divers places, and there shall be famines and troubles: these *are* the beginnings of sorrows.

9 But take heed to yourselves: for they shall deliver you up to councils; and in the synagogues ye shall be beaten: and ye shall be brought before rulers and kings for my sake, for a testimony against them.

10 And the gospel must first be published among all nations.

11 But when they shall lead *you*, and deliver you up, take no thought beforehand what ye shall speak, neither do ye premeditate: but whatsoever shall be given you in that hour, that speak ye: for it is not ye that speak, but the Holy Ghost.

12 Now the brother shall betray the brother to death, and the father the son; and children shall rise up against *their* parents, and shall cause them to be put to death.

13 And ye shall be hated of all *men* for my name's sake: but he that shall endure unto the end, the same shall be saved.

14 But when ye shall see the abomination of desolation, spoken of by Daniel the prophet, standing where it ought not, (let him that readeth understand,) then let them that be in Judaea flee to the mountains:

15 And let him that is on the housetop not go down into the house, neither enter *therein*, to take any thing out of his house:

16 And let him that is in the field not turn back again for to take up his garment.

17 But woe to them that are with child, and to them that give suck in those days!

18 And pray ye that your flight be not in the winter.

19 For *in* those days shall be affliction, such as was not from the beginning of the creation which God created unto this time, neither shall be.

20 And except that the Lord had shortened those days, no flesh should be saved: but for the elect's sake, whom he hath chosen, he hath shortened the days.

21 And then if any man shall say to you, Lo, here *is* Christ; or, lo, *he is* there; believe *him* not:

22 For false Christs and false prophets shall rise, and shall shew signs and wonders, to seduce, if *it were* possible, even the elect.

23 But take ye heed: behold, I have foretold you all things.

24 But in those days, after that tribulation, the sun shall be darkened, and the moon shall not give her light,

25 And the stars of heaven shall fall, and the powers that are in heaven shall be shaken.

26 And then shall they see the Son of man coming in the clouds with great power and glory.

27 And then shall he send his angels, and shall gather together his elect from the four winds, from the uttermost part of the earth to the uttermost part of heaven.

28 Now learn a parable of the fig tree; When her branch is yet tender, and putteth forth leaves, ye know that summer is near:

29 So ye in like manner, when ye shall see these things come to pass, know that it is nigh, *even* at the doors.

30 Verily I say unto you, that this generation shall not pass, till all these things be done.

31 Heaven and earth shall pass away: but my words shall not pass away.

32 But of that day and *that* hour knoweth no man, no, not the angels which are in heaven, neither the Son, but the Father.

33 Take ye heed, watch and pray: for ye know not when the time is.

34 *For the Son of man is* as a man taking a far journey, who left his house, and gave authority to his servants, and to every man his work, and commanded the porter to watch.

35 Watch ye therefore: for ye know not when the master of the house cometh, at even, or at midnight, or at the cockcrowing, or in the morning:

36 Lest coming suddenly he find you sleeping.

37 And what I say unto you I say unto all, Watch.

14 After two days was *the feast of* the passover, and of unleavened bread: and the chief priests and the scribes sought how they might take him by craft, and put *him* to death.

2 But they said, Not on the feast *day*, lest there be an uproar of the people.

3 And being in Bethany in the house of Simon the leper, as he sat at meat, there came a woman having an alabaster box of ointment of spikenard very precious; and she brake the box, and poured *it* on his head.

⁴ And there were some that had indignation within themselves, and said, Why was this waste of the ointment made?

⁵ For it might have been sold for more than three hundred pence, and have been given to the poor. And they murmured against her.

⁶ And Jesus said, Let her alone; why trouble ye her? she hath wrought a good work on me.

⁷ For ye have the poor with you always, and whensoever ye will ye may do them good: but me ye have not always.

⁸ She hath done what she could: she is come aforehand to anoint my body to the burying.

⁹ Verily I say unto you, Wheresoever this gospel shall be preached throughout the whole world, *this* also that she hath done shall be spoken of for a memorial of her.

¹⁰ And Judas Iscariot, one of the twelve, went unto the chief priests, to betray him unto them.

¹¹ And when they heard *it*, they were glad, and promised to give him money. And he sought how he might conveniently betray him.

¹² And the first day of unleavened bread, when they killed the passover, his disciples said unto him, Where wilt thou that we go and prepare that thou mayest eat the passover?

¹³ And he sendeth forth two of his disciples, and saith unto them, Go ye into the city, and there shall meet you a man bearing a pitcher of water: follow him.

¹⁴ And wheresoever he shall go in, say ye to the goodman of the house, The Master saith, Where is the guestchamber, where I shall eat the passover with my disciples?

¹⁵ And he will shew you a large upper room furnished *and* prepared: there make ready for us.

¹⁶ And his disciples went forth, and came into the city, and found as he had said unto them: and they made ready the passover.

¹⁷ And in the evening he cometh with the twelve.

¹⁸ And as they sat and did eat, Jesus said, Verily I say unto you, One of you which eateth with me shall betray me.

¹⁹ And they began to be sorrowful, and to say unto him one by one, *Is* it I? and another *said*, *Is* it I?

²⁰ And he answered and said unto them, *It is* one of the twelve, that dippeth with me in the dish.

²¹ The Son of man indeed goeth, as it is written of him: but woe to that man by whom the Son of man is betrayed! good were it for that man if he had never been born.

²² And as they did eat, Jesus took bread, and blessed, and brake *it*, and gave to them, and said, Take, eat: this is my body.

²³ And he took the cup, and when he had given thanks, he gave *it* to them: and they all drank of it.

²⁴ And he said unto them, This is my blood of the new testament, which is shed for many.

²⁵ Verily I say unto you, I will drink no more of the fruit of the vine, until that day that I drink it new in the kingdom of God.

²⁶ And when they had sung an hymn, they went out into the mount of Olives.

²⁷ And Jesus saith unto them, All ye shall be offended because of me this night: for it is written, I will smite the shepherd, and the sheep shall be scattered.

²⁸ But after that I am risen, I will go before you into Galilee.

²⁹ But Peter said unto him, Although all shall be offended, yet *will* not I.

³⁰ And Jesus saith unto him, Verily I say unto thee, That this day, *even* in this night, before the cock crow twice, thou shalt deny me thrice.

³¹ But he spake the more vehemently, If I should die with thee, I will not deny thee in any wise. Likewise also said they all.

³² And they came to a place which was named Gethsemane: and he saith to his disciples, Sit ye here, while I shall pray.

³³ And he taketh with him Peter and James and John, and began to be sore amazed, and to be very heavy;

³⁴ And saith unto them, My soul is exceeding sorrowful unto death: tarry ye here, and watch.

³⁵ And he went forward a little, and fell on the ground, and prayed that, if it were possible, the hour might pass from him.

³⁶ And he said, Abba, Father, all things *are* possible unto thee; take away this cup from me: nevertheless not what I will, but what thou wilt.

³⁷ And he cometh, and findeth them sleeping, and saith unto Peter, Simon, sleepest thou? couldest not thou watch one hour?

³⁸ Watch ye and pray, lest ye enter into temptation. The spirit truly *is* ready, but the flesh *is* weak.

³⁹ And again he went away, and prayed, and spake the same words.

⁴⁰ And when he returned, he found them

asleep again, (for their eyes were heavy,) neither wist they what to answer him.

⁴¹ And he cometh the third time, and saith unto them, Sleep on now, and take *your* rest: it is enough, the hour is come; behold, the Son of man is betrayed into the hands of sinners.

⁴² Rise up, let us go; lo, he that betrayeth me is at hand.

⁴³ And immediately, while he yet spake, cometh Judas, one of the twelve, and with him a great multitude with swords and staves, from the chief priest and the scribes and the elders.

⁴⁴ And he that betrayed him had given them a token, saying, Whomsoever I shall kiss, that same is he; take him, and lead *him* away safely.

⁴⁵ And as soon as he was come, he goeth straightway to him, and saith, Master, master; and kissed him.

⁴⁶ And they laid their hands on him, and took him.

⁴⁷ And one of them that stood by drew a sword, and smote a servant of the high priest, and cut off his ear.

⁴⁸ And Jesus answered and said unto them, Are ye come out, as against a thief, with swords and *with* staves to take me?

⁴⁹ I was daily with you in the temple teaching, and ye took me not: but the scriptures must be fulfilled.

⁵⁰ And they all forsook him, and fled.

⁵¹ And there followed him a certain young man, having a linen cloth cast about *his* naked *body*; and the young men laid hold on him:

⁵² And he left the linen cloth, and fled from them naked.

⁵³ And they led Jesus away to the high priest: and with him were assembled all the chief priests and the elders and the scribes.

⁵⁴ And Peter followed him afar off, even into the palace of the high priest: and he sat with the servants, and warmed himself at the fire.

⁵⁵ And the chief priests and all the council sought for witness against Jesus to put him to death; and found none.

⁵⁶ For many bare false witness against him, but their witness agreed not together.

⁵⁷ And there arose certain, and bare false witness against him, saying,

⁵⁸ We heard him say, I will destroy this temple that is made with hands, and within three days I will build another made without hands.

⁵⁹ But neither so did their witness agree together.

⁶⁰ And the high priest stood up in the midst, and asked Jesus, saying, Answerest thou nothing? what *is it which* these witness against thee?

⁶¹ But he held his peace, and answered nothing. Again the high priest asked him, and said unto him, Art thou the Christ, the Son of the Blessed?

⁶² And Jesus said, I am: and ye shall see the Son of man sitting on the right hand of power, and coming in the clouds of heaven.

⁶³ Then the high priest rent his clothes, and saith, What need we any further witnesses?

⁶⁴ Ye have heard the blasphemy: what think ye? And they all condemned him to be guilty of death.

⁶⁵ And some began to spit on him, and to cover his face, and to buffet him, and to say unto him, Prophesy: and the servants did strike him with the palms of their hands.

⁶⁶ And as Peter was beneath in the palace, there cometh one of the maids of the high priest:

⁶⁷ And when she saw Peter warming himself, she looked upon him, and said, And thou also wast with Jesus of Nazareth.

⁶⁸ But he denied, saying, I know not, neither understand I what thou sayest. And he went out into the porch; and the cock crew.

⁶⁹ And a maid saw him again, and began to say to them that stood by, This is *one* of them.

⁷⁰ And he denied it again. And a little after, they that stood by said again to Peter, Surely thou art *one* of them: for thou art a Galilaean, and thy speech agreeth *thereto*.

⁷¹ But he began to curse and to swear, *saying,* I know not this man of whom ye speak.

⁷² And the second time the cock crew. And Peter called to mind the word that Jesus said unto him, Before the cock crow twice, thou shalt deny me thrice. And when he thought thereon, he wept.

15 And straightway in the morning the chief priests held a consultation with the elders and scribes and the whole council, and bound Jesus, and carried *him* away, and delivered *him* to Pilate.

² And Pilate asked him, Art thou the King of the Jews? And he answering said unto him, Thou sayest *it.*

³ And the chief priests accused him of many things: but he answered nothing.

⁴ And Pilate asked him again, saying, Answerest thou nothing? behold how many things they witness against thee.

5 But Jesus yet answered nothing; so that Pilate marvelled.

6 Now at *that* feast he released unto them one prisoner, whomsoever they desired.

7 And there was *one* named Barabbas, *which lay* bound with them that had made insurrection with him, who had committed murder in the insurrection.

8 And the multitude crying aloud began to desire *him to do* as he had ever done unto them.

9 But Pilate answered them, saying, Will ye that I release unto you the King of the Jews?

10 For he knew that the chief priests had delivered him for envy.

11 But the chief priests moved the people, that he should rather release Barabbas unto them.

12 And Pilate answered and said again unto them, What will ye then that I shall do *unto him* whom ye call the King of the Jews?

13 And they cried out again, Crucify him.

14 Then Pilate said unto them, Why, what evil hath he done? And they cried out the more exceedingly, Crucify him.

15 And *so* Pilate, willing to content the people, released Barabbas unto them, and delivered Jesus, when he had scourged *him*, to be crucified.

16 And the soldiers led him away into the hall, called Praetorium; and they call together the whole band.

17 And they clothed him with purple, and platted a crown of thorns, and put it about his *head*,

18 And began to salute him, Hail, King of the Jews!

19 And they smote him on the head with a reed, and did spit upon him, and bowing *their* knees worshipped him.

20 And when they had mocked him, they took off the purple from him, and put his own clothes on him, and led him out to crucify him.

21 And they compel one Simon a Cyrenian, who passed by, coming out of the country, the father of Alexander and Rufus, to bear his cross.

22 And they bring him unto the place Golgotha, which is, being interpreted, The place of a skull.

23 And they gave him to drink wine mingled with myrrh: but he received *it* not.

24 And when they had crucified him, they parted his garments, casting lots upon them, what every man should take.

25 And it was the third hour, and they crucified him.

26 And the superscription of his accusation was written over, THE KING OF THE JEWS.

27 And with him they crucify two thieves; the one on his right hand, and the other on his left.

28 And the scripture was fulfilled, which saith, And he was numbered with the transgressors.

29 And they that passed by railed on him, wagging their heads, and saying, Ah, thou that destroyest the temple, and buildest *it* in three days,

30 Save thyself, and come down from the cross.

31 Likewise also the chief priests mocking said among themselves with the scribes, He saved others; himself he cannot save.

32 Let Christ the King of Israel descend now from the cross, that we may see and believe. And they that were crucified with him reviled him.

33 And when the sixth hour was come, there was darkness over the whole land until the ninth hour.

34 And at the ninth hour Jesus cried with a loud voice, saying, Eloi, Eloi, lama sabachthani? which is, being interpreted, My God, my God, why hast thou forsaken me?

35 And some of them that stood by, when they heard *it*, said, Behold, he calleth Elias.

36 And one ran and filled a spunge full of vinegar, and put *it* on a reed, and gave him to drink, saying, Let alone; let us see whether Elias will come to take him down.

37 And Jesus cried with a loud voice, and gave up the ghost.

38 And the veil of the temple was rent in twain from the top to the bottom.

39 And when the centurion, which stood over against him, saw that he so cried out, and gave up the ghost, he said, Truly this man was the Son of God.

40 There were also women looking on afar off: among whom was Mary Magdalene, and Mary the mother of James the less and of Joses, and Salome;

41 (Who also, when he was in Galilee, followed him, and ministered unto him;) and many other women which came up with him unto Jerusalem.

42 And now when the even was come, because it was the preparation, that is, the day before the sabbath,

43 Joseph of Arimathaea, an honourable counsellor, which also waited for the kingdom of

God, came, and went in boldly unto Pilate, and craved the body of Jesus.

⁴⁴ And Pilate marvelled if he were already dead: and calling *unto him* the centurion, he asked him whether he had been any while dead.

⁴⁵ And when he knew *it* of the centurion, he gave the body to Joseph.

⁴⁶ And he bought fine linen, and took him down, and wrapped him in the linen, and laid him in a sepulchre which was hewn out of a rock, and rolled a stone unto the door of the sepulchre.

⁴⁷ And Mary Magdalene and Mary *the mother* of Joses beheld where he was laid.

16 And when the sabbath was past, Mary Magdalene, and Mary the *mother* of James, and Salome, had bought sweet spices, that they might come and anoint him.

² And very early in the morning the first *day* of the week, they came unto the sepulchre at the rising of the sun.

³ And they said among themselves, Who shall roll us away the stone from the door of the sepulchre?

⁴ And when they looked, they saw that the stone was rolled away: for it was very great.

⁵ And entering into the sepulchre, they saw a young man sitting on the right side, clothed in a long white garment; and they were affrighted.

⁶ And he saith unto them, Be not affrighted: Ye seek Jesus of Nazareth, which was crucified: he is risen; he is not here: behold the place where they laid him.

⁷ But go your way, tell his disciples and Peter that he goeth before you into Galilee: there shall ye see him, as he said unto you.

⁸ And they went out quickly, and fled from the sepulchre; for they trembled and were amazed: neither said they any thing to any *man;* for they were afraid.

⁹ Now when *Jesus* was risen early the first *day* of the week, he appeared first to Mary Magdalene, out of whom he had cast seven devils.

¹⁰ *And* she went and told them that had been with him, as they mourned and wept.

¹¹ And they, when they had heard that he was alive, and had been seen of her, believed not.

¹² After that he appeared in another form unto two of them, as they walked, and went into the country.

¹³ And they went and told *it* unto the residue: neither believed they them.

¹⁴ Afterward he appeared unto the eleven as they sat at meat, and upbraided them with their unbelief and hardness of heart, because they believed not them which had seen him after he was risen.

¹⁵ And he said unto them, Go ye into all the world, and preach the gospel to every creature.

¹⁶ He that believeth and is baptized shall be saved; but he that believeth not shall be damned.

¹⁷ And these signs shall follow them that believe; In my name shall they cast out devils; they shall speak with new tongues;

¹⁸ They shall take up serpents; and if they drink any deadly thing, it shall not hurt them; they shall lay hands on the sick, and they shall recover.

¹⁹ So then after the Lord had spoken unto them, he was received up into heaven, and sat on the right hand of God.

²⁰ And they went forth, and preached every where, the Lord working with *them,* and confirming the word with signs following. Amen.

Luke

1 Forasmuch as many have taken in hand to set forth in order a declaration of those things which are most surely believed among us,

2 Even as they delivered them unto us, which from the beginning were eyewitnesses, and ministers of the word;

3 It seemed good to me also, having had perfect understanding of all things from the very first, to write unto thee in order, most excellent Theophilus,

4 That thou mightest know the certainty of those things, wherein thou hast been instructed.

5 There was in the days of Herod, the king of Judaea, a certain priest named Zacharias, of the course of Abia: and his wife *was* of the daughters of Aaron, and her name *was* Elisabeth.

6 And they were both righteous before God, walking in all the commandments and ordinances of the Lord blameless.

7 And they had no child, because that Elisabeth was barren, and they both were *now* well stricken in years.

8 And it came to pass, that while he executed the priest's office before God in the order of his course,

9 According to the custom of the priest's office, his lot was to burn incense when he went into the temple of the Lord.

10 And the whole multitude of the people were praying without at the time of incense.

11 And there appeared unto him an angel of the Lord standing on the right side of the altar of incense.

12 And when Zacharias saw *him,* he was troubled, and fear fell upon him.

13 But the angel said unto him, Fear not, Zacharias: for thy prayer is heard; and thy wife Elisabeth shall bear thee a son, and thou shalt call his name John.

14 And thou shalt have joy and gladness; and many shall rejoice at his birth.

15 For he shall be great in the sight of the Lord, and shall drink neither wine nor strong drink; and he shall be filled with the Holy Ghost, even from his mother's womb.

16 And many of the children of Israel shall he turn to the Lord their God.

17 And he shall go before him in the spirit and power of Elias, to turn the hearts of the fathers to the children, and the disobedient to the wisdom of the just; to make ready a people prepared for the Lord.

18 And Zacharias said unto the angel, Whereby shall I know this? for I am an old man, and my wife well stricken in years.

19 And the angel answering said unto him, I am Gabriel, that stand in the presence of God; and am sent to speak unto thee, and to shew thee these glad tidings.

20 And, behold, thou shalt be dumb, and not able to speak, until the day that these things shall be performed, because thou believest not my words, which shall be fulfilled in their season.

21 And the people waited for Zacharias, and marvelled that he tarried so long in the temple.

22 And when he came out, he could not speak unto them: and they perceived that he had seen a vision in the temple: for he beckoned unto them, and remained speechless.

23 And it came to pass, that, as soon as the days of his ministration were accomplished, he departed to his own house.

24 And after those days his wife Elisabeth conceived, and hid herself five months, saying,

25 Thus hath the Lord dealt with me in the days wherein he looked on *me,* to take away my reproach among men.

26 And in the sixth month the angel Gabriel was sent from God unto a city of Galilee, named Nazareth,

27 To a virgin espoused to a man whose name was Joseph, of the house of David; and the virgin's name *was* Mary.

28 And the angel came in unto her, and said, Hail, *thou that art* highly favoured, the Lord *is* with thee: blessed *art* thou among women.

29 And when she saw *him,* she was troubled at

his saying, and cast in her mind what manner of salutation this should be.

³⁰ And the angel said unto her, Fear not, Mary: for thou hast found favour with God.

³¹ And, behold, thou shalt conceive in thy womb, and bring forth a son, and shalt call his name JESUS.

³² He shall be great, and shall be called the Son of the Highest: and the Lord God shall give unto him the throne of his father David:

³³ And he shall reign over the house of Jacob for ever; and of his kingdom there shall be no end.

³⁴ Then said Mary unto the angel, How shall this be, seeing I know not a man?

³⁵ And the angel answered and said unto her, The Holy Ghost shall come upon thee, and the power of the Highest shall overshadow thee: therefore also that holy thing which shall be born of thee shall be called the Son of God.

³⁶ And, behold, thy cousin Elisabeth, she hath also conceived a son in her old age: and this is the sixth month with her, who was called barren.

³⁷ For with God nothing shall be impossible.

³⁸ And Mary said, Behold the handmaid of the Lord; be it unto me according to thy word. And the angel departed from her.

³⁹ And Mary arose in those days, and went into the hill country with haste, into a city of Juda;

⁴⁰ And entered into the house of Zacharias, and saluted Elisabeth.

⁴¹ And it came to pass, that, when Elisabeth heard the salutation of Mary, the babe leaped in her womb; and Elisabeth was filled with the Holy Ghost:

⁴² And she spake out with a loud voice, and said, Blessed *art* thou among women, and blessed *is* the fruit of thy womb.

⁴³ And whence *is* this to me, that the mother of my Lord should come to me?

⁴⁴ For, lo, as soon as the voice of thy salutation sounded in mine ears, the babe leaped in my womb for joy.

⁴⁵ And blessed *is* she that believed: for there shall be a performance of those things which were told her from the Lord.

⁴⁶ And Mary said, My soul doth magnify the Lord,

⁴⁷ And my spirit hath rejoiced in God my Saviour.

⁴⁸ For he hath regarded the low estate of his handmaiden: for, behold, from henceforth all generations shall call me blessed.

⁴⁹ For he that is mighty hath done to me great things; and holy *is* his name.

⁵⁰ And his mercy *is* on them that fear him from generation to generation.

⁵¹ He hath shewed strength with his arm; he hath scattered the proud in the imagination of their hearts.

⁵² He hath put down the mighty from *their* seats, and exalted them of low degree.

⁵³ He hath filled the hungry with good things; and the rich he hath sent empty away.

⁵⁴ He hath holpen his servant Israel, in remembrance of *his* mercy;

⁵⁵ As he spake to our fathers, to Abraham, and to his seed for ever.

⁵⁶ And Mary abode with her about three months, and returned to her own house.

⁵⁷ Now Elisabeth's full time came that she should be delivered; and she brought forth a son.

⁵⁸ And her neighbours and her cousins heard how the Lord had shewed great mercy upon her; and they rejoiced with her.

⁵⁹ And it came to pass, that on the eighth day they came to circumcise the child; and they called him Zacharias, after the name of his father.

⁶⁰ And his mother answered and said, Not *so*; but he shall be called John.

⁶¹ And they said unto her, There is none of thy kindred that is called by this name.

⁶² And they made signs to his father, how he would have him called.

⁶³ And he asked for a writing table, and wrote, saying, His name is John. And they marvelled all.

⁶⁴ And his mouth was opened immediately, and his tongue *loosed*, and he spake, and praised God.

⁶⁵ And fear came on all that dwelt round about them: and all these sayings were noised abroad throughout all the hill country of Judaea.

⁶⁶ And all they that heard *them* laid *them* up in their hearts, saying, What manner of child shall this be! And the hand of the Lord was with him.

⁶⁷ And his father Zacharias was filled with the Holy Ghost, and prophesied, saying,

⁶⁸ Blessed *be* the Lord God of Israel; for he hath visited and redeemed his people,

⁶⁹ And hath raised up an horn of salvation for us in the house of his servant David;

⁷⁰ As he spake by the mouth of his holy prophets, which have been since the world began:

⁷¹ That we should be saved from our enemies, and from the hand of all that hate us;

⁷² To perform the mercy *promised* to our fathers, and to remember his holy covenant;

⁷³ The oath which he sware to our father Abraham,

⁷⁴ That he would grant unto us, that we being delivered out of the hand of our enemies might serve him without fear,

⁷⁵ In holiness and righteousness before him, all the days of our life.

⁷⁶ And thou, child, shalt be called the prophet of the Highest: for thou shalt go before the face of the Lord to prepare his ways;

⁷⁷ To give knowledge of salvation unto his people by the remission of their sins,

⁷⁸ Through the tender mercy of our God; whereby the dayspring from on high hath visited us,

⁷⁹ To give light to them that sit in darkness and *in* the shadow of death, to guide our feet into the way of peace.

⁸⁰ And the child grew, and waxed strong in spirit, and was in the deserts till the day of his shewing unto Israel.

2 And it came to pass in those days, that there went out a decree from Caesar Augustus, that all the world should be taxed.

²(*And* this taxing was first made when Cyrenius was governor of Syria.)

³ And all went to be taxed, every one into his own city.

⁴ And Joseph also went up from Galilee, out of the city of Nazareth, into Judaea, unto the city of David, which is called Bethlehem; (because he was of the house and lineage of David:)

⁵ To be taxed with Mary his espoused wife, being great with child.

⁶ And so it was, that, while they were there, the days were accomplished that she should be delivered.

⁷ And she brought forth her firstborn son, and wrapped him in swaddling clothes, and laid him in a manger; because there was no room for them in the inn.

⁸ And there were in the same country shepherds abiding in the field, keeping watch over their flock by night.

⁹ And, lo, the angel of the Lord came upon them, and the glory of the Lord shone round about them: and they were sore afraid.

¹⁰ And the angel said unto them, Fear not: for, behold, I bring you good tidings of great joy, which shall be to all people.

¹¹ For unto you is born this day in the city of David a Saviour, which is Christ the Lord.

¹² And this *shall be* a sign unto you; Ye shall find the babe wrapped in swaddling clothes, lying in a manger.

¹³ And suddenly there was with the angel a multitude of the heavenly host praising God, and saying,

¹⁴ Glory to God in the highest, and on earth peace, good will toward men.

¹⁵ And it came to pass, as the angels were gone away from them into heaven, the shepherds said one to another, Let us now go even unto Bethlehem, and see this thing which is come to pass, which the Lord hath made known unto us.

¹⁶ And they came with haste, and found Mary, and Joseph, and the babe lying in a manger.

¹⁷ And when they had seen *it*, they made known abroad the saying which was told them concerning this child.

¹⁸ And all they that heard *it* wondered at those things which were told them by the shepherds.

¹⁹ But Mary kept all these things, and pondered *them* in her heart.

²⁰ And the shepherds returned, glorifying and praising God for all the things that they had heard and seen, as it was told unto them.

²¹ And when eight days were accomplished for the circumcising of the child, his name was called JESUS, which was so named of the angel before he was conceived in the womb.

²² And when the days of her purification according to the law of Moses were accomplished, they brought him to Jerusalem, to present *him* to the Lord;

²³(As it is written in the law of the Lord, Every male that openeth the womb shall be called holy to the Lord;)

²⁴ And to offer a sacrifice according to that which is said in the law of the Lord, A pair of turtledoves, or two young pigeons.

²⁵ And, behold, there was a man in Jerusalem, whose name *was* Simeon; and the same man *was* just and devout, waiting for the consolation of Israel: and the Holy Ghost was upon him.

²⁶ And it was revealed unto him by the Holy Ghost, that he should not see death, before he had seen the Lord's Christ.

²⁷ And he came by the Spirit into the temple:

and when the parents brought in the child Jesus, to do for him after the custom of the law, ²⁸ Then took he him up in his arms, and blessed God, and said,

²⁹ Lord, now lettest thou thy servant depart in peace, according to thy word:

³⁰ For mine eyes have seen thy salvation,

³¹ Which thou hast prepared before the face of all people;

³² A light to lighten the Gentiles, and the glory of thy people Israel.

³³ And Joseph and his mother marvelled at those things which were spoken of him.

³⁴ And Simeon blessed them, and said unto Mary his mother, Behold, this *child* is set for the fall and rising again of many in Israel; and for a sign which shall be spoken against;

³⁵(Yea, a sword shall pierce through thy own soul also,) that the thoughts of many hearts may be revealed.

³⁶ And there was one Anna, a prophetess, the daughter of Phanuel, of the tribe of Aser: she was of a great age, and had lived with an husband seven years from her virginity;

³⁷ And she *was* a widow of about fourscore and four years, which departed not from the temple, but served *God* with fastings and prayers night and day.

³⁸ And she coming in that instant gave thanks likewise unto the Lord, and spake of him to all them that looked for redemption in Jerusalem.

³⁹ And when they had performed all things according to the law of the Lord, they returned into Galilee, to their own city Nazareth.

⁴⁰ And the child grew, and waxed strong in spirit, filled with wisdom: and the grace of God was upon him.

⁴¹ Now his parents went to Jerusalem every year at the feast of the passover.

⁴² And when he was twelve years old, they went up to Jerusalem after the custom of the feast.

⁴³ And when they had fulfilled the days, as they returned, the child Jesus tarried behind in Jerusalem; and Joseph and his mother knew not *of it.*

⁴⁴ But they, supposing him to have been in the company, went a day's journey; and they sought him among *their* kinsfolk and acquaintance.

⁴⁵ And when they found him not, they turned back again to Jerusalem, seeking him.

⁴⁶ And it came to pass, that after three days they found him in the temple, sitting in the midst of the doctors, both hearing them, and asking them questions.

⁴⁷ And all that heard him were astonished at his understanding and answers.

⁴⁸ And when they saw him, they were amazed: and his mother said unto him, Son, why hast thou thus dealt with us? behold, thy father and I have sought thee sorrowing.

⁴⁹ And he said unto them, How is it that ye sought me? wist ye not that I must be about my Father's business?

⁵⁰ And they understood not the saying which he spake unto them.

⁵¹ And he went down with them, and came to Nazareth, and was subject unto them: but his mother kept all these sayings in her heart.

⁵² And Jesus increased in wisdom and stature, and in favour with God and man.

3 Now in the fifteenth year of the reign of Tiberius Caesar, Pontius Pilate being governor of Judaea, and Herod being tetrarch of Galilee, and his brother Philip tetrarch of Ituraea and of the region of Trachonitis, and Lysanias the tetrarch of Abilene,

² Annas and Caiaphas being the high priests, the word of God came unto John the son of Zacharias in the wilderness.

³ And he came into all the country about Jordan, preaching the baptism of repentance for the remission of sins;

⁴ As it is written in the book of the words of Esaias the prophet, saying, The voice of one crying in the wilderness, Prepare ye the way of the Lord, make his paths straight.

⁵ Every valley shall be filled, and every mountain and hill shall be brought low; and the crooked shall be made straight, and the rough ways *shall be* made smooth;

⁶ And all flesh shall see the salvation of God.

⁷ Then said he to the multitude that came forth to be baptized of him, O generation of vipers, who hath warned you to flee from the wrath to come?

⁸ Bring forth therefore fruits worthy of repentance, and begin not to say within yourselves, We have Abraham to *our* father: for I say unto you, That God is able of these stones to raise up children unto Abraham.

⁹ And now also the axe is laid unto the root of the trees: every tree therefore which bringeth not forth good fruit is hewn down, and cast into the fire.

10 And the people asked him, saying, What shall we do then?

11 He answereth and saith unto them, He that hath two coats, let him impart to him that hath none; and he that hath meat, let him do likewise.

12 Then came also publicans to be baptized, and said unto him, Master, what shall we do?

13 And he said unto them, Exact no more than that which is appointed you.

14 And the soldiers likewise demanded of him, saying, And what shall we do? And he said unto them, Do violence to no man, neither accuse *any* falsely; and be content with your wages.

15 And as the people were in expectation, and all men mused in their hearts of John, whether he were the Christ, or not;

16 John answered, saying unto *them* all, I indeed baptize you with water; but one mightier than I cometh, the latchet of whose shoes I am not worthy to unloose: he shall baptize you with the Holy Ghost and with fire:

17 Whose fan *is* in his hand, and he will throughly purge his floor, and will gather the wheat into his garner; but the chaff he will burn with fire unquenchable.

18 And many other things in his exhortation preached he unto the people.

19 But Herod the tetrarch, being reproved by him for Herodias his brother Philip's wife, and for all the evils which Herod had done,

20 Added yet this above all, that he shut up John in prison.

21 Now when all the people were baptized, it came to pass, that Jesus also being baptized, and praying, the heaven was opened,

22 And the Holy Ghost descended in a bodily shape like a dove upon him, and a voice came from heaven, which said, Thou art my beloved Son; in thee I am well pleased.

23 And Jesus himself began to be about thirty years of age, being (as was supposed) the son of Joseph, which was *the son* of Heli,

24 Which was *the son* of Matthat, which was *the son* of Levi, which was *the son* of Melchi, which was *the son* of Janna, which was *the son* of Joseph,

25 Which was *the son* of Mattathias, which was *the son* of Amos, which was *the son* of Naum, which was *the son* of Esli, which was *the son* of Nagge,

26 Which was *the son* of Maath, which was *the son* of Mattathias, which was *the son* of Semei,

which was *the son* of Joseph, which was *the son* of Juda,

27 Which was *the son* of Joanna, which was *the son* of Rhesa, which was *the son* of Zorobabel, which was *the son* of Salathiel, which was *the son* of Neri,

28 Which was *the son* of Melchi, which was *the son* of Addi, which was *the son* of Cosam, which was *the son* of Elmodam, which was *the son* of Er,

29 Which was *the son* of Jose, which was *the son* of Eliezer, which was *the son* of Jorim, which was *the son* of Matthat, which was *the son* of Levi,

30 Which was *the son* of Simeon, which was *the son* of Juda, which was *the son* of Joseph, which was *the son* of Jonan, which was *the son* of Eliakim,

31 Which was *the son* of Melea, which was *the son* of Menan, which was *the son* of Mattatha, which was *the son* of Nathan, which was *the son* of David,

32 Which was *the son* of Jesse, which was *the son* of Obed, which was *the son* of Booz, which was *the son* of Salmon, which was *the son* of Naasson,

33 Which was *the son* of Aminadab, which was *the son* of Aram, which was *the son* of Esrom, which was *the son* of Phares, which was *the son* of Juda,

34 Which was *the son* of Jacob, which was *the son* of Isaac, which was *the son* of Abraham, which was *the son* of Thara, which was *the son* of Nachor,

35 Which was *the son* of Saruch, which was *the son* of Ragau, which was *the son* of Phalec, which was *the son* of Heber, which was *the son* of Sala,

36 Which was *the son* of Cainan, which was *the son* of Arphaxad, which was *the son* of Sem, which was *the son* of Noe, which was *the son* of Lamech,

37 Which was *the son* of Mathusala, which was *the son* of Enoch, which was *the son* of Jared, which was *the son* of Maleleel, which was *the son* of Cainan,

38 Which was *the son* of Enos, which was *the son* of Seth, which was *the son* of Adam, which was *the son* of God.

4 And Jesus being full of the Holy Ghost returned from Jordan, and was led by the Spirit into the wilderness,

2 Being forty days tempted of the devil. And in those days he did eat nothing: and when

they were ended, he afterward hungered.
3 And the devil said unto him, If thou be the Son of God, command this stone that it be made bread.

4 And Jesus answered him, saying, It is written, That man shall not live by bread alone, but by every word of God.

5 And the devil, taking him up into an high mountain, shewed unto him all the kingdoms of the world in a moment of time.

6 And the devil said unto him, All this power will I give thee, and the glory of them: for that is delivered unto me; and to whomsoever I will I give it.

7 If thou therefore wilt worship me, all shall be thine.

8 And Jesus answered and said unto him, Get thee behind me, Satan: for it is written, Thou shalt worship the Lord thy God, and him only shalt thou serve.

9 And he brought him to Jerusalem, and set him on a pinnacle of the temple, and said unto him, If thou be the Son of God, cast thyself down from hence:

10 For it is written, He shall give his angels charge over thee, to keep thee:

11 And in *their* hands they shall bear thee up, lest at any time thou dash thy foot against a stone.

12 And Jesus answering said unto him, It is said, Thou shalt not tempt the Lord thy God.

13 And when the devil had ended all the temptation, he departed from him for a season.

14 And Jesus returned in the power of the Spirit into Galilee: and there went out a fame of him through all the region round about.

15 And he taught in their synagogues, being glorified of all.

16 And he came to Nazareth, where he had been brought up: and, as his custom was, he went into the synagogue on the sabbath day, and stood up for to read.

17 And there was delivered unto him the book of the prophet Esaias. And when he had opened the book, he found the place where it was written,

18 The Spirit of the Lord is upon me, because he hath anointed me to preach the gospel to the poor; he hath sent me to heal the brokenhearted, to preach deliverance to the captives, and recovering of sight to the blind, to set at liberty them that are bruised,

19 To preach the acceptable year of the Lord.

20 And he closed the book, and he gave *it* again to the minister, and sat down. And the eyes of all them that were in the synagogue were fastened on him.

21 And he began to say unto them, This day is this scripture fulfilled in your ears.

22 And all bare him witness, and wondered at the gracious words which proceeded out of his mouth. And they said, Is not this Joseph's son?

23 And he said unto them, Ye will surely say unto me this proverb, Physician, heal thyself: whatsoever we have heard done in Capernaum, do also here in thy country.

24 And he said, Verily I say unto you, No prophet is accepted in his own country.

25 But I tell you of a truth, many widows were in Israel in the days of Elias, when the heaven was shut up three years and six months, when great famine was throughout all the land;

26 But unto none of them was Elias sent, save unto Sarepta, *a city* of Sidon, unto a woman *that was* a widow.

27 And many lepers were in Israel in the time of Eliseus the prophet; and none of them was cleansed, saving Naaman the Syrian.

28 And all they in the synagogue, when they heard these things, were filled with wrath,

29 And rose up, and thrust him out of the city, and led him unto the brow of the hill whereon their city was built, that they might cast him down headlong.

30 But he passing through the midst of them went his way,

31 And came down to Capernaum, a city of Galilee, and taught them on the sabbath days.

32 And they were astonished at his doctrine: for his word was with power.

33 And in the synagogue there was a man, which had a spirit of an unclean devil, and cried out with a loud voice,

34 Saying, Let *us* alone; what have we to do with thee, *thou* Jesus of Nazareth? art thou come to destroy us? I know thee who thou art; the Holy One of God.

35 And Jesus rebuked him, saying, Hold thy peace, and come out of him. And when the devil had thrown him in the midst, he came out of him, and hurt him not.

36 And they were all amazed, and spake among themselves, saying, What a word *is* this! for with authority and power he commandeth the unclean spirits, and they come out.

37 And the fame of him went out into every place of the country round about.

³⁸ And he arose out of the synagogue, and entered into Simon's house. And Simon's wife's mother was taken with a great fever; and they besought him for her.

³⁹ And he stood over her, and rebuked the fever; and it left her: and immediately she arose and ministered unto them.

⁴⁰ Now when the sun was setting, all they that had any sick with divers diseases brought them unto him; and he laid his hands on every one of them, and healed them.

⁴¹ And devils also came out of many, crying out, and saying, Thou art Christ the Son of God. And he rebuking *them* suffered them not to speak: for they knew that he was Christ.

⁴² And when it was day, he departed and went into a desert place: and the people sought him, and came unto him, and stayed him, that he should not depart from them.

⁴³ And he said unto them, I must preach the kingdom of God to other cities also: for therefore am I sent.

⁴⁴ And he preached in the synagogues of Galilee.

5 And it came to pass, that, as the people pressed upon him to hear the word of God, he stood by the lake of Gennesaret,

² And saw two ships standing by the lake: but the fishermen were gone out of them, and were washing *their* nets.

³ And he entered into one of the ships, which was Simon's, and prayed him that he would thrust out a little from the land. And he sat down, and taught the people out of the ship.

⁴ Now when he had left speaking, he said unto Simon, Launch out into the deep, and let down your nets for a draught.

⁵ And Simon answering said unto him, Master, we have toiled all the night, and have taken nothing: nevertheless at thy word I will let down the net.

⁶ And when they had this done, they inclosed a great multitude of fishes: and their net brake.

⁷ And they beckoned unto *their* partners, which were in the other ship, that they should come and help them. And they came, and filled both the ships, so that they began to sink.

⁸ When Simon Peter saw *it*, he fell down at Jesus' knees, saying, Depart from me; for I am a sinful man, O Lord.

⁹ For he was astonished, and all that were with him, at the draught of the fishes which they had taken:

¹⁰ And so *was* also James, and John, the sons of Zebedee, which were partners with Simon. And Jesus said unto Simon, Fear not; from henceforth thou shalt catch men.

¹¹ And when they had brought their ships to land, they forsook all, and followed him.

¹² And it came to pass, when he was in a certain city, behold a man full of leprosy: who seeing Jesus fell on *his* face, and besought him, saying, Lord, if thou wilt, thou canst make me clean.

¹³ And he put forth *his* hand, and touched him, saying, I will: be thou clean. And immediately the leprosy departed from him.

¹⁴ And he charged him to tell no man: but go, and shew thyself to the priest, and offer for thy cleansing, according as Moses commanded, for a testimony unto them.

¹⁵ But so much the more went there a fame abroad of him: and great multitudes came together to hear, and to be healed by him of their infirmities.

¹⁶ And he withdrew himself into the wilderness, and prayed.

¹⁷ And it came to pass on a certain day, as he was teaching, that there were Pharisees and doctors of the law sitting by, which were come out of every town of Galilee, and Judaea, and Jerusalem: and the power of the Lord was *present* to heal them.

¹⁸ And, behold, men brought in a bed a man which was taken with a palsy: and they sought *means* to bring him in, and to lay *him* before him.

¹⁹ And when they could not find by what *way* they might bring him in because of the multitude, they went upon the housetop, and let him down through the tiling with *his* couch into the midst before Jesus.

²⁰ And when he saw their faith, he said unto him, Man, thy sins are forgiven thee.

²¹ And the scribes and the Pharisees began to reason, saying, Who is this which speaketh blasphemies? Who can forgive sins, but God alone?

²² But when Jesus perceived their thoughts, he answering said unto them, What reason ye in your hearts?

²³ Whether is easier, to say, Thy sins be forgiven thee; or to say, Rise up and walk?

²⁴ But that ye may know that the Son of man hath power upon earth to forgive sins, (he said unto the sick of the palsy,) I say unto thee, Arise, and take up thy couch, and go into thine house.

²⁵ And immediately he rose up before them, and took up that whereon he lay, and departed to his own house, glorifying God.

²⁶ And they were all amazed, and they glorified God, and were filled with fear, saying, We have seen strange things to day.

²⁷ And after these things he went forth, and saw a publican, named Levi, sitting at the receipt of custom: and he said unto him, Follow me.

²⁸ And he left all, rose up, and followed him.

²⁹ And Levi made him a great feast in his own house: and there was a great company of publicans and of others that sat down with them.

³⁰ But their scribes and Pharisees murmured against his disciples, saying, Why do ye eat and drink with publicans and sinners?

³¹ And Jesus answering said unto them, They that are whole need not a physician; but they that are sick.

³² I came not to call the righteous, but sinners to repentance.

³³ And they said unto him, Why do the disciples of John fast often, and make prayers, and likewise *the disciples* of the Pharisees; but thine eat and drink?

³⁴ And he said unto them, Can ye make the children of the bridechamber fast, while the bridegroom is with them?

³⁵ But the days will come, when the bridegroom shall be taken away from them, and then shall they fast in those days.

³⁶ And he spake also a parable unto them; No man putteth a piece of a new garment upon an old; if otherwise, then both the new maketh a rent, and the piece that was *taken* out of the new agreeth not with the old.

³⁷ And no man putteth new wine into old bottles; else the new wine will burst the bottles, and be spilled, and the bottles shall perish.

³⁸ But new wine must be put into new bottles; and both are preserved.

³⁹ No man also having drunk old *wine* straightway desireth new: for he saith, The old is better.

6 And it came to pass on the second sabbath after the first, that he went through the corn fields; and his disciples plucked the ears of corn, and did eat, rubbing *them* in *their* hands.

² And certain of the Pharisees said unto them, Why do ye that which is not lawful to do on the sabbath days?

³ And Jesus answering them said, Have ye not read so much as this, what David did, when himself was an hungred, and they which were with him;

⁴ How he went into the house of God, and did take and eat the shewbread, and gave also to them that were with him; which it is not lawful to eat but for the priests alone?

⁵ And he said unto them, That the Son of man is Lord also of the sabbath.

⁶ And it came to pass also on another sabbath, that he entered into the synagogue and taught: and there was a man whose right hand was withered.

⁷ And the scribes and Pharisees watched him, whether he would heal on the sabbath day; that they might find an accusation against him.

⁸ But he knew their thoughts, and said to the man which had the withered hand, Rise up, and stand forth in the midst. And he arose and stood forth.

⁹ Then said Jesus unto them, I will ask you one thing; Is it lawful on the sabbath days to do good, or to do evil? to save life, or to destroy *it*?

¹⁰ And looking round about upon them all, he said unto the man, Stretch forth thy hand. And he did so: and his hand was restored whole as the other.

¹¹ And they were filled with madness; and communed one with another what they might do to Jesus.

¹² And it came to pass in those days, that he went out into a mountain to pray, and continued all night in prayer to God.

¹³ And when it was day, he called *unto him* his disciples: and of them he chose twelve, whom also he named apostles;

¹⁴ Simon, (whom he also named Peter,) and Andrew his brother, James and John, Philip and Bartholomew,

¹⁵ Matthew and Thomas, James the *son* of Alphaeus, and Simon called Zelotes,

¹⁶ And Judas *the brother* of James, and Judas Iscariot, which also was the traitor.

¹⁷ And he came down with them, and stood in the plain, and the company of his disciples, and a great multitude of people out of all Judaea and Jerusalem, and from the sea coast of Tyre and Sidon, which came to hear him, and to be healed of their diseases;

¹⁸ And they that were vexed with unclean spirits: and they were healed.

¹⁹ And the whole multitude sought to touch him: for there went virtue out of him, and healed *them* all.

[20] And he lifted up his eyes on his disciples, and said, Blessed *be ye* poor: for yours is the kingdom of God.

[21] Blessed *are ye* that hunger now: for ye shall be filled. Blessed *are ye* that weep now: for ye shall laugh.

[22] Blessed are ye, when men shall hate you, and when they shall separate you *from their company,* and shall reproach *you,* and cast out your name as evil, for the Son of man's sake.

[23] Rejoice ye in that day, and leap for joy: for, behold, your reward *is* great in heaven: for in the like manner did their fathers unto the prophets.

[24] But woe unto you that are rich! for ye have received your consolation.

[25] Woe unto you that are full! for ye shall hunger. Woe unto you that laugh now! for ye shall mourn and weep.

[26] Woe unto you, when all men shall speak well of you! for so did their fathers to the false prophets.

[27] But I say unto you which hear, Love your enemies, do good to them which hate you,

[28] Bless them that curse you, and pray for them which despitefully use you.

[29] And unto him that smiteth thee on the *one* cheek offer also the other; and him that taketh away thy cloke forbid not *to take thy* coat also.

[30] Give to every man that asketh of thee; and of him that taketh away thy goods ask *them* not again.

[31] And as ye would that men should do to you, do ye also to them likewise.

[32] For if ye love them which love you, what thank have ye? for sinners also love those that love them.

[33] And if ye do good to them which do good to you, what thank have ye? for sinners also do even the same.

[34] And if ye lend *to them* of whom ye hope to receive, what thank have ye? for sinners also lend to sinners, to receive as much again.

[35] But love ye your enemies, and do good, and lend, hoping for nothing again; and your reward shall be great, and ye shall be the children of the Highest: for he is kind unto the unthankful and *to* the evil.

[36] Be ye therefore merciful, as your Father also is merciful.

[37] Judge not, and ye shall not be judged: condemn not, and ye shall not be condemned: forgive, and ye shall be forgiven:

[38] Give, and it shall be given unto you; good measure, pressed down, and shaken together, and running over, shall men give into your bosom. For with the same measure that ye mete withal it shall be measured to you again.

[39] And he spake a parable unto them, Can the blind lead the blind? shall they not both fall into the ditch?

[40] The disciple is not above his master: but every one that is perfect shall be as his master.

[41] And why beholdest thou the mote that is in thy brother's eye, but perceivest not the beam that is in thine own eye?

[42] Either how canst thou say to thy brother, Brother, let me pull out the mote that is in thine eye, when thou thyself beholdest not the beam that is in thine own eye? Thou hypocrite, cast out first the beam out of thine own eye, and then shalt thou see clearly to pull out the mote that is in thy brother's eye.

[43] For a good tree bringeth not forth corrupt fruit; neither doth a corrupt tree bring forth good fruit.

[44] For every tree is known by his own fruit. For of thorns men do not gather figs, nor of a bramble bush gather they grapes.

[45] A good man out of the good treasure of his heart bringeth forth that which is good; and an evil man out of the evil treasure of his heart bringeth forth that which is evil: for of the abundance of the heart his mouth speaketh.

[46] And why call ye me, Lord, Lord, and do not the things which I say?

[47] Whosoever cometh to me, and heareth my sayings, and doeth them, I will shew you to whom he is like:

[48] He is like a man which built an house, and digged deep, and laid the foundation on a rock: and when the flood arose, the stream beat vehemently upon that house, and could not shake it: for it was founded upon a rock.

[49] But he that heareth, and doeth not, is like a man that without a foundation built an house upon the earth; against which the stream did beat vehemently, and immediately it fell; and the ruin of that house was great.

7 Now when he had ended all his sayings in the audience of the people, he entered into Capernaum.

[2] And a certain centurion's servant, who was dear unto him, was sick, and ready to die.

[3] And when he heard of Jesus, he sent unto

him the elders of the Jews, beseeching him that he would come and heal his servant.

4 And when they came to Jesus, they besought him instantly, saying, That he was worthy for whom he should do this:

5 For he loveth our nation, and he hath built us a synagogue.

6 Then Jesus went with them. And when he was now not far from the house, the centurion sent friends to him, saying unto him, Lord, trouble not thyself: for I am not worthy that thou shouldest enter under my roof:

7 Wherefore neither thought I myself worthy to come unto thee: but say in a word, and my servant shall be healed.

8 For I also am a man set under authority, having under me soldiers, and I say unto one, Go, and he goeth; and to another, Come, and he cometh; and to my servant, Do this, and he doeth *it*.

9 When Jesus heard these things, he marvelled at him, and turned him about, and said unto the people that followed him, I say unto you, I have not found so great faith, no, not in Israel.

10 And they that were sent, returning to the house, found the servant whole that had been sick.

11 And it came to pass the day after, that he went into a city called Nain; and many of his disciples went with him, and much people.

12 Now when he came nigh to the gate of the city, behold, there was a dead man carried out, the only son of his mother, and she was a widow: and much people of the city was with her.

13 And when the Lord saw her, he had compassion on her, and said unto her, Weep not.

14 And he came and touched the bier: and they that bare *him* stood still. And he said, Young man, I say unto thee, Arise.

15 And he that was dead sat up, and began to speak. And he delivered him to his mother.

16 And there came a fear on all: and they glorified God, saying, That a great prophet is risen up among us; and, That God hath visited his people.

17 And this rumour of him went forth throughout all Judaea, and throughout all the region round about.

18 And the disciples of John shewed him of all these things.

19 And John calling *unto him* two of his disciples sent *them* to Jesus, saying, Art thou he that should come? or look we for another?

20 When the men were come unto him, they said, John Baptist hath sent us unto thee, saying, Art thou he that should come? or look we for another?

21 And in that same hour he cured many of *their* infirmities and plagues, and of evil spirits; and unto many *that were* blind he gave sight.

22 Then Jesus answering said unto them, Go your way, and tell John what things ye have seen and heard; how that the blind see, the lame walk, the lepers are cleansed, the deaf hear, the dead are raised, to the poor the gospel is preached.

23 And blessed is *he,* whosoever shall not be offended in me.

24 And when the messengers of John were departed, he began to speak unto the people concerning John, What went ye out into the wilderness for to see? A reed shaken with the wind?

25 But what went ye out for to see? A man clothed in soft raiment? Behold, they which are gorgeously apparelled, and live delicately, are in kings' courts.

26 But what went ye out for to see? A prophet? Yea, I say unto you, and much more than a prophet.

27 This is *he,* of whom it is written, Behold, I send my messenger before thy face, which shall prepare thy way before thee.

28 For I say unto you, Among those that are born of women there is not a greater prophet than John the Baptist: but he that is least in the kingdom of God is greater than he.

29 And all the people that heard *him,* and the publicans, justified God, being baptized with the baptism of John.

30 But the Pharisees and lawyers rejected the counsel of God against themselves, being not baptized of him.

31 And the Lord said, Whereunto then shall I liken the men of this generation? and to what are they like?

32 They are like unto children sitting in the marketplace, and calling one to another, and saying, We have piped unto you, and ye have not danced; we have mourned to you, and ye have not wept.

33 For John the Baptist came neither eating bread nor drinking wine; and ye say, He hath a devil.

³⁴ The Son of man is come eating and drinking; and ye say, Behold a gluttonous man, and a winebibber, a friend of publicans and sinners!

³⁵ But wisdom is justified of all her children.

³⁶ And one of the Pharisees desired him that he would eat with him. And he went into the Pharisee's house, and sat down to meat.

³⁷ And, behold, a woman in the city, which was a sinner, when she knew that *Jesus* sat at meat in the Pharisee's house, brought an alabaster box of ointment,

³⁸ And stood at his feet behind *him* weeping, and began to wash his feet with tears, and did wipe *them* with the hairs of her head, and kissed his feet, and anointed *them* with the ointment.

³⁹ Now when the Pharisee which had bidden him saw *it,* he spake within himself, saying, This man, if he were a prophet, would have known who and what manner of woman *this is* that toucheth him: for she is a sinner.

⁴⁰ And Jesus answering said unto him, Simon, I have somewhat to say unto thee. And he saith, Master, say on.

⁴¹ There was a certain creditor which had two debtors: the one owed five hundred pence, and the other fifty.

⁴² And when they had nothing to pay, he frankly forgave them both. Tell me therefore, which of them will love him most?

⁴³ Simon answered and said, I suppose that *he,* to whom he forgave most. And he said unto him, Thou hast rightly judged.

⁴⁴ And he turned to the woman, and said unto Simon, Seest thou this woman? I entered into thine house, thou gavest me no water for my feet: but she hath washed my feet with tears, and wiped *them* with the hairs of her head.

⁴⁵ Thou gavest me no kiss: but this woman since the time I came in hath not ceased to kiss my feet.

⁴⁶ My head with oil thou didst not anoint: but this woman hath anointed my feet with ointment.

⁴⁷ Wherefore I say unto thee, Her sins, which are many, are forgiven; for she loved much: but to whom little is forgiven, *the same* loveth little.

⁴⁸ And he said unto her, Thy sins are forgiven.

⁴⁹ And they that sat at meat with him began to say within themselves, Who is this that forgiveth sins also?

⁵⁰ And he said to the woman, Thy faith hath saved thee; go in peace.

8 And it came to pass afterward, that he went throughout every city and village, preaching and shewing the glad tidings of the kingdom of God: and the twelve *were* with him,

² And certain women, which had been healed of evil spirits and infirmities, Mary called Magdalene, out of whom went seven devils,

³ And Joanna the wife of Chuza Herod's steward, and Susanna, and many others, which ministered unto him of their substance.

⁴ And when much people were gathered together, and were come to him out of every city, he spake by a parable:

⁵ A sower went out to sow his seed: and as he sowed, some fell by the way side; and it was trodden down, and the fowls of the air devoured it.

⁶ And some fell upon a rock; and as soon as it was sprung up, it withered away, because it lacked moisture.

⁷ And some fell among thorns; and the thorns sprang up with it, and choked it.

⁸ And other fell on good ground, and sprang up, and bare fruit an hundredfold. And when he had said these things, he cried, He that hath ears to hear, let him hear.

⁹ And his disciples asked him, saying, What might this parable be?

¹⁰ And he said, Unto you it is given to know the mysteries of the kingdom of God: but to others in parables; that seeing they might not see, and hearing they might not understand.

¹¹ Now the parable is this: The seed is the word of God.

¹² Those by the way side are they that hear; then cometh the devil, and taketh away the word out of their hearts, lest they should believe and be saved.

¹³ They on the rock *are they,* which, when they hear, receive the word with joy; and these have no root, which for a while believe, and in time of temptation fall away.

¹⁴ And that which fell among thorns are they, which, when they have heard, go forth, and are choked with cares and riches and pleasures of *this* life, and bring no fruit to perfection.

¹⁵ But that on the good ground are they, which in an honest and good heart, having heard the word, keep *it,* and bring forth fruit with patience.

¹⁶ No man, when he hath lighted a candle, covereth it with a vessel, or putteth *it* under a

bed; but setteth *it* on a candlestick, that they which enter in may see the light.

¹⁷ For nothing is secret, that shall not be made manifest; neither *any thing* hid, that shall not be known and come abroad.

¹⁸ Take heed therefore how ye hear: for whosoever hath, to him shall be given; and whosoever hath not, from him shall be taken even that which he seemeth to have.

¹⁹ Then came to him *his* mother and his brethren, and could not come at him for the press.

²⁰ And it was told him *by certain* which said, Thy mother and thy brethren stand without, desiring to see thee.

²¹ And he answered and said unto them, My mother and my brethren are these which hear the word of God, and do it.

²² Now it came to pass on a certain day, that he went into a ship with his disciples: and he said unto them, Let us go over unto the other side of the lake. And they launched forth.

²³ But as they sailed he fell asleep: and there came down a storm of wind on the lake; and they were filled *with water,* and were in jeopardy.

²⁴ And they came to him, and awoke him, saying, Master, master, we perish. Then he arose, and rebuked the wind and the raging of the water: and they ceased, and there was a calm.

²⁵ And he said unto them, Where is your faith? And they being afraid wondered, saying one to another, What manner of man is this! for he commandeth even the winds and water, and they obey him.

²⁶ And they arrived at the country of the Gadarenes, which is over against Galilee.

²⁷ And when he went forth to land, there met him out of the city a certain man, which had devils long time, and ware no clothes, neither abode in *any* house, but in the tombs.

²⁸ When he saw Jesus, he cried out, and fell down before him, and with a loud voice said, What have I to do with thee, Jesus, *thou* Son of God most high? I beseech thee, torment me not.

²⁹(For he had commanded the unclean spirit to come out of the man. For oftentimes it had caught him: and he was kept bound with chains and in fetters; and he brake the bands, and was driven of the devil into the wilderness.)

³⁰ And Jesus asked him, saying, What is thy name? And he said, Legion: because many devils were entered into him.

³¹ And they besought him that he would not command them to go out into the deep.

³² And there was there an herd of many swine feeding on the mountain: and they besought him that he would suffer them to enter into them. And he suffered them.

³³ Then went the devils out of the man, and entered into the swine: and the herd ran violently down a steep place into the lake, and were choked.

³⁴ When they that fed *them* saw what was done, they fled, and went and told *it* in the city and in the country.

³⁵ Then they went out to see what was done; and came to Jesus, and found the man, out of whom the devils were departed, sitting at the feet of Jesus, clothed, and in his right mind: and they were afraid.

³⁶ They also which saw *it* told them by what means he that was possessed of the devils was healed.

³⁷ Then the whole multitude of the country of the Gadarenes round about besought him to depart from them; for they were taken with great fear: and he went up into the ship, and returned back again.

³⁸ Now the man out of whom the devils were departed besought him that he might be with him: but Jesus sent him away, saying,

³⁹ Return to thine own house, and shew how great things God hath done unto thee. And he went his way, and published throughout the whole city how great things Jesus had done unto him.

⁴⁰ And it came to pass, that, when Jesus was returned, the people *gladly* received him: for they were all waiting for him.

⁴¹ And, behold, there came a man named Jairus, and he was a ruler of the synagogue: and he fell down at Jesus' feet, and besought him that he would come into his house:

⁴² For he had one only daughter, about twelve years of age, and she lay a dying. But as he went the people thronged him.

⁴³ And a woman having an issue of blood twelve years, which had spent all her living upon physicians, neither could be healed of any,

⁴⁴ Came behind *him,* and touched the border of his garment: and immediately her issue of blood stanched.

⁴⁵ And Jesus said, Who touched me? When all

denied, Peter and they that were with him said, Master, the multitude throng thee and press *thee,* and sayest thou, Who touched me?

⁴⁶ And Jesus said, Somebody hath touched me: for I perceive that virtue is gone out of me.

⁴⁷ And when the woman saw that she was not hid, she came trembling, and falling down before him, she declared unto him before all the people for what cause she had touched him and how she was healed immediately.

⁴⁸ And he said unto her, Daughter, be of good comfort: thy faith hath made thee whole; go in peace.

⁴⁹ While he yet spake, there cometh one from the ruler of the synagogue's *house,* saying to him, Thy daughter is dead; trouble not the Master.

⁵⁰ But when Jesus heard *it,* he answered him, saying, Fear not: believe only, and she shall be made whole.

⁵¹ And when he came into the house, he suffered no man to go in, save Peter, and James, and John, and the father and the mother of the maiden.

⁵² And all wept, and bewailed her: but he said, Weep not; she is not dead, but sleepeth.

⁵³ And they laughed him to scorn, knowing that she was dead.

⁵⁴ And he put them all out, and took her by the hand, and called, saying, Maid, arise.

⁵⁵ And her spirit came again, and she arose straightway: and he commanded to give her meat.

⁵⁶ And her parents were astonished: but he charged them that they should tell no man what was done.

9 Then he called his twelve disciples together, and gave them power and authority over all devils, and to cure diseases.

² And he sent them to preach the kingdom of God, and to heal the sick.

³ And he said unto them, Take nothing for *your* journey, neither staves, nor scrip, neither bread, neither money; neither have two coats apiece.

⁴ And whatsoever house ye enter into, there abide, and thence depart.

⁵ And whosoever will not receive you, when ye go out of that city, shake off the very dust from your feet for a testimony against them.

⁶ And they departed, and went through the towns, preaching the gospel, and healing every where.

⁷ Now Herod the tetrarch heard of all that was done by him: and he was perplexed, because that it was said of some, that John was risen from the dead;

⁸ And of some, that Elias had appeared; and of others, that one of the old prophets was risen again.

⁹ And Herod said, John have I beheaded: but who is this, of whom I hear such things? And he desired to see him.

¹⁰ And the apostles, when they were returned, told him all that they had done. And he took them, and went aside privately into a desert place belonging to the city called Bethsaida.

¹¹ And the people, when they knew *it,* followed him: and he received them, and spake unto them of the kingdom of God, and healed them that had need of healing.

¹² And when the day began to wear away, then came the twelve, and said unto him, Send the multitude away, that they may go into the towns and country round about, and lodge, and get victuals: for we are here in a desert place.

¹³ But he said unto them, Give ye them to eat. And they said, We have no more but five loaves and two fishes; except we should go and buy meat for all this people.

¹⁴ For they were about five thousand men. And he said to his disciples, Make them sit down by fifties in a company.

¹⁵ And they did so, and made them all sit down.

¹⁶ Then he took the five loaves and the two fishes, and looking up to heaven, he blessed them, and brake, and gave to the disciples to set before the multitude.

¹⁷ And they did eat, and were all filled: and there was taken up of fragments that remained to them twelve baskets.

¹⁸ And it came to pass, as he was alone praying, his disciples were with him: and he asked them, saying, Whom say the people that I am?

¹⁹ They answering said, John the Baptist; but some *say,* Elias; and others *say,* that one of the old prophets is risen again.

²⁰ He said unto them, But whom say ye that I am? Peter answering said, The Christ of God.

²¹ And he straitly charged them, and commanded *them* to tell no man that thing;

²² Saying, The Son of man must suffer many things, and be rejected of the elders and chief priests and scribes, and be slain, and be raised the third day.

23 And he said to *them* all, If any *man* will come after me, let him deny himself, and take up his cross daily, and follow me.

24 For whosoever will save his life shall lose it: but whosoever will lose his life for my sake, the same shall save it.

25 For what is a man advantaged, if he gain the whole world, and lose himself, or be cast away?

26 For whosoever shall be ashamed of me and of my words, of him shall the Son of man be ashamed, when he shall come in his own glory, and *in his* Father's, and of the holy angels.

27 But I tell you of a truth, there be some standing here, which shall not taste of death, till they see the kingdom of God.

28 And it came to pass about an eight days after these sayings, he took Peter and John and James, and went up into a mountain to pray.

29 And as he prayed, the fashion of his countenance was altered, and his raiment *was* white *and* glistering.

30 And, behold, there talked with him two men, which were Moses and Elias:

31 Who appeared in glory, and spake of his decease which he should accomplish at Jerusalem.

32 But Peter and they that were with him were heavy with sleep: and when they were awake, they saw his glory, and the two men that stood with him.

33 And it came to pass, as they departed from him, Peter said unto Jesus, Master, it is good for us to be here: and let us make three tabernacles; one for thee, and one for Moses, and one for Elias: not knowing what he said.

34 While he thus spake, there came a cloud, and overshadowed them: and they feared as they entered into the cloud.

35 And there came a voice out of the cloud, saying, This is my beloved Son: hear him.

36 And when the voice was past, Jesus was found alone. And they kept *it* close, and told no man in those days any of those things which they had seen.

37 And it came to pass, that on the next day, when they were come down from the hill, much people met him.

38 And, behold, a man of the company cried out, saying, Master, I beseech thee, look upon my son: for he is mine only child.

39 And, lo, a spirit taketh him, and he suddenly crieth out; and it teareth him that he foameth again, and bruising him hardly departeth from him.

40 And I besought thy disciples to cast him out; and they could not.

41 And Jesus answering said, O faithless and perverse generation, how long shall I be with you, and suffer you? Bring thy son hither.

42 And as he was yet a coming, the devil threw him down, and tare *him*. And Jesus rebuked the unclean spirit, and healed the child, and delivered him again to his father.

43 And they were all amazed at the mighty power of God. But while they wondered every one at all things which Jesus did, he said unto his disciples,

44 Let these sayings sink down into your ears: for the Son of man shall be delivered into the hands of men.

45 But they understood not this saying, and it was hid from them, that they perceived it not: and they feared to ask him of that saying.

46 Then there arose a reasoning among them, which of them should be greatest.

47 And Jesus, perceiving the thought of their heart, took a child, and set him by him,

48 And said unto them, Whosoever shall receive this child in my name receiveth me: and whosoever shall receive me receiveth him that sent me: for he that is least among you all, the same shall be great.

49 And John answered and said, Master, we saw one casting out devils in thy name; and we forbad him, because he followeth not with us.

50 And Jesus said unto him, Forbid *him* not: for he that is not against us is for us.

51 And it came to pass, when the time was come that he should be received up, he stedfastly set his face to go to Jerusalem,

52 And sent messengers before his face: and they went, and entered into a village of the Samaritans, to make ready for him.

53 And they did not receive him, because his face was as though he would go to Jerusalem.

54 And when his disciples James and John saw *this*, they said, Lord, wilt thou that we command fire to come down from heaven, and consume them, even as Elias did?

55 But he turned, and rebuked them, and said, Ye know not what manner of spirit ye are of.

56 For the Son of man is not come to destroy men's lives, but to save *them*. And they went to another village.

57 And it came to pass, that, as they went in the

way, a certain *man* said unto him, Lord, I will follow thee whithersoever thou goest.

58 And Jesus said unto him, Foxes have holes, and birds of the air *have* nests; but the Son of man hath not where to lay *his* head.

59 And he said unto another, Follow me. But he said, Lord, suffer me first to go and bury my father.

60 Jesus said unto him, Let the dead bury their dead: but go thou and preach the kingdom of God.

61 And another also said, Lord, I will follow thee; but let me first go bid them farewell, which are at home at my house.

62 And Jesus said unto him, No man, having put his hand to the plough, and looking back, is fit for the kingdom of God.

10 After these things the Lord appointed other seventy also, and sent them two and two before his face into every city and place, whither he himself would come.

2 Therefore said he unto them, The harvest truly *is* great, but the labourers *are* few: pray ye therefore the Lord of the harvest, that he would send forth labourers into his harvest.

3 Go your ways: behold, I send you forth as lambs among wolves.

4 Carry neither purse, nor scrip, nor shoes: and salute no man by the way.

5 And into whatsoever house ye enter, first say, Peace *be* to this house.

6 And if the son of peace be there, your peace shall rest upon it: if not, it shall turn to you again.

7 And in the same house remain, eating and drinking such things as they give: for the labourer is worthy of his hire. Go not from house to house.

8 And into whatsoever city ye enter, and they receive you, eat such things as are set before you:

9 And heal the sick that are therein, and say unto them, The kingdom of God is come nigh unto you.

10 But into whatsoever city ye enter, and they receive you not, go your ways out into the streets of the same, and say,

11 Even the very dust of your city, which cleaveth on us, we do wipe off against you: notwithstanding be ye sure of this, that the kingdom of God is come nigh unto you.

12 But I say unto you, that it shall be more tolerable in that day for Sodom, than for that city.

13 Woe unto thee, Chorazin! woe unto thee, Bethsaida! for if the mighty works had been done in Tyre and Sidon, which have been done in you, they had a great while ago repented, sitting in sackcloth and ashes.

14 But it shall be more tolerable for Tyre and Sidon at the judgment, than for you.

15 And thou, Capernaum, which art exalted to heaven, shalt be thrust down to hell.

16 He that heareth you heareth me; and he that despiseth you despiseth me; and he that despiseth me despiseth him that sent me.

17 And the seventy returned again with joy, saying, Lord, even the devils are subject unto us through thy name.

18 And he said unto them, I beheld Satan as lightning fall from heaven.

19 Behold, I give unto you power to tread on serpents and scorpions, and over all the power of the enemy: and nothing shall by any means hurt you.

20 Notwithstanding in this rejoice not, that the spirits are subject unto you; but rather rejoice, because your names are written in heaven.

21 In that hour Jesus rejoiced in spirit, and said, I thank thee, O Father, Lord of heaven and earth, that thou hast hid these things from the wise and prudent, and hast revealed them unto babes: even so, Father; for so it seemed good in thy sight.

22 All things are delivered to me of my Father: and no man knoweth who the Son is, but the Father; and who the Father is, but the Son, and *he* to whom the Son will reveal *him.*

23 And he turned him unto *his* disciples, and said privately, Blessed *are* the eyes which see the things that ye see:

24 For I tell you, that many prophets and kings have desired to see those things which ye see, and have not seen *them;* and to hear those things which ye hear, and have not heard *them.*

25 And, behold, a certain lawyer stood up, and tempted him, saying, Master, what shall I do to inherit eternal life?

26 He said unto him, What is written in the law? how readest thou?

27 And he answering said, Thou shalt love the Lord thy God with all thy heart, and with all thy soul, and with all thy strength, and with all thy mind; and thy neighbour as thyself.

28 And he said unto him, Thou hast answered right: this do, and thou shalt live.

29 But he, willing to justify himself, said unto Jesus, And who is my neighbour?

30 And Jesus answering said, A certain *man* went down from Jerusalem to Jericho, and fell among thieves, which stripped him of his raiment, and wounded *him*, and departed, leaving *him* half dead.

31 And by chance there came down a certain priest that way: and when he saw him, he passed by on the other side.

32 And likewise a Levite, when he was at the place, came and looked *on him*, and passed by on the other side.

33 But a certain Samaritan, as he journeyed, came where he was: and when he saw him, he had compassion *on him*,

34 And went to *him*, and bound up his wounds, pouring in oil and wine, and set him on his own beast, and brought him to an inn, and took care of him.

35 And on the morrow when he departed, he took out two pence, and gave *them* to the host, and said unto him, Take care of him; and whatsoever thou spendest more, when I come again, I will repay thee.

36 Which now of these three, thinkest thou, was neighbour unto him that fell among the thieves?

37 And he said, He that shewed mercy on him. Then said Jesus unto him, Go, and do thou likewise.

38 Now it came to pass, as they went, that he entered into a certain village: and a certain woman named Martha received him into her house.

39 And she had a sister called Mary, which also sat at Jesus' feet, and heard his word.

40 But Martha was cumbered about much serving, and came to him, and said, Lord, dost thou not care that my sister hath left me to serve alone? bid her therefore that she help me.

41 And Jesus answered and said unto her, Martha, Martha, thou art careful and troubled about many things:

42 But one thing is needful: and Mary hath chosen that good part, which shall not be taken away from her.

11 And it came to pass, that, as he was praying in a certain place, when he ceased, one of his disciples said unto him, Lord, teach us to pray, as John also taught his disciples.

2 And he said unto them, When ye pray, say, Our Father which art in heaven, Hallowed be thy name. Thy kingdom come. Thy will be done, as in heaven, so in earth.

3 Give us day by day our daily bread.

4 And forgive us our sins; for we also forgive every one that is indebted to us. And lead us not into temptation; but deliver us from evil.

5 And he said unto them, Which of you shall have a friend, and shall go unto him at midnight, and say unto him, Friend, lend me three loaves;

6 For a friend of mine in his journey is come to me, and I have nothing to set before him?

7 And he from within shall answer and say, Trouble me not: the door is now shut, and my children are with me in bed; I cannot rise and give thee.

8 I say unto you, Though he will not rise and give him, because he is his friend, yet because of his importunity he will rise and give him as many as he needeth.

9 And I say unto you, Ask, and it shall be given you; seek, and ye shall find; knock, and it shall be opened unto you.

10 For every one that asketh receiveth; and he that seeketh findeth; and to him that knocketh it shall be opened.

11 If a son shall ask bread of any of you that is a father, will he give him a stone? or if *he ask* a fish, will he for a fish give him a serpent?

12 Or if he shall ask an egg, will he offer him a scorpion?

13 If ye then, being evil, know how to give good gifts unto your children: how much more shall *your* heavenly Father give the Holy Spirit to them that ask him?

14 And he was casting out a devil, and it was dumb. And it came to pass, when the devil was gone out, the dumb spake; and the people wondered.

15 But some of them said, He casteth out devils through Beelzebub the chief of the devils.

16 And others, tempting *him*, sought of him a sign from heaven.

17 But he, knowing their thoughts, said unto them, Every kingdom divided against itself is brought to desolation; and a house *divided* against a house falleth.

18 If Satan also be divided against himself, how shall his kingdom stand? because ye say that I cast out devils through Beelzebub.

19 And if I by Beelzebub cast out devils, by whom do your sons cast *them* out? therefore shall they be your judges.

20 But if I with the finger of God cast out devils, no doubt the kingdom of God is come upon you.

²¹ When a strong man armed keepeth his palace, his goods are in peace:

²² But when a stronger than he shall come upon him, and overcome him, he taketh from him all his armour wherein he trusted, and divideth his spoils.

²³ He that is not with me is against me: and he that gathereth not with me scattereth.

²⁴ When the unclean spirit is gone out of a man, he walketh through dry places, seeking rest; and finding none, he saith, I will return unto my house whence I came out.

²⁵ And when he cometh, he findeth *it* swept and garnished.

²⁶ Then goeth he, and taketh *to him* seven other spirits more wicked than himself; and they enter in, and dwell there: and the last *state* of that man is worse than the first.

²⁷ And it came to pass, as he spake these things, a certain woman of the company lifted up her voice, and said unto him, Blessed is the womb that bare thee, and the paps which thou hast sucked.

²⁸ But he said, Yea rather, blessed *are* they that hear the word of God, and keep it.

²⁹ And when the people were gathered thick together, he began to say, This is an evil generation: they seek a sign; and there shall no sign be given it, but the sign of Jonas the prophet.

³⁰ For as Jonas was a sign unto the Ninevites, so shall also the Son of man be to this generation.

³¹ The queen of the south shall rise up in the judgment with the men of this generation, and condemn them: for she came from the utmost parts of the earth to hear the wisdom of Solomon; and, behold, a greater than Solomon is here.

³² The men of Nineve shall rise up in the judgment with this generation, and shall condemn it: for they repented at the preaching of Jonas; and, behold, a greater than Jonas *is* here.

³³ No man, when he hath lighted a candle, putteth *it* in a secret place, neither under a bushel, but on a candlestick, that they which come in may see the light.

³⁴ The light of the body is the eye: therefore when thine eye is single, thy whole body also is full of light; but when *thine eye* is evil, thy body also *is* full of darkness.

³⁵ Take heed therefore that the light which is in thee be not darkness.

³⁶ If thy whole body therefore *be* full of light, having no part dark, the whole shall be full of light, as when the bright shining of a candle doth give thee light.

³⁷ And as he spake, a certain Pharisee besought him to dine with him: and he went in, and sat down to meat.

³⁸ And when the Pharisee saw *it*, he marvelled that he had not first washed before dinner.

³⁹ And the Lord said unto him, Now do ye Pharisees make clean the outside of the cup and the platter; but your inward part is full of ravening and wickedness.

⁴⁰ *Ye* fools, did not he that made that which is without make that which is within also?

⁴¹ But rather give alms of such things as ye have; and, behold, all things are clean unto you.

⁴² But woe unto you, Pharisees! for ye tithe mint and rue and all manner of herbs, and pass over judgment and the love of God: these ought ye to have done, and not to leave the other undone.

⁴³ Woe unto you, Pharisees! for ye love the uppermost seats in the synagogues, and greetings in the markets.

⁴⁴ Woe unto you, scribes and Pharisees, hypocrites! for ye are as graves which appear not, and the men that walk over *them* are not aware *of them.*

⁴⁵ Then answered one of the lawyers, and said unto him, Master, thus saying thou reproachest us also.

⁴⁶ And he said, Woe unto you also, *ye* lawyers! for ye lade men with burdens grievous to be borne, and ye yourselves touch not the burdens with one of your fingers.

⁴⁷ Woe unto you! for ye build the sepulchres of the prophets, and your fathers killed them.

⁴⁸ Truly ye bear witness that ye allow the deeds of your fathers: for they indeed killed them, and ye build their sepulchres.

⁴⁹ Therefore also said the wisdom of God, I will send them prophets and apostles, and *some* of them they shall slay and persecute:

⁵⁰ That the blood of all the prophets, which was shed from the foundation of the world, may be required of this generation;

⁵¹ From the blood of Abel unto the blood of Zacharias, which perished between the altar and the temple: verily I say unto you, It shall be required of this generation.

⁵² Woe unto you, lawyers! for ye have taken away the key of knowledge: ye entered not in yourselves, and them that were entering in ye hindered.

53 And as he said these things unto them, the scribes and the Pharisees began to urge *him* vehemently, and to provoke him to speak of many things:

54 Laying wait for him, and seeking to catch something out of his mouth, that they might accuse him.

12 In the mean time, when there were gathered together an innumerable multitude of people, insomuch that they trode one upon another, he began to say unto his disciples first of all, Beware ye of the leaven of the Pharisees, which is hypocrisy.

2 For there is nothing covered, that shall not be revealed; neither hid, that shall not be known.

3 Therefore whatsoever ye have spoken in darkness shall be heard in the light; and that which ye have spoken in the ear in closets shall be proclaimed upon the housetops.

4 And I say unto you my friends, Be not afraid of them that kill the body, and after that have no more that they can do.

5 But I will forewarn you whom ye shall fear: Fear him, which after he hath killed hath power to cast into hell; yea, I say unto you, Fear him.

6 Are not five sparrows sold for two farthings, and not one of them is forgotten before God?

7 But even the very hairs of your head are all numbered. Fear not therefore: ye are of more value than many sparrows.

8 Also I say unto you, Whosoever shall confess me before men, him shall the Son of man also confess before the angels of God:

9 But he that denieth me before men shall be denied before the angels of God.

10 And whosoever shall speak a word against the Son of man, it shall be forgiven him: but unto him that blasphemeth against the Holy Ghost it shall not be forgiven.

11 And when they bring you unto the synagogues, and *unto* magistrates, and powers, take ye no thought how or what thing ye shall answer, or what ye shall say:

12 For the Holy Ghost shall teach you in the same hour what ye ought to say.

13 And one of the company said unto him, Master, speak to my brother, that he divide the inheritance with me.

14 And he said unto him, Man, who made me a judge or a divider over you?

15 And he said unto them, Take heed, and beware of covetousness: for a man's life consisteth not in the abundance of the things which he possesseth.

16 And he spake a parable unto them, saying, The ground of a certain rich man brought forth plentifully:

17 And he thought within himself, saying, What shall I do, because I have no room where to bestow my fruits?

18 And he said, This will I do: I will pull down my barns, and build greater; and there will I bestow all my fruits and my goods.

19 And I will say to my soul, Soul, thou hast much goods laid up for many years; take thine ease, eat, drink, *and* be merry.

20 But God said unto him, *Thou* fool, this night thy soul shall be required of thee: then whose shall those things be, which thou hast provided?

21 So *is* he that layeth up treasure for himself, and is not rich toward God.

22 And he said unto his disciples, Therefore I say unto you, Take no thought for your life, what ye shall eat; neither for the body, what ye shall put on.

23 The life is more than meat, and the body *is more* than raiment.

24 Consider the ravens: for they neither sow nor reap; which neither have storehouse nor barn; and God feedeth them: how much more are ye better than the fowls?

25 And which of you with taking thought can add to his stature one cubit?

26 If ye then be not able to do that thing which is least, why take ye thought for the rest?

27 Consider the lilies how they grow: they toil not, they spin not; and yet I say unto you, that Solomon in all his glory was not arrayed like one of these.

28 If then God so clothe the grass, which is to day in the field, and to morrow is cast into the oven; how much more *will he clothe* you, O ye of little faith?

29 And seek not ye what ye shall eat, or what ye shall drink, neither be ye of doubtful mind.

30 For all these things do the nations of the world seek after: and your Father knoweth that ye have need of these things.

31 But rather seek ye the kingdom of God; and all these things shall be added unto you.

32 Fear not, little flock; for it is your Father's good pleasure to give you the kingdom.

33 Sell that ye have, and give alms; provide yourselves bags which wax not old, a treasure in the heavens that faileth not, where no thief approacheth, neither moth corrupteth.

³⁴ For where your treasure is, there will your heart be also.

³⁵ Let your loins be girded about, and *your* lights burning;

³⁶ And ye yourselves like unto men that wait for their lord, when he will return from the wedding; that when he cometh and knocketh, they may open unto him immediately.

³⁷ Blessed *are* those servants, whom the lord when he cometh shall find watching: verily I say unto you, that he shall gird himself, and make them to sit down to meat, and will come forth and serve them.

³⁸ And if he shall come in the second watch, or come in the third watch, and find *them* so, blessed are those servants.

³⁹ And this know, that if the goodman of the house had known what hour the thief would come, he would have watched, and not have suffered his house to be broken through.

⁴⁰ Be ye therefore ready also: for the Son of man cometh at an hour when ye think not.

⁴¹ Then Peter said unto him, Lord, speakest thou this parable unto us, or even to all?

⁴² And the Lord said, Who then is that faithful and wise steward, whom *his* lord shall make ruler over his household, to give *them* *their* portion of meat in due season?

⁴³ Blessed *is* that servant, whom his lord when he cometh shall find so doing.

⁴⁴ Of a truth I say unto you, that he will make him ruler over all that he hath.

⁴⁵ But and if that servant say in his heart, My lord delayeth his coming; and shall begin to beat the menservants and maidens, and to eat and drink, and to be drunken;

⁴⁶ The lord of that servant will come in a day when he looketh not for *him,* and at an hour when he is not aware, and will cut him in sunder, and will appoint him his portion with the unbelievers.

⁴⁷ And that servant, which knew his lord's will, and prepared not *himself,* neither did according to his will, shall be beaten with many *stripes.*

⁴⁸ But he that knew not, and did commit things worthy of stripes, shall be beaten with few *stripes.* For unto whomsoever much is given, of him shall be much required: and to whom men have committed much, of him they will ask the more.

⁴⁹ I am come to send fire on the earth; and what will I if it be already kindled?

⁵⁰ But I have a baptism to be baptized with; and how am I straitened till it be accomplished!

⁵¹ Suppose ye that I am come to give peace on earth? I tell you, Nay; but rather division:

⁵² For from henceforth there shall be five in one house divided, three against two, and two against three.

⁵³ The father shall be divided against the son, and the son against the father; the mother against the daughter, and the daughter against the mother; the mother in law against her daughter in law, and the daughter in law against her mother in law.

⁵⁴ And he said also to the people, When ye see a cloud rise out of the west, straightway ye say, There cometh a shower; and so it is.

⁵⁵ And when *ye see* the south wind blow, ye say, There will be heat; and it cometh to pass.

⁵⁶ *Ye* hypocrites, ye can discern the face of the sky and of the earth; but how is it that ye do not discern this time?

⁵⁷ Yea, and why even of yourselves judge ye not what is right?

⁵⁸ When thou goest with thine adversary to the magistrate, *as thou art* in the way, give diligence that thou mayest be delivered from him; lest he hale thee to the judge, and the judge deliver thee to the officer, and the officer cast thee into prison.

⁵⁹ I tell thee, thou shalt not depart thence, till thou hast paid the very last mite.

13 There were present at that season some that told him of the Galilaeans, whose blood Pilate had mingled with their sacrifices.

² And Jesus answering said unto them, Suppose ye that these Galilaeans were sinners above all the Galilaeans, because they suffered such things?

³ I tell you, Nay: but, except ye repent, ye shall all likewise perish.

⁴ Or those eighteen, upon whom the tower in Siloam fell, and slew them, think ye that they were sinners above all men that dwelt in Jerusalem?

⁵ I tell you, Nay: but, except ye repent, ye shall all likewise perish.

⁶ He spake also this parable; A certain *man* had a fig tree planted in his vineyard; and he came and sought fruit thereon, and found none.

⁷ Then said he unto the dresser of his vineyard, Behold, these three years I come seeking

fruit on this fig tree, and find none: cut it down; why cumbereth it the ground?

8 And he answering said unto him, Lord, let it alone this year also, till I shall dig about it, and dung *it:*

9 And if it bear fruit, *well:* and if not, *then* after that thou shalt cut it down.

10 And he was teaching in one of the synagogues on the sabbath.

11 And, behold, there was a woman which had a spirit of infirmity eighteen years, and was bowed together, and could in no wise lift up *herself.*

12 And when Jesus saw her, he called *her to him,* and said unto her, Woman, thou art loosed from thine infirmity.

13 And he laid *his* hands on her: and immediately she was made straight, and glorified God.

14 And the ruler of the synagogue answered with indignation, because that Jesus had healed on the sabbath day, and said unto the people, There are six days in which men ought to work: in them therefore come and be healed, and not on the sabbath day.

15 The Lord then answered him, and said, *Thou* hypocrite, doth not each one of you on the sabbath loose his ox or *his* ass from the stall, and lead *him* away to watering?

16 And ought not this woman, being a daughter of Abraham, whom Satan hath bound, lo, these eighteen years, be loosed from this bond on the sabbath day?

17 And when he had said these things, all his adversaries were ashamed: and all the people rejoiced for all the glorious things that were done by him.

18 Then said he, Unto what is the kingdom of God like? and whereunto shall I resemble it?

19 It is like a grain of mustard seed, which a man took, and cast into his garden; and it grew, and waxed a great tree; and the fowls of the air lodged in the branches of it.

20 And again he said, Whereunto shall I liken the kingdom of God?

21 It is like leaven, which a woman took and hid in three measures of meal, till the whole was leavened.

22 And he went through the cities and villages, teaching, and journeying toward Jerusalem.

23 Then said one unto him, Lord, are there few that be saved? And he said unto them,

24 Strive to enter in at the strait gate: for many, I say unto you, will seek to enter in, and shall not be able.

25 When once the master of the house is risen up, and hath shut to the door, and ye begin to stand without, and to knock at the door, saying, Lord, Lord, open unto us; and he shall answer and say unto you, I know you not whence ye are:

26 Then shall ye begin to say, We have eaten and drunk in thy presence, and thou hast taught in our streets.

27 But he shall say, I tell you, I know you not whence ye are; depart from me, all *ye* workers of iniquity.

28 There shall be weeping and gnashing of teeth, when ye shall see Abraham, and Isaac, and Jacob, and all the prophets, in the kingdom of God, and you *yourselves* thrust out.

29 And they shall come from the east, and *from* the west, and from the north, and *from* the south, and shall sit down in the kingdom of God.

30 And, behold, there are last which shall be first, and there are first which shall be last.

31 The same day there came certain of the Pharisees, saying unto him, Get thee out, and depart hence: for Herod will kill thee.

32 And he said unto them, Go ye, and tell that fox, Behold, I cast out devils, and I do cures to day and to morrow, and the third *day* I shall be perfected.

33 Nevertheless I must walk to day, and to morrow, and the *day* following: for it cannot be that a prophet perish out of Jerusalem.

34 O Jerusalem, Jerusalem, which killest the prophets, and stonest them that are sent unto thee; how often would I have gathered thy children together, as a hen *doth gather* her brood under *her* wings, and ye would not!

35 Behold, your house is left unto you desolate: and verily I say unto you, Ye shall not see me, until *the time* come when ye shall say, Blessed *is* he that cometh in the name of the Lord.

14 And it came to pass, as he went into the house of one of the chief Pharisees to eat bread on the sabbath day, that they watched him.

2 And, behold, there was a certain man before him which had the dropsy.

3 And Jesus answering spake unto the lawyers and Pharisees, saying, Is it lawful to heal on the sabbath day?

4 And they held their peace. And he took *him,* and healed him, and let him go;

5 And answered them, saying, Which of you shall have an ass or an ox fallen into a pit, and

will not straightway pull him out on the sabbath day?

⁶ And they could not answer him again to these things.

⁷ And he put forth a parable to those which were bidden, when he marked how they chose out the chief rooms; saying unto them,

⁸ When thou art bidden of any *man* to a wedding, sit not down in the highest room; lest a more honourable man than thou be bidden of him;

⁹ And he that bade thee and him come and say to thee, Give this man place; and thou begin with shame to take the lowest room.

¹⁰ But when thou art bidden, go and sit down in the lowest room; that when he that bade thee cometh, he may say unto thee, Friend, go up higher: then shalt thou have worship in the presence of them that sit at meat with thee.

¹¹ For whosoever exalteth himself shall be abased; and he that humbleth himself shall be exalted.

¹² Then said he also to him that bade him, When thou makest a dinner or a supper, call not thy friends, nor thy brethren, neither thy kinsmen, nor *thy* rich neighbours; lest they also bid thee again, and a recompence be made thee.

¹³ But when thou makest a feast, call the poor, the maimed, the lame, the blind:

¹⁴ And thou shalt be blessed; for they cannot recompense thee: for thou shalt be recompensed at the resurrection of the just.

¹⁵ And when one of them that sat at meat with him heard these things, he said unto him, Blessed *is* he that shall eat bread in the kingdom of God.

¹⁶ Then said he unto him, A certain man made a great supper, and bade many:

¹⁷ And sent his servant at supper time to say to them that were bidden, Come; for all things are now ready.

¹⁸ And they all with one *consent* began to make excuse. The first said unto him, I have bought a piece of ground, and I must needs go and see it: I pray thee have me excused.

¹⁹ And another said, I have bought five yoke of oxen, and I go to prove them: I pray thee have me excused.

²⁰ And another said, I have married a wife, and therefore I cannot come.

²¹ So that servant came, and shewed his lord these things. Then the master of the house being angry said to his servant, Go out quickly into the streets and lanes of the city, and bring in hither the poor, and the maimed, and the halt, and the blind.

²² And the servant said, Lord, it is done as thou hast commanded, and yet there is room.

²³ And the lord said unto the servant, Go out into the highways and hedges, and compel *them* to come in, that my house may be filled.

²⁴ For I say unto you, That none of those men which were bidden shall taste of my supper.

²⁵ And there went great multitudes with him: and he turned, and said unto them,

²⁶ If any *man* come to me, and hate not his father, and mother, and wife, and children, and brethren, and sisters, yea, and his own life also, he cannot be my disciple.

²⁷ And whosoever doth not bear his cross, and come after me, cannot be my disciple.

²⁸ For which of you, intending to build a tower, sitteth not down first, and counteth the cost, whether he have *sufficient* to finish *it?*

²⁹ Lest haply, after he hath laid the foundation, and is not able to finish *it,* all that behold *it* begin to mock him,

³⁰ Saying, This man began to build, and was not able to finish.

³¹ Or what king, going to make war against another king, sitteth not down first, and consulteth whether he be able with ten thousand to meet him that cometh against him with twenty thousand?

³² Or else, while the other is yet a great way off, he sendeth an ambassage, and desireth conditions of peace.

³³ So likewise, whosoever he be of you that forsaketh not all that he hath, he cannot be my disciple.

³⁴ Salt *is* good: but if the salt have lost his savour, wherewith shall it be seasoned?

³⁵ It is neither fit for the land, nor yet for the dunghill; *but* men cast it out. He that hath ears to hear, let him hear.

15 Then drew near unto him all the publicans and sinners for to hear him.

² And the Pharisees and scribes murmured, saying, This man receiveth sinners, and eateth with them.

³ And he spake this parable unto them, saying,

⁴ What man of you, having an hundred sheep, if he lose one of them, doth not leave the ninety and nine in the wilderness, and go after that which is lost, until he find it?

5 And when he hath found *it*, he layeth *it* on his shoulders, rejoicing.

6 And when he cometh home, he calleth together *his* friends and neighbours, saying unto them, Rejoice with me; for I have found my sheep which was lost.

7 I say unto you, that likewise joy shall be in heaven over one sinner that repenteth, more than over ninety and nine just persons, which need no repentance.

8 Either what woman having ten pieces of silver, if she lose one piece, doth not light a candle, and sweep the house, and seek diligently till she find *it*?

9 And when she hath found *it*, she calleth *her* friends and *her* neighbours together, saying, Rejoice with me; for I have found the piece which I had lost.

10 Likewise, I say unto you, there is joy in the presence of the angels of God over one sinner that repenteth.

11 And he said, A certain man had two sons:

12 And the younger of them said to *his* father, Father, give me the portion of goods that falleth *to me*. And he divided unto them *his* living.

13 And not many days after the younger son gathered all together, and took his journey into a far country, and there wasted his substance with riotous living.

14 And when he had spent all, there arose a mighty famine in that land; and he began to be in want.

15 And he went and joined himself to a citizen of that country; and he sent him into his fields to feed swine.

16 And he would fain have filled his belly with the husks that the swine did eat: and no man gave unto him.

17 And when he came to himself, he said, How many hired servants of my father's have bread enough and to spare, and I perish with hunger!

18 I will arise and go to my father, and will say unto him, Father, I have sinned against heaven, and before thee,

19 And am no more worthy to be called thy son: make me as one of thy hired servants.

20 And he arose, and came to his father. But when he was yet a great way off, his father saw him, and had compassion, and ran, and fell on his neck, and kissed him.

21 And the son said unto him, Father, I have sinned against heaven, and in thy sight, and am no more worthy to be called thy son.

22 But the father said to his servants, Bring forth the best robe, and put *it* on him; and put a ring on his hand, and shoes on *his* feet:

23 And bring hither the fatted calf, and kill *it*; and let us eat, and be merry:

24 For this my son was dead, and is alive again; he was lost, and is found. And they began to be merry.

25 Now his elder son was in the field: and as he came and drew nigh to the house, he heard musick and dancing.

26 And he called one of the servants, and asked what these things meant.

27 And he said unto him, Thy brother is come; and thy father hath killed the fatted calf, because he hath received him safe and sound.

28 And he was angry, and would not go in: therefore came his father out, and intreated him.

29 And he answering said to *his* father, Lo, these many years do I serve thee, neither transgressed I at any time thy commandment: and yet thou never gavest me a kid, that I might make merry with my friends:

30 But as soon as this thy son was come, which hath devoured thy living with harlots, thou hast killed for him the fatted calf.

31 And he said unto him, Son, thou art ever with me, and all that I have is thine.

32 It was meet that we should make merry, and be glad: for this thy brother was dead, and is alive again; and was lost, and is found.

16 And he said also unto his disciples, There was a certain rich man, which had a steward; and the same was accused unto him that he had wasted his goods.

2 And he called him, and said unto him, How is it that I hear this of thee? give an account of thy stewardship; for thou mayest be no longer steward.

3 Then the steward said within himself, What shall I do? for my lord taketh away from me the stewardship: I cannot dig; to beg I am ashamed.

4 I am resolved what to do, that, when I am put out of the stewardship, they may receive me into their houses.

5 So he called every one of his lord's debtors *unto him*, and said unto the first, How much owest thou unto my lord?

6 And he said, An hundred measures of oil. And he said unto him, Take thy bill, and sit down quickly, and write fifty.

7 Then said he to another, And how much owest thou? And he said, An hundred measures of wheat. And he said unto him, Take thy bill, and write fourscore.

⁸ And the lord commended the unjust steward, because he had done wisely: for the children of this world are in their generation wiser than the children of light.

⁹ And I say unto you, Make to yourselves friends of the mammon of unrighteousness; that, when ye fail, they may receive you into everlasting habitations.

¹⁰ He that is faithful in that which is least is faithful also in much: and he that is unjust in the least is unjust also in much.

¹¹ If therefore ye have not been faithful in the unrighteous mammon, who will commit to your trust the true *riches?*

¹² And if ye have not been faithful in that which is another man's, who shall give you that which is your own?

¹³ No servant can serve two masters: for either he will hate the one, and love the other; or else he will hold to the one, and despise the other. Ye cannot serve God and mammon.

¹⁴ And the Pharisees also, who were covetous, heard all these things: and they derided him.

¹⁵ And he said unto them, Ye are they which justify yourselves before men; but God knoweth your hearts: for that which is highly esteemed among men is abomination in the sight of God.

¹⁶ The law and the prophets *were* until John: since that time the kingdom of God is preached, and every man presseth into it.

¹⁷ And it is easier for heaven and earth to pass, than one tittle of the law to fail.

¹⁸ Whosoever putteth away his wife, and marrieth another, committeth adultery: and whosoever marrieth her that is put away from *her* husband committeth adultery.

¹⁹ There was a certain rich man, which was clothed in purple and fine linen, and fared sumptuously every day:

²⁰ And there was a certain beggar named Lazarus, which was laid at his gate, full of sores,

²¹ And desiring to be fed with the crumbs which fell from the rich man's table: moreover the dogs came and licked his sores.

²² And it came to pass, that the beggar died, and was carried by the angels into Abraham's bosom: the rich man also died, and was buried;

²³ And in hell he lift up his eyes, being in torments, and seeth Abraham afar off, and Lazarus in his bosom.

²⁴ And he cried and said, Father Abraham, have mercy on me, and send Lazarus, that he may dip the tip of his finger in water, and cool my tongue; for I am tormented in this flame.

²⁵ But Abraham said, Son, remember that thou in thy lifetime receivedst thy good things, and likewise Lazarus evil things: but now he is comforted, and thou art tormented.

²⁶ And beside all this, between us and you there is a great gulf fixed: so that they which would pass from hence to you cannot; neither can they pass to us, that *would come* from thence.

²⁷ Then he said, I pray thee therefore, father, that thou wouldest send him to my father's house:

²⁸ For I have five brethren; that he may testify unto them, lest they also come into this place of torment.

²⁹ Abraham saith unto him, They have Moses and the prophets; let them hear them.

³⁰ And he said, Nay, father Abraham: but if one went unto them from the dead, they will repent.

³¹ And he said unto him, If they hear not Moses and the prophets, neither will they be persuaded, though one rose from the dead.

17 Then said he unto the disciples, It is impossible but that offences will come: but woe *unto him,* through whom they come!

² It were better for him that a millstone were hanged about his neck, and he cast into the sea, than that he should offend one of these little ones.

³ Take heed to yourselves: If thy brother trespass against thee, rebuke him; and if he repent, forgive him.

⁴ And if he trespass against thee seven times in a day, and seven times in a day turn again to thee, saying, I repent; thou shalt forgive him.

⁵ And the apostles said unto the Lord, Increase our faith.

⁶ And the Lord said, If ye had faith as a grain of mustard seed, ye might say unto this sycamine tree, Be thou plucked up by the root, and be thou planted in the sea; and it should obey you.

⁷ But which of you, having a servant plowing or feeding cattle, will say unto him by and by, when he is come from the field, Go and sit down to meat?

⁸ And will not rather say unto him, Make ready wherewith I may sup, and gird thyself, and serve me, till I have eaten and drunken; and afterward thou shalt eat and drink?

⁹ Doth he thank that servant because he

did the things that were commanded him? I trow not.

¹⁰ So likewise ye, when ye shall have done all those things which are commanded you, say, We are unprofitable servants: we have done that which was our duty to do.

¹¹ And it came to pass, as he went to Jerusalem, that he passed through the midst of Samaria and Galilee.

¹² And as he entered into a certain village, there met him ten men that were lepers, which stood afar off:

¹³ And they lifted up *their* voices, and said, Jesus, Master, have mercy on us.

¹⁴ And when he saw *them,* he said unto them, Go shew yourselves unto the priests. And it came to pass, that, as they went, they were cleansed.

¹⁵ And one of them, when he saw that he was healed, turned back, and with a loud voice glorified God,

¹⁶ And fell down on *his* face at his feet, giving him thanks: and he was a Samaritan.

¹⁷ And Jesus answering said, Were there not ten cleansed? but where *are* the nine?

¹⁸ There are not found that returned to give glory to God, save this stranger.

¹⁹ And he said unto him, Arise, go thy way: thy faith hath made thee whole.

²⁰ And when he was demanded of the Pharisees, when the kingdom of God should come, he answered them and said, The kingdom of God cometh not with observation:

²¹ Neither shall they say, Lo here! or, lo there! for, behold, the kingdom of God is within you.

²² And he said unto the disciples, The days will come, when ye shall desire to see one of the days of the Son of man, and ye shall not see *it.*

²³ And they shall say to you, See here; or, see there: go not after *them,* nor follow *them.*

²⁴ For as the lightning, that lighteneth out of the one *part* under heaven, shineth unto the other *part* under heaven; so shall also the Son of man be in his day.

²⁵ But first must he suffer many things, and be rejected of this generation.

²⁶ And as it was in the days of Noe, so shall it be also in the days of the Son of man.

²⁷ They did eat, they drank, they married wives, they were given in marriage, until the day that Noe entered into the ark, and the flood came, and destroyed them all.

²⁸ Likewise also as it was in the days of Lot; they did eat, they drank, they bought, they sold, they planted, they builded;

²⁹ But the same day that Lot went out of Sodom it rained fire and brimstone from heaven, and destroyed *them* all.

³⁰ Even thus shall it be in the day when the Son of man is revealed.

³¹ In that day, he which shall be upon the housetop, and his stuff in the house, let him not come down to take it away: and he that is in the field, let him likewise not return back.

³² Remember Lot's wife.

³³ Whosoever shall seek to save his life shall lose it; and whosoever shall lose his life shall preserve it.

³⁴ I tell you, in that night there shall be two *men* in one bed; the one shall be taken, and the other shall be left.

³⁵ Two *women* shall be grinding together; the one shall be taken, and the other left.

³⁶ Two *men* shall be in the field; the one shall be taken, and the other left.

³⁷ And they answered and said unto him, Where, Lord? And he said unto them, Wheresoever the body is, thither will the eagles be gathered together.

18 And he spake a parable unto them *to this end,* that men ought always to pray, and not to faint;

² Saying, There was in a city a judge, which feared not God, neither regarded man:

³ And there was a widow in that city; and she came unto him, saying, Avenge me of mine adversary.

⁴ And he would not for a while: but afterward he said within himself, Though I fear not God, nor regard man;

⁵ Yet because this widow troubleth me, I will avenge her, lest by her continual coming she weary me.

⁶ And the Lord said, Hear what the unjust judge saith.

⁷ And shall not God avenge his own elect, which cry day and night unto him, though he bear long with them?

⁸ I tell you that he will avenge them speedily. Nevertheless when the Son of man cometh, shall he find faith on the earth?

⁹ And he spake this parable unto certain which trusted in themselves that they were righteous, and despised others:

¹⁰ Two men went up into the temple to pray; the one a Pharisee, and the other a publican.

11 The Pharisee stood and prayed thus with himself, God, I thank thee, that I am not as other men *are,* extortioners, unjust, adulterers, or even as this publican.

12 I fast twice in the week, I give tithes of all that I possess.

13 And the publican, standing afar off, would not lift up so much as *his* eyes unto heaven, but smote upon his breast, saying, God be merciful to me a sinner.

14 I tell you, this man went down to his house justified *rather* than the other: for every one that exalteth himself shall be abased; and he that humbleth himself shall be exalted.

15 And they brought unto him also infants, that he would touch them: but when *his* disciples saw *it,* they rebuked them.

16 But Jesus called them *unto him,* and said, Suffer little children to come unto me, and forbid them not: for of such is the kingdom of God.

17 Verily I say unto you, Whosoever shall not receive the kingdom of God as a little child shall in no wise enter therein.

18 And a certain ruler asked him, saying, Good Master, what shall I do to inherit eternal life?

19 And Jesus said unto him, Why callest thou me good? none *is* good, save one, *that is,* God.

20 Thou knowest the commandments, Do not commit adultery, Do not kill, Do not steal, Do not bear false witness, Honour thy father and thy mother.

21 And he said, All these have I kept from my youth up.

22 Now when Jesus heard these things, he said unto him, Yet lackest thou one thing: sell all that thou hast, and distribute unto the poor, and thou shalt have treasure in heaven: and come, follow me.

23 And when he heard this, he was very sorrowful: for he was very rich.

24 And when Jesus saw that he was very sorrowful, he said, How hardly shall they that have riches enter into the kingdom of God!

25 For it is easier for a camel to go through a needle's eye, than for a rich man to enter into the kingdom of God.

26 And they that heard *it* said, Who then can be saved?

27 And he said, The things which are impossible with men are possible with God.

28 Then Peter said, Lo, we have left all, and followed thee.

29 And he said unto them, Verily I say unto you, There is no man that hath left house, or parents, or brethren, or wife, or children, for the kingdom of God's sake,

30 Who shall not receive manifold more in this present time, and in the world to come life everlasting.

31 Then he took *unto him* the twelve, and said unto them, Behold, we go up to Jerusalem, and all things that are written by the prophets concerning the Son of man shall be accomplished.

32 For he shall be delivered unto the Gentiles, and shall be mocked, and spitefully entreated, and spitted on:

33 And they shall scourge *him,* and put him to death: and the third day he shall rise again.

34 And they understood none of these things: and this saying was hid from them, neither knew they the things which were spoken.

35 And it came to pass, that as he was come nigh unto Jericho, a certain blind man sat by the way side begging:

36 And hearing the multitude pass by, he asked what it meant.

37 And they told him, that Jesus of Nazareth passeth by.

38 And he cried, saying, Jesus, *thou* Son of David, have mercy on me.

39 And they which went before rebuked him, that he should hold his peace: but he cried so much the more, *Thou* Son of David, have mercy on me.

40 And Jesus stood, and commanded him to be brought unto him: and when he was come near, he asked him,

41 Saying, What wilt thou that I shall do unto thee? And he said, Lord, that I may receive my sight.

42 And Jesus said unto him, Receive thy sight: thy faith hath saved thee.

43 And immediately he received his sight, and followed him, glorifying God: and all the people, when they saw *it,* gave praise unto God.

19 And *Jesus* entered and passed through Jericho.

2 And, behold, *there was* a man named Zacchaeus, which was the chief among the publicans, and he was rich.

3 And he sought to see Jesus who he was; and could not for the press, because he was little of stature.

4 And he ran before, and climbed up into a sycomore tree to see him: for he was to pass that *way.*

5 And when Jesus came to the place, he

324

looked up, and saw him, and said unto him, Zacchaeus, make haste, and come down; for to day I must abide at thy house.

6 And he made haste, and came down, and received him joyfully.

7 And when they saw *it,* they all murmured, saying, That he was gone to be guest with a man that is a sinner.

8 And Zacchaeus stood, and said unto the Lord; Behold, Lord, the half of my goods I give to the poor; and if I have taken any thing from any man by false accusation, I restore *him* fourfold.

9 And Jesus said unto him, This day is salvation come to this house, forsomuch as he also is a son of Abraham.

10 For the Son of man is come to seek and to save that which was lost.

11 And as they heard these things, he added and spake a parable, because he was nigh to Jerusalem, and because they thought that the kingdom of God should immediately appear.

12 He said therefore, A certain nobleman went into a far country to receive for himself a kingdom, and to return.

13 And he called his ten servants, and delivered them ten pounds, and said unto them, Occupy till I come.

14 But his citizens hated him, and sent a message after him, saying, We will not have this *man* to reign over us.

15 And it came to pass, that when he was returned, having received the kingdom, then he commanded these servants to be called unto him, to whom he had given the money, that he might know how much every man had gained by trading.

16 Then came the first, saying, Lord, thy pound hath gained ten pounds.

17 And he said unto him, Well, thou good servant: because thou hast been faithful in a very little, have thou authority over ten cities.

18 And the second came, saying, Lord, thy pound hath gained five pounds.

19 And he said likewise to him, Be thou also over five cities.

20 And another came, saying, Lord, behold, *here is* thy pound, which I have kept laid up in a napkin:

21 For I feared thee, because thou art an austere man: thou takest up that thou layedst not down, and reapest that thou didst not sow.

22 And he saith unto him, Out of thine own mouth will I judge thee, *thou* wicked servant.

Thou knewest that I was an austere man, taking up that I laid not down, and reaping that I did not sow:

23 Wherefore then gavest not thou my money into the bank, that at my coming I might have required mine own with usury?

24 And he said unto them that stood by, Take from him the pound, and give *it* to him that hath ten pounds.

25 (And they said unto him, Lord, he hath ten pounds.)

26 For I say unto you, That unto every one which hath shall be given; and from him that hath not, even that he hath shall be taken away from him.

27 But those mine enemies, which would not that I should reign over them, bring hither, and slay *them* before me.

28 And when he had thus spoken, he went before, ascending up to Jerusalem.

29 And it came to pass, when he was come nigh to Bethphage and Bethany, at the mount called *the mount* of Olives, he sent two of his disciples,

30 Saying, Go ye into the village over against *you;* in the which at your entering ye shall find a colt tied, whereon yet never man sat: loose him, and bring *him hither.*

31 And if any man ask you, Why do ye loose *him?* thus shall ye say unto him, Because the Lord hath need of him.

32 And they that were sent went their way, and found even as he had said unto them.

33 And as they were loosing the colt, the owners thereof said unto them, Why loose ye the colt?

34 And they said, The Lord hath need of him.

35 And they brought him to Jesus: and they cast their garments upon the colt, and they set Jesus thereon.

36 And as he went, they spread their clothes in the way.

37 And when he was come nigh, even now at the descent of the mount of Olives, the whole multitude of the disciples began to rejoice and praise God with a loud voice for all the mighty works that they had seen;

38 Saying, Blessed *be* the King that cometh in the name of the Lord: peace in heaven, and glory in the highest.

39 And some of the Pharisees from among the multitude said unto him, Master, rebuke thy disciples.

40 And he answered and said unto them, I tell

you that, if these should hold their peace, the stones would immediately cry out.

⁴¹ And when he was come near, he beheld the city, and wept over it,

⁴² Saying, If thou hadst known, even thou, at least in this thy day, the things *which belong* unto thy peace! but now they are hid from thine eyes.

⁴³ For the days shall come upon thee, that thine enemies shall cast a trench about thee, and compass thee round, and keep thee in on every side,

⁴⁴ And shall lay thee even with the ground, and thy children within thee; and they shall not leave in thee one stone upon another; because thou knewest not the time of thy visitation.

⁴⁵ And he went into the temple, and began to cast out them that sold therein, and them that bought;

⁴⁶ Saying unto them, It is written, My house is the house of prayer: but ye have made it a den of thieves.

⁴⁷ And he taught daily in the temple. But the chief priests and the scribes and the chief of the people sought to destroy him,

⁴⁸ And could not find what they might do: for all the people were very attentive to hear him.

20 And it came to pass, *that* on one of those days, as he taught the people in the temple, and preached the gospel, the chief priests and the scribes came upon *him* with the elders,

² And spake unto him, saying, Tell us, by what authority doest thou these things? or who is he that gave thee this authority?

³ And he answered and said unto them, I will also ask you one thing; and answer me:

⁴ The baptism of John, was it from heaven, or of men?

⁵ And they reasoned with themselves, saying, If we shall say, From heaven; he will say, Why then believed ye him not?

⁶ But and if we say, Of men; all the people will stone us: for they be persuaded that John was a prophet.

⁷ And they answered, that they could not tell whence *it was.*

⁸ And Jesus said unto them, Neither tell I you by what authority I do these things.

⁹ Then began he to speak to the people this parable; A certain man planted a vineyard, and let it forth to husbandmen, and went into a far country for a long time.

¹⁰ And at the season he sent a servant to the husbandmen, that they should give him of the fruit of the vineyard: but the husbandmen beat him, and sent *him* away empty.

¹¹ And again he sent another servant: and they beat him also, and entreated *him* shamefully, and sent *him* away empty.

¹² And again he sent a third: and they wounded him also, and cast *him* out.

¹³ Then said the lord of the vineyard, What shall I do? I will send my beloved son: it may be they will reverence *him* when they see him.

¹⁴ But when the husbandmen saw him, they reasoned among themselves, saying, This is the heir: come, let us kill him, that the inheritance may be ours.

¹⁵ So they cast him out of the vineyard, and killed *him.* What therefore shall the lord of the vineyard do unto them?

¹⁶ He shall come and destroy these husbandmen, and shall give the vineyard to others. And when they heard *it,* they said, God forbid.

¹⁷ And he beheld them, and said, What is this then that is written, The stone which the builders rejected, the same is become the head of the corner?

¹⁸ Whosoever shall fall upon that stone shall be broken; but on whomsoever it shall fall, it will grind him to powder.

¹⁹ And the chief priests and the scribes the same hour sought to lay hands on him; and they feared the people: for they perceived that he had spoken this parable against them.

²⁰ And they watched *him,* and sent forth spies, which should feign themselves just men, that they might take hold of his words, that so they might deliver him unto the power and authority of the governor.

²¹ And they asked him, saying, Master, we know that thou sayest and teachest rightly, neither acceptest thou the person *of any,* but teachest the way of God truly:

²² Is it lawful for us to give tribute unto Caesar, or no?

²³ But he perceived their craftiness, and said unto them, Why tempt ye me?

²⁴ Shew me a penny. Whose image and superscription hath it? They answered and said, Caesar's.

²⁵ And he said unto them, Render therefore unto Caesar the things which be Caesar's, and unto God the things which be God's.

²⁶ And they could not take hold of his words before the people: and they marvelled at his answer, and held their peace.

²⁷ Then came to *him* certain of the Sadducees,

which deny that there is any resurrection; and they asked him,

²⁸ Saying, Master, Moses wrote unto us, If any man's brother die, having a wife, and he die without children, that his brother should take his wife, and raise up seed unto his brother.

²⁹ There were therefore seven brethren: and the first took a wife, and died without children.

³⁰ And the second took her to wife, and he died childless.

³¹ And the third took her; and in like manner the seven also: and they left no children, and died.

³² Last of all the woman died also.

³³ Therefore in the resurrection whose wife of them is she? for seven had her to wife.

³⁴ And Jesus answering said unto them, The children of this world marry, and are given in marriage:

³⁵ But they which shall be accounted worthy to obtain that world, and the resurrection from the dead, neither marry, nor are given in marriage:

³⁶ Neither can they die any more: for they are equal unto the angels; and are the children of God, being the children of the resurrection.

³⁷ Now that the dead are raised, even Moses shewed at the bush, when he calleth the Lord the God of Abraham, and the God of Isaac, and the God of Jacob.

³⁸ For he is not a God of the dead, but of the living: for all live unto him.

³⁹ Then certain of the scribes answering said, Master, thou hast well said.

⁴⁰ And after that they durst not ask him any *question at all.*

⁴¹ And he said unto them, How say they that Christ is David's son?

⁴² And David himself saith in the book of Psalms, The LORD said unto my Lord, Sit thou on my right hand,

⁴³ Till I make thine enemies thy footstool.

⁴⁴ David therefore calleth him Lord, how is he then his son?

⁴⁵ Then in the audience of all the people he said unto his disciples,

⁴⁶ Beware of the scribes, which desire to walk in long robes, and love greetings in the markets, and the highest seats in the synagogues, and the chief rooms at feasts;

⁴⁷ Which devour widows' houses, and for a shew make long prayers: the same shall receive greater damnation.

21 And he looked up, and saw the rich men casting their gifts into the treasury.

² And he saw also a certain poor widow casting in thither two mites.

³ And he said, Of a truth I say unto you, that this poor widow hath cast in more than they all:

⁴ For all these have of their abundance cast in unto the offerings of God: but she of her penury hath cast in all the living that she had.

⁵ And as some spake of the temple, how it was adorned with goodly stones and gifts, he said,

⁶ *As for* these things which ye behold, the days will come, in the which there shall not be left one stone upon another, that shall not be thrown down.

⁷ And they asked him, saying, Master, but when shall these things be? and what sign *will there be* when these things shall come to pass?

⁸ And he said, Take heed that ye be not deceived: for many shall come in my name, saying, I am *Christ;* and the time draweth near: go ye not therefore after them.

⁹ But when ye shall hear of wars and commotions, be not terrified: for these things must first come to pass; but the end *is* not by and by.

¹⁰ Then said he unto them, Nation shall rise against nation, and kingdom against kingdom:

¹¹ And great earthquakes shall be in divers places, and famines, and pestilences; and fearful sights and great signs shall there be from heaven.

¹² But before all these, they shall lay their hands on you, and persecute *you,* delivering *you* up to the synagogues, and into prisons, being brought before kings and rulers for my name's sake.

¹³ And it shall turn to you for a testimony.

¹⁴ Settle *it* therefore in your hearts, not to meditate before what ye shall answer:

¹⁵ For I will give you a mouth and wisdom, which all your adversaries shall not be able to gainsay nor resist.

¹⁶ And ye shall be betrayed both by parents, and brethren, and kinsfolks, and friends; and *some* of you shall they cause to be put to death.

¹⁷ And ye shall be hated of all *men* for my name's sake.

¹⁸ But there shall not an hair of your head perish.

¹⁹ In your patience possess ye your souls.

²⁰ And when ye shall see Jerusalem compassed with armies, then know that the desolation thereof is nigh.

²¹ Then let them which are in Judaea flee to the

mountains; and let them which are in the midst of it depart out; and let not them that are in the countries enter thereinto.

22 For these be the days of vengeance, that all things which are written may be fulfilled.

23 But woe unto them that are with child, and to them that give suck, in those days! for there shall be great distress in the land, and wrath upon this people.

24 And they shall fall by the edge of the sword, and shall be led away captive into all nations: and Jerusalem shall be trodden down of the Gentiles, until the times of the Gentiles be fulfilled.

25 And there shall be signs in the sun, and in the moon, and in the stars; and upon the earth distress of nations, with perplexity; the sea and the waves roaring;

26 Men's hearts failing them for fear, and for looking after those things which are coming on the earth: for the powers of heaven shall be shaken.

27 And then shall they see the Son of man coming in a cloud with power and great glory.

28 And when these things begin to come to pass, then look up, and lift up your heads; for your redemption draweth nigh.

29 And he spake to them a parable; Behold the fig tree, and all the trees;

30 When they now shoot forth, ye see and know of your own selves that summer is now nigh at hand.

31 So likewise ye, when ye see these things come to pass, know ye that the kingdom of God is nigh at hand.

32 Verily I say unto you, This generation shall not pass away, till all be fulfilled.

33 Heaven and earth shall pass away: but my words shall not pass away.

34 And take heed to yourselves, lest at any time your hearts be overcharged with surfeiting, and drunkenness, and cares of this life, and so that day come upon you unawares.

35 For as a snare shall it come on all them that dwell on the face of the whole earth.

36 Watch ye therefore, and pray always, that ye may be accounted worthy to escape all these things that shall come to pass, and to stand before the Son of man.

37 And in the day time he was teaching in the temple; and at night he went out, and abode in the mount that is called *the mount* of Olives.

38 And all the people came early in the morning to him in the temple, for to hear him.

22

Now the feast of unleavened bread drew nigh, which is called the Passover.

2 And the chief priests and scribes sought how they might kill him; for they feared the people.

3 Then entered Satan into Judas surnamed Iscariot, being of the number of the twelve.

4 And he went his way, and communed with the chief priests and captains, how he might betray him unto them.

5 And they were glad, and covenanted to give him money.

6 And he promised, and sought opportunity to betray him unto them in the absence of the multitude.

7 Then came the day of unleavened bread, when the passover must be killed.

8 And he sent Peter and John, saying, Go and prepare us the passover, that we may eat.

9 And they said unto him, Where wilt thou that we prepare?

10 And he said unto them, Behold, when ye are entered into the city, there shall a man meet you, bearing a pitcher of water; follow him into the house where he entereth in.

11 And ye shall say unto the goodman of the house, The Master saith unto thee, Where is the guestchamber, where I shall eat the passover with my disciples?

12 And he shall shew you a large upper room furnished: there make ready.

13 And they went, and found as he had said unto them: and they made ready the passover.

14 And when the hour was come, he sat down, and the twelve apostles with him.

15 And he said unto them, With desire I have desired to eat this passover with you before I suffer:

16 For I say unto you, I will not any more eat thereof, until it be fulfilled in the kingdom of God.

17 And he took the cup, and gave thanks, and said, Take this, and divide *it* among yourselves:

18 For I say unto you, I will not drink of the fruit of the vine, until the kingdom of God shall come.

19 And he took bread, and gave thanks, and brake *it,* and gave unto them, saying, This is my body which is given for you: this do in remembrance of me.

20 Likewise also the cup after supper, saying,

This cup *is* the new testament in my blood, which is shed for you.

²¹ But, behold, the hand of him that betrayeth me *is* with me on the table.

²² And truly the Son of man goeth, as it was determined: but woe unto that man by whom he is betrayed!

²³ And they began to enquire among themselves, which of them it was that should do this thing.

²⁴ And there was also a strife among them, which of them should be accounted the greatest.

²⁵ And he said unto them, The kings of the Gentiles exercise lordship over them; and they that exercise authority upon them are called benefactors.

²⁶ But ye *shall* not *be* so: but he that is greatest among you, let him be as the younger; and he that is chief, as he that doth serve.

²⁷ For whether *is* greater, he that sitteth at meat, or he that serveth? *is* not he that sitteth at meat? but I am among you as he that serveth.

²⁸ Ye are they which have continued with me in my temptations.

²⁹ And I appoint unto you a kingdom, as my Father hath appointed unto me;

³⁰ That ye may eat and drink at my table in my kingdom, and sit on thrones judging the twelve tribes of Israel.

³¹ And the Lord said, Simon, Simon, behold, Satan hath desired *to have* you, that he may sift *you* as wheat:

³² But I have prayed for thee, that thy faith fail not: and when thou art converted, strengthen thy brethren.

³³ And he said unto him, Lord, I am ready to go with thee, both into prison, and to death.

³⁴ And he said, I tell thee, Peter, the cock shall not crow this day, before that thou shalt thrice deny that thou knowest me.

³⁵ And he said unto them, When I sent you without purse, and scrip, and shoes, lacked ye any thing? And they said, Nothing.

³⁶ Then said he unto them, But now, he that hath a purse, let him take *it,* and likewise *his* scrip: and he that hath no sword, let him sell his garment, and buy one.

³⁷ For I say unto you, that this that is written must yet be accomplished in me, And he was reckoned among the transgressors: for the things concerning me have an end.

³⁸ And they said, Lord, behold, here *are* two swords. And he said unto them, It is enough.

³⁹ And he came out, and went, as he was wont, to the mount of Olives; and his disciples also followed him.

⁴⁰ And when he was at the place, he said unto them, Pray that ye enter not into temptation.

⁴¹ And he was withdrawn from them about a stone's cast, and kneeled down, and prayed,

⁴² Saying, Father, if thou be willing, remove this cup from me: nevertheless not my will, but thine, be done.

⁴³ And there appeared an angel unto him from heaven, strengthening him.

⁴⁴ And being in an agony he prayed more earnestly: and his sweat was as it were great drops of blood falling down to the ground.

⁴⁵ And when he rose up from prayer, and was come to his disciples, he found them sleeping for sorrow,

⁴⁶ And said unto them, Why sleep ye? rise and pray, lest ye enter into temptation.

⁴⁷ And while he yet spake, behold a multitude, and he that was called Judas, one of the twelve, went before them, and drew near unto Jesus to kiss him.

⁴⁸ But Jesus said unto him, Judas, betrayest thou the Son of man with a kiss?

⁴⁹ When they which were about him saw what would follow, they said unto him, Lord, shall we smite with the sword?

⁵⁰ And one of them smote the servant of the high priest, and cut off his right ear.

⁵¹ And Jesus answered and said, Suffer ye thus far. And he touched his ear, and healed him.

⁵² Then Jesus said unto the chief priests, and captains of the temple, and the elders, which were come to him, Be ye come out, as against a thief, with swords and staves?

⁵³ When I was daily with you in the temple, ye stretched forth no hands against me: but this is your hour, and the power of darkness.

⁵⁴ Then took they him, and led *him,* and brought him into the high priest's house. And Peter followed afar off.

⁵⁵ And when they had kindled a fire in the midst of the hall, and were set down together, Peter sat down among them.

⁵⁶ But a certain maid beheld him as he sat by the fire, and earnestly looked upon him, and said, This man was also with him.

⁵⁷ And he denied him, saying, Woman, I know him not.

⁵⁸ And after a little while another saw him, and said, Thou art also of them. And Peter said, Man, I am not.

⁵⁹ And about the space of one hour after another confidently affirmed, saying, Of a truth this *fellow* also was with him: for he is a Galilaean.

⁶⁰ And Peter said, Man, I know not what thou sayest. And immediately, while he yet spake, the cock crew.

⁶¹ And the Lord turned, and looked upon Peter. And Peter remembered the word of the Lord, how he had said unto him, Before the cock crow, thou shalt deny me thrice.

⁶² And Peter went out, and wept bitterly.

⁶³ And the men that held Jesus mocked him, and smote *him.*

⁶⁴ And when they had blindfolded him, they struck him on the face, and asked him, saying, Prophesy, who is it that smote thee?

⁶⁵ And many other things blasphemously spake they against him.

⁶⁶ And as soon as it was day, the elders of the people and the chief priests and the scribes came together, and led him into their council, saying,

⁶⁷ Art thou the Christ? tell us. And he said unto them, If I tell you, ye will not believe:

⁶⁸ And if I also ask *you,* ye will not answer me, nor let *me* go.

⁶⁹ Hereafter shall the Son of man sit on the right hand of the power of God.

⁷⁰ Then said they all, Art thou then the Son of God? And he said unto them, Ye say that I am.

⁷¹ And they said, What need we any further witness? for we ourselves have heard of his own mouth.

23 And the whole multitude of them arose, and led him unto Pilate.

² And they began to accuse him, saying, We found this *fellow* perverting the nation, and forbidding to give tribute to Caesar, saying that he himself is Christ a King.

³ And Pilate asked him, saying, Art thou the King of the Jews? And he answered him and said, Thou sayest *it.*

⁴ Then said Pilate to the chief priests and *to* the people, I find no fault in this man.

⁵ And they were the more fierce, saying, He stirreth up the people, teaching throughout all Jewry, beginning from Galilee to this place.

⁶ When Pilate heard of Galilee, he asked whether the man were a Galilaean.

⁷ And as soon as he knew that he belonged unto Herod's jurisdiction, he sent him to Herod, who himself also was at Jerusalem at that time.

⁸ And when Herod saw Jesus, he was exceeding glad: for he was desirous to see him of a long *season,* because he had heard many things of him; and he hoped to have seen some miracle done by him.

⁹ Then he questioned with him in many words; but he answered him nothing.

¹⁰ And the chief priests and scribes stood and vehemently accused him.

¹¹ And Herod with his men of war set him at nought, and mocked *him,* and arrayed him in a gorgeous robe, and sent him again to Pilate.

¹² And the same day Pilate and Herod were made friends together: for before they were at enmity between themselves.

¹³ And Pilate, when he had called together the chief priests and the rulers and the people,

¹⁴ Said unto them, Ye have brought this man unto me, as one that perverteth the people: and, behold, I, having examined *him* before you, have found no fault in this man touching those things whereof ye accuse him:

¹⁵ No, nor yet Herod: for I sent you to him; and, lo, nothing worthy of death is done unto him.

¹⁶ I will therefore chastise him, and release *him.*

¹⁷(For of necessity he must release one unto them at the feast.)

¹⁸ And they cried out all at once, saying, Away with this *man,* and release unto us Barabbas:

¹⁹(Who for a certain sedition made in the city, and for murder, was cast into prison.)

²⁰ Pilate therefore, willing to release Jesus, spake again to them.

²¹ But they cried, saying, Crucify *him,* crucify him.

²² And he said unto them the third time, Why, what evil hath he done? I have found no cause of death in him: I will therefore chastise him, and let *him* go.

²³ And they were instant with loud voices, requiring that he might be crucified. And the voices of them and of the chief priests prevailed.

²⁴ And Pilate gave sentence that it should be as they required.

²⁵ And he released unto them him that for sedition and murder was cast into prison, whom they had desired; but he delivered Jesus to their will.

²⁶ And as they led him away, they laid hold upon one Simon, a Cyrenian, coming out of the country, and on him they laid the cross, that he might bear *it* after Jesus.

²⁷ And there followed him a great company of

people, and of women, which also bewailed and lamented him.

²⁸ But Jesus turning unto them said, Daughters of Jerusalem, weep not for me, but weep for yourselves, and for your children.

²⁹ For, behold, the days are coming, in the which they shall say, Blessed *are* the barren, and the wombs that never bare, and the paps which never gave suck.

³⁰ Then shall they begin to say to the mountains, Fall on us; and to the hills, Cover us.

³¹ For if they do these things in a green tree, what shall be done in the dry?

³² And there were also two others, malefactors, led with him to be put to death.

³³ And when they were come to the place, which is called Calvary, there they crucified him, and the malefactors, one on the right hand, and the other on the left.

³⁴ Then said Jesus, Father, forgive them; for they know not what they do. And they parted his raiment, and cast lots.

³⁵ And the people stood beholding. And the rulers also with them derided *him,* saying, He saved others; let him save himself, if he be Christ, the chosen of God.

³⁶ And the soldiers also mocked him, coming to him, and offering him vinegar,

³⁷ And saying, If thou be the king of the Jews, save thyself.

³⁸ And a superscription also was written over him in letters of Greek, and Latin, and Hebrew, THIS IS THE KING OF THE JEWS.

³⁹ And one of the malefactors which were hanged railed on him, saying, If thou be Christ, save thyself and us.

⁴⁰ But the other answering rebuked him, saying, Dost not thou fear God, seeing thou art in the same condemnation?

⁴¹ And we indeed justly; for we receive the due reward of our deeds: but this man hath done nothing amiss.

⁴² And he said unto Jesus, Lord, remember me when thou comest into thy kingdom.

⁴³ And Jesus said unto him, Verily I say unto thee, To day shalt thou be with me in paradise.

⁴⁴ And it was about the sixth hour, and there was a darkness over all the earth until the ninth hour.

⁴⁵ And the sun was darkened, and the veil of the temple was rent in the midst.

⁴⁶ And when Jesus had cried with a loud voice, he said, Father, into thy hands I commend my spirit: and having said thus, he gave up the ghost.

⁴⁷ Now when the centurion saw what was done, he glorified God, saying, Certainly this was a righteous man.

⁴⁸ And all the people that came together to that sight, beholding the things which were done, smote their breasts, and returned.

⁴⁹ And all his acquaintance, and the women that followed him from Galilee, stood afar off, beholding these things.

⁵⁰ And, behold, *there was* a man named Joseph, a counsellor; *and he was* a good man, and a just:

⁵¹(The same had not consented to the counsel and deed of them;) *he was* of Arimathaea, a city of the Jews: who also himself waited for the kingdom of God.

⁵² This *man* went unto Pilate, and begged the body of Jesus.

⁵³ And he took it down, and wrapped it in linen, and laid it in a sepulchre that was hewn in stone, wherein never man before was laid.

⁵⁴ And that day was the preparation, and the sabbath drew on.

⁵⁵ And the women also, which came with him from Galilee, followed after, and beheld the sepulchre, and how his body was laid.

⁵⁶ And they returned, and prepared spices and ointments; and rested the sabbath day according to the commandment.

24 Now upon the first *day* of the week, very early in the morning, they came unto the sepulchre, bringing the spices which they had prepared, and certain *others* with them.

² And they found the stone rolled away from the sepulchre.

³ And they entered in, and found not the body of the Lord Jesus.

⁴ And it came to pass, as they were much perplexed thereabout, behold, two men stood by them in shining garments:

⁵ And as they were afraid, and bowed down *their* faces to the earth, they said unto them, Why seek ye the living among the dead?

⁶ He is not here, but is risen: remember how he spake unto you when he was yet in Galilee,

⁷ Saying, The Son of man must be delivered into the hands of sinful men, and be crucified, and the third day rise again.

⁸ And they remembered his words,

⁹ And returned from the sepulchre, and told all these things unto the eleven, and to all the rest.

¹⁰ It was Mary Magdalene, and Joanna, and Mary *the mother* of James, and other *women that were* with them, which told these things unto the apostles.

¹¹ And their words seemed to them as idle tales, and they believed them not.

¹² Then arose Peter, and ran unto the sepulchre; and stooping down, he beheld the linen clothes laid by themselves, and departed, wondering in himself at that which was come to pass.

¹³ And, behold, two of them went that same day to a village called Emmaus, which was from Jerusalem *about* threescore furlongs.

¹⁴ And they talked together of all these things which had happened.

¹⁵ And it came to pass, that, while they communed *together* and reasoned, Jesus himself drew near, and went with them.

¹⁶ But their eyes were holden that they should not know him.

¹⁷ And he said unto them, What manner of communications *are* these that ye have one to another, as ye walk, and are sad?

¹⁸ And the one of them, whose name was Cleopas, answering said unto him, Art thou only a stranger in Jerusalem, and hast not known the things which are come to pass there in these days?

¹⁹ And he said unto them, What things? And they said unto him, Concerning Jesus of Nazareth, which was a prophet mighty in deed and word before God and all the people:

²⁰ And how the chief priests and our rulers delivered him to be condemned to death, and have crucified him.

²¹ But we trusted that it had been he which should have redeemed Israel: and beside all this, to day is the third day since these things were done.

²² Yea, and certain women also of our company made us astonished, which were early at the sepulchre;

²³ And when they found not his body, they came, saying, that they had also seen a vision of angels, which said that he was alive.

²⁴ And certain of them which were with us went to the sepulchre, and found *it* even so as the women had said: but him they saw not.

²⁵ Then he said unto them, O fools, and slow of heart to believe all that the prophets have spoken:

²⁶ Ought not Christ to have suffered these things, and to enter into his glory?

²⁷ And beginning at Moses and all the prophets, he expounded unto them in all the scriptures the things concerning himself.

²⁸ And they drew nigh unto the village, whither they went: and he made as though he would have gone further.

²⁹ But they constrained him, saying, Abide with us: for it is toward evening, and the day is far spent. And he went in to tarry with them.

³⁰ And it came to pass, as he sat at meat with them, he took bread, and blessed *it*, and brake, and gave to them.

³¹ And their eyes were opened, and they knew him; and he vanished out of their sight.

³² And they said one to another, Did not our heart burn within us, while he talked with us by the way, and while he opened to us the scriptures?

³³ And they rose up the same hour, and returned to Jerusalem, and found the eleven gathered together, and them that were with them,

³⁴ Saying, The Lord is risen indeed, and hath appeared to Simon.

³⁵ And they told what things *were done* in the way, and how he was known of them in breaking of bread.

³⁶ And as they thus spake, Jesus himself stood in the midst of them, and saith unto them, Peace *be* unto you.

³⁷ But they were terrified and affrighted, and supposed that they had seen a spirit.

³⁸ And he said unto them, Why are ye troubled? and why do thoughts arise in your hearts?

³⁹ Behold my hands and my feet, that it is I myself: handle me, and see; for a spirit hath not flesh and bones, as ye see me have.

⁴⁰ And when he had thus spoken, he shewed them *his* hands and *his* feet.

⁴¹ And while they yet believed not for joy, and wondered, he said unto them, Have ye here any meat?

⁴² And they gave him a piece of a broiled fish, and of an honeycomb.

⁴³ And he took *it*, and did eat before them.

⁴⁴ And he said unto them, These *are* the words which I spake unto you, while I was yet with you, that all things must be fulfilled, which were written in the law of Moses, and *in* the prophets, and *in* the psalms, concerning me.

⁴⁵ Then opened he their understanding, that they might understand the scriptures,

⁴⁶ And said unto them, Thus it is written, and

thus it behoved Christ to suffer, and to rise from the dead the third day:

⁴⁷ And that repentance and remission of sins should be preached in his name among all nations, beginning at Jerusalem.

⁴⁸ And ye are witnesses of these things.

⁴⁹ And, behold, I send the promise of my Father upon you: but tarry ye in the city of Jerusalem, until ye be endued with power from on high.

⁵⁰ And he led them out as far as to Bethany, and he lifted up his hands, and blessed them.

⁵¹ And it came to pass, while he blessed them, he was parted from them, and carried up into heaven.

⁵² And they worshipped him, and returned to Jerusalem with great joy:

⁵³ And were continually in the temple, praising and blessing God. Amen.

John

1 In the beginning was the Word, and the Word was with God, and the Word was God.

2 The same was in the beginning with God.

3 All things were made by him; and without him was not any thing made that was made.

4 In him was life; and the life was the light of men.

5 And the light shineth in darkness; and the darkness comprehended it not.

6 There was a man sent from God, whose name *was* John.

7 The same came for a witness, to bear witness of the Light, that all *men* through him might believe.

8 He was not that Light, but *was sent* to bear witness of that Light.

9 *That* was the true Light, which lighteth every man that cometh into the world.

10 He was in the world, and the world was made by him, and the world knew him not.

11 He came unto his own, and his own received him not.

12 But as many as received him, to them gave he power to become the sons of God, *even* to them that believe on his name:

13 Which were born, not of blood, nor of the will of the flesh, nor of the will of man, but of God.

14 And the Word was made flesh, and dwelt among us, (and we beheld his glory, the glory as of the only begotten of the Father,) full of grace and truth.

15 John bare witness of him, and cried, saying, This was he of whom I spake, He that cometh after me is preferred before me: for he was before me.

16 And of his fulness have all we received, and grace for grace.

17 For the law was given by Moses, *but* grace and truth came by Jesus Christ.

18 No man hath seen God at any time; the only begotten Son, which is in the bosom of the Father, he hath declared *him.*

19 And this is the record of John, when the Jews sent priests and Levites from Jerusalem to ask him, Who art thou?

20 And he confessed, and denied not; but confessed, I am not the Christ.

21 And they asked him, What then? Art thou Elias? And he saith, I am not. Art thou that prophet? And he answered, No.

22 Then said they unto him, Who art thou? that we may give an answer to them that sent us. What sayest thou of thyself?

23 He said, I *am* the voice of one crying in the wilderness, Make straight the way of the Lord, as said the prophet Esaias.

24 And they which were sent were of the Pharisees.

25 And they asked him, and said unto him, Why baptizest thou then, if thou be not that Christ, nor Elias, neither that prophet?

26 John answered them, saying, I baptize with water: but there standeth one among you, whom ye know not;

27 He it is, who coming after me is preferred before me, whose shoe's latchet I am not worthy to unloose.

28 These things were done in Bethabara beyond Jordan, where John was baptizing.

29 The next day John seeth Jesus coming unto him, and saith, Behold the Lamb of God, which taketh away the sin of the world.

30 This is he of whom I said, After me cometh a man which is preferred before me: for he was before me.

31 And I knew him not: but that he should be made manifest to Israel, therefore am I come baptizing with water.

32 And John bare record, saying, I saw the Spirit descending from heaven like a dove, and it abode upon him.

33 And I knew him not: but he that sent me to baptize with water, the same said unto me, Upon whom thou shalt see the Spirit descending, and remaining on him, the same is he which baptizeth with the Holy Ghost.

34 And I saw, and bare record that this is the Son of God.

35 Again the next day after John stood, and two of his disciples;

36 And looking upon Jesus as he walked, he saith, Behold the Lamb of God!

37 And the two disciples heard him speak, and they followed Jesus.

38 Then Jesus turned, and saw them following, and saith unto them, What seek ye? They said unto him, Rabbi, (which is to say, being interpreted, Master,) where dwellest thou?

39 He saith unto them, Come and see. They came and saw where he dwelt, and abode with him that day: for it was about the tenth hour.

40 One of the two which heard John *speak*, and followed him, was Andrew, Simon Peter's brother.

41 He first findeth his own brother Simon, and saith unto him, We have found the Messias, which is, being interpreted, the Christ.

42 And he brought him to Jesus. And when Jesus beheld him, he said, Thou art Simon the son of Jona: thou shalt be called Cephas, which is by interpretation, A stone.

43 The day following Jesus would go forth into Galilee, and findeth Philip, and saith unto him, Follow me.

44 Now Philip was of Bethsaida, the city of Andrew and Peter.

45 Philip findeth Nathanael, and saith unto him, We have found him, of whom Moses in the law, and the prophets, did write, Jesus of Nazareth, the son of Joseph.

46 And Nathanael said unto him, Can there any good thing come out of Nazareth? Philip saith unto him, Come and see.

47 Jesus saw Nathanael coming to him, and saith of him, Behold an Israelite indeed, in whom is no guile!

48 Nathanael saith unto him, Whence knowest thou me? Jesus answered and said unto him, Before that Philip called thee, when thou wast under the fig tree, I saw thee.

49 Nathanael answered and saith unto him, Rabbi, thou art the Son of God; thou art the King of Israel.

50 Jesus answered and said unto him, Because I said unto thee, I saw thee under the fig tree, believest thou? thou shalt see greater things than these.

51 And he saith unto him, Verily, verily, I say unto you, Hereafter ye shall see heaven open, and the angels of God ascending and descending upon the Son of man.

2 And the third day there was a marriage in Cana of Galilee; and the mother of Jesus was there:

2 And both Jesus was called, and his disciples, to the marriage.

3 And when they wanted wine, the mother of Jesus saith unto him, They have no wine.

4 Jesus saith unto her, Woman, what have I to do with thee? mine hour is not yet come.

5 His mother saith unto the servants, Whatsoever he saith unto you, do *it*.

6 And there were set there six waterpots of stone, after the manner of the purifying of the Jews, containing two or three firkins apiece.

7 Jesus saith unto them, Fill the waterpots with water. And they filled them up to the brim.

8 And he saith unto them, Draw out now, and bear unto the governor of the feast. And they bare *it*.

9 When the ruler of the feast had tasted the water that was made wine, and knew not whence it was: (but the servants which drew the water knew;) the governor of the feast called the bridegroom,

10 And saith unto him, Every man at the beginning doth set forth good wine; and when men have well drunk, then that which is worse: *but* thou hast kept the good wine until now.

11 This beginning of miracles did Jesus in Cana of Galilee, and manifested forth his glory; and his disciples believed on him.

12 After this he went down to Capernaum, he, and his mother, and his brethren, and his disciples: and they continued there not many days.

13 And the Jews' passover was at hand, and Jesus went up to Jerusalem,

14 And found in the temple those that sold oxen and sheep and doves, and the changers of money sitting:

15 And when he had made a scourge of small cords, he drove them all out of the temple, and the sheep, and the oxen; and poured out the changers' money, and overthrew the tables;

16 And said unto them that sold doves, Take these things hence; make not my Father's house an house of merchandise.

17 And his disciples remembered that it was written, The zeal of thine house hath eaten me up.

18 Then answered the Jews and said unto him,

What sign shewest thou unto us, seeing that thou doest these things?

¹⁹ Jesus answered and said unto them, Destroy this temple, and in three days I will raise it up. ²⁰ Then said the Jews, Forty and six years was this temple in building, and wilt thou rear it up in three days? ²¹ But he spake of the temple of his body. ²² When therefore he was risen from the dead, his disciples remembered that he had said this unto them; and they believed the scripture, and the word which Jesus had said. ²³ Now when he was in Jerusalem at the passover, in the feast *day,* many believed in his name, when they saw the miracles which he did. ²⁴ But Jesus did not commit himself unto them, because he knew all *men,* ²⁵ And needed not that any should testify of man: for he knew what was in man.

3 There was a man of the Pharisees, named Nicodemus, a ruler of the Jews: ² The same came to Jesus by night, and said unto him, Rabbi, we know that thou art a teacher come from God: for no man can do these miracles that thou doest, except God be with him. ³ Jesus answered and said unto him, Verily, verily, I say unto thee, Except a man be born again, he cannot see the kingdom of God. ⁴ Nicodemus saith unto him, How can a man be born when he is old? can he enter the second time into his mother's womb, and be born? ⁵ Jesus answered, Verily, verily, I say unto thee, Except a man be born of water and *of* the Spirit, he cannot enter into the kingdom of God. ⁶ That which is born of the flesh is flesh; and that which is born of the Spirit is spirit. ⁷ Marvel not that I said unto thee, Ye must be born again. ⁸ The wind bloweth where it listeth, and thou hearest the sound thereof, but canst not tell whence it cometh, and whither it goeth: so is every one that is born of the Spirit. ⁹ Nicodemus answered and said unto him, How can these things be? ¹⁰ Jesus answered and said unto him, Art thou a master of Israel, and knowest not these things? ¹¹ Verily, verily, I say unto thee, We speak that we do know, and testify that we have seen; and ye receive not our witness. ¹² If I have told you earthly things, and ye believe not, how shall ye believe, if I tell you *of* heavenly things? ¹³ And no man hath ascended up to heaven, but he that came down from heaven, *even* the Son of man which is in heaven. ¹⁴ And as Moses lifted up the serpent in the wilderness, even so must the Son of man be lifted up: ¹⁵ That whosoever believeth in him should not perish, but have eternal life. ¹⁶ For God so loved the world, that he gave his only begotten Son, that whosoever believeth in him should not perish, but have everlasting life. ¹⁷ For God sent not his Son into the world to condemn the world; but that the world through him might be saved. ¹⁸ He that believeth on him is not condemned: but he that believeth not is condemned already, because he hath not believed in the name of the only begotten Son of God. ¹⁹ And this is the condemnation, that light is come into the world, and men loved darkness rather than light, because their deeds were evil. ²⁰ For every one that doeth evil hateth the light, neither cometh to the light, lest his deeds should be reproved. ²¹ But he that doeth truth cometh to the light, that his deeds may be made manifest, that they are wrought in God.

²² After these things came Jesus and his disciples into the land of Judaea; and there he tarried with them, and baptized. ²³ And John also was baptizing in Aenon near to Salim, because there was much water there: and they came, and were baptized. ²⁴ For John was not yet cast into prison. ²⁵ Then there arose a question between *some* of John's disciples and the Jews about purifying. ²⁶ And they came unto John, and said unto him, Rabbi, he that was with thee beyond Jordan, to whom thou barest witness, behold, the same baptizeth, and all *men* come to him. ²⁷ John answered and said, A man can receive nothing, except it be given him from heaven. ²⁸ Ye yourselves bear me witness, that I said, I am not the Christ, but that I am sent before him. ²⁹ He that hath the bride is the bridegroom: but the friend of the bridegroom, which standeth and heareth him, rejoiceth greatly because of the bridegroom's voice: this my joy therefore is fulfilled. ³⁰ He must increase, but I *must* decrease. ³¹ He that cometh from above is above all: he

that is of the earth is earthly, and speaketh of the earth: he that cometh from heaven is above all.

³² And what he hath seen and heard, that he testifieth; and no man receiveth his testimony.

³³ He that hath received his testimony hath set to his seal that God is true.

³⁴ For he whom God hath sent speaketh the words of God: for God giveth not the Spirit by measure *unto him*.

³⁵ The Father loveth the Son, and hath given all things into his hand.

³⁶ He that believeth on the Son hath everlasting life: and he that believeth not the Son shall not see life; but the wrath of God abideth on him.

4 When therefore the Lord knew how the Pharisees had heard that Jesus made and baptized more disciples than John,

²(Though Jesus himself baptized not, but his disciples,)

³ He left Judaea, and departed again into Galilee.

⁴ And he must needs go through Samaria.

⁵ Then cometh he to a city of Samaria, which is called Sychar, near to the parcel of ground that Jacob gave to his son Joseph.

⁶ Now Jacob's well was there. Jesus therefore, being wearied with *his* journey, sat thus on the well: *and* it was about the sixth hour.

⁷ There cometh a woman of Samaria to draw water: Jesus saith unto her, Give me to drink.

⁸(For his disciples were gone away unto the city to buy meat.)

⁹ Then saith the woman of Samaria unto him, How is it that thou, being a Jew, askest drink of me, which am a woman of Samaria? for the Jews have no dealings with the Samaritans.

¹⁰ Jesus answered and said unto her, If thou knewest the gift of God, and who it is that saith to thee, Give me to drink; thou wouldest have asked of him, and he would have given thee living water.

¹¹ The woman saith unto him, Sir, thou hast nothing to draw with, and the well is deep: from whence then hast thou that living water?

¹² Art thou greater than our father Jacob, which gave us the well, and drank thereof himself, and his children, and his cattle?

¹³ Jesus answered and said unto her, Whosoever drinketh of this water shall thirst again:

¹⁴ But whosoever drinketh of the water that I shall give him shall never thirst; but the water that I shall give him shall be in him a well of water springing up into everlasting life.

¹⁵ The woman saith unto him, Sir, give me this water, that I thirst not, neither come hither to draw.

¹⁶ Jesus saith unto her, Go, call thy husband, and come hither.

¹⁷ The woman answered and said, I have no husband. Jesus said unto her, Thou hast well said, I have no husband:

¹⁸ For thou hast had five husbands; and he whom thou now hast is not thy husband: in that saidst thou truly.

¹⁹ The woman saith unto him, Sir, I perceive that thou art a prophet.

²⁰ Our fathers worshipped in this mountain; and ye say, that in Jerusalem is the place where men ought to worship.

²¹ Jesus saith unto her, Woman, believe me, the hour cometh, when ye shall neither in this mountain, nor yet at Jerusalem, worship the Father.

²² Ye worship ye know not what: we know what we worship: for salvation is of the Jews.

²³ But the hour cometh, and now is, when the true worshippers shall worship the Father in spirit and in truth: for the Father seeketh such to worship him.

²⁴ God *is* a Spirit: and they that worship him must worship *him* in spirit and in truth.

²⁵ The woman saith unto him, I know that Messias cometh, which is called Christ: when he is come, he will tell us all things.

²⁶ Jesus saith unto her, I that speak unto thee am *he*.

²⁷ And upon this came his disciples, and marvelled that he talked with the woman: yet no man said, What seekest thou? or, Why talkest thou with her?

²⁸ The woman then left her waterpot, and went her way into the city, and saith to the men,

²⁹ Come, see a man, which told me all things that ever I did: is not this the Christ?

³⁰ Then they went out of the city, and came unto him.

³¹ In the mean while his disciples prayed him, saying, Master, eat.

³² But he said unto them, I have meat to eat that ye know not of.

³³ Therefore said the disciples one to another, Hath any man brought him *ought* to eat?

³⁴ Jesus saith unto them, My meat is to do

the will of him that sent me, and to finish his work.

³⁵ Say not ye, There are yet four months, and *then* cometh harvest? behold, I say unto you, Lift up your eyes, and look on the fields; for they are white already to harvest.

³⁶ And he that reapeth receiveth wages, and gathereth fruit unto life eternal: that both he that soweth and he that reapeth may rejoice together.

³⁷ And herein is that saying true, One soweth, and another reapeth.

³⁸ I sent you to reap that whereon ye bestowed no labour: other men laboured, and ye are entered into their labours.

³⁹ And many of the Samaritans of that city believed on him for the saying of the woman, which testified, He told me all that ever I did.

⁴⁰ So when the Samaritans were come unto him, they besought him that he would tarry with them: and he abode there two days.

⁴¹ And many more believed because of his own word;

⁴² And said unto the woman, Now we believe, not because of thy saying: for we have heard *him* ourselves, and know that this is indeed the Christ, the Saviour of the world.

⁴³ Now after two days he departed thence, and went into Galilee.

⁴⁴ For Jesus himself testified, that a prophet hath no honour in his own country.

⁴⁵ Then when he was come into Galilee, the Galilaeans received him, having seen all the things that he did at Jerusalem at the feast: for they also went unto the feast.

⁴⁶ So Jesus came again into Cana of Galilee, where he made the water wine. ℞ And there was a certain nobleman, whose son was sick at Capernaum.

⁴⁷ When he heard that Jesus was come out of Judaea into Galilee, he went unto him, and besought him that he would come down, and heal his son: for he was at the point of death.

⁴⁸ Then said Jesus unto him, Except ye see signs and wonders, ye will not believe.

⁴⁹ The nobleman saith unto him, Sir, come down ere my child die.

⁵⁰ Jesus saith unto him, Go thy way; thy son liveth. And the man believed the word that Jesus had spoken unto him, and he went his way.

⁵¹ And as he was now going down, his servants met him, and told *him,* saying, Thy son liveth.

⁵² Then enquired he of them the hour when he began to amend. And they said unto him, Yesterday at the seventh hour the fever left him.

⁵³ So the father knew that *it was* at the same hour, in the which Jesus said unto him, Thy son liveth: and himself believed, and his whole house.

⁵⁴ This *is* again the second miracle *that* Jesus did, when he was come out of Judaea into Galilee.

5 After this there was a feast of the Jews; and Jesus went up to Jerusalem. ℞

² Now there is at Jerusalem by the sheep *market* a pool, which is called in the Hebrew tongue Bethesda, having five porches.

³ In these lay a great multitude of impotent folk, of blind, halt, withered, waiting for the moving of the water.

⁴ For an angel went down at a certain season into the pool, and troubled the water: whosoever then first after the troubling of the water stepped in was made whole of whatsoever disease he had.

⁵ And a certain man was there, which had an infirmity thirty and eight years.

⁶ When Jesus saw him lie, and knew that he had been now a long time *in that case,* he saith unto him, Wilt thou be made whole?

⁷ The impotent man answered him, Sir, I have no man, when the water is troubled, to put me into the pool: but while I am coming, another steppeth down before me.

⁸ Jesus saith unto him, Rise, take up thy bed, and walk.

⁹ And immediately the man was made whole, and took up his bed, and walked: and on the same day was the sabbath.

¹⁰ The Jews therefore said unto him that was cured, It is the sabbath day: it is not lawful for thee to carry *thy* bed.

¹¹ He answered them, He that made me whole, the same said unto me, Take up thy bed, and walk.

¹² Then asked they him, What man is that which said unto thee, Take up thy bed, and walk?

¹³ And he that was healed wist not who it was: for Jesus had conveyed himself away, a multitude being in *that* place.

¹⁴ Afterward Jesus findeth him in the temple, and said unto him, Behold, thou art made whole: sin no more, lest a worse thing come unto thee.

¹⁵ The man departed, and told the Jews that it was Jesus, which had made him whole.

16 And therefore did the Jews persecute Jesus, and sought to slay him, because he had done these things on the sabbath day.

17 But Jesus answered them, My Father worketh hitherto, and I work.

18 Therefore the Jews sought the more to kill him, because he not only had broken the sabbath, but said also that God was his Father, making himself equal with God.

19 Then answered Jesus and said unto them, Verily, verily, I say unto you, The Son can do nothing of himself, but what he seeth the Father do: for what things soever he doeth, these also doeth the Son likewise.

20 For the Father loveth the Son, and sheweth him all things that himself doeth: and he will shew him greater works than these, that ye may marvel.

21 For as the Father raiseth up the dead, and quickeneth *them;* even so the Son quickeneth whom he will.

22 For the Father judgeth no man, but hath committed all judgment unto the Son:

23 That all *men* should honour the Son, even as they honour the Father. He that honoureth not the Son honoureth not the Father which hath sent him.

24 Verily, verily, I say unto you, He that heareth my word, and believeth on him that sent me, hath everlasting life, and shall not come into condemnation; but is passed from death unto life.

25 Verily, verily, I say unto you, The hour is coming, and now is, when the dead shall hear the voice of the Son of God: and they that hear shall live.

26 For as the Father hath life in himself; so hath he given to the Son to have life in himself;

27 And hath given him authority to execute judgment also, because he is the Son of man.

28 Marvel not at this: for the hour is coming, in the which all that are in the graves shall hear his voice,

29 And shall come forth; they that have done good, unto the resurrection of life; and they that have done evil, unto the resurrection of damnation.

30 I can of mine own self do nothing: as I hear, I judge: and my judgment is just; because I seek not mine own will, but the will of the Father which hath sent me.

31 If I bear witness of myself, my witness is not true.

32 There is another that beareth witness of me; and I know that the witness which he witnesseth of me is true.

33 Ye sent unto John, and he bare witness unto the truth.

34 But I receive not testimony from man: but these things I say, that ye might be saved.

35 He was a burning and a shining light: and ye were willing for a season to rejoice in his light.

36 But I have greater witness than *that* of John: for the works which the Father hath given me to finish, the same works that I do, bear witness of me, that the Father hath sent me.

37 And the Father himself, which hath sent me, hath borne witness of me. Ye have neither heard his voice at any time, nor seen his shape.

38 And ye have not his word abiding in you: for whom he hath sent, him ye believe not.

39 Search the scriptures; for in them ye think ye have eternal life: and they are they which testify of me.

40 And ye will not come to me, that ye might have life.

41 I receive not honour from men.

42 But I know you, that ye have not the love of God in you.

43 I am come in my Father's name, and ye receive me not: if another shall come in his own name, him ye will receive.

44 How can ye believe, which receive honour one of another, and seek not the honour that *cometh* from God only?

45 Do not think that I will accuse you to the Father: there is *one* that accuseth you, *even* Moses, in whom ye trust.

46 For had ye believed Moses, ye would have believed me: for he wrote of me.

47 But if ye believe not his writings, how shall ye believe my words?

6 After these things Jesus went over the sea of Galilee, which is *the sea* of Tiberias.

2 And a great multitude followed him, because they saw his miracles which he did on them that were diseased.

3 And Jesus went up into a mountain, and there he sat with his disciples.

4 And the passover, a feast of the Jews, was nigh.

5 When Jesus then lifted up *his* eyes, and saw a great company come unto him, he saith unto Philip, Whence shall we buy bread, that these may eat?

6 And this he said to prove him: for he himself knew what he would do.

7 Philip answered him, Two hundred pennyworth of bread is not sufficient for them, that every one of them may take a little.

8 One of his disciples, Andrew, Simon Peter's brother, saith unto him,

9 There is a lad here, which hath five barley loaves, and two small fishes: but what are they among so many?

10 And Jesus said, Make the men sit down. Now there was much grass in the place. So the men sat down, in number about five thousand.

11 And Jesus took the loaves; and when he had given thanks, he distributed to the disciples, and the disciples to them that were set down; and likewise of the fishes as much as they would.

12 When they were filled, he said unto his disciples, Gather up the fragments that remain, that nothing be lost.

13 Therefore they gathered *them* together, and filled twelve baskets with the fragments of the five barley loaves, which remained over and above unto them that had eaten.

14 Then those men, when they had seen the miracle that Jesus did, said, This is of a truth that prophet that should come into the world.

15 When Jesus therefore perceived that they would come and take him by force, to make him a king, he departed again into a mountain himself alone.

16 And when even was *now* come, his disciples went down unto the sea,

17 And entered into a ship, and went over the sea toward Capernaum. And it was now dark, and Jesus was not come to them.

18 And the sea arose by reason of a great wind that blew.

19 So when they had rowed about five and twenty or thirty furlongs, they see Jesus walking on the sea, and drawing nigh unto the ship: and they were afraid.

20 But he saith unto them, It is I; be not afraid.

21 Then they willingly received him into the ship: and immediately the ship was at the land whither they went.

22 The day following, when the people which stood on the other side of the sea saw that there was none other boat there, save that one whereinto his disciples were entered, and that Jesus went not with his disciples into the boat, but *that* his disciples were gone away alone;

23 (Howbeit there came other boats from Tiberias nigh unto the place where they did eat bread, after that the Lord had given thanks:)

24 When the people therefore saw that Jesus was not there, neither his disciples, they also took shipping, and came to Capernaum, seeking for Jesus.

25 And when they had found him on the other side of the sea, they said unto him, Rabbi, when camest thou hither?

26 Jesus answered them and said, Verily, verily, I say unto you, Ye seek me, not because ye saw the miracles, but because ye did eat of the loaves, and were filled.

27 Labour not for the meat which perisheth, but for that meat which endureth unto everlasting life, which the Son of man shall give unto you: for him hath God the Father sealed.

28 Then said they unto him, What shall we do, that we might work the works of God?

29 Jesus answered and said unto them, This is the work of God, that ye believe on him whom he hath sent.

30 They said therefore unto him, What sign shewest thou then, that we may see, and believe thee? what dost thou work?

31 Our fathers did eat manna in the desert; as it is written, He gave them bread from heaven to eat.

32 Then Jesus said unto them, Verily, verily, I say unto you, Moses gave you not that bread from heaven; but my Father giveth you the true bread from heaven.

33 For the bread of God is he which cometh down from heaven, and giveth life unto the world.

34 Then said they unto him, Lord, evermore give us this bread.

35 And Jesus said unto them, I am the bread of life: he that cometh to me shall never hunger; and he that believeth on me shall never thirst.

36 But I said unto you, That ye also have seen me, and believe not.

37 All that the Father giveth me shall come to me; and him that cometh to me I will in no wise cast out.

38 For I came down from heaven, not to do mine own will, but the will of him that sent me.

39 And this is the Father's will which hath sent me, that of all which he hath given me I should lose nothing, but should raise it up again at the last day.

40 And this is the will of him that sent me, that every one which seeth the Son, and believeth

on him, may have everlasting life: and I will raise him up at the last day.

⁴¹ The Jews then murmured at him, because he said, I am the bread which came down from heaven.

⁴² And they said, Is not this Jesus, the son of Joseph, whose father and mother we know? how is it then that he saith, I came down from heaven?

⁴³ Jesus therefore answered and said unto them, Murmur not among yourselves.

⁴⁴ No man can come to me, except the Father which hath sent me draw him: and I will raise him up at the last day.

⁴⁵ It is written in the prophets, And they shall be all taught of God. Every man therefore that hath heard, and hath learned of the Father, cometh unto me.

⁴⁶ Not that any man hath seen the Father, save he which is of God, he hath seen the Father.

⁴⁷ Verily, verily, I say unto you, He that believeth on me hath everlasting life.

⁴⁸ I am that bread of life.

⁴⁹ Your fathers did eat manna in the wilderness, and are dead.

⁵⁰ This is the bread which cometh down from heaven, that a man may eat thereof, and not die.

⁵¹ I am the living bread which came down from heaven: if any man eat of this bread, he shall live for ever: and the bread that I will give is my flesh, which I will give for the life of the world.

⁵² The Jews therefore strove among themselves, saying, How can this man give us *his* flesh to eat?

⁵³ Then Jesus said unto them, Verily, verily, I say unto you, Except ye eat the flesh of the Son of man, and drink his blood, ye have no life in you.

⁵⁴ Whoso eateth my flesh, and drinketh my blood, hath eternal life; and I will raise him up at the last day.

⁵⁵ For my flesh is meat indeed, and my blood is drink indeed.

⁵⁶ He that eateth my flesh, and drinketh my blood, dwelleth in me, and I in him.

⁵⁷ As the living Father hath sent me, and I live by the Father: so he that eateth me, even he shall live by me.

⁵⁸ This is that bread which came down from heaven: not as your fathers did eat manna, and are dead: he that eateth of this bread shall live for ever.

⁵⁹ These things said he in the synagogue, as he taught in Capernaum.

⁶⁰ Many therefore of his disciples, when they had heard *this*, said, This is an hard saying; who can hear it?

⁶¹ When Jesus knew in himself that his disciples murmured at it, he said unto them, Doth this offend you?

⁶² *What* and if ye shall see the Son of man ascend up where he was before?

⁶³ It is the spirit that quickeneth; the flesh profiteth nothing: the words that I speak unto you, *they* are spirit, and *they* are life.

⁶⁴ But there are some of you that believe not. For Jesus knew from the beginning who they were that believed not, and who should betray him.

⁶⁵ And he said, Therefore said I unto you, that no man can come unto me, except it were given unto him of my Father.

⁶⁶ From that *time* many of his disciples went back, and walked no more with him.

⁶⁷ Then said Jesus unto the twelve, Will ye also go away?

⁶⁸ Then Simon Peter answered him, Lord, to whom shall we go? thou hast the words of eternal life.

⁶⁹ And we believe and are sure that thou art that Christ, the Son of the living God.

⁷⁰ Jesus answered them, Have not I chosen you twelve, and one of you is a devil?

⁷¹ He spake of Judas Iscariot *the son* of Simon: for he it was that should betray him, being one of the twelve.

7 After these things Jesus walked in Galilee: for he would not walk in Jewry, because the Jews sought to kill him.

² Now the Jews' feast of tabernacles was at hand.

³ His brethren therefore said unto him, Depart hence, and go into Judaea, that thy disciples also may see the works that thou doest.

⁴ For *there is* no man *that* doeth any thing in secret, and he himself seeketh to be known openly. If thou do these things, shew thyself to the world.

⁵ For neither did his brethren believe in him.

⁶ Then Jesus said unto them, My time is not yet come: but your time is alway ready.

⁷ The world cannot hate you; but me it hateth, because I testify of it, that the works thereof are evil.

⁸ Go ye up unto this feast: I go not up yet unto this feast; for my time is not yet full come.

9 When he had said these words unto them, he abode *still* in Galilee.

10 But when his brethren were gone up, then went he also up unto the feast, not openly, but as it were in secret.

11 Then the Jews sought him at the feast, and said, Where is he?

12 And there was much murmuring among the people concerning him: for some said, He is a good man: others said, Nay; but he deceiveth the people.

13 Howbeit no man spake openly of him for fear of the Jews.

14 Now about the midst of the feast Jesus went up into the temple, and taught.

15 And the Jews marvelled, saying, How knoweth this man letters, having never learned?

16 Jesus answered them, and said, My doctrine is not mine, but his that sent me.

17 If any man will do his will, he shall know of the doctrine, whether it be of God, or *whether* I speak of myself.

18 He that speaketh of himself seeketh his own glory: but he that seeketh his glory that sent him, the same is true, and no unrighteousness is in him.

19 Did not Moses give you the law, and *yet* none of you keepeth the law? Why go ye about to kill me?

20 The people answered and said, Thou hast a devil: who goeth about to kill thee?

21 Jesus answered and said unto them, I have done one work, and ye all marvel.

22 Moses therefore gave unto you circumcision; (not because it is of Moses, but of the fathers;) and ye on the sabbath day circumcise a man.

23 If a man on the sabbath day receive circumcision, that the law of Moses should not be broken; are ye angry at me, because I have made a man every whit whole on the sabbath day?

24 Judge not according to the appearance, but judge righteous judgment.

25 Then said some of them of Jerusalem, Is not this he, whom they seek to kill?

26 But, lo, he speaketh boldly, and they say nothing unto him. Do the rulers know indeed that this is the very Christ?

27 Howbeit we know this man whence he is: but when Christ cometh, no man knoweth whence he is.

28 Then cried Jesus in the temple as he taught, saying, Ye both know me, and ye know whence I am: and I am not come of myself, but he that sent me is true, whom ye know not.

29 But I know him: for I am from him, and he hath sent me.

30 Then they sought to take him: but no man laid hands on him, because his hour was not yet come.

31 And many of the people believed on him, and said, When Christ cometh, will he do more miracles than these which this *man* hath done?

32 The Pharisees heard that the people murmured such things concerning him; and the Pharisees and the chief priests sent officers to take him.

33 Then said Jesus unto them, Yet a little while am I with you, and *then* I go unto him that sent me.

34 Ye shall seek me, and shall not find *me:* and where I am, *thither* ye cannot come.

35 Then said the Jews among themselves, Whither will he go, that we shall not find him? will he go unto the dispersed among the Gentiles, and teach the Gentiles?

36 What *manner of* saying is this that he said, Ye shall seek me, and shall not find *me:* and where I am, *thither* ye cannot come?

37 In the last day, that great *day* of the feast, Jesus stood and cried, saying, If any man thirst, let him come unto me, and drink.

38 He that believeth on me, as the scripture hath said, out of his belly shall flow rivers of living water.

39 (But this spake he of the Spirit, which they that believe on him should receive: for the Holy Ghost was not yet *given;* because that Jesus was not yet glorified.)

40 Many of the people therefore, when they heard this saying, said, Of a truth this is the Prophet.

41 Others said, This is the Christ. But some said, Shall Christ come out of Galilee?

42 Hath not the scripture said, That Christ cometh of the seed of David, and out of the town of Bethlehem, where David was?

43 So there was a division among the people because of him.

44 And some of them would have taken him; but no man laid hands on him.

45 Then came the officers to the chief priests and Pharisees; and they said unto them, Why have ye not brought him?

⁴⁶ The officers answered, Never man spake like this man.

⁴⁷ Then answered them the Pharisees, Are ye also deceived?

⁴⁸ Have any of the rulers or of the Pharisees believed on him?

⁴⁹ But this people who knoweth not the law are cursed.

⁵⁰ Nicodemus saith unto them, (he that came to Jesus by night, being one of them,)

⁵¹ Doth our law judge *any* man, before it hear him, and know what he doeth?

⁵² They answered and said unto him, Art thou also of Galilee? Search, and look: for out of Galilee ariseth no prophet.

⁵³ And every man went unto his own house.

8 Jesus went unto the mount of Olives.

² And early in the morning he came again into the temple, and all the people came unto him; and he sat down, and taught them.

³ And the scribes and Pharisees brought unto him a woman taken in adultery; and when they had set her in the midst,

⁴ They say unto him, Master, this woman was taken in adultery, in the very act.

⁵ Now Moses in the law commanded us, that such should be stoned: but what sayest thou?

⁶ This they said, tempting him, that they might have to accuse him. But Jesus stooped down, and with *his* finger wrote on the ground, *as though he heard them not.*

⁷ So when they continued asking him, he lifted up himself, and said unto them, He that is without sin among you, let him first cast a stone at her.

⁸ And again he stooped down, and wrote on the ground.

⁹ And they which heard *it,* being convicted by *their own* conscience, went out one by one, beginning at the eldest, *even* unto the last: and Jesus was left alone, and the woman standing in the midst.

¹⁰ When Jesus had lifted up himself, and saw none but the woman, he said unto her, Woman, where are those thine accusers? hath no man condemned thee?

¹¹ She said, No man, Lord. And Jesus said unto her, Neither do I condemn thee: go, and sin no more.

¹² Then spake Jesus again unto them, saying, I am the light of the world: he that followeth me shall not walk in darkness, but shall have the light of life.

¹³ The Pharisees therefore said unto him, Thou bearest record of thyself; thy record is not true.

¹⁴ Jesus answered and said unto them, Though I bear record of myself, *yet* my record is true: for I know whence I came, and whither I go; but ye cannot tell whence I come, and whither I go.

¹⁵ Ye judge after the flesh; I judge no man.

¹⁶ And yet if I judge, my judgment is true: for I am not alone, but I and the Father that sent me.

¹⁷ It is also written in your law, that the testimony of two men is true.

¹⁸ I am one that bear witness of myself, and the Father that sent me beareth witness of me.

¹⁹ Then said they unto him, Where is thy Father? Jesus answered, Ye neither know me, nor my Father: if ye had known me, ye should have known my Father also.

²⁰ These words spake Jesus in the treasury, as he taught in the temple: and no man laid hands on him; for his hour was not yet come.

²¹ Then said Jesus again unto them, I go my way, and ye shall seek me, and shall die in your sins: whither I go, ye cannot come.

²² Then said the Jews, Will he kill himself? because he saith, Whither I go, ye cannot come.

²³ And he said unto them, Ye are from beneath; I am from above: ye are of this world; I am not of this world.

²⁴ I said therefore unto you, that ye shall die in your sins: for if ye believe not that I am *he,* ye shall die in your sins.

²⁵ Then said they unto him, Who art thou? And Jesus saith unto them, Even *the same* that I said unto you from the beginning.

²⁶ I have many things to say and to judge of you: but he that sent me is true; and I speak to the world those things which I have heard of him.

²⁷ They understood not that he spake to them of the Father.

²⁸ Then said Jesus unto them, When ye have lifted up the Son of man, then shall ye know that I am *he,* and *that* I do nothing of myself; but as my Father hath taught me, I speak these things.

²⁹ And he that sent me is with me: the Father hath not left me alone; for I do always those things that please him.

³⁰ As he spake these words, many believed on him.

³¹ Then said Jesus to those Jews which believed on him, If ye continue in my word, *then* are ye my disciples indeed;

32 And ye shall know the truth, and the truth shall make you free.

33 They answered him, We be Abraham's seed, and were never in bondage to any man: how sayest thou, Ye shall be made free?

34 Jesus answered them, Verily, verily, I say unto you, Whosoever committeth sin is the servant of sin.

35 And the servant abideth not in the house for ever: *but* the Son abideth ever.

36 If the Son therefore shall make you free, ye shall be free indeed.

37 I know that ye are Abraham's seed; but ye seek to kill me, because my word hath no place in you.

38 I speak that which I have seen with my Father: and ye do that which ye have seen with your father.

39 They answered and said unto him, Abraham is our father. Jesus saith unto them, If ye were Abraham's children, ye would do the works of Abraham.

40 But now ye seek to kill me, a man that hath told you the truth, which I have heard of God: this did not Abraham.

41 Ye do the deeds of your father. Then said they to him, We be not born of fornication; we have one Father, *even* God.

42 Jesus said unto them, If God were your Father, ye would love me: for I proceeded forth and came from God; neither came I of myself, but he sent me.

43 Why do ye not understand my speech? *even* because ye cannot hear my word.

44 Ye are of your father the devil, and the lusts of *your* father ye will do. He was a murderer from the beginning, and abode not in the truth, because there is no truth in him. When he speaketh a lie, he speaketh of his own: for he is a liar, and the father of it.

45 And because I tell *you* the truth, ye believe me not.

46 Which of you convinceth me of sin? And if I say the truth, why do ye not believe me?

47 He that is of God heareth God's words: ye therefore hear *them* not, because ye are not of God.

48 Then answered the Jews, and said unto him, Say we not well that thou art a Samaritan, and hast a devil?

49 Jesus answered, I have not a devil; but I honour my Father, and ye do dishonour me.

50 And I seek not mine own glory: there is one that seeketh and judgeth.

51 Verily, verily, I say unto you, If a man keep my saying, he shall never see death.

52 Then said the Jews unto him, Now we know that thou hast a devil. Abraham is dead, and the prophets; and thou sayest, If a man keep my saying, he shall never taste of death.

53 Art thou greater than our father Abraham, which is dead? and the prophets are dead: whom makest thou thyself?

54 Jesus answered, If I honour myself, my honour is nothing: it is my Father that honoureth me; of whom ye say, that he is your God:

55 Yet ye have not known him; but I know him: and if I should say, I know him not, I shall be a liar like unto you: but I know him, and keep his saying.

56 Your father Abraham rejoiced to see my day: and he saw *it*, and was glad.

57 Then said the Jews unto him, Thou art not yet fifty years old, and hast thou seen Abraham?

58 Jesus said unto them, Verily, verily, I say unto you, Before Abraham was, I am.

59 Then took they up stones to cast at him: but Jesus hid himself, and went out of the temple, going through the midst of them, and so passed by.

9 And as *Jesus* passed by, he saw a man which was blind from *his* birth.

2 And his disciples asked him, saying, Master, who did sin, this man, or his parents, that he was born blind?

3 Jesus answered, Neither hath this man sinned, nor his parents: but that the works of God should be made manifest in him.

4 I must work the works of him that sent me, while it is day: the night cometh, when no man can work.

5 As long as I am in the world, I am the light of the world.

6 When he had thus spoken, he spat on the ground, and made clay of the spittle, and he anointed the eyes of the blind man with the clay,

7 And said unto him, Go, wash in the pool of Siloam, (which is by interpretation, Sent.) He went his way therefore, and washed, and came seeing.

8 The neighbours therefore, and they which before had seen him that he was blind, said, Is not this he that sat and begged?

9 Some said, This is he: others *said*, He is like him: *but* he said, I am *he*.

10 Therefore said they unto him, How were thine eyes opened?

11 He answered and said, A man that is called Jesus made clay, and anointed mine eyes, and said unto me, Go to the pool of Siloam, and wash: and I went and washed, and I received sight.

12 Then said they unto him, Where is he? He said, I know not.

13 They brought to the Pharisees him that aforetime was blind.

14 And it was the sabbath day when Jesus made the clay, and opened his eyes.

15 Then again the Pharisees also asked him how he had received his sight. He said unto them, He put clay upon mine eyes, and I washed, and do see.

16 Therefore said some of the Pharisees, This man is not of God, because he keepeth not the sabbath day. Others said, How can a man that is a sinner do such miracles? And there was a division among them.

17 They say unto the blind man again, What sayest thou of him, that he hath opened thine eyes? He said, He is a prophet.

18 But the Jews did not believe concerning him, that he had been blind, and received his sight, until they called the parents of him that had received his sight.

19 And they asked them, saying, Is this your son, who ye say was born blind? how then doth he now see?

20 His parents answered them and said, We know that this is our son, and that he was born blind:

21 But by what means he now seeth, we know not; or who hath opened his eyes, we know not: he is of age; ask him: he shall speak for himself.

22 These words spake his parents, because they feared the Jews: for the Jews had agreed already, that if any man did confess that he was Christ, he should be put out of the synagogue.

23 Therefore said his parents, He is of age; ask him.

24 Then again called they the man that was blind, and said unto him, Give God the praise: we know that this man is a sinner.

25 He answered and said, Whether he be a sinner or no, I know not: one thing I know, that, whereas I was blind, now I see.

26 Then said they to him again, What did he to thee? how opened he thine eyes?

27 He answered them, I have told you already, and ye did not hear: wherefore would ye hear it again? will ye also be his disciples?

28 Then they reviled him, and said, Thou art his disciple; but we are Moses' disciples.

29 We know that God spake unto Moses: as for this fellow, we know not from whence he is.

30 The man answered and said unto them, Why herein is a marvellous thing, that ye know not from whence he is, and yet he hath opened mine eyes.

31 Now we know that God heareth not sinners: but if any man be a worshipper of God, and doeth his will, him he heareth.

32 Since the world began was it not heard that any man opened the eyes of one that was born blind.

33 If this man were not of God, he could do nothing.

34 They answered and said unto him, Thou wast altogether born in sins, and dost thou teach us? And they cast him out.

35 Jesus heard that they had cast him out; and when he had found him, he said unto him, Dost thou believe on the Son of God?

36 He answered and said, Who is he, Lord, that I might believe on him?

37 And Jesus said unto him, Thou hast both seen him, and it is he that talketh with thee.

38 And he said, Lord, I believe. And he worshipped him.

39 And Jesus said, For judgment I am come into this world, that they which see not might see; and that they which see might be made blind.

40 And some of the Pharisees which were with him heard these words, and said unto him, Are we blind also?

41 Jesus said unto them, If ye were blind, ye should have no sin: but now ye say, We see; therefore your sin remaineth.

10 Verily, verily, I say unto you, He that entereth not by the door into the sheepfold, but climbeth up some other way, the same is a thief and a robber.

2 But he that entereth in by the door is the shepherd of the sheep.

3 To him the porter openeth; and the sheep hear his voice: and he calleth his own sheep by name, and leadeth them out.

4 And when he putteth forth his own sheep, he goeth before them, and the sheep follow him: for they know his voice.

5 And a stranger will they not follow, but will flee from him: for they know not the voice of strangers.

⁶ This parable spake Jesus unto them: but they understood not what things they were which he spake unto them.

⁷ Then said Jesus unto them again, Verily, verily, I say unto you, I am the door of the sheep.

⁸ All that ever came before me are thieves and robbers: but the sheep did not hear them.

⁹ I am the door: by me if any man enter in, he shall be saved, and shall go in and out, and find pasture.

¹⁰ The thief cometh not, but for to steal, and to kill, and to destroy: I am come that they might have life, and that they might have *it* more abundantly.

¹¹ I am the good shepherd: the good shepherd giveth his life for the sheep.

¹² But he that is an hireling, and not the shepherd, whose own the sheep are not, seeth the wolf coming, and leaveth the sheep, and fleeth: and the wolf catcheth them, and scattereth the sheep.

¹³ The hireling fleeth, because he is an hireling, and careth not for the sheep.

¹⁴ I am the good shepherd, and know my *sheep*, and am known of mine.

¹⁵ As the Father knoweth me, even so know I the Father: and I lay down my life for the sheep.

¹⁶ And other sheep I have, which are not of this fold: them also I must bring, and they shall hear my voice; and there shall be one fold, *and* one shepherd.

¹⁷ Therefore doth my Father love me, because I lay down my life, that I might take it again.

¹⁸ No man taketh it from me, but I lay it down of myself. I have power to lay it down, and I have power to take it again. This commandment have I received of my Father.

¹⁹ There was a division therefore again among the Jews for these sayings.

²⁰ And many of them said, He hath a devil, and is mad; why hear ye him?

²¹ Others said, These are not the words of him that hath a devil. Can a devil open the eyes of the blind?

²² And it was at Jerusalem the feast of the dedication, and it was winter.

²³ And Jesus walked in the temple in Solomon's porch.

²⁴ Then came the Jews round about him, and said unto him, How long dost thou make us to doubt? If thou be the Christ, tell us plainly.

²⁵ Jesus answered them, I told you, and ye believed not: the works that I do in my Father's name, they bear witness of me.

²⁶ But ye believe not, because ye are not of my sheep, as I said unto you.

²⁷ My sheep hear my voice, and I know them, and they follow me:

²⁸ And I give unto them eternal life; and they shall never perish, neither shall any *man* pluck them out of my hand.

²⁹ My Father, which gave *them* me, is greater than all; and no *man* is able to pluck *them* out of my Father's hand.

³⁰ I and *my* Father are one.

³¹ Then the Jews took up stones again to stone him.

³² Jesus answered them, Many good works have I shewed you from my Father; for which of those works do ye stone me?

³³ The Jews answered him, saying, For a good work we stone thee not; but for blasphemy; and because that thou, being a man, makest thyself God.

³⁴ Jesus answered them, Is it not written in your law, I said, Ye are gods?

³⁵ If he called them gods, unto whom the word of God came, and the scripture cannot be broken;

³⁶ Say ye of him, whom the Father hath sanctified, and sent into the world, Thou blasphemest; because I said, I am the Son of God?

³⁷ If I do not the works of my Father, believe me not.

³⁸ But if I do, though ye believe not me, believe the works: that ye may know, and believe, that the Father is in me, and I in him.

³⁹ Therefore they sought again to take him: but he escaped out of their hand,

⁴⁰ And went away again beyond Jordan into the place where John at first baptized; and there he abode.

⁴¹ And many resorted unto him, and said, John did no miracle: but all things that John spake of this man were true.

⁴² And many believed on him there.

11 Now a certain *man* was sick, *named* Lazarus, of Bethany, the town of Mary and her sister Martha.

²(It was *that* Mary which anointed the Lord with ointment, and wiped his feet with her hair, whose brother Lazarus was sick.)

³ Therefore his sisters sent unto him, saying, Lord, behold, he whom thou lovest is sick.

⁴ When Jesus heard *that*, he said, This sickness

is not unto death, but for the glory of God, that the Son of God might be glorified thereby.

5 Now Jesus loved Martha, and her sister, and Lazarus.

6 When he had heard therefore that he was sick, he abode two days still in the same place where he was.

7 Then after that saith he to *his* disciples, Let us go into Judaea again.

8 *His* disciples say unto him, Master, the Jews of late sought to stone thee; and goest thou thither again?

9 Jesus answered, Are there not twelve hours in the day? If any man walk in the day, he stumbleth not, because he seeth the light of this world.

10 But if a man walk in the night, he stumbleth, because there is no light in him.

11 These things said he: and after that he saith unto them, Our friend Lazarus sleepeth; but I go, that I may awake him out of sleep.

12 Then said his disciples, Lord, if he sleep, he shall do well.

13 Howbeit Jesus spake of his death: but they thought that he had spoken of taking of rest in sleep.

14 Then said Jesus unto them plainly, Lazarus is dead.

15 And I am glad for your sakes that I was not there, to the intent ye may believe; nevertheless let us go unto him.

16 Then said Thomas, which is called Didymus, unto his fellowdisciples, Let us also go, that we may die with him.

17 Then when Jesus came, he found that he had *lain* in the grave four days already.

18 Now Bethany was nigh unto Jerusalem, about fifteen furlongs off:

19 And many of the Jews came to Martha and Mary, to comfort them concerning their brother.

20 Then Martha, as soon as she heard that Jesus was coming, went and met him: but Mary sat *still* in the house.

21 Then said Martha unto Jesus, Lord, if thou hadst been here, my brother had not died.

22 But I know, that even now, whatsoever thou wilt ask of God, God will give *it* thee.

23 Jesus saith unto her, Thy brother shall rise again.

24 Martha saith unto him, I know that he shall rise again in the resurrection at the last day.

25 Jesus said unto her, I am the resurrection, and the life: he that believeth in me, though he were dead, yet shall he live:

26 And whosoever liveth and believeth in me shall never die. Believest thou this?

27 She saith unto him, Yea, Lord: I believe that thou art the Christ, the Son of God, which should come into the world.

28 And when she had so said, she went her way, and called Mary her sister secretly, saying, The Master is come, and calleth for thee.

29 As soon as she heard *that,* she arose quickly, and came unto him.

30 Now Jesus was not yet come into the town, but was in that place where Martha met him.

31 The Jews then which were with her in the house, and comforted her, when they saw Mary, that she rose up hastily and went out, followed her, saying, She goeth unto the grave to weep there.

32 Then when Mary was come where Jesus was, and saw him, she fell down at his feet, saying unto him, Lord, if thou hadst been here, my brother had not died.

33 When Jesus therefore saw her weeping, and the Jews also weeping which came with her, he groaned in the spirit, and was troubled,

34 And said, Where have ye laid him? They said unto him, Lord, come and see.

35 Jesus wept.

36 Then said the Jews, Behold how he loved him!

37 And some of them said, Could not this man, which opened the eyes of the blind, have caused that even this man should not have died?

38 Jesus therefore again groaning in himself cometh to the grave. It was a cave, and a stone lay upon it.

39 Jesus said, Take ye away the stone. Martha, the sister of him that was dead, saith unto him, Lord, by this time he stinketh: for he hath been *dead* four days.

40 Jesus saith unto her, Said I not unto thee, that, if thou wouldest believe, thou shouldest see the glory of God?

41 Then they took away the stone *from the place* where the dead was laid. And Jesus lifted up *his* eyes, and said, Father, I thank thee that thou hast heard me.

42 And I knew that thou hearest me always: but because of the people which stand by I said *it,* that they may believe that thou hast sent me.

43 And when he thus had spoken, he cried with a loud voice, Lazarus, come forth.

44 And he that was dead came forth, bound hand and foot with graveclothes: and his face

was bound about with a napkin. Jesus saith unto them, Loose him, and let him go.

⁴⁵ Then many of the Jews which came to Mary, and had seen the things which Jesus did, believed on him.

⁴⁶ But some of them went their ways to the Pharisees, and told them what things Jesus had done.

⁴⁷ Then gathered the chief priests and the Pharisees a council, and said, What do we? for this man doeth many miracles.

⁴⁸ If we let him thus alone, all *men* will believe on him: and the Romans shall come and take away both our place and nation.

⁴⁹ And one of them, *named* Caiaphas, being the high priest that same year, said unto them, Ye know nothing at all,

⁵⁰ Nor consider that it is expedient for us, that one man should die for the people, and that the whole nation perish not.

⁵¹ And this spake he not of himself: but being high priest that year, he prophesied that Jesus should die for that nation;

⁵² And not for that nation only, but that also he should gather together in one the children of God that were scattered abroad.

⁵³ Then from that day forth they took counsel together for to put him to death.

⁵⁴ Jesus therefore walked no more openly among the Jews; but went thence unto a country near to the wilderness, into a city called Ephraim, and there continued with his disciples.

⁵⁵ And the Jews' passover was nigh at hand: and many went out of the country up to Jerusalem before the passover, to purify themselves.

⁵⁶ Then sought they for Jesus, and spake among themselves, as they stood in the temple, What think ye, that he will not come to the feast?

⁵⁷ Now both the chief priests and the Pharisees had given a commandment, that, if any man knew where he were, he should shew *it*, that they might take him.

12 Then Jesus six days before the passover came to Bethany, where Lazarus was which had been dead, whom he raised from the dead.

² There they made him a supper; and Martha served: but Lazarus was one of them that sat at the table with him.

³ Then took Mary a pound of ointment of spikenard, very costly, and anointed the feet of Jesus, and wiped his feet with her hair: and the house was filled with the odour of the ointment.

⁴ Then saith one of his disciples, Judas Iscariot, Simon's *son,* which should betray him,

⁵ Why was not this ointment sold for three hundred pence, and given to the poor?

⁶ This he said, not that he cared for the poor; but because he was a thief, and had the bag, and bare what was put therein.

⁷ Then said Jesus, Let her alone: against the day of my burying hath she kept this.

⁸ For the poor always ye have with you; but me ye have not always.

⁹ Much people of the Jews therefore knew that he was there: and they came not for Jesus' sake only, but that they might see Lazarus also, whom he had raised from the dead.

¹⁰ But the chief priests consulted that they might put Lazarus also to death;

¹¹ Because that by reason of him many of the Jews went away, and believed on Jesus.

¹² On the next day much people that were come to the feast, when they heard that Jesus was coming to Jerusalem,

¹³ Took branches of palm trees, and went forth to meet him, and cried, Hosanna: Blessed *is* the King of Israel that cometh in the name of the Lord.

¹⁴ And Jesus, when he had found a young ass, sat thereon; as it is written,

¹⁵ Fear not, daughter of Sion: behold, thy King cometh, sitting on an ass's colt.

¹⁶ These things understood not his disciples at the first: but when Jesus was glorified, then remembered they that these things were written of him, and *that* they had done these things unto him.

¹⁷ The people therefore that was with him when he called Lazarus out of his grave, and raised him from the dead, bare record.

¹⁸ For this cause the people also met him, for that they heard that he had done this miracle.

¹⁹ The Pharisees therefore said among themselves, Perceive ye how ye prevail nothing? behold, the world is gone after him.

²⁰ And there were certain Greeks among them that came up to worship at the feast:

²¹ The same came therefore to Philip, which was of Bethsaida of Galilee, and desired him, saying, Sir, we would see Jesus.

²² Philip cometh and telleth Andrew: and again Andrew and Philip tell Jesus.

23 And Jesus answered them, saying, The hour is come, that the Son of man should be glorified.

24 Verily, verily, I say unto you, Except a corn of wheat fall into the ground and die, it abideth alone: but if it die, it bringeth forth much fruit.

25 He that loveth his life shall lose it; and he that hateth his life in this world shall keep it unto life eternal.

26 If any man serve me, let him follow me; and where I am, there shall also my servant be: if any man serve me, him will *my* Father honour.

27 Now is my soul troubled; and what shall I say? Father, save me from this hour: but for this cause came I unto this hour.

28 Father, glorify thy name. Then came there a voice from heaven, *saying*, I have both glorified *it*, and will glorify *it* again.

29 The people therefore, that stood by, and heard *it*, said that it thundered: others said, An angel spake to him.

30 Jesus answered and said, This voice came not because of me, but for your sakes.

31 Now is the judgment of this world: now shall the prince of this world be cast out.

32 And I, if I be lifted up from the earth, will draw all *men* unto me.

33 This he said, signifying what death he should die.

34 The people answered him, We have heard out of the law that Christ abideth for ever: and how sayest thou, The Son of man must be lifted up? who is this Son of man?

35 Then Jesus said unto them, Yet a little while is the light with you. Walk while ye have the light, lest darkness come upon you: for he that walketh in darkness knoweth not whither he goeth.

36 While ye have light, believe in the light, that ye may be the children of light. These things spake Jesus, and departed, and did hide himself from them.

37 But though he had done so many miracles before them, yet they believed not on him:

38 That the saying of Esaias the prophet might be fulfilled, which he spake, Lord, who hath believed our report? and to whom hath the arm of the Lord been revealed?

39 Therefore they could not believe, because that Esaias said again,

40 He hath blinded their eyes, and hardened their heart; that they should not see with *their* eyes, nor understand with *their* heart, and be converted, and I should heal them.

41 These things said Esaias, when he saw his glory, and spake of him.

42 Nevertheless among the chief rulers also many believed on him; but because of the Pharisees they did not confess *him*, lest they should be put out of the synagogue:

43 For they loved the praise of men more than the praise of God.

44 Jesus cried and said, He that believeth on me, believeth not on me, but on him that sent me.

45 And he that seeth me seeth him that sent me.

46 I am come a light into the world, that whosoever believeth on me should not abide in darkness.

47 And if any man hear my words, and believe not, I judge him not: for I came not to judge the world, but to save the world.

48 He that rejecteth me, and receiveth not my words, hath one that judgeth him: the word that I have spoken, the same shall judge him in the last day.

49 For I have not spoken of myself; but the Father which sent me, he gave me a commandment, what I should say, and what I should speak.

50 And I know that his commandment is life everlasting: whatsoever I speak therefore, even as the Father said unto me, so I speak.

13 Now before the feast of the passover, when Jesus knew that his hour was come that he should depart out of this world unto the Father, having loved his own which were in the world, he loved them unto the end.

2 And supper being ended, the devil having now put into the heart of Judas Iscariot, Simon's *son*, to betray him;

3 Jesus knowing that the Father had given all things into his hands, and that he was come from God, and went to God;

4 He riseth from supper, and laid aside his garments; and took a towel, and girded himself.

5 After that he poureth water into a bason, and began to wash the disciples' feet, and to wipe *them* with the towel wherewith he was girded.

6 Then cometh he to Simon Peter: and Peter saith unto him, Lord, dost thou wash my feet?

7 Jesus answered and said unto him, What I do thou knowest not now; but thou shalt know hereafter.

8 Peter saith unto him, Thou shalt never wash my feet. Jesus answered him, If I wash thee not, thou hast no part with me.

9 Simon Peter saith unto him, Lord, not my feet only, but also *my* hands and *my* head.

10 Jesus saith to him, He that is washed needeth not save to wash *his* feet, but is clean every whit: and ye are clean, but not all.

11 For he knew who should betray him; therefore said he, Ye are not all clean.

12 So after he had washed their feet, and had taken his garments, and was set down again, he said unto them, Know ye what I have done to you?

13 Ye call me Master and Lord: and ye say well; for so I am.

14 If I then, *your* Lord and Master, have washed your feet; ye also ought to wash one another's feet.

15 For I have given you an example, that ye should do as I have done to you.

16 Verily, verily, I say unto you, The servant is not greater than his lord; neither he that is sent greater than he that sent him.

17 If ye know these things, happy are ye if ye do them.

18 I speak not of you all: I know whom I have chosen: but that the scripture may be fulfilled, He that eateth bread with me hath lifted up his heel against me.

19 Now I tell you before it come, that, when it is come to pass, ye may believe that I am *he*.

20 Verily, verily, I say unto you, He that receiveth whomsoever I send receiveth me; and he that receiveth me receiveth him that sent me.

21 When Jesus had thus said, he was troubled in spirit, and testified, and said, Verily, verily, I say unto you, that one of you shall betray me.

22 Then the disciples looked one on another, doubting of whom he spake.

23 Now there was leaning on Jesus' bosom one of his disciples, whom Jesus loved.

24 Simon Peter therefore beckoned to him, that he should ask who it should be of whom he spake.

25 He then lying on Jesus' breast saith unto him, Lord, who is it?

26 Jesus answered, He it is, to whom I shall give a sop, when I have dipped *it*. And when he had dipped the sop, he gave *it* to Judas Iscariot, *the son* of Simon.

27 And after the sop Satan entered into him. Then said Jesus unto him, That thou doest, do quickly.

28 Now no man at the table knew for what intent he spake this unto him.

29 For some *of them* thought, because Judas had the bag, that Jesus had said unto him, Buy *those things* that we have need of against the feast; or, that he should give something to the poor.

30 He then having received the sop went immediately out: and it was night.

31 Therefore, when he was gone out, Jesus said, Now is the Son of man glorified, and God is glorified in him.

32 If God be glorified in him, God shall also glorify him in himself, and shall straightway glorify him.

33 Little children, yet a little while I am with you. Ye shall seek me: and as I said unto the Jews, Whither I go, ye cannot come; so now I say to you.

34 A new commandment I give unto you, That ye love one another; as I have loved you, that ye also love one another.

35 By this shall all *men* know that ye are my disciples, if ye have love one to another.

36 Simon Peter said unto him, Lord, whither goest thou? Jesus answered him, Whither I go, thou canst not follow me now; but thou shalt follow me afterwards.

37 Peter said unto him, Lord, why cannot I follow thee now? I will lay down my life for thy sake.

38 Jesus answered him, Wilt thou lay down thy life for my sake? Verily, verily, I say unto thee, The cock shall not crow, till thou hast denied me thrice.

14 Let not your heart be troubled: ye believe in God, believe also in me.

2 In my Father's house are many mansions: if *it were* not so, I would have told you. I go to prepare a place for you.

3 And if I go and prepare a place for you, I will come again, and receive you unto myself; that where I am, *there* ye may be also.

4 And whither I go ye know, and the way ye know.

5 Thomas saith unto him, Lord, we know not whither thou goest; and how can we know the way?

6 Jesus saith unto him, I am the way, the truth, and the life: no man cometh unto the Father, but by me.

7 If ye had known me, ye should have known my Father also: and from henceforth ye know him, and have seen him.

8 Philip saith unto him, Lord, shew us the Father, and it sufficeth us.

9 Jesus saith unto him, Have I been so

long time with you, and yet hast thou not known me, Philip? he that hath seen me hath seen the Father; and how sayest thou *then,* Shew us the Father?

¹⁰ Believest thou not that I am in the Father, and the Father in me? the words that I speak unto you I speak not of myself: but the Father that dwelleth in me, he doeth the works.

¹¹ Believe me that I *am* in the Father, and the Father in me: or else believe me for the very works' sake.

¹² Verily, verily, I say unto you, He that believeth on me, the works that I do shall he do also; and greater *works* than these shall he do; because I go unto my Father.

¹³ And whatsoever ye shall ask in my name, that will I do, that the Father may be glorified in the Son.

¹⁴ If ye shall ask any thing in my name, I will do *it.*

¹⁵ If ye love me, keep my commandments.

¹⁶ And I will pray the Father, and he shall give you another Comforter, that he may abide with you for ever;

¹⁷ *Even* the Spirit of truth; whom the world cannot receive, because it seeth him not, neither knoweth him: but ye know him; for he dwelleth with you, and shall be in you.

¹⁸ I will not leave you comfortless: I will come to you.

¹⁹ Yet a little while, and the world seeth me no more; but ye see me: because I live, ye shall live also.

²⁰ At that day ye shall know that I *am* in my Father, and ye in me, and I in you.

²¹ He that hath my commandments, and keepeth them, he it is that loveth me: and he that loveth me shall be loved of my Father, and I will love him, and will manifest myself to him.

²² Judas saith unto him, not Iscariot, Lord, how is it that thou wilt manifest thyself unto us, and not unto the world?

²³ Jesus answered and said unto him, If a man love me, he will keep my words: and my Father will love him, and we will come unto him, and make our abode with him.

²⁴ He that loveth me not keepeth not my sayings: and the word which ye hear is not mine, but the Father's which sent me.

²⁵ These things have I spoken unto you, being *yet* present with you.

²⁶ But the Comforter, *which is* the Holy Ghost, whom the Father will send in my name, he shall teach you all things, and bring all things to your remembrance, whatsoever I have said unto you.

²⁷ Peace I leave with you, my peace I give unto you: not as the world giveth, give I unto you. Let not your heart be troubled, neither let it be afraid.

²⁸ Ye have heard how I said unto you, I go away, and come *again* unto you. If ye loved me, ye would rejoice, because I said, I go unto the Father: for my Father is greater than I.

²⁹ And now I have told you before it come to pass, that, when it is come to pass, ye might believe.

³⁰ Hereafter I will not talk much with you: for the prince of this world cometh, and hath nothing in me.

³¹ But that the world may know that I love the Father; and as the Father gave me commandment, even so I do. Arise, let us go hence.

15 I am the true vine, and my Father is the husbandman.

² Every branch in me that beareth not fruit he taketh away: and every *branch* that beareth fruit, he purgeth it, that it may bring forth more fruit.

³ Now ye are clean through the word which I have spoken unto you.

⁴ Abide in me, and I in you. As the branch cannot bear fruit of itself, except it abide in the vine; no more can ye, except ye abide in me.

⁵ I am the vine, ye *are* the branches: He that abideth in me, and I in him, the same bringeth forth much fruit: for without me ye can do nothing.

⁶ If a man abide not in me, he is cast forth as a branch, and is withered; and men gather them, and cast *them* into the fire, and they are burned.

⁷ If ye abide in me, and my words abide in you, ye shall ask what ye will, and it shall be done unto you.

⁸ Herein is my Father glorified, that ye bear much fruit; so shall ye be my disciples.

⁹ As the Father hath loved me, so have I loved you: continue ye in my love.

¹⁰ If ye keep my commandments, ye shall abide in my love; even as I have kept my Father's commandments, and abide in his love.

¹¹ These things have I spoken unto you, that my joy might remain in you, and *that* your joy might be full.

¹² This is my commandment, That ye love one another, as I have loved you.

13 Greater love hath no man than this, that a man lay down his life for his friends.

14 Ye are my friends, if ye do whatsoever I command you.

15 Henceforth I call you not servants; for the servant knoweth not what his lord doeth: but I have called you friends; for all things that I have heard of my Father I have made known unto you.

16 Ye have not chosen me, but I have chosen you, and ordained you, that ye should go and bring forth fruit, and *that* your fruit should remain: that whatsoever ye shall ask of the Father in my name, he may give it you.

17 These things I command you, that ye love one another.

18 If the world hate you, ye know that *it hated* me before it hated you.

19 If ye were of the world, the world would love his own: but because ye are not of the world, but I have chosen you out of the world, therefore the world hateth you.

20 Remember the word that I said unto you, The servant is not greater than his lord. If they have persecuted me, they will also persecute you; if they have kept my saying, they will keep yours also.

21 But all these things will they do unto you for my name's sake, because they know not him that sent me.

22 If I had not come and spoken unto them, they had not had sin: but now they have no cloke for their sin.

23 He that hateth me hateth my Father also.

24 If I had not done among them the works which none other man did, they had not had sin: but now have they both seen and hated both me and my Father.

25 But *this cometh to pass,* that the word might be fulfilled that is written in their law, They hated me without a cause.

26 But when the Comforter is come, whom I will send unto you from the Father, *even* the Spirit of truth, which proceedeth from the Father, he shall testify of me:

27 And ye also shall bear witness, because ye have been with me from the beginning.

16 These things have I spoken unto you, that ye should not be offended.

2 They shall put you out of the synagogues: yea, the time cometh, that whosoever killeth you will think that he doeth God service.

3 And these things will they do unto you, because they have not known the Father, nor me.

4 But these things have I told you, that when the time shall come, ye may remember that I told you of them. And these things I said not unto you at the beginning, because I was with you.

5 But now I go my way to him that sent me; and none of you asketh me, Whither goest thou?

6 But because I have said these things unto you, sorrow hath filled your heart.

7 Nevertheless I tell you the truth; It is expedient for you that I go away: for if I go not away, the Comforter will not come unto you; but if I depart, I will send him unto you.

8 And when he is come, he will reprove the world of sin, and of righteousness, and of judgment:

9 Of sin, because they believe not on me;

10 Of righteousness, because I go to my Father, and ye see me no more;

11 Of judgment, because the prince of this world is judged.

12 I have yet many things to say unto you, but ye cannot bear them now.

13 Howbeit when he, the Spirit of truth, is come, he will guide you into all truth: for he shall not speak of himself; but whatsoever he shall hear, *that* shall he speak: and he will shew you things to come.

14 He shall glorify me: for he shall receive of mine, and shall shew *it* unto you.

15 All things that the Father hath are mine: therefore said I, that he shall take of mine, and shall shew *it* unto you.

16 A little while, and ye shall not see me: and again, a little while, and ye shall see me, because I go to the Father.

17 Then said *some* of his disciples among themselves, What is this that he saith unto us, A little while, and ye shall not see me: and again, a little while, and ye shall see me: and, Because I go to the Father?

18 They said therefore, What is this that he saith, A little while? we cannot tell what he saith.

19 Now Jesus knew that they were desirous to ask him, and said unto them, Do ye enquire among yourselves of that I said, A little while, and ye shall not see me: and again, a little while, and ye shall see me?

20 Verily, verily, I say unto you, That ye shall weep and lament, but the world shall rejoice: and ye shall be sorrowful, but your sorrow shall be turned into joy.

21 A woman when she is in travail hath sorrow,

because her hour is come: but as soon as she is delivered of the child, she remembereth no more the anguish, for joy that a man is born into the world.

22 And ye now therefore have sorrow: but I will see you again, and your heart shall rejoice, and your joy no man taketh from you.

23 And in that day ye shall ask me nothing. Verily, verily, I say unto you, Whatsoever ye shall ask the Father in my name, he will give *it* you.

24 Hitherto have ye asked nothing in my name: ask, and ye shall receive, that your joy may be full.

25 These things have I spoken unto you in proverbs: but the time cometh, when I shall no more speak unto you in proverbs, but I shall shew you plainly of the Father.

26 At that day ye shall ask in my name: and I say not unto you, that I will pray the Father for you:

27 For the Father himself loveth you, because ye have loved me, and have believed that I came out from God.

28 I came forth from the Father, and am come into the world: again, I leave the world, and go to the Father.

29 His disciples said unto him, Lo, now speakest thou plainly, and speakest no proverb.

30 Now are we sure that thou knowest all things, and needest not that any man should ask thee: by this we believe that thou camest forth from God.

31 Jesus answered them, Do ye now believe?

32 Behold, the hour cometh, yea, is now come, that ye shall be scattered, every man to his own, and shall leave me alone: and yet I am not alone, because the Father is with me.

33 These things I have spoken unto you, that in me ye might have peace. In the world ye shall have tribulation: but be of good cheer; I have overcome the world.

17 These words spake Jesus, and lifted up his eyes to heaven, and said, Father, the hour is come; glorify thy Son, that thy Son also may glorify thee:

2 As thou hast given him power over all flesh, that he should give eternal life to as many as thou hast given him.

3 And this is life eternal, that they might know thee the only true God, and Jesus Christ, whom thou hast sent.

4 I have glorified thee on the earth: I have finished the work which thou gavest me to do.

5 And now, O Father, glorify thou me with thine own self with the glory which I had with thee before the world was.

6 I have manifested thy name unto the men which thou gavest me out of the world: thine they were, and thou gavest them me; and they have kept thy word.

7 Now they have known that all things whatsoever thou hast given me are of thee.

8 For I have given unto them the words which thou gavest me; and they have received *them*, and have known surely that I came out from thee, and they have believed that thou didst send me.

9 I pray for them: I pray not for the world, but for them which thou hast given me; for they are thine.

10 And all mine are thine, and thine are mine; and I am glorified in them.

11 And now I am no more in the world, but these are in the world, and I come to thee. Holy Father, keep through thine own name those whom thou hast given me, that they may be one, as we *are*.

12 While I was with them in the world, I kept them in thy name: those that thou gavest me I have kept, and none of them is lost, but the son of perdition; that the scripture might be fulfilled.

13 And now come I to thee; and these things I speak in the world, that they might have my joy fulfilled in themselves.

14 I have given them thy word; and the world hath hated them, because they are not of the world, even as I am not of the world.

15 I pray not that thou shouldest take them out of the world, but that thou shouldest keep them from the evil.

16 They are not of the world, even as I am not of the world.

17 Sanctify them through thy truth: thy word is truth.

18 As thou hast sent me into the world, even so have I also sent them into the world.

19 And for their sakes I sanctify myself, that they also might be sanctified through the truth.

20 Neither pray I for these alone, but for them also which shall believe on me through their word;

21 That they all may be one; as thou, Father, *art* in me, and I in thee, that they also may be one in us: that the world may believe that thou hast sent me.

22 And the glory which thou gavest me I have

given them; that they may be one, even as we are one:

23 I in them, and thou in me, that they may be made perfect in one; and that the world may know that thou hast sent me, and hast loved them, as thou hast loved me.

24 Father, I will that they also, whom thou hast given me, be with me where I am; that they may behold my glory, which thou hast given me: for thou lovedst me before the foundation of the world.

25 O righteous Father, the world hath not known thee: but I have known thee, and these have known that thou hast sent me.

26 And I have declared unto them thy name, and will declare *it:* that the love wherewith thou hast loved me may be in them, and I in them.

18 When Jesus had spoken these words, he went forth with his disciples over the brook Cedron, where was a garden, into the which he entered, and his disciples.

2 And Judas also, which betrayed him, knew the place: for Jesus ofttimes resorted thither with his disciples.

3 Judas then, having received a band *of men* and officers from the chief priests and Pharisees, cometh thither with lanterns and torches and weapons.

4 Jesus therefore, knowing all things that should come upon him, went forth, and said unto them, Whom seek ye?

5 They answered him, Jesus of Nazareth. Jesus saith unto them, I am *he.* And Judas also, which betrayed him, stood with them.

6 As soon then as he had said unto them, I am *he,* they went backward, and fell to the ground.

7 Then asked he them again, Whom seek ye? And they said, Jesus of Nazareth.

8 Jesus answered, I have told you that I am *he:* if therefore ye seek me, let these go their way:

9 That the saying might be fulfilled, which he spake, Of them which thou gavest me have I lost none.

10 Then Simon Peter having a sword drew it, and smote the high priest's servant, and cut off his right ear. The servant's name was Malchus.

11 Then said Jesus unto Peter, Put up thy sword into the sheath: the cup which my Father hath given me, shall I not drink it?

12 Then the band and the captain and officers of the Jews took Jesus, and bound him,

13 And led him away to Annas first; for he was father in law to Caiaphas, which was the high priest that same year.

14 Now Caiaphas was he, which gave counsel to the Jews, that it was expedient that one man should die for the people.

15 And Simon Peter followed Jesus, and *so did* another disciple: that disciple was known unto the high priest, and went in with Jesus into the palace of the high priest.

16 But Peter stood at the door without. Then went out that other disciple, which was known unto the high priest, and spake unto her that kept the door, and brought in Peter.

17 Then saith the damsel that kept the door unto Peter, Art not thou also *one* of this man's disciples? He saith, I am not.

18 And the servants and officers stood there, who had made a fire of coals; for it was cold: and they warmed themselves: and Peter stood with them, and warmed himself.

19 The high priest then asked Jesus of his disciples, and of his doctrine.

20 Jesus answered him, I spake openly to the world; I ever taught in the synagogue, and in the temple, whither the Jews always resort; and in secret have I said nothing.

21 Why askest thou me? ask them which heard me, what I have said unto them: behold, they know what I said.

22 And when he had thus spoken, one of the officers which stood by struck Jesus with the palm of his hand, saying, Answerest thou the high priest so?

23 Jesus answered him, If I have spoken evil, bear witness of the evil: but if well, why smitest thou me?

24 Now Annas had sent him bound unto Caiaphas the high priest.

25 And Simon Peter stood and warmed himself. They said therefore unto him, Art not thou also *one* of his disciples? He denied *it,* and said, I am not.

26 One of the servants of the high priest, being *his* kinsman whose ear Peter cut off, saith, Did not I see thee in the garden with him?

27 Peter then denied again: and immediately the cock crew.

28 Then led they Jesus from Caiaphas unto the hall of judgment: and it was early; and they themselves went not into the judgment hall, lest they should be defiled; but that they might eat the passover.

29 Pilate then went out unto them, and said, What accusation bring ye against this man?

30 They answered and said unto him, If he were not a malefactor, we would not have delivered him up unto thee.

31 Then said Pilate unto them, Take ye him, and judge him according to your law. The Jews therefore said unto him, It is not lawful for us to put any man to death:

32 That the saying of Jesus might be fulfilled, which he spake, signifying what death he should die.

33 Then Pilate entered into the judgment hall again, and called Jesus, and said unto him, Art thou the King of the Jews?

34 Jesus answered him, Sayest thou this thing of thyself, or did others tell it thee of me?

35 Pilate answered, Am I a Jew? Thine own nation and the chief priests have delivered thee unto me: what hast thou done?

36 Jesus answered, My kingdom is not of this world: if my kingdom were of this world, then would my servants fight, that I should not be delivered to the Jews: but now is my kingdom not from hence.

37 Pilate therefore said unto him, Art thou a king then? Jesus answered, Thou sayest that I am a king. To this end was I born, and for this cause came I into the world, that I should bear witness unto the truth. Every one that is of the truth heareth my voice.

38 Pilate saith unto him, What is truth? And when he had said this, he went out again unto the Jews, and saith unto them, I find in him no fault *at all*.

39 But ye have a custom, that I should release unto you one at the passover: will ye therefore that I release unto you the King of the Jews?

40 Then cried they all again, saying, Not this man, but Barabbas. Now Barabbas was a robber.

19 Then Pilate therefore took Jesus, and scourged *him*.

2 And the soldiers platted a crown of thorns, and put *it* on his head, and they put on him a purple robe,

3 And said, Hail, King of the Jews! and they smote him with their hands.

4 Pilate therefore went forth again, and saith unto them, Behold, I bring him forth to you, that ye may know that I find no fault in him.

5 Then came Jesus forth, wearing the crown of thorns, and the purple robe. And *Pilate* saith unto them, Behold the man!

6 When the chief priests therefore and officers saw him, they cried out, saying, Crucify *him*, crucify *him*. Pilate saith unto them, Take ye him, and crucify *him*: for I find no fault in him.

7 The Jews answered him, We have a law, and by our law he ought to die, because he made himself the Son of God.

8 When Pilate therefore heard that saying, he was the more afraid;

9 And went again into the judgment hall, and saith unto Jesus, Whence art thou? But Jesus gave him no answer.

10 Then saith Pilate unto him, Speakest thou not unto me? knowest thou not that I have power to crucify thee, and have power to release thee?

11 Jesus answered, Thou couldest have no power *at all* against me, except it were given thee from above: therefore he that delivered me unto thee hath the greater sin.

12 And from thenceforth Pilate sought to release him: but the Jews cried out, saying, If thou let this man go, thou art not Caesar's friend: whosoever maketh himself a king speaketh against Caesar.

13 When Pilate therefore heard that saying, he brought Jesus forth, and sat down in the judgment seat in a place that is called the Pavement, but in the Hebrew, Gabbatha.

14 And it was the preparation of the passover, and about the sixth hour: and he saith unto the Jews, Behold your King!

15 But they cried out, Away with *him,* away with *him,* crucify him. Pilate saith unto them, Shall I crucify your King? The chief priests answered, We have no king but Caesar.

16 Then delivered he him therefore unto them to be crucified. And they took Jesus, and led *him* away.

17 And he bearing his cross went forth into a place called *the place* of a skull, which is called in the Hebrew Golgotha:

18 Where they crucified him, and two others with him, on either side one, and Jesus in the midst.

19 And Pilate wrote a title, and put *it* on the cross. And the writing was, JESUS OF NAZARETH THE KING OF THE JEWS.

20 This title then read many of the Jews: for the place where Jesus was crucified was nigh to the city: and it was written in Hebrew, *and* Greek, *and* Latin.

21 Then said the chief priests of the Jews to Pilate, Write not, The King of the Jews; but that he said, I am King of the Jews.

²² Pilate answered, What I have written I have written.

²³ Then the soldiers, when they had crucified Jesus, took his garments, and made four parts, to every soldier a part; and also *his* coat: now the coat was without seam, woven from the top throughout.

²⁴ They said therefore among themselves, Let us not rend it, but cast lots for it, whose it shall be: that the scripture might be fulfilled, which saith, They parted my raiment among them, and for my vesture they did cast lots. These things therefore the soldiers did.

²⁵ Now there stood by the cross of Jesus his mother, and his mother's sister, Mary the *wife* of Cleophas, and Mary Magdalene.

²⁶ When Jesus therefore saw his mother, and the disciple standing by, whom he loved, he saith unto his mother, Woman, behold thy son!

²⁷ Then saith he to the disciple, Behold thy mother! And from that hour that disciple took her unto his own *home.*

²⁸ After this, Jesus knowing that all things were now accomplished, that the scripture might be fulfilled, saith, I thirst.

²⁹ Now there was set a vessel full of vinegar: and they filled a spunge with vinegar, and put *it* upon hyssop, and put *it* to his mouth.

³⁰ When Jesus therefore had received the vinegar, he said, It is finished: and he bowed his head, and gave up the ghost.

³¹ The Jews therefore, because it was the preparation, that the bodies should not remain upon the cross on the sabbath day, (for that sabbath day was an high day,) besought Pilate that their legs might be broken, and *that* they might be taken away.

³² Then came the soldiers, and brake the legs of the first, and of the other which was crucified with him.

³³ But when they came to Jesus, and saw that he was dead already, they brake not his legs:

³⁴ But one of the soldiers with a spear pierced his side, and forthwith came there out blood and water.

³⁵ And he that saw *it* bare record, and his record is true: and he knoweth that he saith true, that ye might believe.

³⁶ For these things were done, that the scripture should be fulfilled, A bone of him shall not be broken.

³⁷ And again another scripture saith, They shall look on him whom they pierced.

³⁸ And after this Joseph of Arimathaea, being a disciple of Jesus, but secretly for fear of the Jews, besought Pilate that he might take away the body of Jesus: and Pilate gave *him* leave. He came therefore, and took the body of Jesus.

³⁹ And there came also Nicodemus, which at the first came to Jesus by night, and brought a mixture of myrrh and aloes, about an hundred pound *weight.*

⁴⁰ Then took they the body of Jesus, and wound it in linen clothes with the spices, as the manner of the Jews is to bury.

⁴¹ Now in the place where he was crucified there was a garden; and in the garden a new sepulchre, wherein was never man yet laid.

⁴² There laid they Jesus therefore because of the Jews' preparation *day;* for the sepulchre was nigh at hand.

20 The first *day* of the week cometh Mary Magdalene early, when it was yet dark, unto the sepulchre, and seeth the stone taken away from the sepulchre.

² Then she runneth, and cometh to Simon Peter, and to the other disciple, whom Jesus loved, and saith unto them, They have taken away the Lord out of the sepulchre, and we know not where they have laid him.

³ Peter therefore went forth, and that other disciple, and came to the sepulchre.

⁴ So they ran both together: and the other disciple did outrun Peter, and came first to the sepulchre.

⁵ And he stooping down, *and looking in,* saw the linen clothes lying; yet went he not in.

⁶ Then cometh Simon Peter following him, and went into the sepulchre, and seeth the linen clothes lie,

⁷ And the napkin, that was about his head, not lying with the linen clothes, but wrapped together in a place by itself.

⁸ Then went in also that other disciple, which came first to the sepulchre, and he saw, and believed.

⁹ For as yet they knew not the scripture, that he must rise again from the dead.

¹⁰ Then the disciples went away again unto their own home.

¹¹ But Mary stood without at the sepulchre weeping: and as she wept, she stooped down, *and looked* into the sepulchre,

¹² And seeth two angels in white sitting, the one at the head, and the other at the feet, where the body of Jesus had lain.

¹³ And they say unto her, Woman, why

weepest thou? She saith unto them, Because they have taken away my Lord, and I know not where they have laid him.

¹⁴ And when she had thus said, she turned herself back, and saw Jesus standing, and knew not that it was Jesus.

¹⁵ Jesus saith unto her, Woman, why weepest thou? whom seekest thou? She, supposing him to be the gardener, saith unto him, Sir, if thou have borne him hence, tell me where thou hast laid him, and I will take him away.

¹⁶ Jesus saith unto her, Mary. She turned herself, and saith unto him, Rabboni; which is to say, Master.

¹⁷ Jesus saith unto her, Touch me not; for I am not yet ascended to my Father: but go to my brethren, and say unto them, I ascend unto my Father, and your Father; and *to* my God, and your God.

¹⁸ Mary Magdalene came and told the disciples that she had seen the Lord, and *that* he had spoken these things unto her.

¹⁹ Then the same day at evening, being the first *day* of the week, when the doors were shut where the disciples were assembled for fear of the Jews, came Jesus and stood in the midst, and saith unto them, Peace *be* unto you.

²⁰ And when he had so said, he shewed unto them *his* hands and his side. Then were the disciples glad, when they saw the Lord.

²¹ Then said Jesus to them again, Peace *be* unto you: as *my* Father hath sent me, even so send I you.

²² And when he had said this, he breathed on *them,* and saith unto them, Receive ye the Holy Ghost:

²³ Whose soever sins ye remit, they are remitted unto them; *and* whose soever *sins* ye retain, they are retained.

²⁴ But Thomas, one of the twelve, called Didymus, was not with them when Jesus came.

²⁵ The other disciples therefore said unto him, We have seen the Lord. But he said unto them, Except I shall see in his hands the print of the nails, and put my finger into the print of the nails, and thrust my hand into his side, I will not believe.

²⁶ And after eight days again his disciples were within, and Thomas with them: *then* came Jesus, the doors being shut, and stood in the midst, and said, Peace *be* unto you.

²⁷ Then saith he to Thomas, reach hither thy finger, and behold my hands; and reach hither thy hand, and thrust *it* into my side: and be not faithless, but believing.

²⁸ And Thomas answered and said unto him, My Lord and my God.

²⁹ Jesus saith unto him, Thomas, because thou hast seen me, thou hast believed: blessed *are* they that have not seen, and *yet* have believed.

³⁰ And many other signs truly did Jesus in the presence of his disciples, which are not written in this book:

³¹ But these are written, that ye might believe that Jesus is the Christ, the Son of God; and that believing ye might have life through his name.

21 After these things Jesus shewed himself again to the disciples at the sea of Tiberias; and on this wise shewed he *himself.*

² There were together Simon Peter, and Thomas called Didymus, and Nathanael of Cana in Galilee, and the *sons* of Zebedee, and two other of his disciples.

³ Simon Peter saith unto them, I go a fishing. They say unto him, We also go with thee. They went forth, and entered into a ship immediately; and that night they caught nothing.

⁴ But when the morning was now come, Jesus stood on the shore: but the disciples knew not that it was Jesus.

⁵ Then Jesus saith unto them, Children, have ye any meat? They answered him, No.

⁶ And he said unto them, Cast the net on the right side of the ship, and ye shall find. They cast therefore, and now they were not able to draw it for the multitude of fishes.

⁷ Therefore that disciple whom Jesus loved saith unto Peter, It is the Lord. Now when Simon Peter heard that it was the Lord, he girt *his* fisher's coat *unto him,* (for he was naked,) and did cast himself into the sea.

⁸ And the other disciples came in a little ship; (for they were not far from land, but as it were two hundred cubits,) dragging the net with fishes.

⁹ As soon then as they were come to land, they saw a fire of coals there, and fish laid thereon, and bread.

¹⁰ Jesus saith unto them, Bring of the fish which ye have now caught.

¹¹ Simon Peter went up, and drew the net to land full of great fishes, and hundred and fifty and three: and for all there were so many, yet was not the net broken.

¹² Jesus saith unto them, Come *and* dine. And none of the disciples durst ask him, Who art thou? knowing that it was the Lord.

¹³ Jesus then cometh, and taketh bread, and giveth them, and fish likewise.

¹⁴ This is now the third time that Jesus shewed himself to his disciples, after that he was risen from the dead.

¹⁵ So when they had dined, Jesus saith to Simon Peter, Simon, *son* of Jonas, lovest thou me more than these? He saith unto him, Yea, Lord; thou knowest that I love thee. He saith unto him, Feed my lambs.

¹⁶ He saith to him again the second time, Simon, *son* of Jonas, lovest thou me? He saith unto him, Yea, Lord; thou knowest that I love thee. He saith unto him, Feed my sheep.

¹⁷ He saith unto him the third time, Simon, *son* of Jonas, lovest thou me? Peter was grieved because he said unto him the third time, Lovest thou me? And he said unto him, Lord, thou knowest all things; thou knowest that I love thee. Jesus saith unto him, Feed my sheep.

¹⁸ Verily, verily, I say unto thee, When thou wast young, thou girdedst thyself, and walkedst whither thou wouldest: but when thou shalt be old, thou shalt stretch forth thy hands, and another shall gird thee, and carry *thee* whither thou wouldest not.

¹⁹ This spake he, signifying by what death he should glorify God. And when he had spoken this, he saith unto him, Follow me.

²⁰ Then Peter, turning about, seeth the disciple whom Jesus loved following; which also leaned on his breast at supper, and said, Lord, which is he that betrayeth thee?

²¹ Peter seeing him saith to Jesus, Lord, and what *shall* this man *do?*

²² Jesus saith unto him, If I will that he tarry till I come, what *is that* to thee? follow thou me.

²³ Then went this saying abroad among the brethren, that that disciple should not die: yet Jesus said not unto him, He shall not die; but, If I will that he tarry till I come, what *is that* to thee?

²⁴ This is the disciple which testifieth of these things, and wrote these things: and we know that his testimony is true.

²⁵ And there are also many other things which Jesus did, the which, if they should be written every one, I suppose that even the world itself could not contain the books that should be written. Amen.

About the Author

Rodney Howard-Browne was raised in a godly home, giving his life to Jesus Christ at the tender age of five and being filled with the Holy Spirit at eight. He met and married his lovely wife Adonica on October 3, 1981, and they began to minister throughout the region of Southern Africa.

In 1987 they moved to the United States with their three young children, Kirsten, Kelly, and Kenneth, after feeling the call to come as missionaries to America. They arrived with $300 in their pockets and began to travel across the USA. In 1989 a revival broke out in upstate New York with unusual manifestations of the Holy Spirit. There were many conversions, miracles, healings, and great joy. Over the last ten years Rodney and Adonica have held crusades in over 130 cities in the USA and many countries around the world.

As Revival Ministries International ("RMI"), an association of churches encompassing many denominations, Rodney focuses on what God is doing today — bringing revival to the world. In 1996, Rodney and Adonica pioneered The River at Tampa Bay, and in 1997, they began River Bible Institute, which is dedicated to training revivalists for the 21st century. In 1998, RMI founded Acres of Love, a home for abandoned aids babies located in Bryanston, South Africa.

The newest addition to the ministry is Good News America, a soul-winning organization designed to sweep cities with the good news of the Gospel through massive evangelistic crusades. Their first crusade begins in the summer of 1999 in New York City's Madison Square Garden.

Dr. Howard-Browne has authored nearly twenty books, most which have been translated into many languages. Their bimonthly newspaper, *Chronicles of Revival,* is sent out to 200,000 people around the world. Their ministry headquarters is in Tampa, Florida, with offices in Vancouver, BC, Canada; Melbourne, Australia; Manila, Philippines; London, England; Johannesburg, South Africa; and New York, New York.

You may contact Dr. Howard-Browne by writing:

P. O. Box 292888

Tampa, Florida 33687

or telephone (USA):

813-971-9999

or visiting his website:

http://www.revival.com.